MIDDLE EAST FOREIGN POLICY

Issues and Processes

R. D. McLaurin
Don Peretz, Lewis W. Snider

PRAEGER

PRAEGER SPECIAL STUDIES • PRAEGER SCIENTIFIC

Library of Congress Cataloging in Publication Data

McLaurin, R. D. (Ronald De), 1944–
    Middle East foreign policy.

    Bibliography: p.
    Includes index.
    1. Near East—Foreign relations—Addresses,
essays, lectures.   I. Peretz, Don, 1922–
II. Snider, Lewis W.   III. Title.
DS63.1.M385   1982   327.56   82-13137
ISBN 0-03-057753-5
ISBN 0-03-057754-3 (pbk.)

Published in 1982 by Praeger Publishers
CBS Educational and Professional Publishing
a Division of CBS Inc.
521 Fifth Avenue, New York, New York 10175 U.S.A.

© 1982 by Praeger Publishers

23456789 052 987654321
Printed in the United States of America

PREFACE

Perhaps no area remains as critical to global security and as much the focus of international attention as the Middle East. It is the authors' contention that the dynamics of the Middle East in the 1980s is a function of interactive pressures, especially domestic pressures, and foreign policy processes. The present work brings together analyses of the dynamics of foreign policy in the Middle East by three authors, each with an emphasis on specific regional states. The authors share many views, and differ in some areas. Chapters 1, 2, 6, 7, and 8 were the responsibility of Ron McLaurin; Chapters 3 and 4, of Lewis Snider; Chapter 5, of Don Peretz.

Many individuals, both in the United States and the Middle East, have made significant contributions to the authors' understanding of the problems involved. Without the initial support of Robert H. Kubal, Office of the Assistant Secretary of Defense (International Security Affairs), the original edition of this book would not have been prepared. The research and preparation of this work have benefited immeasurably from the aid and counsel of Paul A. Jureidini of Abbott Associates, Inc.; Edward E. Azar, University of Maryland; Edmund Ghareeb, School of Advanced International Studies, Johns Hopkins University; and Mohammed Mughisuddin, American University, whose new duties precluded his preparation of chapters for which he was responsible in the previous edition. The authors would also like to express their appreciation to Mazher Hameed, Alaeddin S. Hreib, Sami Khoury, and Nikolaos van Dam for their helpful views on a range of issues.

Betsy Brown, our editor at Praeger, has helped at every stage of this project from its inception. We are grateful for her ideas, her follow-through, and, alas, her patience. In this book and in our previous collaboration, Betsy has always been a real gem.

While each of these individuals has made a contribution to this work, the authors bear sole responsibility for any errors of fact or judgment.

CONTENTS

CHAPTER
1

INTRODUCTION

BACKGROUND

The modern history of the Middle East could start at any one of many points, from the late nineteenth century to the post-World War II era. Whichever initial point is chosen, it is safe to state that since then the region has been characterized by substantial political change and spasmodic outbreaks of political violence.

This book is not intended as a political history of Egypt, Iraq, Israel, Saudi Arabia, or Syria. Even less is it a regional history. Still, it is important to give at least some recent historical perspective to this analysis of the five states' foreign-policy processes, and that perspective must of necessity revolve around phenomena that have significantly influenced the course and direction of developments in the region since the late 1940s — the evolution of Arab nationalism, the creation of Israel as an independent state, and the sudden burgeoning of wealthy petroleum economies in the Gulf.

Arab Nationalism

No attempt is made to provide an analysis of Arab nationalism here, a task that has been ably performed by others.[1] It is, however, necessary to underscore the importance of this elusive and potent force in postwar Arab political development. In each of the Arab states considered here, Arab nationalism has played a major role; in Egypt, Iraq, and Syria it was intimately associated with the revolutionary experience each underwent. Because this book is concerned with societal and related pressures on foreign-policy decision making, the Arab nationalist Weltanschauung is directly relevant to our subject.

1

As independence came to the Arab states of the Middle East, the nationalist phenomenon encountered several major problems of which two are especially relevant to this book: the conflict between pan-Arab nationalism and regional (state) nationalisms; and the conflict between Western-style modernization and Islamic values.

Pan-Arabism has been a strong impulse at the very heart of Arab nationalist thought. However, as the Arab states were granted independence, local interests and traditions impeded the realization of pan-Arab unity. For decades this frustration was widely perceived, at the mass level, as a series of temporary procedural setbacks. Yet, pan-Arab nationalism, while it played a significant part in establishing the identity and facilitating the communication of nationalist groups, and represented the touchstone commonalities of the Arab experience, was silent on many local aspirations, blind to local conflicts, and empirically less relevant than local nationalism to the actual process of decolonization. Instead, it was the local or regional national movements that dealt with these challenges in a manner acceptable to their various constituencies. After independence, Arab governments rarely gave serious thought to the abnegation of their own power and "national" independence in favor of a pan-Arab entity.

The foregoing is not to suggest, however, that Arab unity was a meaningless shibboleth, as many Western observers concluded. On the contrary, it was both a significant long-term political objective and a pregnant symbol of identity. If in succeeding years the concept of Arab unity has lost its appeal as a meaningful political goal, it is still, despite the growth of disintegrative factors across the Middle East (see below), reflective of a powerful and profound sense of common heritage and identity.

The era of independence witnessed, then, the clash between state nationalism and Arab nationalism. It also witnessed a more fundamental problem — the inability of nationalist ideologies, at either level, to resolve the conflict between modernization and the societal values (especially Islamic values) and social structure on which Arab society was based. Modernization was understood only in a framework of Westernization. That the leading supporters of modernization were educated in or identified with the West assured this characterization and weakened these supporters' credentials in periods of challenge. The postcolonial period brought new but still important issues of decolonization in the social and economic domains. Nowhere in the Arab Middle East was an acceptable and enduring compromise struck between the dedication of societies to socioeconomic objectives based on Western values and experience (modernization), and the dedication of the same societies to the elimination of Western socioeconomic domination. The anti-Western strain so visible in the foreign policies of the region considered here is often a political reflection of the determination to avoid social and cultural domination by the West.

The Arab-Israeli Problem

The Arab-Israeli and Palestinian problems began as a conflict between the Arab and Jewish populations of Palestine. At that time, the Palestinian Arab community was supported by the rest of the Arab world, but was divided (as it has continued to be) in many ways. From 1919 until 1948, this issue was viewed by both Arab and Jew as colonial in nature. As the Zionists believed the British were responsible for blocking the open-ended Jewish immigration into Palestine, which they believed was authorized by the terms of both the Balfour Declaration and League of Nations' mandate agreement (under which the United Kingdom administered Palestine), the Arab community and the Arab world believed the British were responsible for allowing Jewish immigration at a level far above what was reasonable, just, or authorized by the mandate. Zionists pressured the government in London to relax restrictions; Arabs pressured the local administration to enlarge and enforce restrictions.

From the Arab perspective, Palestine was a classic colonialist intervention in the Arab world. Did the Zionist movement not look to the Western countries — to Europe and the United States — to effect the Jewish colonization of Palestine? Palestine was a part of the Arab Islamic sphere, part of *dar al-Islam*. The Palestine problem, then, was seen as a Western attempt to dismember the Arab world and to foist a foreign presence on it, to remove Palestine from *dar al-Islam*.[2]

Jewish nationalism in Palestine, Zionism, and the history of Israel's creation have also been chronicled elsewhere.[3] Apart from their importance in understanding current Israeli policy, they have had a far-reaching effect on the evolution of the Middle East, particularly the Levant area. Israel's existence and its military strength also have had significant effects on the nature of bilateral relations between various Arab states and foreign powers external to the region.

For a variety of reasons, the process by which Israel was established as a modern state (or reborn, from the Israeli viewpoint) was not accepted as legitimate by any Arab state. This perceived illegitimacy was, however, only in part a function of the "Palestine problem." That Israel was viewed as a foreign creation, a dagger in the heart of the Arab nation — and thus an enemy of Arab nationalism — was also a critical consideration. In the Arab view, Israel was a price the Arabs were forced to pay for the sins of the Nazi holocaust in which the Arab states had had no part. Because of all Israel represented, because of the presence of millions of Palestinians without their own national home, and because of the perceived "indecisive" military outcome of the 1948 war, the hope that the Israeli state could be eradicated was virtually universal among Arabs. Even after the 1956 rout of Egypt by British, French, and Israeli forces, there was still no consensus in the Arab world that Israel's military power was preponderant over any likely coalition of major Arab forces.

The 1950 Tripartite Agreement on arms transfers to the Middle East was negated by the Soviet arms deals with Egypt and Syria in 1955-56. In 1955 a major regional arms race began that continues to the present. When the June 1967 war broke out, few believed Israel would be able to overwhelm the Arabs as totally or as quickly as it did.

The political and military lessons of the 1967 conflict in the Middle East have been analyzed by many writers — Arab, Israeli, Western, and Soviet. But the most important conclusion Arab elites were to draw from the 1967 conflict crept into their consciousness only subtly over the succeeding six years — Israel was there to stay. Whatever the changes in the details of the regional military equation, no combination of Arab forces would be able to disestablish Israel as a regional state in the foreseeable future. The development of an Israeli nuclear weapons capability[4] — never completely confirmed but almost universally believed to exist — served to underscore the accuracy and impact of this conclusion.

At the same time, the June War created a set of new facts. It was one thing for Egyptians, Lebanese, Syrians, Jordanians, Iraqis, Moroccans, and other Arab citizens of extant states to "accept" the inevitability of the existence of Israel on "Palestinian land" held by Israel since 1948, but quite another for Egyptians, Syrians, and Palestinian-Jordanians to accept indefinite occupation by Israel of Egyptian, Syrian, and (Palestinian) Jordanian land never allotted to Israel under the U.N. partition plan and never claimed by Israel. Even beyond the merits of the Palestinian claims perceived by Arab governments, those regimes supported the Palestinian resistance movement for their own political ends. By 1970 the primary Arab issue in Arab-Israeli relations had passed from recognition of "Palestinian rights" to return of Arab lands (in the Sinai, West Bank, and Golan Heights) captured in 1967. This was demonstrated by the various exchanges of Gunnar Jarring's unsuccessful mission; the circumstances surrounding the proposal, consideration, and collapse of the Rogers Peace Plan; and Arab strategic planning preceding the October 1973 War.[5]

Although the years from 1967 to 1973 seemed to be characterized by stagnation in terms of Arab-Israeli bilateral developments, they were a period of major political change within several Arab countries, including all of the Arab confrontation states and Iraq. In Egypt, Iraq, and Syria, ideological rhetoricians gave way to more pragmatic leadership that laid the groundwork and gave the impetus for economic development, political institutionalization, and perhaps, in Iraq and Syria, greater political stability. Meanwhile, in Jordan the civil war of 1969-70 led to the eviction of most of the activist Palestinian elements from that country, and in Lebanon clashes between Palestinians and Lebanese furthered the process of political decay that would lead to civil war.[6]

The death of Gamal Abdel Nasser in 1970 brought Anwar Sadat, another pragmatist, to the Egyptian presidency. Only a few weeks before Nasser's death, Syria's leadership had passed from Salah Jadid to Hafez Assad in a coup that was merely the final act in a transfer of power begun more than a year earlier. Over the next two-and-a-half years, Syria, Egypt, and Jordan watched the 1967 cease-fire become a no-war, no-peace political fact, with the appearance of permanence more firmly established with the passing of each day.

Sadat's expulsion of most of Egypt's Soviet technicians in 1972 was but one of several Egyptian attempts to break the stalemate.[7] Within some six months, after it had become clear that nothing short of war could bring about movement toward a return of the occupied territories, Sadat decided on such a course.[8] Egyptian-Syrian coordination proceeded well at the national strategic level, but progressed only minimally from the point of view of detailed military coordination.[9]

The October War and the events surrounding its outbreak and aftermath have been chronicled even more widely than the 1967 conflict.[10] For both wars, we refer readers to the extant literature on the war rather than add to it. At the same time, like the June War, the October conflict gave rise to a new set of realities. Whereas by virtue of Israel's overwhelming victory in 1967 most Arab elites grudgingly accepted the fact of Israel's existence and permanence as a state in the Middle East, Israel learned in 1973 that the costs of not achieving some sort of settlement with the Arab states were high militarily and politically. Both sides, at least as far as the confrontation states were concerned, perceived important benefits to be derived from a settlement.

Oil in the Gulf

Coincident with the interwar development of anticolonial Arab nationalism and Zionist consciousness and migration to Palestine, was the slow beginning of the extraction of petroleum from oil fields, then still largely uncharted, in the Gulf. As older and more established fields in the United States, Eastern Europe, and Venezuela were exhausted, and some idea of the magnitude of Gulf oil reserves emerged, the importance of the Arab oil producers increased. The result was essentially a struggle between the oil companies and the Middle East governments whose oil was being exploited, an economic and political struggle that developed quickly in the 1960s and early 1970s.[11]

Even before the sudden, large increase in the price of petroleum following the October 1973 War and the Arab oil embargo it engendered, a few Western experts had begun to grapple with the implications of rapidly growing Western dependence on imports of oil from the Middle East and the dimensions of the influx of revenue to Arab oil-producing countries,[12] some of the most important of which have very small populations. Yet, no one foresaw the speed of the increase in oil prices; nor, therefore, did anyone accurately predict the magnitude of oil revenues.

The dynamism of the Gulf economies and the dearth of labor have brought about the transfer of well over a million Arabs to the labor forces of the oil exporters.[13] The rapid influx of foreign business and of expatriate remittances, the size of capital flows from the oil producers to other Arab states, and the multiplier effect resulting from oil price increases have made inflation a major problem in many Arab countries. Moreover, while the Gulf and Levant remained rather insulated from each other before the October War, the two subregions became much more heavily interdependent after 1973.[14]

PUBLICS, POLICIES, AND GOVERNMENT IN THE DEVELOPING COUNTRIES

It is our belief that the governments of the Middle East, like the democracies of the West, cannot be analyzed, nor their policies understood, without reference to the publics they speak for and answer to. This is not to say that politics in the two areas is essentially the same, only that interests, interest groups, and interest articulation are necessarily central in both. Indeed, we are quick to agree that these similarities exist *in spite* of several fundamental differences between Middle Eastern and Western political systems.

Understanding the nature of political processes in developing countries is complicated by the nature of the relationship between society and government in the third world. When assessing political phenomena, Western analysts are trained to think, and have become accustomed even to intuit, within the narrow parameters of Western experience. That is, even though they recognize the obvious structural differences between developed-country political systems and those of the developing countries, the similarity of these structures is still great enough that they overlook the much more profound functional distinctions that are based on fundamental differences in identity, loyalty, and authority patterns.

Across the Middle East — except in Israel — the national government is an artificial structure designed to interact with other similar institutions elsewhere. These structures developed during the colonial period even in those countries never subjected to colonization. Their purpose was and is to maintain domestic legitimacy and international credibility. These institutions do allocate material resources in both spheres and, because they reveal certain patterns of domestic political alignment and power, they *are* important. Most of the time, these governments reflect more or less directly the dominance of one or more national interest groups. (Interest groups, for these purposes, are associations of individuals according to some ascriptive or other identification.) However, these groups, like the national government itself, are neither representative of nor directly responsive to the national population.

Thus, for example, political change in developing countries arises in one of three ways. First, an interest group opposed to the existing political order may initiate direct action to alter that situation. (Such action is exemplified in coups d'etat, assassinations, or other abrupt, nonroutine attempts to alter the distribution of power in the country.) Second, an interest group may seek to indirectly alter the status quo by besieging the government through legal or illegal means with stimuli either so numerous or so serious that the existing order may be unable to cope with them. (Strikes, riots, or other violence are illegal stimuli, but accusations in the press, forced resignations, and other legal action may have the same result.) Finally, an interest group seeking to unravel the existing political order can undertake to mobilize the entire population (rather than a small cross-section of it) against the government. (Popular mobilization may be called a revolution for present purposes, although we do not necessarily impute to the succeeding political order the new sociological or political goals usually associated with "revolutions.") Given the unrepresentativeness of most political interest groups in the third world, and the limited degree of popular identification with the state, general mobilization of a national population is extraordinarily difficult and rare. Finding symbols that cut across conflicting identities and loyalties is almost impossible in the Middle East.

Although members and employees of "government" grow to overlook the nature of the relationship between government and society, and often sincerely believe themselves legitimate in the public consciousness, this set of institutions has relatively little to do with the day-to-day identities of the people who live within national boundaries. Neither the "government" nor the "country" represents the locus of primary or even secondary loyalties of the affected populace.

Understanding the relationship between people and government in the Middle East is absolutely critical to conceptualizing a means to understand the political process there and the nature of what we call politics. Much of the day-to-day political behavior taking place within the institutional parameters of the government is supremely irrelevant to the functioning of political reality. Thus, the primitiveness of our own concepts of politics, economics, and even social affairs within these countries becomes manifest. Public opinion can be mobilized to discard a regime or government, as it can be mobilized to support one – but only ephemerally, and generally ineffectively. The key to stability (and instability) lies not in public opinion, but rather in the attitudes, alliances, and communications of key interest groups. The general public and public opinion are exploited and manipulated by various interest groups and can be mobilized by them. Public attitudes and opinions are not a major factor in political stability, even when the government or regime enjoys widespread popularity.

Additionally, political expression is tightly controlled or suppressed altogether in many Middle East countries. Therefore, traditional indicators of interest articulation and even issue identification are substantially confounded. While a distinction may be drawn between relatively "open" and "closed" societies in the Middle East, none of the Arab countries permits a wide range of truly free political expression, and those dissident voices permitted to speak are carefully monitored. The fact that tolerated opposition is aware of such supervision directly affects the nature and content of appeals.

Israel alone of the countries covered in this book has developed a system of government that has strong roots in the public and is wholly "legitimate" in its eyes. Whether such legitimacy would withstand the disintegrative pressures of peace as it has taken root in the integrative pressures of war is questioned by some. For the present, though, the relationship of people and government in Israel is unique in the Middle East, the role of publics and policy processes both more open and accepted.

INTRODUCTION

The countries we shall be studying here, like all the other states of the Middle East except Iran and Turkey, are relatively new. Although Egyptian, Iraqi, Israeli, and Syrian traditions go back to some of the earliest recorded civilizations, the modern states we now call Egypt, Iraq, Israel, and Syria all occupy territory that for many years prior to World War II was under some form of foreign control. The Saudi case differs in the sense that Saudi Arabia was never colonized by a Western state, and only small parts of contemporary Saudi Arabia were ever under Ottoman control. Nevertheless, each of the five states has expended considerable effort in developing a sense of nationhood, of national identity. Each — including Saudi Arabia — has minority groups and subcultures whose relationships to the nation as a whole are important both to the national identity and to national policies. Indeed, minority issues in Iraq, Israel, and Syria have been among the most important problems facing those countries.[15]

Today's Middle East is, then, a vast complex of publics or constituencies. National leaders' decisions must be placed in the context of their need to maintain their domestic power positions by influencing constituent alignments, as well as in that of their intentions to realize Egyptian, Iraqi, Israeli, Jordanian, Saudi, Syrian, or some other "national interest." This book discusses these critical regional actors in terms of the publics and processes that shape national policies.

In political systems resembling those of the West, systems such as Israel's, the role and power of interest groups are clear since they operate openly as the aggregation of specific publics that individually or severally possess finite, measurable claims on the allocation of resources. Under systems with no pretense of democracy, irrespective of the degree of benevolence inherent in the system, many observers overlook or underestimate the role of key groups or publics. Yet, since these groups represent real, competing demands, and since the institutions to channel claims on and allocation of political goods possess less legitimacy, it can be argued that sensitivity to these group interests is even more important to political stability. It is our conviction that all five political systems under study here manifest different but real concerns about the attitudes, opinions, needs, and perceptions of key publics within their respective populations.

ORGANIZATION

This book is presented in eight chapters. Chapter 1 has consisted of a general sketch that seeks to introduce the subject matter of the rest of the book.

Chapter 2 addresses the regional environment with which Egypt, Iraq, Israel, Saudi Arabia, and Syria must deal. Middle East countries and interaction patterns that influence the foreign and military policies of these five countries are the focus of Chapter 2.

Chapters 3 to 7 analyze the foreign-policy processes and the foreign policies of Egypt, Iraq, Israel, Saudi Arabia, and Syria, respectively. Recognizing that there are major differences in the structure of and influences on the five governments, we have nevertheless attempted to retain an approach to the five that allows maximum comparability. Each chapter therefore has three primary sections. The first part is a discussion of the internal environment of the national security policy that describes the structure of government, the operation of the political system, and the main interest groups or publics. The second section identifies the major issue areas as they are perceived within each country. Finally, the political and military objectives and policies of each government are described.

Chapter 8 identifies some of the issues raised by the conclusions of Chapters 3 to 7 in the context of the political evolution of the Middle East.

NOTES

1. George Antonius, *The Arab Awakening* (Philadelphia: Lippincott, 1938); Sylvia Haim, *Arab Nationalism: An Anthology* (Berkeley and Los Angeles: University of California Press, 1962); Albert H. Hourani, *Arabic Thought in the Liberal Age, 1798-1939* (New York and London: Oxford University Press, 1962); and Zeine N. Zeine, *The Emergence of Arab Nationalism: With a Background Study of Arab-Turkish Relations in the Near East* (Beirut: Khayats, 1966).

2. Compare, for example, the much less controversial cession of Alexandretta from Arab (Syrian) to Turkish control. One reason for the less vociferous protest (a protest confined much more to Syria) was that the territory and population of Alexandretta remained within the Islamic world. We do not by this argument mean to overlook the substantial Palestinian Christian population that has always played an active political role out of all proportion to its size. Despite the prominence during and after the mandate of the Christian community, Palestine was generally perceived as part of the Arab *Islamic* community.

3. See David Ben-Gurion, *Israel: Years of Challenge* (New York: Holt, Rinehart and Winston, 1963); Ben Halpern, *The Idea of the Jewish State* (Cambridge, Mass.: Harvard University Press, 1961); Walter Z. Laqueur, *A History of Zionism* (New York: Holt, Rinehart and Winston, 1972); and Chaim Weizman, *Trial and Error* (New York: Schocken, 1966).

4. See Robert E. Harkavy, *Spectre of a Middle Eastern Holocaust: The Strategic and Diplomatic Implications of the Israeli Nuclear Weapons Program* (Denver: University of Denver, 1977).

5. The Jarring mission exchanges appear in various U.N. documents and in the *Journal of Palestine Studies* II, 4 (Summer 1973). The essence of the Rogers peace initiatives of 1969 and 1970 is framed in Rogers's speech of December 9, 1969, reprinted in U.S. Senate, Committee on Foreign Relations, *A Select Chronology and Background Documents Relating to the Middle East* 2d ed., rev. (Washington, D. C.: U.S. Government Printing Office, 1975). There is a wealth of literature on the strategic and tactical prelude to the October War. See especially Chaim Herzog, *The War of Atonement: October 1973* (Boston: Little, Brown, 1975), Heikal, *The Road to Ramadan*, and other sources listed in note 10 below.

6. For the military aspects of the Jordanian civil war, see Paul A. Jureidini and William E. Hazen, *Six Clashes: An Analysis of the Relationship between the Palestinian Guerrilla Movement and the Governments of Jordan and Lebanon* (Kensington, Md.: American Institutes for Research, 1971) or the summary in their *The Palestinian Movement in Politics* (Lexington, Mass.: Heath, 1976), pp. 41-76; and, for the political aspects, William B. Quandt, Fuad Jabber, and Ann Mosely Lesch, *The Politics of Palestinian Nationalism* (Berkeley and Los Angeles: University of California Press, 1973). The best English-language sources on the Lebanese conflict are Marius Deeb, *The Lebanese Civil War* (New York: Praeger, 1980), Walid Khalidi, *Conflict and Violence in Lebanon: Confrontation in the Middle East* (Cambridge, Mass.: Harvard University Center for International Affairs, 1979), and P. Edward Haley and Lewis W. Snider, eds., *Lebanon in Crisis: Participants and Issues* (Syracuse: Syracuse University Press, 1979). Military operations are analyzed in Paul A. Jureidini, R. D. McLaurin, and James M. Price, *Military Operations in Selected Lebanese Built-Up Areas, 1975-1978* (Aberdeen, Md.: Aberdeen Proving Grounds, 1979).

7. See Abraham S. Becker, "The Superpowers and the Arab-Israeli Conflict, 1970-1973," Rand Corporation paper, December 1973; and Heikal, *The Road to Ramadan*.

8. Charles Wakebridge, "The Egyptian Staff Solution," *Military Review*, LV, 3 (March 1975), pp. 3-11.

9. Ibid. The nature of the Egyptian and Syrian attacks was totally different, and coordination was poor beyond the timing of the initial assault.

10. Avraham (Bren) Adan, *On the Banks of Suez* (San Rafael: Presidio, 1980); J. S. Arora, *West Asia War 1973: That Shook the World and Brought Us to the Brink of the Third World War* (New Delhi: New Light Publishers, n. d.); Hassan el Badri, Taha el Magdoub, and Mohammed Din el Din Zohdy, *The Ramadan War, 1973* (Dunn Loring, Va.: T. N. Dupuy Associates, 1978); Yeshoyahu Ben Porat et al., *Kippur* (Tel Aviv: Special Edition Publishers, 1973); Riad N. el-Rayyes and Dunia Nahas, eds., *The October War: Documents, Personalities, Analyses and Maps* (Beirut: An-Nahar, 1974); Louis Williams, ed., *Military Aspects of the Israeli-Arab Conflict* (Tel Aviv: University Publishing Projects, 1975); Edgar O'Ballance, *No Victor, No Vanquished: The Yom Kippur War* (San Rafael: Presidio, 1978); D. K. Palit, *Return to Sinai: The Arab Offensive, October 1973* (New Delhi: Palit and Palit, 1974); Zeev Schiff, *October Earthquake*

(Tel Aviv: University Publishing Projects, 1974); Saad el Shazly, *The Crossing of the Suez* (San Francisco: American Mideast Research, 1980); Lester A. Sobel, ed., *Israel and the Arabs: The October 1973 War* (New York: Facts on File, 1974); and Lawrence L. Whetten, *The Canal War: Four Power Conflict in the Middle East* (Cambridge, Mass.: MIT Press, 1974).

11. See Louis Turner, *Oil Companies in the International System* (London: George Allen Unwin for the Royal Institute of International Affairs, 1978); Dan-Kwart A. Rustow and John F. Mugno, *OPEC: Success and Prospects* (New York: NYU Press, 1976); and Fariborz Ghadar, *The Evolution of OPEC Strategy* (Lexington, Mass.: Heath, 1977).

12. Only the most well-known example is James E. Akins, "The Oil Crisis: This Time the Wolf Is Here," *Foreign Affairs*, LI, 3 (April 1973), pp. 462-90.

13. See Nazli Choucri, "Demographic Changes in the Middle East," *The Political Economy of the Middle East: 1973-78* (Washington, D. C.: U.S. Government Printing Office for the Joint Economic Committee of the Congress of the United States, 1980), pp. 25-54, and sources cited therein, for detailed consideration of the intraregional migration and some treatment of migration from outside the Middle East. In fact, there are probably over one million Yemenis in Saudi Arabia alone.

14. See Paul A. Jureidini and R. D. McLaurin, *Beyond Camp David: Emerging Alignments and Leaders in the Middle East* (Syracuse: Syracuse University Press, 1981), Chap. 1.

15. Cf. R. D. McLaurin, ed., *The Political Role of Minority Groups in the Middle East* (New York: Praeger, 1979), Chaps. 2-5.

CHAPTER
2

THE REGIONAL ENVIRONMENT

Since 1948, foreign policies in the central Middle East — the Eastern Mediterranean area and Egypt — have been concerned with factors related to the Arab-Israeli conflict.[1] Alignment, armament, and domestic political patterns have been affected more by the rigidities caused by that problem than by any other external factor. This chapter discusses the recent politics of the region as *external* influences on the policies of Egypt, Iraq, Israel, Saudi Arabia, and Syria.

THE EASTERN MEDITERRANEAN

Although the Middle East is synonymous with government instability in the minds of many, there have been few examples of illegal government turnovers, and none in the Levant, since 1970. Relationships among the diverse states have nevertheless remained volatile, with fluid alignments the rule rather than the exception. The one constant factor in the Eastern Mediterranean from 1948 to 1977 was the solidarity of the Arab alliance against Israel. Despite several covert Israeli attempts to establish a modus vivendi with Jordan or Lebanon,[2] all Arab peoples and governments retained an unswerving official hostility[3] toward Israel either as "confrontation" or "supporting" states.[4]

In the first chapter, we suggested that the two wars of June 1967 and October 1973 brought about conditions in which a settlement could emerge.[5]

Another regional turning point or key date is clearly November 1977 and the Anwar Sadat trip to Israel. The emerging Egyptian policy[6] to first challenge the Arab coalition and then, if that failed, to defy and take leave of it, has had a fundamental impact on Levantine politics, for no longer can the Arab coalition against Israel be taken for granted. Moreover, if the Camp David accords should lead to meaningful progress toward Palestinian autonomy, other Arab governments must participate or be left behind by the process (though not necessarily the peace). The rules of the game are unattractive to most Arab governments, but the alternatives appear no more appealing.[7]

The Arab-Israeli issue is not, however, the only regional problem. During the last decade in the Eastern Mediterranean, most Arab governments have felt some of the impact of the petroleum capital influx. All have seen skilled, semi-skilled, and unskilled labor emigrate to the Gulf,[8] and all have had to battle the general regional inflation the capital inflow has engendered.[9] At the same time, the oil producers have also provided substantial economic transfusions to Egypt, Jordan, Lebanon, and Syria, for a wide variety of reasons and under a wider variety of conditions.[10]

Finally, the unwonted political stability of the past decade is ending. Civil war has ended Lebanon's life as it was constituted before 1975. The conclusion of the conflict will find Lebanon partitioned into confederal states totally dominated by a Maronite-Shi'a-Druze alliance (the principal section controlled by the Maronites) all living more or less under Israeli protection.[11] Even Hussein bin Talal, the king of Jordan, has lost much of the near-mystical hold he once had over the Jordanian people.[12] While the Hashemite kingdom is not presently threatened, such a change cannot be excluded in the future. Forces of political disintegration will constitute a major challenge to Iran, the United Arab Emirates, and Syria, and to the foreign policy of each of the five states we are studying.

THE GULF/ARABIAN PENINSULA

Before the 1973 war and the subsequent rapid rise in oil prices, the Gulf/Peninsula subregion was insulated as well as conceptually discrete from the Levant.[13] Of the states in this subregion, only Iraq was also very active in the Arab-Israeli environment, and Iraq has historically vacillated in orientation and interest between west (the Levant) and south (the Gulf).[14] On the one hand, it is true that these two areas were more closely linked after 1973. On the other, it is also evident that the influence and impact of the Gulf increased vis-a-vis the Eastern Mediterranean in international councils. Since the mid-1970s, Gulf/Peninsula oil producers have become significant actors in international finance,[15] in Western and Japanese social structures,[16] and in regional politics.[17]

Under circumstances where the more established states of the region and the highly developed countries of the world look to them for decisions and behavioral patterns,[18] where petroleum revenues generate unabsorbable income the task of managing which exceeds the reservoirs of time and skill available,[19] and where education and other processes are producing pressures for social change which, if not properly channeled, may explode[20] — under these circumstances, the inadequate, ill-trained, shallow, and often irrelevant administrative institutions of most Gulf and Peninsula states are greatly overtaxed. These strains are very real for Bahrain and Oman, but are even more pressing for Kuwait, Qatar, Saudi Arabia, and the United Arab Emirates. These problems suggest a substantial potential for political instability and government change in the subregion[21] – all of which certainly affects Saudi and Iraqi foreign policy even today.

Partially in view of the foregoing, and in part just because such a large portion of the earth's energy reservoir is concentrated along the narrow Arabian/ Persian Gulf, all the Gulf's countries have been deeply concerned about Gulf security.[22] American policy foresaw Iran and Saudi Arabia as the two pillars of Gulf security,[23] much to the dismay of Iraqi (and other Arab) leaders.[24] Only the ambitious shah of Iran and Iraq's government seemed willing to take an active role in the Gulf, one that did not back away from military force. However, Iran's credentials as guarantor of Gulf security were tarnished in view of the country's seizure of three Arab islands.[25] No one doubted the shah's determination to maintain a conservative hue in Gulf politics,[26] but the sheikhdoms and Saudi Arabia made little secret of their concern over the continuing acquisitions – and hence purpose – of Iran's military establishment.[27] The construction of the world's largest fleet of air cushion vehicles persuaded many that the shah fully intended to expand his empire across the Gulf when Iran's oil ran out.[28]

The end of the shah's rule evoked a mixture of relief and surprise from Saudi Arabia and the smaller Gulf countries – relief at the passing of one threat, surprise at the speed with which the Pahlavi dynasty, with far more military muscle than any of their own regimes, was swept away.[29] Both these sensations were eclipsed by concern when the new Islamic regime in Tehran began to export religious unrest and revolutionary fervor.[30] Thus, during late 1979 and 1980, even before the outbreak of war between Iran and Iraq, attention to regime security became a far more common preoccupation of the Gulf governments than attention to Gulf security.[31] There can be little doubt that concern about the dynamism (exportability) of Iran's revolution, on the one hand, and about Iran's centrifugation, on the other, will play a major role in shaping regional foreign policies in the Gulf.

POWER CENTERS

The key countries in the Middle East today are, primarily, Israel; secondarily, Egypt, Iran, Iraq, and Saudi Arabia; and thirdly, Algeria and Syria. From a regional perspective, the Eastern Mediterranean, traditionally perceived to be the core of the Arab world, has generally been viewed as the most powerful subregion. Yet, the rapid growth in oil revenues generated initially by increases in Western and world demand and, after 1973, by rapid price rises resulted in a shift in the perceived locus of power east and southward toward the Arab/ Persian Gulf, particularly to Iraq and Saudi Arabia.

Israel is unquestionably the most powerful state in the Middle East from a military standpoint.[32] Israel's conventional materiel inventories are the largest in most categories of equipment of any regional state,[33] and excellent maintenance keeps a high proportion of all equipment operational.[34] Much of the equipment is highly sophisticated, either state of the art or as advanced as the equipment of that type deployed anywhere in the world. Israeli military manpower is also of the highest quality, far more capable of optimally operating and effectively maintaining equipment than the manpower of any other country in the region.[35] Tactics and doctrine are highly developed, well thought out, and admirably suited both to the quality of manpower and materiel and to the various threat environments. Military leadership and training are comparable to the best in the world and bear little similarity to those of other regional states.[36]

Because of the relatively small population of Israel, there exists a low ceiling on the size of active forces. Under these circumstances, the IDF has stressed rapid mobilization through which full mobilized strength can be reached in three days,[37] certainly the fastest full mobilization period of any major armed force in the world. Israel relies on highly competent intelligence services to provide sufficient warning to ensure full mobilization prior to the onset of hostilities.[38]

Israel's military capabilities are a principal reason for the country's image as a key power center. Unlike the region's other military powers, political and economic influence are strictly limited (by Israel's isolation) to the impact flowing from its military strength. Arab foreign policies have often been based upon the conviction that Israel is dependent upon and therefore can be directed by the United States.[39] (In fact, Israeli political culture, reflecting Jewish history, has placed a premium upon independence from other countries.[40])

No other single country in the Middle East can boast Israel's military capabilities or preparedness. Indeed, no other Middle East state can defend itself against any likely attacker. The two Arab states closest to this condition are Egypt and Iraq, either of which can adequately protect its territorial integrity against any likely opponent *except* Israel.

Egypt has the largest armed forces in the Middle East[41] and one of the largest armies in the world. Unlike Israel, however, Egypt's power derives more from its size than its military capabilities. The largest of the Arab states, Egypt's population represents about 40 percent of total Arab population, and Egypt's skilled and unskilled manpower therefore represents a substantial part of total Arab labor. The country has been a primary political, educational, and religious leader of the Arab world, exporting teachers as well as laborers, and providing important religious institutions and instruction. The Arab world needs Egypt more than Egypt needs the rest of the Arab world.[42]

Although current Eygptian policies vis-a-vis Israel have temporarily isolated Eygpt in the Arab world, Cairo is still the single most influential capital in the political domain. No other Arab country alone could have pursued a separate peace with Israel. In part, Egypt's independence derives from the perceptions of the Egyptian people, whose Arab loyalties are less pronounced than those of many other Arab groups; who feel little kinship with or understanding of Iraqis, Syrians, Saudis, or other Arab peoples that seem far away and peripheral to Egypt; and whose political culture has been characterized by greater stability and regime legitimacy than that of other Arab countries.[43] It is their neighbor to the south — the Sudan — that Egyptians feel most sensitive about, for the Nile, vital to Egypt, flows through the Sudan.[44]

Iraq is the new Arab power, succeeding Syria in the Levant and in some respects surpassing the influence of Saudi Arabia as well.[45] Iraq's power ranking and stability may be dramatically altered, however, depending upon the outcome of the Gulf war. Iraq's probable oil reserves are enormous, second only to those of Saudi Arabia in the Middle East, and possibly larger than the Saudis'.[46] Unlike Saudi Arabia, however, Iraq has a population of about 13 million,[47] and despite substantial poverty and illiteracy in the country, parts of Iraq have a history of sophistication and culture.

The Iraqi active-duty armed forces before the war with Iran were the third largest in the Middle East,[48] and boast the largest Arab inventories of operable equipment in some categories.[49] Moreover, the Iraqi army has undergone extensive changes since its poor showing in the October 1973 War.[50] It is now somewhat more mobile, and marginally better trained than in the past.[51] Ground forces are the best equipped Arab army in the region.[52] Like the army, Iraq's air forces are well equipped, and Iraq was one of the first countries in the world to acquire the supersonic and nuclear-capable Tu-22 bomber in 1973.[53] Ground-based air defense has grown markedly since 1973 as well.[54] Nevertheless, Iraqi armed forces have a marginal capability to project power or sustain a military offensive. It is likely that Iraq will learn many lessons from its 1980-1982 war with Iran and that its ground forces will improve markedly as a result of this first and costly experience as a principal combatant. At the same time, however, a number of deficiencies will require years to remedy, and the remedies may in any event be politically unacceptable to the government. Principal among these shortcomings is command/control/communications, modernization of which would decentralize military power in excess of government wishes. However, other problem areas — air defense, tactical mobility, gunnery — may well improve. Much depends upon political changes that may result from the war.

The economic base of Iraqi power results from rapidly increasing oil revenue and sound planning. Since the major petroleum price increases have provided Iraq's capital wealth over the last decade, the country's commerce and the economy as a whole have swung from the East to a strongly Western orientation.[55] Moreover, the Iraqis have been more careful than many regimes in the Organization of Petroleum Exporting Countries (OPEC) in their international financial commitments; they have generally met these commitments promptly and fully.[56]

From a political standpoint, the Ba'ath government of Iraq is narrowly based in ethnic, regional, and religious terms,[57] but has proved to be both pragmatic and stable.[58] That the Steadfastness Front (opposed to the Camp David accords) met in Baghdad, and that Iraq was able to secure a truce in the 1979 Yemen war while Saudi Arabia failed, are indicative of Iraq's new role in the area.

Saudi Arabia's regional power depends almost solely upon its financial base.[59] For several years, the Saudi kingdom has been the principal oil exporter in OPEC, and has constituted the single most important voice in price setting, often being able to stalemate OPEC even when greatly outnumbered by members demanding higher price increases.[60] Because Mecca is in Saudi Arabia and, to some extent, because the late King Faisal was such a respected figure, the Saudis also advance a religious claim to leadership of the Muslim world. But while the Wahhabi House of Saud has controlled the country since its integration in the 1920s, it should be noted that Saudi regional influence has grown largely apace with the increase in oil revenues and oil power.

Saudi Arabia is a traditionalist monarchy, socially conservative even relative to most other Arab societies.[61] Despite good relations with the Soviet Union in the early years of the kingdom, Saudi elites are vehemently anticommunist, strongly anti-Soviet, and highly distrustful of socialist or other reformist or revolutionary ideologies.[62] The country has used its financial and religious resources increasingly in recent years to play an active role in regional affairs, exploiting these tools to both affect international relations and to influence the course of events within other Middle East states.[63]

By contrast, Syria's leadership star is on the wane. For reasons discussed in Chapter 7, Syria's government is precarious, and its influence declining. Syria remains a key country, and Syria's future will have a significant effect on the Levant in general and on the future of the Arab-Israeli conflict in particular.

ALIGNMENTS AND RIVALRIES

The one stable, indeed rigid, relationship in the Middle East was that between Israel and the Arab states. Before 1975, no Arab state was prepared to acknowledge Israel's presence and future publicly; before 1977, no Arab country officially entertained full peace talks and plans with Israel. Clearly, this pattern ended with the agreement between Anwar Sadat and Menachem Begin at Camp David and the subsequent signature of the Egyptian-Israeli peace treaty on March 26, 1979.[64] The treaty represents Egypt's willingness to formalize a radically new approach to the Israel-Palestine problem; it was a far-reaching commitment by Sadat's government, a commitment to the United States at least as much as to Israel.[65]

The implications of the Egyptian-Israeli treaty go well beyond a one-front peace. No coalition of Arab states without Egypt can present a credible conventional strategic threat to Israel.[66] Thus, Israel is relatively as secure as, or more secure than, other countries with respect to conventional war. Moreover, because Arab reactions to the Sadat approach and to the peace treaty were predictable and anticipated,[67] the responses have tended to underscore the salience and meaningfulness of Sadat's political strategy, a strategy that is generally accepted in Egypt. Israel, therefore, is no longer isolated in an Arab Middle East, and in fact, the Arab response has made a nonbelligerency into something akin to a limited, quasipolitical alliance.

In addition to the Egyptian normalization process, Israel's northern border has, with IDF help, come under the control of "Free Lebanon," a Christian[68] Lebanese secessionist polity that in reality is an Israeli protectorate. To the east is Jordan, a militarily weak state in the Arab-Israeli balance, but long a moderate on the issue of Israel's future role in the region. Jordan has opposed the Egyptian-Israeli treaty but has never completely rejected associating itself with the peace process.[69] In addition, prospects for the breakup of Syria and even the end of Syria itself are considerable.[70] A Lebanese-Israeli-Egyptian zone of peace with which Jordan and part of Syria might associate themselves may be emerging. Certainly, it can be said that Israel has broken through the Arab containment and, conversely, the Arab coalition against Israel has divided. The spring of 1982 also brought important developments that will determine or affect events for years to come.

From 1975 to 1979 Jordan and Syria maintained a close and cooperative relationship based upon the personal trust of Hafez Assad and King Hussein.[71] This alliance involved more than political coordination, stretching to economic and even military cooperation.[72] Jordan's king, recognizing his country's military weakness, always seeks to ensure that Jordan has a protector.[73] From 1975 to 1979 that protector was Syria. With Assad's future clearly limited, King Hussein and Jordan consequently moved toward better and closer relations with Iraq, Syria's enemy.[74] With Jordan, Iraqi relationships have improved rapidly due partly to common interests in the Gulf and on the Peninsula,[75] partly to the disintegration of Syria, and partly to Jordan's image as a window to the West (particularly the United States).[76]

Iraq remains a critical junction of the Eastern Mediterranean and the Gulf. Its alignment pattern reflects the country's historic ambivalence in this regard. On the one hand, Iraq's political power had begun to be strongly felt in the Levant, where Baghdad was a key leader in opposing the Camp David accords[77] and where the heat of its friction with Syria has once again increased. On the other hand, and more importantly at present, Iraq has made a conscious and to date very successful effort to improve its relations with the countries of the Arabian Peninsula,[78] particularly Jordan and Saudi Arabia; to reinforce the voices of the OPEC price moderates;[79] and to speak forcefully in favor of Gulf security and stability.[80] The 1980 Iraqi attack on Iran was widely seen in the Gulf as Iraq's response to the destabilizing calls for Islamic (read, Shi'a) revolution emanating from Tehran. As we have indicated, Iraq, although not bordering on the Mediterranean, is an actor in both the Eastern Mediterranean subregion and the Gulf. The importance of these two arenas to Iraqi decision elites has varied, but today there is no question that Iraq's primary attention is directed toward the Gulf. In large part, the Gulf interest may be a reaction to the deposition of the shah of Iran. No great friend of Iraq,[81] the shah and the Iraqi leadership had reached a mutually acceptable accommodation in 1975 that both parties sincerely endeavored to honor.[82] The overthrow of the shah brought forth a religious government that promoted the regional political consciousness of the Shi'a Muslim sect, a minority in the Muslim world, but a majority in both Iraq and Iran.[83] Because Shi'as are greatly underrepresented and socially underprivileged in Iraq,[84] the government has been extremely sensitive to Iran's attempts to mobilize Iraqi Shi'as.[85] When the animosity that characterized Iranian-Iraqi relations for years before 1975 returned, Iran raised the Iraqi Shi'a issue while Iraq encouraged Kurdish unrest in Iran,[86] demanded a return to the historic Shatt al-'Arab boundary rather than the one established under the 1975 treaty,[87] continued to claim Khuzistan (Iran's oil province),[88] and insisted that Iran withdraw from three Arab islands seized in 1971 and occupied since.[89] Then, the war.

Yet, Iraq's policy for the Gulf emphasizes the stability and security in that region vital to the continuation of the oil commerce that is an Iraqi economic necessity.[90] The war was expected — erroneously, it turns out — to be a brief anomaly. Relations with Jordan have improved in large part because Jordan's credibility to and relationship with the smaller Gulf countries is seen as a means of enlisting their cooperation with Baghdad.[91] Moreover, Iraq and Saudi Arabia have begun to overcome past differences and are coordinating policies on a number of issues both openly and secretly.[92] And when the People's Democratic Republic of Yemen (PDRY) attacked the Yemen Arab Republic (YAR) in early 1979, it was Aden's former ally that succeeded in halting the attack and later in forcing a withdrawal.[93]

Never trusted by the Arab states, Iran under the new Islamic republic has further isolated itself from its fellow littoral states of the Gulf by exporting Shi'a consciousness.[94] Since many of the smaller sheikhdoms have sizable Shi'a communities (in some cases, Iranian),[95] their governments view increased sectarian consciousness with great suspicion.[96] Iran's continued occupation of Abu Musa and the Tunbs and the resurfacing of claims (that the shah's government had disavowed) to Bahrain[97] have excited renewed Arab concern for security and stability in the Gulf. Thus, while the Iran-Saudi and Iran-Iraq rivalry for Gulf leadership have evaporated as a result of the deposition of the imperial Iranian government, conflicts between Iran and the Arab Gulf states remain active.

Saudi allies have then also begun to shift — toward Iraq, away from Egypt. (However, Egyptian alignment with the United States and opposition to the Soviet Union will ultimately serve as a strong attraction to Riyadh.) Improving relations with Iraq are important, since Iraq and Saudi Arabia were the dominant powers of the Gulf from 1979 to 1981, are still major actors there, and remain two of the three principal Arab powers. By contrast with its ties to the north,

Saudi relations with the Yemen Arab Republic are deteriorating.[98] Long a satellite of Saudi Arabia, Yemen is experiencing substantial disenchantment with that role because many Yemenis feel their country and people are taken for granted and resent Saudi domination and interference.[99] South Yemen (or PDRY) has been a principal Saudi antagonist for years, and has become one of the Soviet Union's more dependable clients, providing port and base privileges and playing host to a substantial number of Cuban and Soviet military personnel.[100]

Relationships in North Africa are far less intense and complicated. Morocco and Tunisia have been among the most consistently moderate and pro-Western regimes in the Arab world, and have generally enjoyed very good, if not very intense, relations.[101] Algeria, however, has been at odds with Morocco for Maghreb leadership ever since Algerian independence in 1962, a rivalry that has taken on several manifestations — border disputes, territorial conflicts over irredentist claims, and ideological skirmishes — and even erupted into open warfare. Libya, too, though not particularly close to Algeria, has long been aligned against Morocco and particularly against its king, Hassan.[102] Both Algeria and Libya have had acceptable relations with weak Tunisia, though the latter has always considered one of the two to be its prime external threat. And both Algeria and Libya have supported the Polisario, a nationalist group fighting Morocco over the status of the former Spanish Sahara.

In spite of Libya's problem with Morocco and intermittent differences with Tunisia, its principal adversary has for years been Egypt. The two states have maintained unremitting and intense verbal combat for years, and engaged in short-lived hostilities in 1977.[103] To the extent the Egyptian-Libyan confrontation forced underpopulated and then-lightly-armed Libya to turn to the Soviet Union for military support, it is ironic that Moscow's response — massive arms transfers and a very large Soviet presence[104] — sharply increased the conflict intensity, since Sadat was convinced Libya's Soviet relationship is part of the USSR's strategy to threaten Egypt and its new policies.[105] The Egyptian-Libyan rivalry is particularly important to the issue of nuclear proliferation because human and mineral resource disparities have the effect of increasing the economic and political attractiveness to Egypt of the military option and decreasing the military cost. It is, therefore, hardly surprising that Libya's mercurial, unofficial (but real) leader, Muammar Qaddafi, has openly sought the acquisition of a nuclear capability.[106] Although he claims to seek nuclear weapons for the Arab-Israeli conflict, Qaddafi probably sees a more immediate threat in Egypt, and a much safer target for political uses of the nuclear poker chip.

REGIONAL ECONOMY AND NATIONAL ECONOMIES

The Middle East is a region of developing economies, with only one (Israel) having many of the characteristics of a developed economy. The largest employment sector is generally agriculture, but Middle Eastern agriculture is notoriously inefficient. Yet, unquestionably the dominant factor in the regional economy today, and the reason for its vital role in the international economy, is petroleum.[107]

Almost a decade ago, before the 1973-74 oil embargo and price increases, James Akins wrote prophetically about the influx of power and wealth into the Middle East, and especially the Gulf, that was likely to occur from the petroleum supply picture then still forming.[108] Since then, oil and the oil trade have completely altered the face of the Middle East economy. Every country in the area, whether a petroleum exporter or not, has been directly and significantly affected by the petroleum situation.[109] In this section, we provide an overview of only the most important economic developments.

Oil and other natural resources are located quite unevenly in the Middle East, and are located principally where people are not — Algeria, Iran, and Iraq being the exceptions. They are located away from the major regional centers of learning, away from the areas of literacy — Cairo, Beirut, Damascus, and Israel generally. Thus, the "absorptive capacity" of technology and petroleum revenue is limited by manpower shortages or skills shortages or both. Another harsh reality of Middle East development is that high fertility rates have created extraordinarily young populations throughout the region (except, again, in Israel), taxing the ability of the working-age population to improve national standards of living.[110] Among nonoil producers, economies and development prospects are best understood in the light of the level of infrastructural development. This would also be the case to a large extent for the petroleum producers in the absence of their primary export.

Thus, four or five Middle East countries have major advantages in the struggle to develop — a reasonable population base and a strong capital base — and another (Israel) is already substantially developed. Five or six oil producers have abundant capital but serious shortages of manpower. Six others are more or less typical third world countries with fair to good development prospects. The Yemens are probably closest to fourth world membership.[111]

It cannot be excluded that the frustration of development aspirations may lead to increasing regional conflict. Leaders of all the oil-producing countries, for example, believe their new wealth must and will pave the road to development. Yet, despite remarkable changes in the face of these nations, it is unclear that they are making real progress toward literacy, health, and self-sustaining economies.[112] Since popular aspirations in many of these countries have evolved into expectations, the demands on the political system may conduce to internal conflict in some countries, which will inevitably affect the foreign policies of others.

Finally, while oil is located unevenly in the Middle East, most of the region has felt the impact of the petroleum trade. Nonoil countries like Jordan and Lebanon have experienced an unprecedented influx of capital — Lebanon in spite of its internal conflict — *and* concomitant inflation. Japanese and Western investment is ubiquitous. The price of oil for nonproducers has had a seriously adverse impact upon budgets and development planning.

SOCIAL ENVIRONMENT AND INTERDEPENDENCE

The social environment is important to the understanding of politics in the Middle East. Particularly in the case of issues that strike the boundaries of the possible, social realities in the Middle East contribute to the establishment of the parameters of behavior.

The dominant social reality in the Middle East is an overwhelming sense of regional kinship among the peoples from Morocco in the west to Iraq and the western Gulf countries in the east, excepting only Israel. Throughout this entire sweep of territory, the majority of the population is Arab. "Arabism" is not easy to define: it is a question of self-identity. Arabs are Semitic peoples, but are heavily intermixed with Hamitic stock all across North Africa. They are mostly Islamic, but include members of many other religions as well (especially in Iraq, Lebanon, and Syria).

Egypt, the most populous Arab country, while self-avowedly Arab is probably as little so as any Arab society. Yet, it is the Levantine Arabs, not the Egyptians, who question Egypt's "Arabism." Morocco, Algeria, Tunisia, and Libya manifest symptoms of insecurity about their Arab credentials — they work very hard at being true Arabs. Lebanese Christians are more ambiguous about their identity. Tracing their lineage to the Phoenicians, they tend to see themselves as Arabs in most contexts, but often as non-Arabs when their religious community is threatened.

We *are* arguing that Arab consciousness does have meaning, and that it is a more robust explanatory variable for perceptual commonalities than most outside observers realize. For all the arguments between Arabs, their sense of community is deep, broad, and pervasive vis-a-vis the outside world. Moreover, the constant interchange across all levels of society is a phenomenon unique in the modern world. Students, laborers, politicians, philosophers, linguists, scientists — all groups travel frequently, and not infrequently spend much or most of their lives in Arab countries other than their own.

This population exchange leads to subtle dependencies not easily discerned by the usual measures (such as trade patterns or migration). Labor and student exchanges, for example, are of such magnitude that even as major an issue as disagreement over the Camp David accords has not been allowed to affect them: Egyptian teachers and laborers continue to work throughout the Arab world; Arab students continue to study by the tens of thousands in Cairo.[113] Trade routes (including extralegal trade), pipelines, wellhead-refinery linkages, agriculture, and water resources all manifest significant transnationalism in the Middle East.

NOTES

1. The literature on the Arab-Israeli conflict is voluminous. Two of the most useful references on the subject are Fred John Khouri, *The Arab-Israeli Dilemma* (Syracuse: Syracuse University Press, 1968) and John Norton Moore, ed., *The Arab-Israeli Conflict*, 3 vols. (Princeton: Princeton University Press, 1974).

2. *Time*, September 11, 1972, and October 3, 1977, provides some details concerning alleged clandestine meetings between King Hussein and Israeli leaders.

3. Indeed, the secret nature of Arab talks with Israel demonstrates the official rejection of the Jewish state.

4. The "confrontation" or "front-line" Arab states included Egypt before 1979, Syria, and Jordan, although Jordan's status became more that of a "supporting" state after 1970-71. "Supporting" states included all the other Arab countries from virtually neutral Lebanon, geographically on the "front-line," to participant Iraq, which behaved in many respects more like a confrontation state.

5. We have made this point in R. D. McLaurin, Mohammed Mughisuddin, and Abraham R. Wagner, *Foreign Policy Making in the Middle East* (New York: Praeger, 1977), pp. 2-3.

6. See Thomas W. Lippman, "Sadat's Strategy Emerges," *Washington Post*, December 4, 1977, p. A1.

7. Cf. Paul A. Jureidini and R. D. McLaurin, *Beyond Camp David: Emerging Alignments and Leaders in the Middle East* (Syracuse: Syracuse University Press, forthcoming), passim.

8. Nazli Choucri, "Demographic Changes in the Middle East," *The Political Economy of the Middle East: 1973-78* (Washington, D.C.: U.S. Government Printing Office for the Joint Economic Committee, Congress of the United States, 1980), pp. 43ff; Nazli Choucri, *Labor Transfers in the Arab World* (Cambridge: Center for International Studies, MIT, 1979).

9. Charles Issawi, "Economic Trends in the Middle East and Future Prospects," *The Political Economy*, pp. 16, 24.

10. R. D. McLaurin and James M. Price, "OPEC Current Account Surpluses: Assistance to the Arab Front-Line States," *Oriente Moderno*, LVIII, no. 11 (November 1978), pp. 533-46.

11. Jureidini and McLaurin, *Beyond Camp David*, pp. 63-64.

12. Paul A. Jureidini, R. D. McLaurin, and James M. Price, "The Structures and Parameters of U.S.-Jordan Relations," Abbott Associates SR52 (August 1979).

13. An insulation that U.S. policy consciously sought to reinforce.

14. Paul A. Jureidini and R. D. McLaurin, "Inside and Outside Iraq," Abbott Associates SR54 (January 1980) and sources cited there.

15. David Curry, "Petrodollars and the International Payments System," *The Political Economy*, pp. 306-12.

16. See the comments of Walter J. Levy, "Oil and the Decline of the West," *Foreign Affairs* LVIII, no. 5 (Summer 1980), pp. 999-1015, and of "Bridget Gail" (pseud.), "The West's Jugular Vein: Arab Oil," *Armed Forces Journal International*, August 1978, pp. 18ff.

17. Jureidini and McLaurin, *Beyond Camp David*, passim.

18. E.g., the sources in note 16 above.

19. Willard A. Beling, ed., *King Faisal and the Modernization of Saudi Arabia* (Boulder: Westview, 1980) and Chap. 6 of this book. See, however, Fern Racine Gold and Charles K. Ebinger, "Economic Change in the Oil Exporting Countries of the Middle East," *The Political Economy*, pp. 91-101.

20. See the statement of Assistant Secretary of State Harold H. Saunders before the Subcommittee on Europe and the Middle East of the House Committee on Foreign Affairs, July 26, 1979.

21. Jureidini and McLaurin, *Beyond Camp David*, passim.

22. Gulf security is the dominant foreign policy theme of public statements of *all* of the smaller countries of the Gulf, and has been a preoccupation of Iraq for some years as well. Under the shah, Iran, too, was heavily concerned with the issue of Gulf security.

23. Emile A. Nakhleh, "Future Direction of U.S. Policy in the Arabian Peninsula and the Gulf: Prospects and Reflections," *The Arabian Peninsula, Red Sea, and Gulf: Strategic Considerations*, ed. Enver M. Koury and Emile A. Nakhleh (Bethesda: Institute of Middle Eastern and North African Affairs, 1979), Chap. V; National Security Decision Memorandum (NDSM) 92.

24. See Edmund Ghareeb, "Iraq and Gulf Security," *The Impact of the Iranian Events upon Persian Gulf and United States Security*, ed. Z. Michael Szaz (Washington, D.C.: American Foreign Policy Institute, 1979), pp. 39-64.

25. In 1971 Iran's armed forces captured the islands of Abu Musa, Big Tunb, and Little Tunb. These islands were nominally under the sovereignty of the United Arab Emirates. See "The Role of Sheikh Saqr," *An Nahar Arab Report*, II, no. 50 (December 13, 1971), pp. 2-3; "New Arab State," ibid., II, no. 49 (December 6, 1971), pp. 3-4.

26. See Rouhollah K. Ramazani, *The Persian Gulf: Iran's Role* (Charlottesville, Va.: University Press of Virginia, 1972), Shahram Chubin and Sepehr Zabi, *The Foreign Relations of Iran: A Developing State in a Zone of Great Power Conflict* (Berkeley, Los Angeles: University of California, 1974), or any of Alvin Cottrell's numerous publications on the shah's security perceptions.

27. Dale R. Tahtinen, *National Security Challenges to Saudi Arabia* (Washington, D.C.: American Enterprise Institute, 1978), p. 5.

28. Lewis W. Snider and R. D. McLaurin, *Saudi Arabia's Air Defense in the 1980s* (Alexandria, Va.: Abbott Associates, 1979), pp. 14-15, 35-39.

29. Cf. Drew Middleton, "Fall of Shah in Iran Unnerving to Saudis," *New York Times*, June 14, 1979, p. 5.

30. Drew Middleton, "Turmoil in Iran is Breaking up Patterns in Gulf," ibid., p. 13; James McCartney, "Persian Gulf Politics Hold the Key to Much of the Future of the U.S." *Philadephia Inquirer*, December 26, 1979, p. 17-A.

31. James M. Markham, "Kuwait is Calming down after Jitters about Iran," *New York Times*, June 28, 1979, p. 18; Emile A. Nakhleh, "Securing the Gulf," ibid., January 8, 1980, p. 19.

32. Anthony H. Cordesman, "The Arab-Israeli Balance: How Much Is Too Much?" *Armed Forces Journal International*, October 1977, pp. 32-39; W. Seth Carus, "The Military Balance of Power in the Middle East," *Current History*, LXXIV, no. 1 (January 1978), pp. 29ff.

33. International Institute for Strategic Studies (IISS), *The Military Balance, 1979-80* (1979).

34. Anthony Pascal et al., *Men and Arms in the Middle East: The Human Factor in Military Modernization* (Santa Monica: Rand, 1979), Chapter II.

35. Ibid., Geoffrey Kemp and Michael Vlahos, "The Military Balance in the Middle East in 1978," *The Political Economy of the Middle East: 1973-78*, pp. 430-33.

36. Kemp and Vlahos, "The Military Balance," pp. 434-37; Amos Perlmutter, "The Arab-Israeli Conflict: Strategic Concepts and Practices," ibid., pp. 486-502.

37. IISS, *The Military Balance*.

38. Cf. the articles by Zeev Schiff on the failure of Israeli intelligence in October 1973, *Haaretz*, June 22-June 27, 1974; Steven J. Rosen, "What the Next Arab-Israeli War Might Look Like," *International Security*, II, no. 4 (Spring 1978); Steven J. Rosen and Martin Indyk, "The Temptation to Pre-empt in a Fifth Arab-Israeli War," *Orbis*, XX, no. 2 (Summer 1976), pp. 265-85. Since the October War, a substantial literature has grown up in open sources over surprise, deception, and intelligence failure. See, e.g., Michael I. Handel, "Perception, Deception and Surprise: The Case of the Yom Kippur War," *Jerusalem Papers on Peace Problems*, 19 (1976); Abraham Ben-Zvi, "Hindsight and Foresight: A Conceptual Framework for the Analysis of Surprise Attacks," *World Politics*, XXVIII, no. 3 (April 1976), pp. 381-95; Avraham Shlaim, "Failures in National Intelligence Estimates: The Case of the Yom Kippur War," ibid., pp. 348-80; Michael I. Handel, "Surprise and Change in International Politics," *International Security*, IV, no. 4 (Spring 1980), pp. 57-85; Shlomo Gazit, "Estimates and Fortune Telling in Intelligence Work," ibid., pp. 36-56; Michael I. Handel, "The Yom Kippur War and the Inevitability of Surprise," *International Studies Quarterly*, XXI, no. 3 (September 1977), pp. 461-501; Richard K. Betts, "Analysis, War and Decision: Why Intelligence Failures are Inevitable," *World Politics*, XXXI, no. 1 (October 1978), pp. 61-89.

39. While this image has started to change, the concomitant of the change has been a feeling that the United States is less powerful and less important than previously thought.

40. This notion is an inherent element of historical Zionism, reflecting the Jewish experience in the Diaspora. See Theodor Herzl, *The Jewish State* (New York: Herzl Press, 1970), a translation of Herzl's original pamphlet, *Der Judenstaat*.

41. IISS, *The Military Balance*.

42. However, we hasten to add that even Egypt can remain isolated from the remainder of the Arab world for only a limited period. Pressures to return to boundaries of Arab acceptance are inherent in all Arab states.

43. Jureidini and McLaurin, *Beyond Camp David*, pp. 2-3, 27-29.

44. Ibid., p. 28.

45. Jureidini and McLaurin, "Inside"; Claudia Wright, "Iraq – New Power in the Middle East," *Foreign Affairs*, LVIII, no. 2 (Winter 1979/80), pp. 257-77.

46. "Proven reserves" refers to petroleum that is feasibly exploited with current technology at present prices. However, countries with a favorable reserves-to-production ratio tend to be greatly underexplored. This is particularly

applicable in the case of Iraq, since the country was boycotted after its national-ization of foreign petroleum holdings.

47. U.S. Central Intelligence Agency (CIA), *National Basic Intelligence Factbook* (Washington, D.C., July 1979).

48. IISS, *The Military Balance*.

49. E.g., modern tanks. Ibid.

50. See Trevor N. Dupuy, *Elusive Victory: The Arab-Israeli Wars 1947-1974* (New York: Harper & Row, 1970), pp. 467-68.

51. Drew Middleton, "Iraqis Hold Military Edge in Confrontation with Iranians," *New York Times*, April 13, 1980, p. 14.

52. Amos Perlmutter, "The Courtship of Iraq," *New Republic*, May 3, 1980, pp. 19-22.

53. Roger F. Pajak, "Soviet Arms Aid in the Middle East since the October War," *The Political Economy*, p. 469.

54. Middleton, "Iraqis Hold Military Edge."

55. J. P. Smith, "Oil Wealth Causing a Shift in Iraq's Foreign Policy," *Washington Post*, August 8, 1978, p. A14.

56. Jureidini and McLaurin, *Beyond Camp David*.

57. Jureidini and McLaurin, "Inside and Outside Iraq," p. 2.

58. McLaurin, Mughisuddin, and Wagner, *Foreign Policy Making*, Chap. 4.

59. By this we mean simply that on the basis of the standard measures of power, Saudi Arabia has few resources − population, industrial production, military capabilities − to exert influence. Within the region the Saudi asset that confers power is the country's financial resources, which permit substantial aid flows.

60. Until 1979-80, Saudi power derived from its ability to unilaterally increase production (and thus drive down prices) as well as its production margin over any other OPEC country. The rapid decrease in Iranian output, however, reduced Saudi flexibility.

61. The founder of the Saudi monarchy represented Wahhabism, a funda-mentalist Sunni movement. Consequently, Wahhabi principles today underline the Saudi value structure and pose significant constraints on both domestic and foreign policies and actions.

62. See Adeed Dawisha, "Saudi Arabia's Search for Security," *Adelphi Papers*, 158 (Winter 1979-80), p. 20.

63. Ibid., pp. 19-24.

64. See Paul A. Jureidini, R. D. McLaurin, and James M. Price, "Arab Reactions to the Egyptian-Israeli Peace Treaty," Abbott Associates SR48 (March 1979).

65. Jureidini and McLaurin, *Beyond Camp David*.

66. Kemp and Vlahos, "The Military Balance"; Rosen, "What the Next."

67. Jureidini, McLaurin, and Price, "Arab Reactions."

68. "Free Lebanon" was established by Lebanese Army Major Saad Haddad, a Christian. However, the region included in "Free Lebanon" is pre-dominantly Shi'a.

69. E.g., Jonathan Randal, "Jordan Seeks Wider Talks," *Washington Post*, October 2, 1970, pp. 1, 16; Christopher S. Wren, "Hussein Calling on Arabs to Offer Their Own Framework for Peace," *New York Times*, October 29, 1979, p. 3.

70. Jureidini and McLaurin, "Political Disintegration and Conflict Reduction in the Eastern Mediterranean Area," Abbott Associates SR51 (October 1979).

71. Avigdor Haselkorn, R. D. McLaurin, and Abraham R. Wagner, *Middle East Net Assessment: Regional Threat Perceptions* (Marina del Rey: Analytical Assessments Corporation, 1979), p. 58.

72. Paul A. Jureidini and R. D. McLaurin, "The Hashemite Kingdom of Jordan," *Lebanon in Crisis: Participants and Issues*, ed. P. Edward Haley and Lewis W. Snider (Syracuse: Syracuse University Press, 1979), pp. 153, 198; Fehmi Saddy, *The Eastern Front: Implications of the Syrian/Palestinian/Jordanian Entente and the Lebanese Civil War* (Alexandria, Va.: Abbott Associates, 1976), pp. 13-16.

73. Jureidini and McLaurin, "The Hashemite Kingdom," p. 148.

74. Jureidini and McLaurin, *Beyond Camp David*.

75. Jureidini and McLaurin, *Beyond Camp David*, Chap. IV.

76. Ibid.

77. Indeed, it was at Baghdad that the united Arab opposition to Camp David formulated its strategy of opposition to the accords and "punishment" of Egypt.

78. "Le Jeu d'Irak," *L'Express*, December 1, 1979, p. 68; Marwan Iskander, "The Jordanian Example," *An Nahar Arab Report & Memo*, IV, no. 4 (January 21, 1980), pp. 1-2.

79. "Iraq: East or West," *An Nahar Arab Report & Memo*, III, no. 24 (June 11, 1979); Dusko Doder, "4 OPEC Nations Reported Setting Record Oil Prices," *Washington Post*, December 29, 1979, p. A1.

80. Jureidini and McLaurin, "Inside and Outside," p. 9.

81. As we have indicated, Iran-Iraq rivalry is traditional. Thus, under the shah, Iran supported the Kurdish insurgency against the Iraqi central government and conducted many other unfriendly acts directed against Baghdad. However, these acts took place before the 1975 agreement.

82. By the terms of the 1975 accord between Iran and Iraq, the former terminated its support for dissident Iraqi Kurds while the latter relinquished its claim to the entire Shatt al-Arab waterway under a four-decades-old treaty. Although there were other provisions, this quid pro quo was the key element of the agreement.

83. Exact population figures are unknown in the Middle East, and those contained in even Iran's census are highly questionable. (For example, the number of Arabs according to Iranian official census figures is probably less than 10 percent of the actual total.) Reasonable estimates of Shi'a population percentages are 88 percent in Iran, 53 percent in Iraq. R. D. McLaurin, ed., *The Political Role of the Minority Groups in the Middle East* (New York: Praeger, 1979), pp. 271-72. Accuracy in estimating Shi'a population figures is also complicated by the common Shi'a practice of dissimulation.

84. James M. Markham, "Arab Countries Fear Spread of Iran's Shiite Revolt," *New York Times*, January 29, 1979, p. 3.

85. Ibid.

86. Jonathan C. Randal, "Iraq Moves to Sever 1975 Border Accord with Iran," *Washington Post*, November 1, 1979, p. A29; FBIS, June 14, 1979,

pp. R5-6. Iranian Kurds have been armed by Iraq, and leading Iranian dissidents are in Iraqi Kurdistan — armed and prepared to assist in deposing Khomeini.

87. Randal, "Iraq Moves."

88. The status of this claim is not clear. Most Iraqi comments suggest that Khuzistan ("Arabistan," as Iraqis call it) is part of the Arab nation. They speak of liberating its inhabitants. The focus is on "Arab" not "Iraqi" character. See, e.g., FBIS, April 18, 1980, p. E-2.

89. Ibid., April 17, 1980, p. E-4, and April 6, 1980, p. E-3.

90. Article by Kenan Akin, *Tercuman*, February 29, 1980, p. 6.

91. Jureidini and McLaurin, *Beyond Camp David*, Chap. IV.

92. "Le Jeu d'Irak."

93. The importance of the Iraqi role was not merely its power in stopping the soi-disant Marxist regime in Aden. The fact that Iraq succeeded where others, like Saudi Arabia, failed is also noteworthy.

94. See Emile A. Nakhleh, "Islamic Revolution: Dangerous Export," *Washington Post*, October 22, 1979, p.. A16; Markham, "Arab Countries Fear Spread," p. 3.

95. McLaurin, *The Political Role*, appendices.

96. See references in note 94 above.

97. William Branigin, "Iran Charges New Iraqi Air Raid, Renews Bahrain Claim," *Washington Post*, June 16, 1979, p. A18. In fact, the claim to Bahrain remains unofficial, but is clearly officially "inspired."

98. While Yemeni policy before 1962 and after 1967 was heavily influenced by Saudi Arabia, recent Yemeni initiatives — such as the brief flirtation with the USSR in 1979-80 — have been independent of Saudi Arabia.

99. Discussions with senior Yemenis in interviews in January 1980.

100. E.g., U.S. Central Intelligence Agency, National Foreign Assessment Center, *Communist Aid Activities in Non-Communist Less Developed Countries 1978* (Washington, D.C., 1979), ER 79-10412U, pp. 34-35.

101. Kerr, "Political Trends," passim.

102. Indeed, Muammar Qaddafi, Libya's leader, has financed efforts aimed at the assassination of King Hassan.

103. The short border war has not been widely discussed in the literature, and in fact even today the only detailed accounts are those filed by journalists who were not present.

104. U.S. CIA, *Communist Aid Activities.* See also the predecessors to this report in the same series.

105. Dennis Chaplin, "Libya: Military Spearhead against Sadat," *Military Review*, LIX, no. 11 (November 1979), pp. 42-50.

106. E.g., Mohamed Heikal, *The Road to Ramadan* (New York: Quadrangle, 1975), pp. 76-77; Paul Jabber, "A Nuclear Middle East," ACIS Working Paper 6 (Los Angeles: Center for Arms Control and International Security, UCLA, 1977), p. 13; "Rumors of Libyan Atomic Bomb Quest Raise Fears," *Washington Post*, July 30, 1979, p. A9

107. We do not overlook the financial importance of the region in saying this, since the financial strength of the Middle East lies in its control of most of the world's known oil reserves and its wealth results from that petroleum concentration.

108. James E. Akins, "The Oil Crisis: This Time the Wolf is Here," *Foreign Affairs*, LI, no. 3 (April 1973), pp. 462-90.

109. Some of the telling results of the oil trade are inflation and the migration of skilled personnel to the Gulf. Unfortunately, these concomitants of the economic boom have affected Arab countries otherwise unaffected by the new capital influx.

110. John Waterbury and Ragaei El Mallakh, *The Middle East in the Coming Decade: From Wellhead to Well-Being?* (New York: McGraw-Hill, 1978), p. 28.

111. The "fourth world" is the natural extension of the "third world" idea. If the third world is "developing," the fourth world is possibly beyond developmental hope.

112. Waterbury and El Mallakh, *The Middle East*, Part 1. Cf. Charles Issawi, "Economic Trends in the Middle East and Future Prospects," *The Political Economy*, pp. 7-24; and R. S. Eckaus, "An Overview of Real Economic Development in the Middle East, ibid., pp. 55-90.

113. Cf. Nazli Choucri, "Demographic Changes in the Middle East," *The Political Economy*, pp. 43ff and United Nations, *UNESCO Statistical Yearbook*.

EGYPTIAN FOREIGN POLICYMAKING

ENVIRONMENT

Like many third world countries, Egypt's foreign policy is made in an environment characterized by rather weak political institutions where political authority and effective power are concentrated in the hands of one man, the president. The president may delegate some powers in certain domestic arenas such as agriculture, industrial development, or social affairs. However, he retains full decision-making power in the two critical areas of defense and foreign policy. Although the consultative machinery appears to be in place in the form of a cabinet (including a foreign-policy advisor) and a parliament (the People's Assembly), the role of such formally constituted bodies, if any, in making foreign policy is confined to discussions taken in these areas after decisions have been made. Furthermore, the existence of a People's Assembly and the proliferation of political parties notwithstanding, the power of the president depends ultimately on the support he enjoys from the military.[1]

The power of the president in defense and foreign policymaking is illustrated by such facts as the following:

• Only 14 people were informed in advance of President Gamel Abdel Nasser's decision to nationalize the Suez Canal Company in 1956;
• President Anwar Sadat's decision to join Egypt with Libya and Syria in the Federation of Arab Republics in 1971 was taken without any consultations;
• Only two people knew in advance of Sadat's decision to expel some 21,000 Soviet advisors and technicians from Egypt in July 1972, and they were informed only a few hours before the Soviet ambassador was informed;

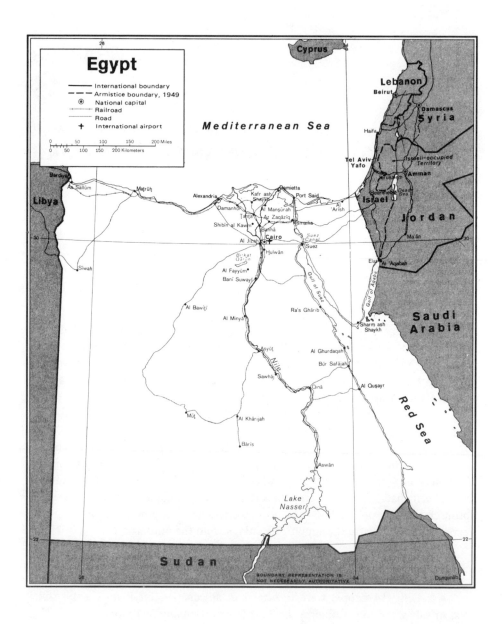

Egypt

—— International boundary
- - - Armistice boundary, 1949
⊛ National capital
┼┼┼┼ Railroad
········ Road
✛ International airport

0   50   100   150   200 Miles
0 50 100 150 200 Kilometers

Mediterranean Sea

Cyprus

Lebanon
Beirut

Damascus
Syria

Haifa

Tel Aviv-
Yafo

Israeli-occupied
Territory

Jerusalem
Amman

Bardiyah

Aş Sallūm

Maţrūḥ

Damietta

Alexandria

Kafr ash
Shaykh

Port Said

Al
'Arīsh

Libya

Damanhūr

Al Manşūrah

Az Zaqāzīq

Ismailia

Israel
Beersheba

Dead
Sea

Jordan

Tanta

Shibīn al Kawm

Banhā

Al Jīzah

Cairo

Suez
Canal

Suez

Ma'ān

30

30

Birkat
Qārūn

Ḩulwān

Elat

Al 'Aqabah

Sīwah

Al Fayyūm

Banī Suwayf

Al Bawīţī

Al Minyā

Ra's Ghārib

**Saudi
Arabia**

Sharm ash
Shaykh

Asyūţ

Al Ghurdaqah

Būr Safājah

Sawhāj

Qinā

Al Quşayr

Red Sea

Mūţ

Al Khārijah

Bāris

Aswān

*Lake
Nasser*

22

22

Sudan

BOUNDARY REPRESENTATION IS
NOT NECESSARILY AUTHORITATIVE

Dunqunāb

32

- Sadat's selection of October 6, 1973 as D-Day for launching Operation Badr against Israel was taken in consultation with Syria's President Assad on August 28-29, 1973, and only later did Sadat inform his own senior staff;
- Only one person, the foreign minister, knew of Sadat's decision to go to Jerusalem in November 1977.

All these decisions had a decisive impact on war and peace in the Middle East and on Egypt's political destiny. None of these decisions was taken arbitrarily or haphazardly, but the fact that they were largely undertaken by one man underscores the fact that in Egypt the president is the final and sole arbiter of all major decisions affecting defense and foreign policy.

The foregoing remarks do not mean that foreign-policy decisions are taken in an institutional vacuum. However, the momentum and effectiveness of Egypt's institutional structure depend upon presidential direction and control. The political structure that has evolved since the 1950s has been geared to supporting a strong presidency with enough power to make formal decisions without much intrusion from other institutions. This condition partly derives from the fact that Egypt's decision-making structures have not achieved a very high degree of institutionalization. That is, in a highly institutionalized decision-making environment, the chief executive derives his authority from the perceived legitimacy of the political system. In Egypt, however, the legitimacy of the political institutions still derives from the prestige and charisma of the chief executive. For example, the legitimacy of Sadat in the period immediately following Nasser's death was not based so much on any independently derived legal or institutional sanctions as it was on Sadat's long and close association with Nasser. Sadat had to establish his own independently derived authority largely through successes in the foreign-policy domain. Until that was accomplished, Sadat could scarcely deviate from Nasser's policies, which were grounded on the principles of pan-Arabism, anticolonialism, and Egypt's leadership of the Arab revolutionary struggle.

Similarly, Husni Mubarak's legitimacy derives more from an association with Sadat that began in the 1950s and from the fact that Sadat was grooming him to be his successor than from the formal authority vested in the presidency. Until he can establish his own independent authority, Mubarak is unlikely to deviate significantly from Sadat's policies, which were based on Egyptian patriotism, the Open Door Policy to the West (*infitah*), a peaceful resolution of the Arab-Israeli conflict, and the continued centrality of Egypt in the Arab world. Like Sadat and Nasser before him, Mubarak's success in establishing his own authority will likely depend on success in the foreign-policy arena. To appreciate why this is so requires an understanding of the primacy that defense and foreign affairs occupy in Egypt's policy environment and how foreign policy has been instrumental in legitimizing the authority of the chief executive since the middle 1950s.

In retrospect, the primacy that defense and foreign policy occupy in Egypt's policy environment stems from the fact that while Nasser and the other members of the Revolutionary Command Council were dedicated to modernization and domestic reform, defense and foreign policy continued to absorb most of their attention and energy: the continuous need to resist U.S. pressures, beginning in 1953, to join a Western-sponsored collective security pact; the negotiation of Britain's withdrawal from the Suez Canal Zone in 1954; the urgency of finding a reliable source of arms after the conclusion of the Baghdad Pact and Israel's attack on Khan Yunis in Gaza in 1955; the need to negotiate international financing of the High Dam at Aswan; the Suez crisis in 1956 and the subsequent Anglo-French-Israeli invasion of Egypt the same year; the U.S. attempt to isolate Egypt from potential Arab allies with the Eisenhower Doctrine in 1957, followed by the formation of the United Arab Republic in 1958 and the American military intervention in Lebanon the same year.

This brief review of foreign-policy events illuminates an important link between the foreign-policy environment and the establishment of the legitimacy and authority of the chief executive. Nasser's and later Sadat's authority in Egypt did not derive from any spectacular accomplishments in domestic economic affairs. Their political leadership was secured mainly through perceived success in foreign policy. For Nasser, the first arms deal with the Soviet Union, the nationalization of the Suez Canal Company, and his conduct of the Suez crisis generated far more enthusiasm for his leadership than the enactment of the Agrarian Reform Law, the socialist decrees and the National Charter, or the completion of the High Dam.[2] Nasser's weathering of the Suez crisis and the tripartite invasion is thought to be the decisive event in establishing his leadership in the eyes of his colleagues and the Egyptian people.[3]

Similarly, Sadat's dramatic expulsion of some 21,000 Soviet personnel from Egypt in July 1972 considerably increased his prestige within his own country. The process of establishing his own authority and consolidating his power was completed after Egypt's successes in the October War, which were attributed to Sadat's courageous and decisive leadership.

A third reason for the primacy of foreign policy is the perception by both Nasser and Sadat that foreign policy could be used to extract the financial resources needed to develop the Egyptian economy, and that Egypt could not achieve its development goals if it relied solely on domestic resources. Mohamed Hasanein Heikal has characterized Egyptian foreign policy under Nasser as the "motive force for the Egyptian economy."[4] Miles Copeland, a former employee of the CIA and State Department and a close observer of Nasser, characterizes Nasser's policy of positive neutralism not as an objective, but as a strategy for extracting the maximum amount of economic aid and technical assistance. Copeland estimates this strategy yielded ten times the amount of aid Egypt would have received — not to mention military aid, without which the regime might not have survived — if Nasser had aligned Egypt with the West as Secretary of State John Foster Dulles wanted.[5]

The benefit of using foreign-policy activism to generate resources from abroad was not lost on Anwar Sadat. He has candidly acknowledged that without the October War Egypt would have been unable to meet its debt installments due in January 1974. Not only did the war regain for Egypt the initiative in foreign affairs, but, Sadat pointed out, as soon as the war ended, the Arab countries came to Egypt's aid with $500 million that they would not otherwise have provided.[6] That one of the reasons for launching the October War was the need to reverse Egypt's desperate economic situation is suggested by a speech Sadat gave to his National Security Council on September 30, 1973:

> let me tell you that our economy has fallen below zero. We have commitments (to the banks, and so on) which we should but cannot meet by the end of the year. In three months' time, by, say, 1974, we shan't have enough money for bread in the pantry! I cannot ask the Arabs for a single dollar more; they say they have been paying us the aid in lieu of the lost [Suez] Canal revenue, although we didn't, or wouldn't fight.[7]

With the termination of the war and newfound wealth from the Arab oil-producing states, a new set of priorities emerged. Regaining the rest of the Sinai and the liberation of the other occupied territories were relegated to a secondary or tertiary objective, while an intense, new emphasis was placed on economic and social development. The extent of Egypt's initial political realignment with the United States and Western Europe and the conservative regimes of the Persian Gulf would not have been necessary to keep the United States actively involved in securing a disengagement agreement with Israel. Indeed, Sadat might have held out the prospect of such a realignment with the West as an incentive to the United States to continue pressuring Israel into a settlement that Egypt could accept. The realignment was necessary, however, if Egypt was to tap U.S. and European investment capital and secure unencumbered access to Western technology. Similarly, initiating the policy of *infitah* to the West, shortly after the end of the October War, had the advantage of sustaining the Egyptian people's hopes for economic improvement based on external resources. In this way Sadat's abrupt realignment with the United States and its allies was associated with the prospect of economic prosperity. A similar association was established between Sadat's trip to Jerusalem and the prospect of near-term economic abundance, as well as with the Camp David accords.

Again, as was the case with the October War, Sadat's dramatic visit to Jerusalem on November 19, 1977, and his signing of the Camp David agreements in September 1978, were in keeping with the pattern of using foreign policy to enhance the leader's popularity and to consolidate his control over the domestic situation. Sadat's strong position in the autumn of 1978 contrasted sharply with what it had been in January 1977. At that time his domestic position had sunk to the lowest point since the October War. This decline in Sadat's prestige resulted mainly from unfulfilled expectations of the postwar period. His Open Door Policy had not brought the vast majority of Eygptians any observable relief from the economic hardship they had been suffering with increasing severity since 1967: inflation, low wages, unemployment, supply shortages, and nonresponsive public services. Indeed, the Open Door and the various austerity measures designed to alleviate these problems only increased the burden on the public and intensified popular discontent. The liberalization of the economy accomplished by the Open Door Policy intensified social tensions, as this merely facilitated the enrichment of a small class of entrepreneurs and middlemen, and encouraged the ostentatious display of wealth by privileged Egyptians and foreigners. The frustrations resulting from the combination of vulgar affluence by the privileged few and the continuing decline of the standard of living of the vast majority of Eygptians erupted in the food riots of January 18-19, 1977, which undermined Sadat's political position and his prestige. Indeed, Sadat's visit to Jerusalem was motivated as much by these mounting domestic problems as by a genuine desire to settle the Arab-Israeli conflict. He sincerely believed that with peace would come instant prosperity.[8]

Sadat's visit to Jerusalem produced a sense of euphoria unknown in Egypt since the October War.[9] Public appreciation was expressed in the enthusiastic welcome Sadat received when he returned from Jerusalem on November 21, 1977. The signing of the Camp David accords in September 1978 further revived popular support for Sadat's policy. However, even though the lack of progress in the negotiations between Egypt and Israel in 1979 contributed once again to public disappointment and a renewed preoccupation with economic problems, public discontent was not translated into criticism of Sadat and his policies. Instead it was focused mainly on Israel, which was seen as intransigent, inflexible, or clinging to outdated conceptions.

One requirement of using foreign policy to generate resources from abroad is the need to maintain a high degree of political flexibility and latitude for tactical movement on the part of Egypt's top political leadership. Such tactical mobility could only be achieved by insulating foreign policy from the potential constraints imposed by domestic, political, and societal pressures. This require- ment was initially met by Nasser when he based his regime on the military and a dependent administrative apparatus.[10] Nasser's approach was continued by Sadat, which helps to account for his ability to abruptly alter Eygpt's alignment from the Soviet Union and the "revolutionary" Arab regimes to the United States and the conservative Arab oil-producing countries and to undertake his historical peace initiative by travelling to Jerusalem.

None of the foregoing discussion is intended to suggest that the Egyptian president does not have to contend with opposition to his defense and foreign policies or that he does not have to account to any foreign-policy constituencies. For example, various sectors of the bureaucracy undoubtedly took strong exception to Sadat's Open Door Policy as this policy weakened the bureau- cracy's control over many activities in the public sector. Similarly, Ismail Fahmi resigned as foreign minister just prior to Sadat's trip to Jerusalem out of his opposition to Sadat's peace initiative. When Sadat accepted Fahmi's resignation and appointed his deputy, Mohamed Riad, to succeed him, Riad, too, declined. Yet neither these individuals nor the bureaucracy represented a coherent foreign-policy constituency or interest group. More serious foreign-policy interest groups[11] are discussed in the next section. What is more important, however, is that expressions of public support for Sadat, and Nasser before him (particularly when Nasser offered to resign after Eygpt's defeat in 1967), were directed at the president as leader, and did not necessarily reflect strong public commitment to the regime. Since the president is the focus of public support as well as criticism, the future stability and vitality of the Egyptian government will depend on the success or failure of the president's policies. If Husni Mubarak fails to regain the rest of the Sinai Peninsula from Israel or experiences some other significant policy setback and so loses his legitimacy and the support of the military, the Egyptian government structure might undergo a radical change in both substance and personnel.

STRUCTURE OF THE GOVERNMENT

Egypt is governed in a republican form with executive powers concentrated in the presidency (see Figure 3.1). The president is commander-in-chief of the armed forces as well as commander of the national police force. In short, he controls the state's monopoly of coercive power. In formulating and implementing the state's policies, the president is assisted by a council of ministers, which he appoints under a prime minister, whom he also appoints. The president also appoints the governors of Egypt's 24 governorates or provinces. The council of ministers, including the prime minister, is confirmed by the People's Assembly. The president is nominated for a six-year term by a two-thirds vote of the People's Assembly, and is confirmed in a national plebiscite in which he must receive an absolute majority of votes of those participating. He may be reelected for a second term.[12] Sadat was elected twice in unopposed elections, with the people asked to vote yes or no on his candidacy. Mubarak was elected to succeed Sadat in the same manner. Article 74 of the constitution provides that the "President of the Republic in the event of a danger threatening national unity or the security of the homeland, or impeding the institutions of the State from fulfilling their constitutional role may take speedy measures to face that danger."[13] The same article obliges the president to hold a referendum on the measures taken within 60 days from the date of their initiation. In a sense the referendum allows the president to circumvent parliamentary or other sources of opposition and to call for a vote of confidence from the people. Sadat, for example, held just such a referendum on his foreign policy and the Camp David accords in April 1979.

This article has the effect of institutionalizing a direct charismatic relationship between the president and the people creating a direct linkage between

FIGURE 3.1
Structure of the Egyptian Government

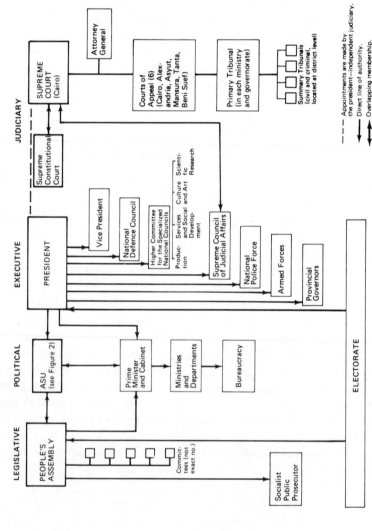

Source: Constitution of the Arab Republic of Egypt, as amended April 30, 1980.

38

the two that not only circumvents important institutions, but seriously weakens them as independent, power-wielding, decision-making organs. One effect is the weakening of the power to question, probe, disagree, modify, or change policy either in the predecisional or postdecisional stages of policymaking. Instead, where foreign policy is concerned, the role of other institutions, including the cabinet, is limited pretty much to applauding and endorsing decisions already taken.[14]

Although cabinet members have participated more actively in the execution and even the formulation of policy under Sadat than under Nasser, the cabinet has traditionally been subservient to the president for at least three reasons.

First, during the critical period in the 1950s when Nasser was establishing his leadership and authority, the cabinet was filled with Nasser's trusted friends. These were either long-time associates from the Free Officers group or they were civilians who supported Nasser's policies and objectives from the time the Free Officers seized power in 1952.[15] Consequently, there was very little disagreement on the broad outlines of policy or on the vision of Eygpt's future. This homogeneity of views enabled Nasser to act independently, particularly in the defense and foreign-policy areas.

Sadat has continued the practice of appointing trusted individuals who share his policy views and vision of Egypt's future. One observable indicator of this practice is the fact that the highest rates of cabinet turnover appear to be associated with policy changes.[16] Thus, there remain very few situations of potential conflict arising from broad policy disagreements.

A second main reason for the subservience of the cabinet to the presidency concerns the strong emphasis on specialization in Egyptian cabinets. Individual cabinet ministers can and do exert influence on the president in matters directly pertaining to their own ministries. Collectively, however, the cabinet members have very little influence on broad policy matters, particularly concerning defense and foreign policy. This tradition also began under Nasser, who on principle never liked his ministers to intervene in discussions that were not strictly related to their own departments.[17] While Sadat apparently delegated more responsibility in foreign policy to his chief lieutenants (for example, Vice-President Husni Mubarak and Prime Ministers Mamduh Salim and Abdel Aziz Hegazi) than Nasser did, the formulation and conduct of foreign policy is still essentially determined by presidential decision.

A third reason for the subservience of the cabinet to the presidency derives from the second. Because the cabinet is basically a collection of heads of specialized departments, the president and his staff are usually the only ones who have the necessary information necessary for policy discussion. Heikal, for example, points out that since the consultative bodies in Egypt are not in possession of the facts leading up to a foreign-policy decision, "their discussions are thus ineffectual, perfunctory affairs that affect the decisionmaking process not at all."[18]

The legislative branch of the Egyptian governmental structure is dominated by the People's Assembly, whose members are directly elected through general elections and a secret ballot. The influence of the People's Assembly in foreign policy, however, is minimal at best. It was created by the leadership and is therefore dependent upon the executive branch. The People's Assembly, like the ruling National Democratic Party (NDP) and the Arab Socialist Union that the NDP replaced, functions primarily as a mobilizational and legitimizing agency for the executive branch (see Figure 3.1). However, the parliament played a more active role during Sadat's tenure than under Nasser's. Since the early 1970s the People's Assembly has played an increasingly assertive role in reviewing and criticizing policy. There are implicit ground rules that limit the scope and subject matter of parliamentary debate, limits that Sadat occasionally indicated had been transgressed. For example, seldom has debate focused very critically on foreign policy. On those rare occasions when this has occurred, the political position of the president was at a very weak point. One prominent incident took place in December 1972, when the government came under fire from the Assembly for asserting that Egypt was ready for war with Israel when the facts indicated otherwise.[19] Yet even in this rare expression of criticism the Assembly's anger was directed at Prime Minister Aziz Sidqi, not at Sadat himself.

Generally, however, the Assembly's assertiveness has been confined to investigatory activities and exposing abuses and wrongdoing in the government rather than censuring specific officials or reversing policy. One close observer of Egyptian politics summarized the Assembly's deliberation on policy as follows:

> The normal pattern . . . has been to tear a given policy to pieces in committee . . . , to give ample newspaper coverage to the findings, and then to have the Assembly as a whole approve the policy with marginal modifications.[20]

On the whole, the People's Assembly has tended to reflect and confirm presidential decisions.

The legitimacy of the government structure should not be confused with the Egyptian public's acceptance of Nasser's and Sadat's authority, nor with the popularity of the regime's broad policies and objectives. A major impediment to the establishment of the regime's legitimacy has been the understanding that real political power did not lie with the formal civilian structures where it was officially declared to rest. Military and security officials, aided by docile technocrats, hold the key positions and make the critical decisions. The extent to which individuals or institutions participated in the decision-making process appears to be almost entirely dependent upon their accessibility to the president.[21] The personalization of power under Nasser and Sadat means that leadership has yet to be effectively institutionalized. That is, the Egyptian people have yet to accept controversial or unpopular measures — either in the domestic or foreign-policy arena — that have been formulated and carried out by public officials whose stature is nowhere as great as Nasser's or Sadat's, and who act according to authority and responsibility vested in their offices, not in accordance with their accessibility to the president.

OPERATION OF THE EGYPTIAN POLITICAL SYSTEM

Before proceeding further, it should be pointed out that a term such as "interest groups" does not connote the same potential impact on decision making in Egypt that it does in the West. It should be kept in mind that Egyptian political culture encourages a strong centralized authority. The Egyptian Revolution, the structure of government, and even the legally sanctioned opposition groups have originated with the top leadership. Interest groups as defined here refer to self-differentiating sectional groups, ad hoc clusters or organizations bound by vocational and/or associational interests who seek to influence policies and decisions. Ordinarily, this definition would exclude groups that participate in the decision-making process such as political parties, and, in Egypt's case, the defense establishment. The concern here is with influence attempts emanating from outside the formal decision-making structure. However, it was mentioned earlier that political power is concentrated elsewhere than where it is formally proclaimed to rest, and that foreign-policy decision making is almost exclusively the prerogative of the president and his staff. Therefore, political parties and the defense establishment do constitute "interest groups" in the sense that the phrase is used here. Also, by definition, an interest group's concerns and policy preference are not identical with the regime's.

Toward A Multiparty System

Until 1977 the Arab Socialist Union (ASU) was the sole political party sanctioned under the Egyptian constitution. Politically active groups were expected to keep their activities within the prescribed limits and organizational structure of the ASU, which was supposed to represent the "alliance" of the peasants, workers, soldiers, intelligentsia, and national capitalists. However, like the parliament, the principal function of the ASU was that of a mobilizational and legitimizing agency, as evidenced by the fact that the governmental and party hierarchies converged at the top.[22]

Because the top leadership of the ASU, the People's Assembly, and the executive branch (including the council of ministers) overlapped, there were visible signs of close cooperation between the political party and the executive and legislative branches. It was not uncommon to see the Executive Committee of the ASU, which had as its members cabinet ministers and key legislators, make a statement of goals that would later be adopted as a government policy to be implemented by the bureaucracy. Also, a cabinet decision might as easily be accepted and adopted by the ASU Executive Committee or the Central Committee, which might then advise its political and administrative machinery to disseminate the information for a "popular" response to the government's policy.

The ASU, however, was not necessarily a vanguard for recruiting top political leadership for the executive branch. Indeed, at times the ASU threatened to become a potential rival power center.[23] On the contrary, Dekmejian has shown that of the 131 ministers who served in the cabinet between 1952 and 1968, only three held positions in the political organization prior to becoming ministers, while more than 80 held a party position either during or after their term as minister.[24] Thus, domestic and political alignments in Egypt could be described as "personal," "ad hoc," and "lacking in solemn commitment to the movement of the party." This system has appropriately been called a "collaboration" movement that conceptually rests on the "principle of power concentration and dispersion." It allowed concentration of power at the national level and permitted subnational leaders residual powers dealing primarily with local and community affairs. This prevents the subnational leader from building a national image and from challenging the top echelon.

In 1976, after a long and bitter debate between the rightists, who favored a return to a multiparty system, and leftists, who supported a single party system, President Sadat created three ideological platforms (*minbars*) within the ASU and the confines of "national consensus": a centrist Arab Socialist Platform, led by Mamduh Salim (who was also Egypt's prime minister) and Mahmoud Abu al-Wafiya (Sadat's brother-in-law), which was fully supported by the government and the bureaucracy; a rightist Liberal Socialist Platform, headed by Mustafa Kamil Murad (a veteran of the Free Officers group), which advocated free enterprise; and a leftist National Progressive Unionist Rally (NPUR) led by Khalid Muhieddin, which represented a Marxist and Nasserist trend. These platforms were eventually transformed into independent political parties in 1977. A draft law regulating the operation of these parties was approved by the People's Assembly on June 20, 1977. A committee consisting of the secretary of the ASU Central Committee, three ministers, and three former heads of the Justice Department was empowered to deal with applications for the establishment of new parties.

The authorization entailed some risk to the regime as it provided an opportunity to three political groups that had previously remained unorganized and ineffective: the Nasserites and Marxists, the Muslim Brethren, and the Wafd. Given this opportunity to institutionalize their existence, these forces appeared to have the potential to pose a serious challenge to the regime, a challenge that included the possibility of exposing Egypt's foreign policy to domestic pressures.

The rightist platform became the Liberal Socialist Party (LSP), from the platform of the same name, and initially won 12 seats in the People's Assembly. The LSP generally endorsed the government's foreign policy, and Sadat regarded it as a "constructive opposition." He even included LSP leader Mustafa Kamil Murad in his entourage during his trip to Jerusalem in November 1977.

The Progressive Unionist Socialist Alignment Party (PUSA) represented the legal left. It was headed by Khalid Muhieddin and started with only two members in the People's Assembly. The party drew its support from the traditionally leftist groups in Egypt — Nasserites, left-leaning students, intellectuals, and workers — and enjoyed extraparliamentary influence out of proportion to its strength in the Assembly. Some of the PUSA's supporters were reportedly members of illegal subversive organizations and were suspected of being among the fomenters of the food riots in January 1977.[25] Unlike the other parties, the PUSA had a well-defined ideology that upheld many elements of Nasser's program and strongly advocated a greater involvement of the state in social and economic affairs. It rejected Sadat's economic Open Door Policy, which it claimed had restored the old bourgeoisie-created noveaux riches who were once more making a conspicuous display of their wealth and power. The main tenets of the PUSA's foreign policy were a more balanced position toward the superpowers, which entailed a rapprochement with the Soviet Union, improved relations with the Steadfastness Front states and the Palestine Liberation Organization, and a renewed commitment to Egypt's role in the Arab world and to the pan-Arab cause.

In 1974 a group of former leading members of the prerevolutionary Wafd Party organized to create a neo-Wafd Party under the leadership of Fuad Siraj al-Din, former secretary of the old Wafd Party and minister of interior. Its application was approved by the ASU on February 4, 1978. The neo-Wafd became Egypt's second largest party almost overnight when 22 members of the People's Assembly joined it. The party soon attracted wide popular support, particularly among young urban educated Egyptians. The text of Siraj al-Din's speech, which had called for the formation of a new national party, reportedly sold almost a quarter of a million copies in just a few weeks. The appeal of the party lay in its appearance as an authentic expression of the call for parliamentary democracy. Although deleted from the draft of the program approved by the ASU, an earlier draft included a declaration that the New Wafd would strive to "put an end to the exclusive powers of the President of the Republic."[26] The neo-Wafd did not oppose the government on foreign-policy issues. It favored a reduced role for Egypt in the Arab world and therefore approved of Sadat's peace initiative with Israel. Foreign-policy issues, however, were of secondary concern to the New Wafd. Its primary objective was in domestic affairs, which involved weakening the power of the president and transforming Egypt into a parliamentary system.

When the multiparty system was first created in 1977, the centrist *minbars* became the new ruling party, and was officially named the Arab Socialist Party of Egypt (ASPE). This party was in reality a reincarnation of the ASU. Led by Prime Minister Mamduh Salim, most of its leading members held high positions in the old Arab Socialist Union. The ASPE generally reflected Sadat's ideas, but permitted some freedom of expression so that occasionally party members voiced opinions that were not in agreement with the president's.

The ASPE, however, was unable to dominate political life. In May 1978 the government cracked down on the New Wafd and the PUSA, accusing them of having conspired together to overthrow the regime. On June 1 the People's Assembly barred the New Wafd from engaging in political activity, and the following day the New Wafd announced its dissolution. On July 22, 1978 Sadat announced the creation of a new political party of his own, which became known as the National Democratic Party (NDP) and which ASPE members joined en bloc. In addition, the ASU's Central Committee was declared abolished, which for all practical purposes put an end to the ASU.[27]

In the speech announcing the creation of his own party, Sadat also announced his intention to amend the law governing the establishment of political parties to facilitate the creation of more political parties. This apparently was an attempt to fragment the opposition.

The foregoing measures had the effect of returning Egypt's political life to the old formula of a ruling party with virtually no legal opposition in the Assembly. There was a very strong overlap between the officers of the NDP's politburo and members of the cabinet in a manner very reminiscent of the old Arab Socialist Union under Nasser.[28]

The timing of the revival of the Wafd in February 1978 and Sadat's crackdown coincided with growing serious criticism in the press and the Assembly, which was an indication that the luster of Sadat's peace initiative was becoming tarnished for want of a positive reciprocating Israeli response. It was one thing when discontent focused on rising prices, but when criticism included foreign policy — Sadat's peace initiative with Israel, relations with the United States and the Soviet Union — as it did in the spring of 1978, Sadat was directly touched and apparently felt that his domestic critics had exceeded tolerable limits with criticism that was inconsistent with the national interest.

INTEREST GROUPS

The Military

Although President Sadat declared in his speech at the NDP Congress that "the army is the property of the people and not of the party," nevertheless, Lieutenant General Ahmad Badawi, the minister of defense, was appointed to the NDP's politburo. His appointment as well as the appointments of other top government officials with military backgrounds — Vice-President Mubarak, Minister of Interior General Nabawi Ismail, Deputy Prime Minister and Minister of Foreign Affairs General Kamal Hassan Ali — to the NDP's politburo (Mubarak was appointed secretary-general) reflects a core principle of Egyptian politics that has carried over from Nasser's time: ultimate power rests with the military. Key policy decisions still require at least military acquiescence.

The military dimension of political power in Egypt has been manifested in the prominence of military men in the decision-making apparatus. During Nasser's tenure, control of the military was ensured by three main approaches: outright takeover of key ministries by top Revolutionary Command Council (RCC) members, who then employed civilian experts in second-echelon positions; the placement of military personnel in the number-two slots in civilian-led ministries (for example, deputy minister or undersecretary); and beginning in the late 1950s, the appointment of a new breed of officer-technocrats in top positions.[29] The last was the most effective device of all since it meant that the military had trained its own experts to manage the complexities of a modern industrialized society, and thus need not rely on civilians. By the early 1960s, the military, through its chief spokesman, Field Marshal Abdel Hakim Amer, was even able to challenge Nasser.[30] Since 1952, the vice-president has been a military man.

The influence of the army in Egyptian foreign policy can be seen in 1959 when Nasser had a falling-out with Khrushchev. The clash was over Soviet support for Iraq at a time when Iraqi-Egyptian relations were very hostile and when Egypt had cracked down on local communists and was accusing Moscow of meddling in its internal affairs. Nasser had responded to the Soviet support of Iraq with a bold verbal counterattack. However, the Egyptian army was heavily dependent on Moscow for spare parts and future arms deliveries. Amer's persuasion, plus evidence of serious unrest in the officer's corps over this issue, prompted Nasser to mend his fences with the Soviets.[31]

Sadat was able to thwart the attempted coup against him in May 1971 because he was able to retain the loyalty of the chief of staff of the army, General Mohamed Ahmed Sadek, and the commander of the presidential guard, General Leithy Nassef. It was only after Sadat had secured their assurance of support that he knew he could move against the conspirators.[32] Apparently Sadat won this support of the military in exchange for promises to refurbish the military's tarnished image and to reinstate the officers purged by Nasser after the 1967 defeat.[33]

Deference to the military in foreign-policy matters was apparent in November 1977 when Sadat made his historic trip to Israel. Particular prominence was given to the support of that decision by the minister of war and commander-in-chief, Mohamed Gamassy, who was pictured in the forefront of officials seeing Sadat off on his historic journey. General Gamassy's message to Sadat was widely quoted:

> The armed forces are aware of the dimensions and responsibilities of the present situation and are closely watching your courageous step toward a just peace. So, march ahead Mr. President, with the blessings of God, and you have, from all the members of the armed forces, greetings, esteem, and prayers for success.[34]

Similarly, considerable prominence was given to expressions of support from Gamassy and other high-ranking Egyptian officers for the Camp David agreements. Thus, Sadat's confidence in the army's support provided him with the freedom to maneuver that he needed to conduct the Camp David negotiations. In addition, the armed forces received repeated assurances that their interests would not be jeopardized by the transition to peace. Prime Minister Mustafa Khalil, for example, opened his government's policy statement in the People's Assembly by pledging full attention to the armed forces and to ensuring the improvement of their combat performance through better training, modernization of weapons, and diversification of their sources of supply.[35]

It would be a mistake, however, to conclude that the military represents a monolithic interest group. Over the years it has probably evolved into a microcosm of the political spectrum that exists in Egyptian society as a whole. Grim support for that assessment lies in the fact that Sadat's assassins were Muslim zealots led by a junior officer.

Ad Hoc Collaborations

Many political alliances are personal or ad hoc collaborations that focus solely on domestic issues. The signing of the Camp David accords, however, illuminated the existence of various groups opposed to the government's foreign policy.

The Camp David accords were severely criticized by the Nationalist Progressive Unionist Grouping (NPUG), which is the former Progressive Unionist Alignment Party, led by Khalid Muhieddin. After the elections of June 1979, it was no longer represented in the Assembly. Having both a Nasserite and a Marxist wing, the NPUG denounced the peace agreement as being against Egypt's national interest and as threatening Egypt's chances for economic development as a consequence of Arab economic isolation. It also criticized the Camp David agreement on the grounds that its purpose was not a comprehensive peace but the formation of a new U.S. security pact in the Middle East. The NPUG also voiced its support for the Iranian revolution and reportedly denounced Sadat's policy toward Iran and the welcome he extended to the shah in Egypt.[36]

The Camp David accords were also criticized by the National Front Party, a parliamentary group set up in August 1978 and led by two former independent deputies, Mumtaz Nasser and Mahmoud Qadi, and by independents associated with the Wafd and the Muslim Brethren. These were reportedly attempts by members of the Assembly to create a front of all the groups in the parliament opposed to the peace agreement, and some 20 members did sign an anti-agreement statement.

The Islamic Opposition

Islamic opposition — namely opposition based on the incompatibility of the regime or of its policies with the teachings of Islam — emanates from a variety of organizations and individuals who share an Islamic fundamentalist outlook. What is important for the purposes of this discussion is that the concern of many of these groups is no longer limited to domestic affairs, but is increasingly extending into the foreign-policy arena as well. In this regard it should be pointed out that the discussion is confined to those Islamic groups who are attempting privately to influence the policies of the incumbent regime, not to overthrow it. By definition, subversive groups whose primary purpose is to replace an existing regime with an alternative are not interested in influencing the policies of the incumbent regime. Consequently, this section does not include a discussion of groups like *al-Takfir wal-al-hijra* (Repentence and Holy Flight), members of which are reportedly responsible for Sadat's assassination.

Probably the best known group is the Muslim Brotherhood (*Ikhwan Muslimin*), a revivalist mass movement founded in Egypt in 1928. The Brotherhood was in the forefront of Egypt's struggle to free itself of British colonial occupation. The Brethren also raised an army of volunteers to fight in Palestine in 1948. This group has always been sensitive to the dangers that Western imperialism (as they saw it) posed to the cultural identity of the Muslim community. Although proscribed under Nasser, the Brotherhood was allowed by Sadat to resume its missionary work, presumably in order to buttress Sadat's de-Nasserization campaign. However, the group has never been given recognition as a political organization.

The Muslim Brotherhood, led by its Supreme Guide, Umar Talimsani, has been critical of the regime on a variety of issues including Sadat's economic Open Door and political, economic, and cultural penetration by the West. The Brotherhood's criticism of the government's peace initiatives with Israel became so severe in late 1978 after the Camp David agreements that it bordered on incitement. The Brotherhood is opposed to the very idea of peace with Israel, arguing that it is incompatible with the Qur'an, which enjoins Muslims to rescue every inch of Muslim land usurped by non-Muslims. It believes that Israel was established in the heart of the Muslim world by the United States and the Soviet Union "in order to liquidate Islam and the Muslims."[37] The Brotherhood has even gone so far as to accuse the Egyptian government of collaborating with Israel and the United States in a plan to destroy the Islamic forces inside Egypt, since they constituted the main obstacle to a peace agreement.[38] In addition, the Brotherhood rejects the official argument that Egypt has sacrificed more than its share of blood and treasure to the cause of the Palestinians.[39]

A more serious and immediate challenge to the government, however, has been the radical and increasingly assertive Muslim youth groups that have become entrenched in Egypt's universities. Composed of student volunteers working to establish their fundamentalist way of life on the campuses, these Islamic youth groups have become increasingly active since the early 1970s. Initially, the government sanctioned and even encouraged their activities, viewing them as a useful counterweight to what was then a leftist-Nasserite dominance of political life in the universities. By 1978, the Islamic groups had succeeded in gaining control of key student bodies by landslide victories in university students' unions and in displacing the Marxist and Nasserite left as the dominant ideological movement in the universities. These students' unions are often an accurate reflection of political trends in Eygptian society at large.

The challenge posed by the Islamic youth groups to the government is that their activities have gone beyond the confines of the campuses. Among the criticisms leveled by these groups at the regime is its hostile position toward the Iranian revolution. Their wall posters not only applauded the Iranian revolution, but also warned that governments that did not apply Islamic law to their societies could face similar public uprisings.[40] Members of these groups demonstrated against the Camp David accords and even against the idea of peace with Israel. The dominance that these groups have achieved on the university campuses puts them in a good position to mobilize student support for their ideas if the government cannot demonstrate that peace with Israel and realignment with the West are yielding positive dividends. Moreover, at the time of Sadat's assassination, the Muslim Brotherhood was reportedly achieving some success in forming tactical alliances and coalitions with other groups, some of them secular.

The history of the Muslim Brotherhood indicates that it has the potential to become a mass movement at the grass-roots level. Its Islamic ideology enjoys cultural legitimacy, particularly since the 1967 war. The Brotherhood's political stands on most current issues reflect all Egyptian patriotisms: independence, nonalignment, anti-Zionism, and anti-imperialism. As of the early 1980s the Brotherhood's image was generally positive, as indicated by its landslide victories in student elections in all Egyptian universities. To the extent that these Muslim opposition groups associate Egypt's foreign policy with the humiliation of Islam at Western and Israeli bidding, they will pose a threat to the insularity of Egyptian foreign policy from societal pressures.

ISSUE AREAS

In a sense, the principal issue areas in Egyptian politics and foreign policy turn on the late Anwar Sadat's vision of Egypt's future: modernized, Western-oriented, militarily powerful, prosperous, and reestablished as the leader of the Arab world. At first glance, this would appear to generate no more controversy than motherhood or the flag. The issues, however, stem from controversy over Sadat's (and initially Mubarak's) policies for realizing this vision. Specifically these are: the challenge posed to Egypt's foreign policy by the rise in Islamic consciousness; the costs and benefits of the peace agreement with Israel; the pro-Western orientation in Egypt's foreign policy, particularly the close alignment with the United States; the economic Open Door Policy.

Peace with Israel

As far as the territorial issues are concerned, there is unanimity among Egyptians: they are firmly committed to a complete recovery of the Arab lands occupied by Israel. Likewise, there is a consensus that considerable progress must be made toward a solution of the Palestinian problem, which should include self-determination and the establishment of some sort of Palestinian national entity and the inclusion of Jerusalem in that entity. The consensus, however, breaks down on the question of whether the Camp David accords are a very effective instrument for achieving these goals.

Part of the problem is what some Egyptians see as Israeli intransigence in implementing that part of the Camp David accords dealing with Palestinian autonomy. Thus, even though all of the Sinai has been returned to Egypt, continuing domestic support for the peace process may begin to erode without some corresponding progress on settling the Palestinian problem. For example, the left-of-center Socialist Labor Party (SLP), led by former Minister of Land Reclamation Ibrahim Shukri, initially supported the government's peace initiative and the Camp David agreement. According to Shukri, this support was given "provided both sides of the accords were implemented." However, the SLP withdrew its support from the peace agreement "after it became clear Israel hadn't implemented anything in respect to the Palestinians."[41]

Islamic Consciousness

The rise of Islamic consciousness in Egypt and in other parts of the Arab world is in no small way a consequence of the outcome of the Arab-Israeli wars of 1967 and 1973. The effect of the Arab defeat in 1967 was particularly devastating for two reasons. One was the loss of Jerusalem, and the other was that the magnitude of the defeat cast doubt on the credibility of the type of secular, pan-Arab nationalism propagated by Nasser. Nasser's death three years later created a secular ideological vacuum that was never filled.

In addition, Islam places a much higher value on military power than do the other major religions. As the heirs to a great military tradition, the defeat in 1967 and Israel's subsequent displays of military superiority placed a particularly heavy burden on Egypt's rulers, many of whom were military rulers. The defeat in 1967 convinced conservative Muslims that the ways of Arab Socialism were not the ways of God. The defeat was interpreted as a punishment from God because Muslims had once more placed their faith in alien systems and devoted their energies to achieving the purposes of these systems rather than working to serve the purposes of God.[42] Conservatives blamed Nasser's crushing military defeat in 1967 on his entire social system, including his socialist policies. The Soviet Union was also blamed because it let the Arabs down in that way. Therefore, socialism, Marxism, and the

Soviet Union gradually became discredited. They were tried and failed to solve Egypt's problems.

The crossing of the Suez Canal in 1973 has been portrayed as a significant religious victory. Prior to the war, Sadat's image among conservative Muslims had been enhanced after he maneuvered to expel the socialists (the Aly Sabry group) in the corrective revolution of May 1971. Sadat's stock went up further when he expelled the Soviets in 1972. The religious significance of the war was reinforced since it began during the Islamic holy month of Ramadan. The code name for the offensive was Badr, named after the first Islamic victory against the forces of apostasy under Muhammad in 623 A.D. Just like its 1973 namesake, this battle was won despite overwhelming odds. Similarly, the battle cry in 1973 was explicitly Muslim: "God is great" (*Allahu Akbar*). It is the battle cry that accompanied the spread of Islam through major portions of the world.[43] By contrast, the battle cry of the Arabs in 1967 was "Land, Sea, Sky," connoting faith in equipment and tactics.[44]

However, Sadat's postwar policies were viewed by conservative Islamic groups as a betrayal of whatever gains were made by the crossing. According to a study of Egyptian militant Islamic groups by Saad Eddin Ibrahim, the growth of Islamic fundamentalism is largely a reaction to Western capitalism and the peace agreement with Israel. The movements themselves predate Sadat's policies, but have gained followers as Westernization and the Camp David agreements have been implemented.[45] All of these are ideologically hostile to any external encroachment — economic, political, military, or cultural — on Muslim society. All of them identify their foreign enemies as Zionism, Western capitalism, and Marxist communism. Most Middle Eastern governments are viewed as convert allies or by-products of one or more of these external enemies.[46]

According to Ibrahim's study, these Islamic movements attract mainly middle-class and lower-class university students from rural or small-town backgrounds, with high achievement motivation, who see little hope for their careers.[47] What is important is that the young people who are attracted to fundamentalist groups are not marginal individuals or social misfits. According to Ibrahim, most of the members of these groups that his team investigated "would normally be considered ideal or model young Egyptians. If they are not typical at all, it was because they were significantly above the average in their generation."[48] In other words, when it comes to compulsory military service, people with just this background are likely candidates for noncommissioned and junior officer slots requiring higher-than-average education and technological aptitude. Such individuals are more likely to join Muslim fundamentalist groups rather than leftist or outright Marxist organizations because these are portrayed as groups of atheists or agents of a foreign power (usually the Soviet Union) who are bent on destroying Islamic culture and the national heritage.

The results of the study suggest that these fundamentalist groups have the potential to attract widespread popular support. Such groups have risen to prominence in the past in conjunction with a sense of national crisis (for example, economic depression, lack of economic or political opportunity) that has been related to foreign encroachment. Thus, many conservative Muslims view the Sadat-Mubarak policies as humiliating concessions to the Christian West (mainly the United States) and Zionism (alias Israel). In their eyes, Sadat had become particularly culpable not only because of his peace initiatives with Israel, but also because of his very open wooing of the United States to become more involved in Egypt.

Against this background, it is understandable that Sadat and then Mubarak gave such high priority to securing Israel's withdrawal from the last portion of Egyptian territory in the Sinai in 1982. Completion of that withdrawal would demonstrate that Camp David removed an Israeli humiliation from Egyptian soil.

Alignment with the West

The foregoing discussion suggests there are many thoughtful Egyptians to whom the benefits of a close political alignment with the United States are not entirely self-evident. Since the end of the October War, the Egyptian leadership has operated on the premise that only the United States could help Egypt regain the rest of its occupied territories. A second premise has been that there were only two sources that could provide sufficient funds to rescue Egypt's economy: U.S. government aid and investment by private American capital were one; Arab oil money from the conservative oil-producing states in the Persian Gulf was the other. Therefore, Egypt had to distance itself from the Soviet Union. The Soviets could provide arms, but not the capital or the technology to revive Egypt's shattered economy. A similar realignment took place at the regional level as well. The Cairo-Damascus-PLO axis that was in force until after the October War was replaced with a Cairo-Riyadh-Tehran axis.

The Egyptian government can claim considerable success from this realignment. Egypt has successfully involved the United States in the peace process in such a way that at times tension between the United States and Israel developed over U.S. efforts to persuade Israel to be more conciliatory to Egypt.[49] American aid to Egypt had jumped from $250 million in 1974-75 to $750 million in 1975-76, and surpassed $1 billion in 1976-77. This included $700 million in bilateral aid and $208 million in a special wheat program; it was more economic assistance than the United States had provided to any single country since the Marshall Plan.[50]

Arab and Iranian financial assistance between 1973 and 1978 was also plentiful and took many forms — grants, cash loans, project and program financing, deposits in the Central Bank of Egypt, and guarantees to underpin borrowing from other sources.[51]

In 1976 Egypt faced an almost calamitous balance-of-payments deficit of $25 billion. By 1979 the debt had been reduced to one-tenth that amount.

Moreover, even the widely publicized economic sanctions imposed on Egypt by most of its fellow Arab nations have had only a marginal impact. Egypt was estimated to be losing about $300 million to $400 million in Arab economic commitments, but these were largely offset by increases in U.S. commodity aid and military credits.[52] Saudi Arabia's decision to withdraw financing of the purchase of U.S. F-5E fighters was compensated for by U.S. military credits that enabled Egypt to purchase F-4Es. The performance of the F-4, which is in Israel's inventory, is superior to the F-5, so neither Sadat nor the Egyptian Air Force could have been disappointed in this outcome.

These and other positive benefits notwithstanding, Egypt's growing political and economic ties to the United States have provoked serious internal criticisms. The point has frequently been made that Egypt was replacing Iran as the United States' policeman for the Middle East. With the upsurge in Islamic fundamentalism, Egypt's growing ties to the West are seen as foreign encroachment in Egypt's cultural values. Close association with the United States has failed to win from the Americans either adequate pressure on Israel concerning the Palestinian issue or substantial investments of the kind most needed to strengthen the Egyptian economy. Egypt's isolation from the rest of the Arab world as a result of Camp David is imposing an onerous burden on Egyptian intellectuals, writers, filmmakers, and businessmen who are accustomed to operating throughout the Arab Middle East and cannot flourish within the narrow confines of the Nile Valley. For other thoughtful Egyptians, the prominence given by the United States to the "Arc of Crisis" in Western Asia and to the Reagan administration's goal of developing a "strategic consensus" in the Middle East against Soviet encroachments, is all too reminiscent of John Foster Dulles's Northern Tier concept in the early 1950s, the Baghdad Pact, and the Eisenhower Doctrine. The frustrations and concerns coalesced into a broad spectrum of opposition by the summer of 1981. One of the leaders of this opposition was Lutfi El-Kholi, an Egyptian leftist who attributed the size and breadth of this opposition partly to growing discontent with Egypt's separate peace with Israel and Egypt's political and economic isolation in the Arab world.[53] The fact that Sadat's crackdown on the opposition in September 1981 was not confined to "religious extremists" but included prominent foreign-policy critics such as Mohamed Hassanein Heikal, top leaders of the Socialist Labor Party, Khalid Muhieddin, leader of the Progressive Unionist Party and even Fuad Siraj al-Din, the old Wafd leader, strongly suggests that opposition to his policies was widespread. Indeed, leftist opposition leaders like Lutfi El-Kholi and Mohammed Sid Ahmed, who escaped arrest, attributed the sectarian strife that erupted in Egypt in the summer of 1981 as one manifestation of the internal unrest nurtured by Sadat's separate peace.[54]

The Open Door Policy

Sadat's Open Door Policy is basically an economic strategy attuned to global and regional opportunities. As mentioned earlier, the regime viewed the opening of Egypt to foreign investment as the most effective way of acquiring the vitally needed capital to rejuvenate Egypt's stagnating economy.

Briefly, the changes in economic policy, collectively known as the "Open Door," began with Law 43 of 1974, which was designed to encourage foreign and domestic private investment and the establishment of free zones (usually in port areas). The law contained a host of special privileges, including tax and tariff concessions and exemptions from labor regulations, such as a 25 percent profit-sharing requirement that applies to all Egyptian enterprises. Projects in the free zones were made entirely exempt from Egyptian profit taxes, and foreign employees were exempted from paying the Egyptian income tax. Banking laws were amended to facilitate the establishment of joint ventures between foreign and domestic banks. Subsequent amendments and regulations allowed foreign investors to calculate investment in Egyptian pounds at a rate of exchange that was much more favorable than the official rate. These favorable rates also applied to the repatriation of profits. Wider participation of Egypt's private sector was encouraged by allowing the private importation of goods on condition that the foreign currency was obtained from sources other than the treasury. Egyptian importers were not required to account for these sources of foreign currency. A major source of imports under this system was the rapidly growing remittances of Egyptians working abroad.[55]

Despite its potential, incentives, and investment guarantees, the Open Door Policy has generally been disappointing. The number of foreign firms that actually undertook projects has been far lower than anticipated, although some firms have shown renewed interest since the Camp David agreement. By June 1975 only ten modest projects had actually begun. Furthermore, nearly 65 percent of all planned investment capital was channeled into tourism, hotels, housing, and construction — areas likely to provide a relatively quick return for foreign investors. In addition, many foreign businesses used the Open Door Policy to provide foreign-made consumer products to satisfy the Egyptian public's pent-up consumer demand. Instead of creating more jobs, the Open Door Policy has been associated with an increase in the migration of Egyptians, many of whom are skilled technicians, for lack of economic opportunity. Arab investment, in particular, was concentrated on middle and upper income housing in Cairo, which led to inflated real estate values that priced Egyptian investors out of the market.[56]

The most serious problem with the Open Door Policy was that the benefits and burdens from economic liberalization were not distributed evenly across the population. The main beneficiaries appeared to be: the old prerevolutionary bourgeoisie; a new class of middlemen and profiteers who, for a fee, acted as expeditors between bewildered foreign investors and the Egyptian bureaucracy; and various bureaucratic strata that benefited from the expansion of corruption attending the influx of foreign money.

Meanwhile, the vast majority of Egyptians had to cope with soaring inflation and more food shortages. Conservative Muslims viewed the Open Door as an invitation to further foreign encroachment on Egypt's cultural values and public morality. The initial results of the Open Door confirmed the fears of the left and the Nasserites that the public sector would be allowed to stagnate or decline while a parallel economy, built around foreign capital and banks working with the Egyptian private sector, would gradually dominate the economy for the benefit of a new "parasitic" middle class.

Indications that the *infitah* has imposed intolerably high social costs on the majority of Egyptians are evident in a series of strikes and riots that occurred in 1974 and 1975. For example, in January 1975 workers from the Helwan iron and steel complex rioted in downtown Cairo, denouncing Sadat for inflation, food shortages, and corruption, which had tarnished his image as the Hero of the Crossing. A more severe judgment was offered two years later during the January 1977 food riots. Finally, the lack of public grief expended at Sadat's death was seen as a further indication of Egyptians' disenchantment with the payoffs from his policies. The scope and intensity of these protests underscore some of the negative consequences of insulating foreign policymaking from domestic pressures. In this regard, it is significant that Sadat's successor has pledged to continue the Open Door Policy, but with a difference: "Infitah," said Mubarak, "means projects will be aimed at meeting basic needs of the working masses, not producing luxury goods that only a minority of Egyptians can afford to buy."[57]

Foreign Relations

This issue area covers such intangible factors as Egyptian perception of the country's role in the Middle East, what constitutes national prestige, and from which directions the country is most seriously threatened and by whom.

One factor on which a high degree of consensus has been maintained throughout the leaderships of Nasser, Sadat, and Mubarak has been the Egyptian elite's perception of their country's leading role in the Arab world. This view is supported by the centrality of Egypt's geographical location, the size and skills of its population, and its military capabilities. This perception is reinforced by other Arab elites. For example, Muhamed Hassanein Heikal reports that during a discussion on the timing of the October operations, the Syrian chief of staff, General Yusuf Shakur, deferred to the H-hour preferred by Egypt's General Ahmed Ismail, saying:

> if there is a failure on the Egyptian front . . . it will be the end of the Arabs which means the end of Syria. If there is failure on the Syrian front this would not be the end. It is on Egypt that all our hopes are pinned . . . if Damascus falls it can be recaptured; if Cairo falls the whole Arab nation falls.[58]

It is important to note that the Arabs accord Egypt a position of centrality whether they have approved or disapproved of Egypt's policies. A prominent example is the reaction of the Arab world, particularly Jordan and Syria, to Egypt's conclusion of a separate peace agreement with Israel. The Arab reaction has been so intensely negative because the Sinai disengagement agreements and Camp David have removed Egypt from any potential military coalition. This, in turn, deprives the other Arab countries of a credible military threat that could be activated if Israel failed to make sufficient concessions in any future peace negotiations. Thus, Egypt's separate peace has in effect deprived the other Arab countries of the critical bargaining strength they believe they need to extract an acceptable settlement from Israel.

The perception of Egypt's regional centrality has at times been expressed in unilateral decisions taken by the Egyptian leadership that suggest a certain hegemonic attitude toward Arab allies. During the planning for the October War, the Egyptians' had promised to give the Syrians five days' notice of D-Day so they would have time to complete the emptying of the oil refineries at Homs. The Egyptians informed the Syrians of the choice of October 6 as D-Day only on October 3. The Syrian chief of staff protested but the date stood. The Syrians were similarly overridden on the question of H-hour. During the war, on October 16, Sadat outlined Egypt's conditions for a cease-fire in a speech to the National Assembly without prior consultations with President Assad. The Syrian president responded with a message that said he had a right to be informed of Egypt's proposals before hearing about them in a broadcast.[59]

Similarly, even though Sadat's decision to visit Jerusalem was announced without any prior consultation with other Arab leaders, an official statement issued before his departure declared that Sadat was traveling to Jerusalem "on behalf of the just and legitimate demands of the entire Arab people."[60]

The belief in Egypt's regional centrality lies in the conviction that the interests and destiny of the Arab world are tied to Egypt's strength and well-being. This is clearly evident in an interview of Sadat and Israel's Prime Minister Menachem Begin by Barbara Walters during Sadat's visit to Jerusalem:

Barbara Walters: Is it true that there cannot be war or peace in the Arab world without Egypt and really that as you go, so ultimately must the rest of the Arab world?

President Sadat: Hush. This is a fact. War or peace is decided in Egypt, because as I told you, we are forty million.[61]

That Sadat expected the Arab world to fall into line behind Egypt's lead is evident in a conversation he had with Ezer Weizman, then Israel's minister of defense. Weizman recalls the following conversation with Sadat during their second meeting:

"suppose we do reach an agreement with you." I said. "What about the Syrians? Don't forget the Jordanians."

[Sadat:]   "The Jordanians will follow in our footsteps. So will the Syrians. Things in the Arab world happen the way Egypt decides."[62]

Compounding this hegemonic attitude is the belief that Egypt has sacrificed enough for the Arab world, and that the value of Egypt's leadership and sacrifice on behalf of the Arab cause has not been given its due. These sentiments are evident in a speech Sadat gave to Egyptian students in 1981:

Enough of them [the Arab governments]. We do not work as gendarmes or as mercenaries for them at all. It is enough for them that we, in the October War and with the blood of our sons, raised the price of their oil from $3 to $40 [per barrel]. Their coffers have been filled to overflowing so far. We have not asked, nor will we ask, for anything from them. But in any dealings in the future, each one of us must know his size and all our actions must be announced to our Arab nations so that it may determine who is right and who is wrong. This is our policy toward our brothers. . . . This is what we in Egypt have done. I have taken up our own cause, so that Egypt will not be in the hands of al-Qadhafi, al-Asad and their ilk, Saddam Husayn and his ilk and Saudi Arabia. I have taken my cause into my own hands.[63]

These words do not indicate an Egyptian rejection of the Arab world. Rather, they reflect Egyptian indignation at the hostility of the Arab governments' response to an initiative that the Egyptians presumably intended to advance the interests of the Arab world as a whole. The passage further suggests that while Egypt had not rejected the Arab world, the Sadat regime was not going to subordinate Egypt's vital interests to Arab pressures.

The fact that the rest of the Arab world has yet to accept Egypt's peace initiative reflects a possible divergence in threat perception between Egypt and the eastern Arab states. This difference derives partly from the geographical fact that Egypt is an African state as well as an Arab state. Less than a month after Israel and Egypt agreed on the basics of a peace treaty, the Egyptian army changed the color of its combat uniforms from desert khaki to jungle green. This switch illustrates, unintentionally perhaps, a fundamental change in Egyptian strategic thinking.

Currently, the principal threat is no longer perceived as coming from the eastern desert (where, despite peaceful withdrawals, Israel retains a formidable armed presence), but from unsettled regions on the African continent to the south and west. The redirection in priorities is based on Egypt's perception that the principal threat to regional stability in the Arab world, particularly in North Africa, is the collaboration of radical revisionist regimes such as Libya and Ethiopia with the Soviet Union to overthrow the more moderate and conservative regimes in the area, particularly Sudan. Sudanese President Jaafar

Numeri has survived three attempted coups during his decade in power, and has been confronted with serious internal problems as well as sporadic pressures from Libya and Ethiopia, both Soviet client states.

In addition, Egypt's reassertion of its African identity and Sadat's emphasis on an "Egypt-first" approach to foreign affairs undoubtedly reflected the regime's determination not to be isolated by the Arab states. Although Egypt's African tie is not new, the emphasis Egypt placed on Africa in general and on the Egyptian-Sudanese tie in particular, increased considerably in the wake of the Arab summit conference of November 1978 and Sadat's reported statements that Egypt cannot be isolated by the Arabs since Egypt and Sudan together comprise a majority of the Arab world's population.[64] Egypt's emphasis on Africa may also reflect a new sense of urgency to come to grips with Egypt's mounting social and economic problems, particularly in the wake of Sadat's assassination and the possibility that the Egyptian army may have been heavily penetrated by Muslim zealots. In this regard, Heikal observes that Egypt's preoccupation with either its eastern (Arab) front or its southern (African) frontier has been a reliable indicator of Egypt's political and social vitality: "the more outgoing and vigorous it is, the more active its policy toward the east; the more introspective and turned in on itself it becomes, the more it looks southward."[65]

EGYPTIAN OBJECTIVES AND POLICIES

In addition to such general and obvious objectives of maintaining territorial integrity, political independence, and a strong national defense — goals pursued by all independent states — Egypt's defense and foreign policies are formulated with a view to achieving the following political objectives:

• Recovering the remaining Egyptian (the Sinai Peninsula) and other Arab territories (the West Bank of the Jordan River, including the Arab section of Jerusalem, plus the Golan Heights) under Israeli occupation since the June War — the first element having now been realized;
• Restoring the political and territorial rights of the Palestinian people;
• Reestablishing Egyptian leadership in the Arab world;
• Attracting private and foreign government investment to finance Egypt's economic and industrial development;
• Restricting Soviet penetration in the Horn of Africa, to prevent what Egypt sees as Moscow's grand design of encirclement — a ring of Soviet client states stretching from Libya to Ethiopia around Egypt and Sudan.

These objectives are presented in a rough order of importance (with emphasis on the "rough"). However, a positive synergism exists among these objectives in the sense that success in achieving one of them (particularly the first two) increases the chances of success in achieving the rest. Similarly, set-backs sustained in pursuit of any one of these policy objectives is likely to diminish the chances for success in any of the others.

Policies formulated to serve these objectives can be divided into "political initiatives" and "military programs." While the separation of foreign from domestic policies can be arbitrary and misleading in that foreign policy — especially Egypt's — may be addressing internal issues, domestic programs will be discussed insofar as they are germane to understanding Egyptian foreign policymaking.

Having said that, one must hasten to add that Egypt's foreign policy is heavily defined and severely constrained by the need to extract resources from the international environment. To a large extent, the amount of financial aid Egypt can obtain from the conservative, oil-rich regimes in the Gulf or from the industrialized West (including Japan), depends on the role Egypt plays in the conflict with Israel, the shaping of inter-Arab politics, and its relations with the superpowers. Alignment with the United States is deemed necessary in order to keep it involved in the peace process on Egypt's behalf and in order to secure U.S. economic and military aid. The extent to which the United States remains involved in the peace process on Egypt's behalf depends upon Washington's perception of Egypt's value as a regional ally; peace with Israel is necessary if Egypt hopes to attract adequate private foreign investment. One way Egypt can continue to receive American political, economic, and military support is to convince the United States that Egypt is *the* key to peace in the Middle East. Similarly, in order to reestablish Egypt's leadership and political centrality in the Arab world, Cairo must demonstrate to the Arab countries that Egypt can secure for them more favorable terms in a peace settlement than they can obtain for themselves using some other approach.

Opposing Soviet penetration in the Horn of Africa not only serves Egypt's immediate security interests, but makes it a more valuable ally to the United States. It enhances Egypt's chances of reestablishing its leadership in the Arab world to the extent that Egypt's resistance to Soviet expansion disrupts Libyan efforts to further isolate Egypt as punishment for Camp David. It also soothes jittery conservative, oil-rich regimes along the Gulf who are concerned about Soviet penetration and Libya's radical activism in Africa and on the Arabian Peninsula.

The pursuit of these policy objectives requires Egypt to conduct an activist foreign policy in regional affairs.

Political Policies

Egypt's primary concern in the Arab confrontation with Israel was the recovery of the remainder of the Sinai Peninsula, occupied by Israel in 1967. However, the return of Egyptian territory alone is not enough. It is essential that

Egypt appear in Arab eyes to have achieved some gains for the Palestinians. This was very much in evidence during the Egyptian-Israeli treaty negotiations following the Camp David accords in September 1978.

It was essential that the framework for any settlement pertaining to the West Bank and the Gaza Strip clearly provide for future Egyptian involvement. This is also the reason that during the negotiations of the draft treaty, Egypt took a firm stand on linking the normalization of relations with Israel to the agreement on autonomy for the West Bank and Gaza. The linkage was eventually retained in the final peace treaty to Egypt's satisfaction.[66]

Egypt's sensitivity to the need to produce results for the Palestinians can be seen in the hardening of Sadat's position on the linkage issue in November 1978. This change reflected shifts in Arab and regional alignments, particularly after the Arab summit conference held in Baghdad in November. The position of the "Steadfastness and Confrontation Front" (Algeria, Libya, South Yemen, and Syria) was strengthened when, at a meeting in Baghdad (October 24-26), Iraq and Syria agreed to put aside their long-standing quarrels and to take joint action against the effects of the Camp David accords. Sudan had begun a rapprochement with Libya that struck a particularly sensitive nerve in Cairo. Saudi Arabia, normally one of Egypt's strongest allies, agreed to provide $1 billion of a $3.5 billion annual fund to support frontline resistance by Syria, Jordan, and the PLO. In the background of this display of Arab solidarity, the growth of revolutionary unrest in Iran rendered the position of the shah, another staunch ally, very precarious.

By mid-1982, the territorial provisions of the Egyptian-Israeli peace treaty were being implemented without a major hitch. Israel had returned the Sinai to Egypt. However, no significant progress had been made on implementing the other portion of the agreement concerning Palestinian autonomy.

Moreover, several events at the close of 1981 underscored the very limited extent of Egyptian control over the implementation of the treaty. In November, Israel lashed back at what it perceived as an American tilt toward Saudi Arabia and a shift away from Israel and the Camp David process. Israel was reacting to the U.S. decision to sell Saudi Arabia five E-3A Sentry AWACS (Airborne Warning and Control System) aircraft in October, followed by the Reagan administration's expression of interest in an eight-point peace proposal by the Saudi prime minister, Crown Prince Fahd. Israel feared that the Fahd plan would become the main pivot of U.S. Middle East policy at Israeli expense once Israel withdrew from the Sinai in April 1982. In order to express its displeasure at this new direction in U.S. policy and to head off the possibility that the United States might try to incorporate parts of the Fahd plan in a wider framework than Camp David in order to solve the Palestinian issue, Israel refused to make any further concessions on Palestinian autonomy.[67] Thus, any further U.S. "pressure" on Israel could jeopardize the return of the Sinai to Egypt on schedule. The new Mubarak government was thus confronted with the possibility of losing the territorial gains for Egypt and failure to obtain anything for the Palestinians, even if it faithfully implemented the provisions of its treaty with Israel.

The most serious threat was Israel's unilateral annexation of the Golan Heights in December. This had the effect of breathing new life into the Steadfastness and Confrontation Front, Egypt's most serious Arab opponent; it spiked any inclination on the part of the PLO or the PLO's two most important sponsors, Saudi Arabia and Syria, toward acceptance of negotiating with Israel; and it appeared to be the first step in an Israeli plan to annex the West Bank after April 1982, when it evacuated the Sinai. With no gains to point to beyond the retrieval of its own occupied territories, Egypt's claim to have been acting on behalf of the Arab world as a whole would be totally undermined. Without being able to produce some gains for the Palestinians or more favorable conditions for Israel's return of the other occupied territories, Egypt has little chance of breaking out of the isolation imposed on it by the Arab countries, much less regaining its preeminent political position in Arab politics in the foreseeable future. Barring success in the Camp David approach, the only other way Egypt can regain its position of political centrality in the Arab world is to demonstrate (or wait for events to demonstrate) that the Arabs will be unable to succeed in isolating Egypt and that they may need Egyptian support in some other conflict or policy domain.

In this regard, Egypt can claim some success in that Arab attempts to isolate Egypt have not been very successful. First, it was already mentioned that the economic impact of the Arab sanctions taken at the 1979 Arab League meeting was not nearly as severe as first anticipated. Since that time the solidarity of Sadat's Arab opposition has weakened as a result of other conflicts: the Iran-Iraq war and the attendant hostility between Iraq and Syria; growing tensions between Syria and Jordan; and increasing tension between Morocco and Algeria over Morocco's attempt to pacify the Western Sahara. Many Arab airlines still were flying to Cairo; Egyptians working abroad in Arab countries were not repatriated nor were their remittances embargoed. The Baghdad summit had not called for action against Egyptian migrant workers who remitted $1.7 billion in 1978 and who constitute an important source of foreign exchange.[68] Though the loss of Arab aid has been a serious blow, increases in U.S. aid were likely to offset some of the impact, as well as bring in technical assistance that was lacking from Arab sources. What at first appeared to be one of the hardest blows was the withdrawal of Saudi Arabia, the United Arab Emirates, and Qatar from the Arab Organization for Industrialization (AOI), the consortium that was developing an armaments industry in Egypt. However, Sadat established an Egyptian Organization for Military Industrialization to take over the consortium's functions and to assume responsiblity for all contracts. Since the Arab withdrawal from AOI was part of the cost to Egypt of concluding a peace settlement, it was not too surprising that the U.S. Agency for International Development agreed in June 1979 to provide the new Egyptian organization a grant of $16 million for the renovation and replacement of factories.[69] The

Carter administration further agreed to help Egypt's arms industry produce airplane and tank engines and to maintain and upgrade Soviet-made equipment that was falling into disrepair.[70] By the end of 1981, the AOI factories were still being run by Egypt, using funds from the original organization. Egypt simply refused to return the group's assets when the consortium's partners demanded them. Normally a decision like that would anger the world banking community and destroy a country's credit rating, but in this case Egypt was reassured by its creditors that they would ignore what everyone recognized as an absolutely essential political decision.[71] In 1981 some Arab nations reportedly were making overtures to Egypt to reestablish AOI after the return of the Sinai by Israel in April 1982.[72]

In addition, Egypt can still exploit its position as the most important military power in the Arab world. It has been sending Iraq Soviet military equipment in its inventory in support of Iraq's war with Iran.[73] Similarly, Iraq is reportedly interested in a new twin-barrel 23mm air defense gun that Egypt is producing.[74] Moreover, whether or not the conservative Arab states like it, Egypt is one of the few states in the region able to aid Oman and Saudi Arabia if they are threatened by the Soviet-supported tripartite alliance of Libya, South Yemen, and Ethiopia.

Egypt's decision to reassert its African ties as a counterweight to isolation in the Arab world soon began to yield political dividends. At the ministerial conference of the Non-Aligned Movement held in Sri Lanka in June 1979, the African states united to resist an Arab effort to obtain Egypt's suspension. An Arab move to ban Egypt from attending the Organization of African Unity conference in Liberia in July of that year also failed. Particularly satisfying to Sadat was the refusal of the African summit to condemn the Camp David accords. Similarly, at the Non-Aligned summit in Havana, an Arab demand to expel Egypt was blocked in the Political Committee (held at the foreign minister level), an outcome that was again due primarily to the position of African states.[75] Most of Egypt's efforts to strengthen its ties to Africa were in the form of offers of technical assistance, coordination of Egyptian and African diplomatic strategies at the U.N., the OAU, and the Havana Non-Aligned summit. However, during the conflict between Tanzania and Uganda in March 1979, in which Libya sent troops to Uganda, Egypt supported Tanzania and even offered ten MiG-17 fighters during a visit to Dar Es-Salaam by Vice-President Mubarak.[76] Egypt declared its full support to the black African cause in Zimbabwe-Rhodesia, Namibia, and South Africa and maintained contacts with the liberation movements there. Similarly, Morocco, never a very enthusiastic member of the "Baghdad camp," was prompted by the deteriorating situation in the war with the Polisario in the Western Sahara and by an increasingly threatening stance by Algeria to ask Egypt for military aid. Egypt, which is eager to exploit any possibility of a split among its opponents, quickly responded, providing military assistance of an undisclosed kind and scope.

Africa has also become a major arena of Egyptian interest and activity for reasons that have little to do with Arab retaliation for Camp David. The growing Soviet influence in Africa and the Red Sea area is viewed in Cairo as a means of encircling Egypt and overthrowing the pro-Egyptian regime in Sudan. This concern has enabled Egypt to claim the role of a regional power, determined to stand up to the Soviet threat and to protect weaker regimes. In pursuit of this objective, Egypt extended military aid of various types to Sudan; to Tanzania in its conflict with the Libyan-supported forces of Idi Amin in Uganda; and to Zaire where Egypt's chief of staff, General Ahmed Badawi, declared that his country would not rest until all African territories were freed from all types of imperialism.[77] The military aid Egypt provided to Somalia reportedly prevented that country from joining the Baghdad camp, produced statements by Somali officials supporting Sadat's peace policy, and prevented Somalia from severing relations with Egypt after the peace treaty with Israel was signed in March 1979.[78] Egypt also provided support to the government of Chad against the Libyan-supported wing of Frolinat, and accused the Soviet Union and Libya of trying to bring the whole of Chad under Soviet domination and use it as a springboard to launch attacks against other West African states.[79] Egypt later acted as a conduit for arms to antigovernment forces in Chad who were fighting the Libyan-backed Chadian government. When Libya withdrew from Chad, Egypt withdrew its support of the insurgents.

Egypt's alignment with the United States has enabled it to gain more foreign economic and military aid than it would have been able to obtain from alternative sources. That by 1979 Egypt had received more U.S. government aid than any single country since the Marshall Plan is a direct consequence of its peace initiatives with Israel. Even if Egypt cannot produce gains for the Palestinians, the Camp David settlements have attracted renewed interest from foreign investors.[80] Similarly, Egypt's military prowess is being maintained and expanded by large amounts of U.S. military credits and technical assistance (which will be discussed further below). Moreover, the Soviet invasion of Afghanistan in 1979, the volatile political situation in Ayatollah Khomeini's revolutionary Iran, the Iran-Iraq war, and rising tensions in the Persian Gulf have combined to sharply increase Egypt's importance as a U.S. ally. American anxiety over the situations in Afghanistan and the Persian Gulf was reflected in the Carter administration's announcement in January 1980 that it would ask Congress for an extra $1.1 billion in military credits for Egypt, in addition to the $1.5 billion arranged in 1979 in connection with Egypt's peace treaty with Israel.[81] A parallel political benefit has been that the United States has appeared to favor Egypt's position as the Palestinian autonomy talks have proceeded. Similarly, growing Israeli intransigence on the subject of Palestinian autonomy, the annexation of the Golan Heights, fresh Israeli military actions in Lebanon, and indications that Israel intends to annex the West Bank and Gaza[82] have persuaded some in the Reagan administration that the Begin government is the principal obstacle to an emerging anti-Soviet strategic alliance in the Middle East.

These and other payoffs from Egypt's political realignment involve heavy political costs and risks that no Egyptian government dares ignore. Egypt is now always in competition with Israel for American support — diplomatic, economic and military. This situation raises the risk that the United States may one day side with Israel on an issue that undermines Egypt's political standing in the Arab world and so make it even more difficult for Egypt to reassert its claim to Arab leadership. In order to avoid this sort of humiliation, Egypt may find itself having to defer to U.S.-Israeli preferences to avoid the appearance of a dispute with Washington or a clear demonstration that Israeli political clout with the United States is still stronger than Cairo's. By preemptively moving to avoid an open split, Egypt is likely to risk further isolation from the Arab world. In addition, this competition with Israel may ultimately limit the extent to which the United States is willing to aid Egypt's expansion of its military capabilities. For example, Egypt has been cleared to purchase the F-15 and F-16, two of the most advanced fighters the United States produces and that Israel has already received. Egypt has not yet decided to buy the F-15, but had it done so, Israel would have launched a vigorous protest to prevent the sale. The political significance of an ultimate Israeli veto on the military equipment Egypt can obtain from the United States is far greater than any increment in military capabilities that a system like the F-15 might confer on the Egyptian air force. One of the most important elements in Egypt's political centrality in the Arab world is its military prowess. If Israel is seen to have an ultimate veto on what weapons systems the United States will provide Egypt, it will have the effect of degrading one of Egypt's most important qualifications for Arab leadership.

The other risk is that too close an association with the United States could further damage Egypt's political position in the Arab world so long as the United States continues to pursue policies that are unpopular in that region. One area concerns tacit U.S. approval of, or acquiescence in, Israeli military action against an Arab country (for example, the Israeli air attack on Iraq's nuclear reactor in June 1981 and the Israeli bombing of Beirut in the summer of 1982) or further territorial seizures such as the Golan Heights, parts of southern Lebanon, or annexation of the West Bank. Another area concerns too close an association with the U.S. notion of an anti-Soviet "strategic consensus." Such an association, particularly Sadat's offer of Egyptian territory to the United States for military operations in times of crisis, could totally discredit Egypt as an Arab leader if it ever places Egypt with the United States against a brother Arab country. These considerations illuminate a policy problem that Egypt has yet to solve. Part of Egypt's value as an ally to the United States is its ability to assert its leadership and influence in the Arab world to nudge Arab countries in directions Washington favors. Part of Egypt's value as a leader in the Arab world is its ability to influence the United States to adopt policy positions the Arab countries favor. Egypt has yet to establish its credentials in either of these arenas.

Military Policies

Egypt's principal strategic problem is that the most vital areas it must defend are located outside Egyptian territory. This is the problem of securing the flow of the Nile River, which originates in Ethiopia, from any threat of disruption within Egyptian territory or outside of it. Thus, even though Egypt has a relatively large land area, Sudan is viewed as providing the necessary strategic depth for Egypt's defense.[83] This concern is reflected in the redirection of Egyptian military priorities since 1975 from an almost exclusive concentration on Israel to

- Defense against Israel but not with the quantity and type of forces required when Egypt was committed to regaining the occupied territories by military means if necessary; and
- The development of a highly mobile intervention force capable of operating in Arab countries, but primarily in the northern and central regions of Africa.

As mentioned earlier, this redirection in priorities is based on Egypt's perception (shared by Morocco, France, and the United States) that the major threat to the Arab world, particularly in North Africa, is the collaboration of the Soviet Union with radical-revisionist regimes like Libya and Ethiopia to overthrow the more moderate and conservative regimes in the region. Egypt maintains that while the United States has focused its attention on the Soviet threat to NATO in Europe, the Soviet Union has maneuvered to threaten vital oil fields in the Persian Gulf by establishing its presence in Libya, Ethiopia, and South Yemen. This threat includes the pre-positioning of a large number of fighter aircraft and armored fighting vehicles in countries where this equipment cannot be operated by indigenous forces since the sheer number of weapons is far more than they can absorb.

The Egyptians identify three main threats to the nation: Libya, with its strong Soviet backing; Ethiopia, with strong Soviet and Cuban support against Sudan and therefore against Egypt itself; and Israel.[84] The threat from Israel is the possibility that in the event of a crisis, Israel will attempt to reoccupy the Sinai and not evacuate it a second time. This threat is likely to materialize if another Arab-Israeli war were to break out, even if Egypt is not initially involved in fighting on the side of the other Arab combatants. However, that Israel as a military threat has been relegated to a secondary level of concern is indicated by the fact that two full divisions have been transferred from Egypt's eastern border with Israel to its western border with Libya.[85]

Within this redirection of commitment and focus, a new force structure is emerging that is consistent with the new defense priorities:

- The acquisition of Lynx and Commando helicopters, C-130 troop transports, planes, SRN-6 hovercraft, and Alpha-jet trainer/strike underscoring the new emphasis on rapid deployment, and
- The concentration on the acquisition of antitank weapons – TOW, Beeswing, Swingfire, and Milan for the army instead of the replacement of the 800+ Soviet tanks lost in the 1973 war; only in 1980 did Egypt belatedly order 244 M-60A3 tanks from the United States, indicating a rate of replacement of three-for-one.
- The acquisition of combat aircraft suitable for relatively long-range ground attack missions such as the F-16, the first 40 of which were delivered in January 1982.

If current trends continue, it can be anticipated that a larger portion of Egypt's defense efforts will be directed away from the armor-oriented front with Israel. Increased emphasis would then be on long-range maritime air transport capabilities in support of operations in Africa at some distance from Egyptian bases, and more concern with interdiction missions for the air force.[86] The emphasis on enhanced interdiction roles for the Egyptian air force is indicated by Egypt's desire to purchase at least 150 F-16s or Mirage 2000s, but only a small number of F-15s (if any). The latter are largely for the purposes of symbolic deterrence of Libyan aircraft piloted by Soviet-bloc mercenaries.

Egypt's weapons purchases (largely from the West) since the October War have been weapons more suited for the low-intensity combat environments likely to be encountered by intervention forces in Africa than to the sophisticated, high-intensity, and deadly combat environment of another Arab-Israeli war. This is a distinctly different force structure from the armor- and artillery-dominated, Soviet-equipped force that was built up over the years to fight Israel. The majority of army officers made their careers in this force and will continue to do so for the foreseeable future. Therefore, partly because of political considerations and partly because a credible defense force against Israel will still be necessary even after peace is established, it is necessary to maintain and refurbish a significant proportion of this "old army."

As a result, the Egyptian command is faced with the twin problem of keeping its Soviet arsenal in working order while introducing American, British, and French equipment, some of it very sophisticated. This transition involves two sets of maintenance procedures and a more complicated logistical organization.

Egypt's approach both to the refurbishment of older equipment and the acquisition of new systems is guided by the principle that "materials sold to Egypt must be produced, at least in part, by Egypt."[87] Regarding the maintenance of Soviet equipment, Egypt has concluded agreements with various Western organizations to refurbish and upgrade its old equipment. The T-55 and T-62 tanks in Egypt's inventory, for example, have been retrofitted with Rolls Royce diesel engines. The MiG-21s have been retrofitted with Rolls Royce turbo-jet engines. Teledyne has a contract to develop and install an identification-friend-or-foe system (IFF) that operates on the Soviet frequency range, thereby making it compatible with other Soviet-built Egyptian equipment. Egypt's Helwan factory is producing new external fuel tanks for the MiG-21, which are larger than the Soviet-built external tanks. Spare parts for Soviet equipment have been obtained from India, Romania, and Iraq before the rift developed over Egypt's peace initiative.

Egypt aims at acquiring technology, not just new weapons, from a variety of sources. Therefore, it has entered into coproduction or licensed production agreements to produce a range of weapons from jeeps (American Motors) to aircraft (Alpha jet, Mirage 2000), radar, helicopters (Lynx), and missiles (Swingfire and improved TOW antitank missiles, and Matra Magic R.550 air-to-air missiles).[88] Egypt is concentrating on custom-designed items such as a 132mm artillery multiple rocket launching system, and a twin-barrel 23mm air-defense gun.

In addition to providing Egypt with advanced technology for military aid and civilian purposes, these programs are making Egypt an important arms manufacturer and supplier which reinforces the country's role as a regional power in Africa or the Arab Middle East.

NOTES

1. See for example, Mohamed Hassanein Heikal, "Egyptian Foreign Policy," *Foreign Affairs*, LVI, no. 4 (July 1978), pp. 714-27; Raymond William Baker, *Egypt's Uncertain Revolution under Nasser and Sadat* (Cambridge, Mass.: Harvard University Press, 1978) Chaps. 4, 6; and A. I. Dawisha, *Egypt in the Arab World: The Elements of Foreign Policy* (New York: Wiley, 1976), Chaps. 8, 13.

2. See Majid Khadduri, *Arab Contemporaries: The Role of Personalities in Politics* (Baltimore and London: Johns Hopkins University Press, 1973), pp. 56-57.

3. For example, Anthony Nutting notes in his biography of Nasser that before the Suez crisis Nasser "had always consulted his colleagues before making any important decisions, he now told them what he wanted done and brooked no argument with his judgment," Nutting, *Nasser* (New York: Dutton, 1972), p. 176.

4. As cited in Baker, *Egypt's Uncertain Revolution*, p. 45.

5. Miles Copeland, *The Game of Nations* (New York: Simon and Schuster, 1969), pp. 170-72.

6. See Baker, *Egypt's Uncertain Revolution*, p. 46.

7. Anwar el-Sadat, *In Search of Identity* (New York: Harper and Row, 1978), p. 245.

8. That Sadat thought his peace initiative would bring prosperity to Egypt is evident in interviews he gave to Anis Mansur and published in the Cairo weekly *October*, December 18 and 25, 1977, as reported in *FBIS*, December 19, 1977, pp. D11-D20, and December 28, 1977, pp. D9-D19. Despite the indifferent success of the open-door policy, Sadat clearly believed his initiative had brought concrete economic gains to Egypt. See his speech to Egyptian students in the United States as reported in *FBIS*, August 12, 1981, pp. D1-D8.

9. *Middle East Contemporary Survey, 1977-78* (New York and London: Holmes and Meier, 1979), p. 369.

10. The negative and positive consequences of insulating foreign policy from societal pressures are discussed by Baker, *Egypt's Uncertain Revolution*, pp. 47-48.

11. "Interest groups" in the sense that these groups' views *as groups* must be taken into consideration by the country's top decision makers.

12. Presidential powers are described in the Constitution of the Arab Republic of Egypt, Part V, Chapter 1. See Albert P. Blaustein and Gisbert H. Flanz, eds., *Constitutions of the World* (Dobbs Ferry, N.Y.: Oceana Publications, 1972).

13. Ibid., p. 11.

14. A more thorough discussion of this point is offered by Dawisha, *Egypt in the Arab World*, Chap. 8.

15. This is not to say that the majority of cabinet members under Nasser were army officers. Indeed, a breakdown of the Nasser cabinets from 1952 to 1969 shows that out of 131 individuals, 33.6 percent were from the military and 66.4 were civilians. However, these proportions are not a valid indicator of the power of the civilian members, since most were subservient to the military members (and ultimately to Nasser). In addition, no civilian member had an independent power base so that none ever emerged as a political leader in his own right. See R. Hrair Dekmejian, *Egypt under Nasir: A Study in Political Dynamics* (Albany, N.Y.: State University of New York Press, 1977), pp. 170-71.

16. See Shahrough Akhavi, "Egypt: Diffused Elite in a Bureaucratic Society," in I. William Zartman et al., *Political Elites in Arab North Africa* (New York and London: Longman, 1982), pp. 237-39.

17. Nutting, *Nasser*, p. 410. See also Dawisha, *Egypt in the Arab World*, pp. 113-15.

18. Heikal, "Egyptian Foreign Policy," p. 715.

19. *New York Times*, December 11, 1972, p. 3.

20. John Waterbury, *Egypt: Burdens of the Past/Options for the Future* (Bloomington and London: Indiana University Press, 1978), p. 250. See also Henry Tanner, "Sadat vs. the Egyptian Assembly," *New York Times*, December 15, 1972, p. 3.

21. See, for example, Dawisha, *Egypt in the Arab World*, pp. 120-22; Dekmejian, *Egypt under Nasir*, pp. 173-75; and Baker, *Egypt's Uncertain Revolution*, p. 161.

22; See Dekmejian, *Egypt under Nasir*, Chap. 10.

23. See Baker, *Egypt's Uncertain Revolution*, pp. 108-13, 124-25; and Mohamed Hassanein Heikal, *The Road to Ramadan* (New York: Quadrangle/New York Times Books, 1975), pp. 125-28.

24. Dekmejian, *Egypt under Nasir*, pp. 192-99.

25. *Middle East Contemporary Survey, 1977-78*, p. 379.

26. As cited in *Middle East Contemporary Survey, 1977-78*, p. 380.

27. The ASU was formally abolished by constitutional amendment April 30, 1980.

28. For a comparison of officials holding both senior government positions and membership in the NDP's politburo, see Akhavi, "Egypt: Diffused Elite," p. 232.

29. See Dekmejian, *Egypt under Nasir*, pp. 172-74.

30. Baker, *Egypt's Uncertain Revolution*, pp. 92-96; Sadat, *In Search of Identity*, pp. 168-70.

31. See Robert St. John, *The Boss* (New York: McGraw-Hill, 1960), pp. 301-3.

32. See Heikal, *The Road to Ramadan*, p. 134.

33. Baker, *Egypt's Uncertain Revolution*, p. 126.

34. As cited ibid., p. 160.

35. See Prime Minister Mustapha Khalil's policy statement to the People's Assembly, November 25, 1978, as reported in *FBIS*, November 27, 1978, p. D1.

36. *Middle East Contemporary Survey, 1978-79*, p. 396.

37. As cited ibid., p. 398.

38. Ibid.

39. Israel Altman, "Islamic Movements in Egypt," *Jerusalem Quarterly*, No. 10 (Winter 1979), p. 95.

40. Ibid., p. 99.

41. Helena Cobban, "Mubarak's Swift Actions Gain Time to Plan Egypt's Future," *Christian Science Monitor*, October 27, 1981, p. 9.

42. Yvonne Haddad, "The Arab-Israeli Wars, Nasserism, and the Affirmation of Islamic Identity," in John L. Esposito, ed., *Islam and Development: Religion and Sociopolitical Change* (Syracuse, N.Y.: Syracuse University Press, 1980), p. 119. See also R. Hrair Dekmejian, "Anatomy of Islamic Revival: Legitimacy Crisis, Ethnic Conflict and the Search for Islamic Alternatives, *Middle East Journal*, vol. 34, no. 1 (Winter 1980), pp. 1-12.

43. An indication of the importance of this battle cry on the morale of Egyptian troops is indicated by their chief of staff, Lt. General Saad El-Shazly, who wanted to distribute loudspeakers the length of the front. During the assault on the east bank of the Suez Canal, they would broadcast only one phrase, *"Allahu Akbar."* "When the men hear that," Shazly said, "they will take up the cry and soon the whole front will be shouting *'Allahu-Akbar'* in unison. The weaker will be swept along by the stronger and the more aggressive." Lt. General Saad El-Shazly, *The Crossing of the Suez* (San Francisco: American Mideast Research, 1980), p. 214.

44. Haddad, "Arab-Israeli Wars, Nasserism, and Islamic Identity," p. 120.

45. Saad Eddin Ibrahim, "Anatomy of Egypt's Militant Islamic Groups," *International Journal of Middle East Studies*, vol. 12, no. 4 (December 1980), pp. 423-53; Geoffrey Godsell, "Muslim Group Penetrates Deep into Egyptian Society: An Analysis," *Christian Science Monitor*, October 13, 1981, p. 14; and John Yemma, "How Many More Istanbulis Are in Egypt's Army?" *Christian Science Monitor*, October 21, 1981, p. 9.

46. The most systematic treatment of Islamic themes is a content analysis of the cassettes of Egypt's most well-known Muslim fundamentalist cleric, the blind Sheikh Kishk. See Paul A. Jureidini, *The Themes and Appeals of Sheikh Abdul Hamid Kishk* (Alexandria, Va.: Abbott Associates, 1980).

47. Ibrahim, "Anatomy of Egypt's Militant Islamic Groups," pp. 440-47.

48. Ibid., p. 440.

49. One of the more prominent examples of tensions between Israel and the United States concerns the U.S. "reassessment" of its Middle East policy in March 1976 in response to Israeli refusal to make adequate concessions to Egypt in order to secure another disengagement agreement. On this point see Matti Golan, *The Secret Conversations of Henry Kissinger* (New York: Quadrangle/ New York Times Books, 1976), pp. 235-47; and Edward R. F. Sheehan, *The Arabs, Israelis, and Kissinger* (New York: Reader's Digest Press, 1976), Chap. 12.

50. *Economist*, November 13, 1976, p. 85.

51. See Khalid Ikram, *Egypt: Economic Management in a Period of Transition* (Baltimore and London: Johns Hopkins University Press, 1980), p. 350.

52. Don A. Schanche, "Despite Arab Sanctions, Egypt Is Getting Stronger," *Los Angeles Times*, July 22, 1979, pp. 1, 15.

53. See Geoffrey Godsell, "Sadat Tries to Rule and Keep His Balance," *Christian Science Monitor*, September 8, 1981, pp. 1, 11; and Joe Stork, "Massive Arrests Precede Sadat's Assassination," *MERIP Reports*, vol. XI, nos. 100-1 (October-December 1981), pp. 43-55.

54. Stork, "Massive Arrests Precede Sadat's Assassination," p. 55.

55. See *Middle East Contemporary Survey, 1978-79*, pp. 353-55.

56. See Waterbury, *Egypt*, pp. 228-29.

57. Olfat M. El-Tohamy, "Mubarak Diverging from Sadat — But Not Camp David," *Christian Science Monitor*, November 19, 1981, pp. 14-15.

58. Heikal, *The Road to Ramadan*, p. 31.

59. Ibid., p. 231.

60. Arab Republic of Egypt, Ministry of Information, *Speeches and Interviews by President Mohamed Anwar El-Sadat on the Occasion of His Visit to Jerusalem* (Cairo: State Information Service, n.d.), p. 140.

61. ABC News transcript of "Barbara Walters' Interview with Prime Minister Begin of Israel and President Sadat of Egypt, November 20, 1977," p. 9.

62. Ezer Weizman, *The Battle for Peace* (New York: Bantam Books, 1981), pp. 88-89.

63. President Sadat's Speech to Egyptian Students in the U.S., August 9, 1981, as reported by *FBIS*, August 12, 1981, pp. D3-D4.

64. For example, in his interview with Barbara Walters in Jerusalem, Walters asked Sadat how he could assure Israelis of their safety when states like Syria and Libya are so opposed. Sadat replied, "Well, I'm always speaking for my people. We are forty million and with Sudan, we are 60,000,000 — 2/3 of the Arab world or about that — and my attitude today was to send the message [peace initiative to Israel] and then I shall be waiting for the response." ABC News, "Barbara Walters' Interview with Prime Minister Begin of Israel and President Sadat of Egypt," p. 9.

65. Heikal, "Egyptian Foreign Policy," p. 717.

66. A complete text of the peace treaty between Egypt and Israel is published in *Middle East Contemporary Survey, 1978-79*, pp. 119-46.

67. See Geoffrey Godsell, "Menachem Begin Trains His Sights on Saudi Peace Plan," *Christian Science Monitor*, November 2, 1981, p. 4; and Ned Temko, "Israel Hits Back against Western 'Tilt' to Saudis," ibid., November 10, 1981, pp. 1, 8.

68. See "Final Statement Issued by the 9th Arab Summit Conference," Baghdad, November 5, 1978, in *FBIS*, No. 215 (November 6, 1978), pp. A13-A15; and "Resolutions of the Arab League Council Following Meetings of the Arab Foreign and Economy Ministers," Baghdad, March 31, 1979 in *FBIS*, No. 064 (April 2, 1979), pp. A1-A5.

69. *Africa Contemporary Record, 1979-80*, p. B41.

70. George C. Wilson, "U.S. Will Help Egypt Revitalize Weapons Output," *Washington Post*, August 9, 1979, pp. A1, A17; see also Clarence A. Robinson, Jr., "Egypt's Technology Shift: U.S. Helps to Update Soviet-Built Weaponry," *Aviation Week and Space Technology*, January 11, 1982, pp. 44-49.

71. Schanche, "Despite Arab Sanctions, Egypt Is Getting Stronger," p. 15.

72. Clarence A. Robinson, Jr., "Egypt's Technology Shift: Nation Seeks Larger Production Base," *Aviation Week and Space Technology*, January 4, 1982, p. 44.

73. See Nathaniel Harrison, "Iraq Gets Arms for Iran War — From Sadat with Love," *Christian Science Monitor*, April 1, 1981, p. 10. Arab sources claim Egypt has been providing aid to Iraq since the beginning of the war.

74. Robinson, "Nation Seeks Larger Production Base," p. 44.

75. *Middle East Contemporary Survey, 1978-79*, pp. 422-23.

76. *Africa Contemporary Record, 1979-80*, pp. B43-B44.

77. *Middle East Contemporary Survey, 1978-79*, p. 421.

78. *Middle East Contemporary Survey, 1978-79*, p. 421.

79. Ibid.

80. These include DuPont, the Crush Company, Coca-Cola, International Paint, Ford, Goodyear, Union Carbide, Colgate-Palmolive, Johnson, Reynolds, Hoechst, Stein-Muller, Siemens, Michelin, Massey Ferguson, Honda, and Volkswagen. A Volkswagen vehicle assembly plant and a Kloeckner-Humboldt Deutz tractor plant are among the industrial projects approved by the Egyptian government in the wake of the signing of the Egyptian-Israeli peace treaty.

81. Bernard Gwertzman, "White House Asking $1.1 Billion Extra in Arms Aid to Cairo," *New York Times*, January 21, 1980, pp. A1, A8.

82. See Geoffrey Godsell, "Israel Girds for Fight to Annex the West Bank," *Christian Science Monitor*, December 28, 1981, pp. 1, 14; Geoffrey Godsell, "Why Feelings Run So Deep in U.S.-Israeli Dispute," ibid., December 22, 1981, pp. 1, 6; and Stephen Webbe, "How Strategic Is Israel to the U.S.?" ibid., July 31, 1981, pp. 1, 6.

83. Egypt's principal military problems are discussed in depth in Lewis W. Snider, R. D. McLaurin, and Paul A. Jureidini, *Middle East Air-Ground Environment Analysis* (Alexandria, Va.: Abbott Associates, September 1981), pp. 33-41.

84. See interview with Egypt's Defense Minister Lt. General Muhammed Abdel Halim Abu Ghazala, in "Soviets Focus on Control of the Region," *Aviation*

Week and Space Technology, December 14, 1981, p. 49; and *African Recorder*, July 1-14, 1980, pp. 5395-96.

85. Ibid., p. 49.

86. Indeed, some minor instances of Egyptian military intervention have occurred. During 1977-78, Egyptian pilots and other military specialists were dispatched to Zaire, alongside French and Moroccan forces, to aid Zaire in repelling an invasion by rebels based in Angola. Egyptian military advisors and supplies have gone to assist the Chad government in resisting attacks by Libyan-backed insurgents. Egyptian military units and advisors have reportedly been sent to Sudan as a deterrent to Ethiopia. Sadat promised to use Egyptian forces to defend Sudan against an attack from Libya and promised arms to any other African country threatened by Libya. See *Middle East Contemporary Survey, 1978-79*, pp. 416-17; and *African Recorder*, February 12-25, p. 5568.

87. *Aviation Week and Space Technology*, January 4, 1982, p. 45.

88. See articles on Egypt's technology shift in *Aviation Week and Space Technology*, December 14, 1981, pp. 40-48 passim; ibid., December 21, 1981, pp. 34-37 passim; ibid., January 4, 1981, pp. 45-47; and ibid., January 11, 1982, pp. 44-58 passim.

IRAQI FOREIGN POLICYMAKING

ENVIRONMENT

Iraq's political boundaries date back only to 1920 and were established to suit the purposes of the European great powers, mainly Britain. They were not intended to reflect any sense of territorial (Iraqi) national sentiment among the mosaic of religious, ethnic, and tribal groups that comprise the country's population. Iraq was created artificially by the merging of three provinces of the defunct Ottoman Empire. Each of these provinces had a different ethnic or sectarian makeup.

The Iraqi state began as a collection of ethnic and sectarian communities that were not accustomed to living together or interacting with one another. Upon them the British imposed an alien institution, kingship, and an alien ruling family – the Hashemites of the Hijaz headed by Emir Faisal, a leader of the Arab Revolt against the Ottoman Turks. This fractionated population generally lacks any tradition of cooperation to achieve a common purpose or a sense of a common national identity that can successfully compete with the claims of region, tribe, ethnic group, or religion on individual loyalties.

Without any well-established political institutions that are the respository of an Iraqi national identity, Iraq has a singular lack of political cohesion that makes it uncommonly difficult to govern, no matter what type of regime is in power. Lacking a common national identity, the Iraqi state has been unable to provide a common basis for the rule of law. Hence political conflict has usually been resolved by violence, rebellion, repression, or coercion. Since its formal independence in 1932, nearly 20 changes in government have occurred. Many of these changes have been violent and virtually none of them has been as a result of a democratic election. In such a political environment,

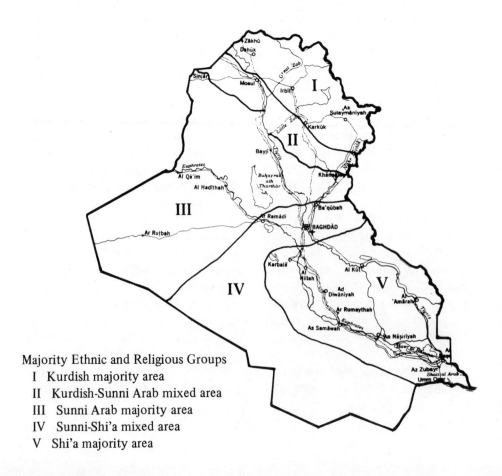

Majority Ethnic and Religious Groups
I   Kurdish majority area
II   Kurdish-Sunni Arab mixed area
III   Sunni Arab majority area
IV   Sunni-Shi'a mixed area
V   Shi'a majority area

the quality of individual leadership has been a far more crucial element in shaping Iraq's political fortunes than is often appreciated. That is particularly true today where, despite the position of the Ba'ath Party and the Revolutionary Command Council in the governmental structure, decision making is concentrated in the hands of one individual, the president, Saddam Hussein Takriti.

Iraq's tradition of confessional and ethnic politics has evolved from a long history of confessional conflicts going back to the days of the Khalif Ali (656-661), who became the patron saint of the first great schismatic sect of Islam, the Shi'as. The Sunnis, the followers of orthodox Islam, have historically held the reins of power, except for the period between 1623 and 1638 when the Shi'a Safavid dynasty of Iran ruled most of what is modern Iraq. The Sunni Ottoman Empire ruled the country between 1534 and 1918. The Sunni Hashemite dynasty, which ruled Iraq from 1921 to 1958, and most of the ruling elites in the republican era since 1958, have been Sunni Muslims. The unwillingness of the Sunni religious minority to share power with the Shi'as, who claim a 60 percent majority in the country,[1] has been one of the major impediments to effecting a political rapprochement between Shi'as and Sunnis, most of whom are ethnically and linguistically Arabs.[2]

Ethnically, the Iraqi population is divided into two major and several minor groups. The Arabs are the dominant ethnic and linguistic group, accounting for about 75 percent of a total estimated population of 13 million. The Kurds are the second major group and comprise about 23 percent of the population. The Kurds are mostly Sunnis, but their religious practices differ in some respects from those of the Sunni Arabs. A breakdown of the population across both sectarian and ethnic lines shows that 53 percent of the Iraqi population is Shi'a Arab, 20 percent is Sunni Arab, and 18 percent Sunni Kurd. Arab Christians comprise about 3 percent. The Turkomans account for another 2.5 percent, which accounts for 96.5 percent of the population. Other groups include Lurs, Armenians, Circassians, and Jews.

The fact that the Arab Sunni minority has been able to consistently dominate successive Iraqi governments regardless of regime is partly explained by the Arab Shi'as' religious heritage and regional concentration. The Shi'a community is located mainly in the southern part of the country in the Basra region. They are particularly concentrated in the areas around the shrine cities of Shi'ism, where the martyrs Ali and Hussein, victims of the first great schism in Islam, were slain in battle and according to Shi'a tradition are buried. Most Shi'a Arabs are farmers, shepherds, or unskilled laborers and are generally the least educated and most impoverished group of Iraqi Muslims. The Shi'as compose most of the remaining nomadic tribes as well.

Their traditional ways of life and religious heritage thus make the Shi'as resistant to change. This conservative outlook is reinforced by their religious heritage, since many Iraqi Shi'as have a closer affinity for their coreligionists in Persian Iran than with their Sunni Arab conationals in Iraq. This affinity has produced an ambivalent attitude toward Arab nationalism in general and toward pan-Arabism in particular. The Shi'as have usually preferred to develop a more parochial Iraqi nationalism, partly out of fear of becoming a minority in a larger Arab state favored by the Sunni elites.[3] The latter, by contrast, have persistently tried to impose a pan-Arab regime of a Ba'athist Nasserite or (under the monarchy) Hashemite persuasion on the country.

Unlike the Shi'as, the Arab Sunnis are found in all strata of Iraqi society and tend to dominate professional life in the larger cities like Baghdad. Enjoying a generally higher level of education than the rural, village-dwelling Shi'as, the Sunnis have been more receptive to modern secular political concepts and ideologies and more successful in assimilating them.

Since the overthrow of the Iranian monarchy, Sunni-Shi'a tensions have intensified. One of the reasons put forward by the Iraqi government for initiating a war with Iran was the Ayatollah Khomeini's incitement of the Iraqi Shi'a population to overthrow the Sunni-dominated regime, and the alleged agitation of Persian Shi'a *ulema* in Iraq for an Iranian-style Islamic revolution there. Since the current government is a narrowly based minority regime dependent upon family and clan ties at the top and a strong, pervasive state security apparatus at the bottom, the Ba'athist regime has been particularly vulnerable to Khomeini's appeals. In the months preceding the war with Iran, some 20,000 to 25,000 ethnic Persians were deported by the Iraqi government to Iran. Similarly, in 1974 when relations between Iraq and Iran were very hostile, the Iraqi government deported some 60,000 ethnic Persians.[4]

Nevertheless, while Iraq is probably unique among the major Arab states for the centrality of the Sunni-Shi'a cleavage in its national politics and foreign policy, these sectarian tensions are generally not overtly hostile. Moreover, the Saddam Hussein government has moved to redress Shi'a grievances, particularly since the revolution in Iran.

Kurdish nationalism has been the most persistent and violent problem in modern Iraq. The Kurdish problem has been a continuous source of strife and political instability, and a serious drain on the country's economic, military, and human resources since Iraq was created. Most of the Iraqi Kurds live in the north and northeast areas of the country, a region that is contiguous to the Kurdish territories in Turkey and Iran.

Since the end of World War I, Kurdish nationalism has been expressed in the form of demands and a struggle for local autonomy and outright independence. Just as Arab nationalism developed partly as a reaction to Turkish nationalism, so Kurdish nationalism after World War II gained momentum in part as a reaction to the Arab nationalism and pan-Arabism that the Kurds perceived as a threat to their identity and status in Iraq.[5]

Kurdish nationalism in Iraq has led to brief periods of Kurdish unity, but the tribal rivalries and conflicts between modern and traditional Kurds often have created problems in negotiating terms of agreement with the Iraqi government. Almost all Kurds agree that Kurdish identity must be preserved and that some of the wealth from Kurdish areas (especially the oil revenues from the

Kirkuk oil fields) ought to be used for development projects in the Kurdish region. Beyond these broad objectives, there is little else that can be construed as a common demand. The Iraqi Kurds have never officially demanded independence from Baghdad, nor have they shown much sustained interest in the idea of a Kurdish state to be carved out of Iraq, Turkey, and Iran.

Until March 1975, the Kurdish problem was a source of bitter tension between Baghdad and Tehran because, for a variety of political and strategic reasons, Iran was using the Kurds to apply pressure on the Ba'athist regime in Baghdad. The Kurdish threat to the Iraqi government significantly diminished after Iran withdrew its support for the Kurds in March 1975. (The Kurdish problem will be discussed in more detail below.) The Kurds, however, have taken advantage of the war between Iraq and Iran to press their demand for autonomy from Iraq. Shortly after hostilities broke out between Iraq and Iran in September 1980, Kurdish tribesmen reportedly opened a new offensive against Iraqi army units in their region.[6] The longer the war drags on, the greater the opportunities for Kurdish guerrilla initiatives against the remaining Iraqi forces in Kurdish territory, and the more serious is the Kurdish threat to the Iraqi government.

After the Kurds, the Turkomans are the largest ethnic minority. About two-thirds of this group are Sunni and one-third is Shi'a. They are far less troublesome politically to the government in Baghdad than the Kurdish people. The Turkomans suffer the misfortune of being wedged between the Arabs and the Kurds, primarily around the Mosul district. Consequently, they have, on occasion, been the victims of Arab-Kurdish hostilities. Since the Iranian revolution, the Turkomans in Iran have been extremely restive and this has created apprehension in Baghdad. As tensions between the Iran and Iraq increased in 1980, many Iraqi Turkomans as well as Kurds were reportedly arrested.[7]

The divisions within the Iraqi population extend beyond religious and ethnic groups. Additional divisions have been created by linguistic, regional, and educational differences. Arabic, for example, is the official language of the country, but at least 20 percent of the Iraqi population speaks Kurdish, Turkoman, or Farsi. Kurdish has been accepted as the primary language of education for the Kurds in regions where they are a local majority. The March 11, 1970 agreement, which temporarily halted the war between the Kurds and the Iraqi government, stipulated, inter alia, that while Kurdish would be taught to Kurdish students in schools in the Kurdish region, Arabic would remain compulsory for all children in Iraqi schools. It was hoped that this provision would satisfy the cultural aspirations of the Kurds while creating a linguistic link between the Arab majority and the Kurdish minority. The provision, however, is not reciprocal. No requirement is imposed on the Arabs living in the Kurdish regions to learn Kurdish. In 1979 the Iraqi government disbanded the Kurdish Academy, which had been established in 1970 to promote Kurdish culture and books.

Regional differences are another source of friction in Iraq. In the absence of strong integrative forces, the traditional rivalry among the urban, rural, and nomadic populations has not been substantially reduced. Despite concerted effort by the Ba'athist regime to reduce these cleavages, each group has remained largely isolated from the others, with each manifesting an attitude of superiority toward the others. In part, this attitude has been reflected in the educational policies of a series of Iraqi regimes, which, being controlled by a relatively small group of urban elites from Baghdad, Mosul, and provincial towns, has not followed a consistent policy of equal education for all Iraqis.[8] The quality of schools has traditionally been highest in major cities such as Baghdad, Mosul, and Kirkuk, and very low in the smaller provincial towns. Since 1970 the expansion of colleges has been extremely rapid. The number of universities has grown from two to five as new ones have been established in Mosul, Basra, and Sulaimaniya provinces. Thus, the proportion of university students in Baghdad has fallen from nearly complete dominance in 1958 to 60 percent in 1969-70 to 40 percent in 1974-75.[9] Iraq has the resources to build schools, laboratories, and other educational facilities, and to pay teachers and instructors. Despite the fact that resistance to change is quite prevalent in the rural areas, Iraqi parents and children do not lack the desire for education. The problem is with staffing small-town and village schools, because most young men and women refuse to work in rural areas after receiving their diplomas. Nevertheless, since 1968 the government has made considerable gains in decreasing the extreme concentration of primary and secondary educational facilities in the main cities, especially Baghdad.

It is only by focusing on the overlapping points of social cohesion and division, including those of locality, kinship, and family, that the Sunni-Shi'a division can be properly understood, including how the Sunni minority has continued to dominate successive governments and regimes in Iraq.

Current Sunni political dominance is based on Sunni urban dominance, supported first by Ottoman and later by British rule.[10] The Sunnis are basically an urban population and constitute the majority of the urban population in every city except Basra. As city dwellers, the Sunnis occupied most of the administrative and military apparatuses under Ottoman, British, and later Hashemite rule. They have thus far been more exposed to secular modernizing influences.

The Shi'as, by contrast, had little interaction with state authorities, be they Ottoman, British, or Arab. Their holy cities of Najaf and Karbala were virtually self-governing entities. Those Shi'as who lived in other urban areas were engaged mainly in commerce or theology rather than government administration. There were very few if any Shi'as among the trained Ottoman officials. Sunni dominance of the machinery of government was reinforced by the fact that schools and other opportunities for secular education were concentrated almost exclusively in the larger towns, particularly Baghdad. Therefore it was the Sunnis, not the Shi'as, who gravitated toward teaching, administrative, and military careers. Meanwhile social conflict under the monarchy developed along class, not sectarian, lines. Sunni and Shi'a tribal sheikhs collaborated clearly in maintaining the status quo. While fundamental social conflict in the north was between Arabs and Kurds, in the south it was between landlord and peasant. Most of the landlords and nearly all of the peasants were Shi'a. Thus, sectarian divisions have traditionally been diluted by class differences and locality.

In addition, the potential of the Shi'a *ulema* for maintaining influence over their followers was weaker than that of their Sunni counterparts. While the monopoly of both Shi'a and Sunni *ulema* to mold the world view of their followers was shattered by the entry of young Muslims into modern schools, the influence of the Shi'a *ulema* over their followers was further weakened by the decline in their income. The Sunni *ulema*, by contrast, maintained control over rich *awqaf*, which are properties or funds bequeathed for pious or charitable purposes. Because of this circumstance, the Shi'a *ulema* were estranged from the government while their Sunni counterparts were not.[11]

The importance of locality has increased since the overthrow of the monarchy in 1958. Although localistic concerns were given added attention under the regime of Abdul al-Karim Qassim (who was of mixed Sunni-Shi'a parentage and who opened public posts more widely to Shi'a than before), they have gained particular prominence under the current Ba'ath regime. While the current regime is largely Sunni, sectarian affiliations appear to have declined in salience relative to kinship ties and locality.

The most prominent example of the importance of locality relative to sect is the "Takriti Connection" — ties with the formerly industrial Sunni Arab town of Takrit in northwestern Iraq. The Takriti affiliation is a dominating influence in the government, the Ba'ath party, and the army. It is discussed further below. Here it is sufficient to point out that there are a large number of Takritis in the military. Their gravitation toward the military is explained largely by the impoverishment of the inhabitants of Takrit caused by the decline in production of *h'alaks* — rafts of inflated skins — for which the town was once renowned in the nineteenth century. Many Takritis migrated to Baghdad in order to earn a living. While some found work in railroad or pipeline construction, many others gained admission to the cost-free Royal Military Academy.[12] In this case the fact that the Takritis are also Sunnis is of secondary importance. Geographically, Takrit is important as it lies at the heart of what one scholar has called a Sunni-Arab "territorial triangle,"[13] defined by Rutba in the west, Baghdad in the south, and Mosul in the north. Baghdad and Mosul are the major centers of political power. Takrit is also the birthplace of one of the most influential members of Faisal's Sherifian forces in Iraq, Mawlud Mukhlis. Mukhlis was an Ottoman officer who defected to the movement for Arab succession under Amir Faisal. He later became a high official in the Iraqi government and a close advisor to the king. Mukhlis used his power and influence for several years to encourage young politically aware residents of Takrit to enroll in the army and police services. Similarly, contemporary officer-politicians such as former president Hassan al-Bakr, who also came from Takrit, have used their influence to place Takritis in government positions.

In addition, there has been a fairly large-scale migration of poor and mostly Shi'a peasants to the cities, particularly to Baghdad, which has nearly doubled in population. This trend has been accompanied since 1968 by the expansion of educational and other social services in the rural areas, reinforced by a more recent program of large-scale industrial investment in the countryside. The cumulative effect of these trends is to weaken the significance and political volatility of the Sunni-Shi'a division. The effect of expanded education and the creation of more job and income opportunities has been to undermine the strength of religious divisions and reduce intercommunal inequities and rivalries. Furthermore, Iraq's population is relatively young. One Iraqi in five is under ten years of age and two out of every three are under 25. Iraqi culture is already far more secular than Iran's or Egypt's. The drawing power of both the Shi'a and Sunni branches of Islam is declining with the youthfulness of the population. With the continuing migration to the cities, sectarian appeal is likely to decline even further. One of the many signs of the weakening of religiosity among the people is that the number of students of religion has been decreasing significantly since the end of World War I. In 1918, for example, there were at least 6,000 students attending the Shi'a theological schools or *madrasahs* in Najaf alone. By 1957 the number of students had diminished to 1,954, only 326 of whom were Iraqis.[14]

Notwithstanding the decline in the importance of Sunni-Shi'a divisions between the leadership and the populace, traditional attitudes, values, and prejudices still play a significant role in the daily lives of the population, especially those living in the provincial towns in the countryside. Although education and the mass media have popularized the concept of territorial nationalism and pan-Arabism among the urbanites (an increasing percentage of which is Shi'a and Kurdish), these concepts are still of marginal importance in the everyday lives of a large portion of the Iraqi populace. Certainly, they have not eliminated the divisions caused by sect, region, ethnicity, or tribe that have retarded the social and political integration of the country. Indeed, the persistence of these divisions is the main reason the concept of an Iraqi national identity remains ambiguous and continues to pose serious political problems.

The sources of Iraq's political identity continue to be partly subnational and partly supranational.[15] In a domestic political context, the average Iraqi is still likely to identify himself as a Baghdadi, a Najafi, a Takriti, a Kurd, an Arab, a Shi'a, or a Sunni. Political alliances are often based on such identifications and affiliations. These subnational commitments make it difficult for Iraq to play a consistent leading role in regional politics despite the Ba'athist regime's strong pan-Arab orientation. This factionalism has been a major source of instability and weakness in Iraqi domestic and foreign policies.

Domestically, it has caused civil strife and has deepened suspicions between the governing elites and various subnational groups. Internationally, the supranationalist Nasserite version of pan-Arabism was one of the inspirations of the coup that overthrew the Iraqi monarchy in 1958. Pan-Arabism in one form or another has been highly attractive to various military and civilian groups in the 1960s and 1970s, notably the Ba'ath party. However, pan-Arabism is far less popular among Iraq Shi'as, with their affinity for Persian Iran, than with the politically dominant Sunnis. It has no appeal whatsoever to the Kurds and other ethnic groups. The pan-Arab element in Iraq's foreign policy has been partly responsible for causing military confrontations, recently with Iran and earlier with Syria and Turkey. This point has been a bone of contention among Sunni elites and masses alike. Pro-union groups have often achieved power in Baghdad, but they have never been able to effect a union with Egypt or Syria, the two most promising partners. Both internal dissension and external circumstances have contributed to frustration of the unionists' political goals.[16]

STRUCTURE OF THE GOVERNMENT

Iraq is a republic ruled by a strong presidential government dominated by the Arab Socialist Ba'ath (Resurrection) Party, which seized power in a coup d'etat in July 1968. Structurally, the system of government has been in a "transitional" phase since then. The government system is based on the Provisional Constitution of July 16, 1970, which is a modification of an earlier constitution issued September 21, 1968.[17]

A formal distinction is maintained between the National Command of the Ba'ath Party, which is responsible for party activities throughout the Arab nation as a whole, and the Regional Command, which is the Iraqi branch of the Ba'ath and formally subordinate to the National Command. Technically, then, the Ba'ath Party in Iraq is a branch of the Ba'ath Party that rules Syria. However, relations between the Iraqi and Syrian regimes seldom have been cordial and the two Ba'ath Regional Commands are separated by strong political, ideological, and personal differences. The titular head of the party's National Command (in Iraq) is Michel Aflaq, a Syrian and one of the party's original founders. At the state level the Regional Command is headed by Iraq's president, Saddam Hussein. Here one can see how the supranational sources of Iraq's political identity are reflected in governmental structure (see Figure 4.1). The Iraqis, however, dominate both commands (Saddam Hussein is deputy secretary general of the National Command), and the Syrians do not recognize the authority of either. (Indeed, Syria has its own version of the National Command.)

Formally, the Ba'ath party maintains a separate identity from the Iraqi government. Theoretically, this is supposed to reduce conflicts of loyalty among party workers, who maintain an elaborate party organization and the state government apparatus.

Formal structures notwithstanding, almost all real political power and decision-making authority are concentrated in the person of — as distinct from the office of — the president, Saddam Hussein al Takriti. In addition to being the chief executive of the government, Hussein is commander-in-chief of the

FIGURE 4.1
Structure of the Iraqi Government

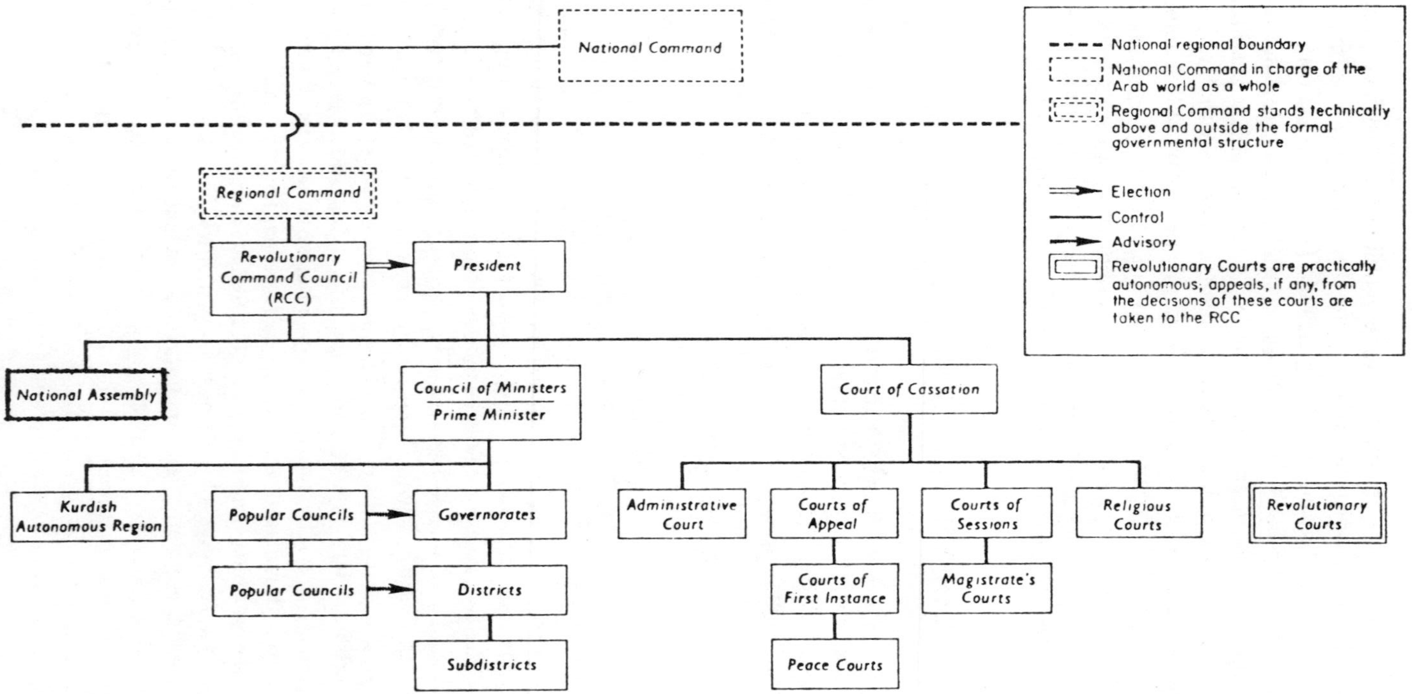

Source: Richard F. Nyrop et al, *Iraq: A Country Study* (Washington, D.C.: U.S. Government Printing Office 1979), p. 187. Reprinted with the permission of the copyright holder, the American University.

82

armed forces and chairman of the Revolutionary Command Council (RCC), the highest executive and legislative body in Iraq. He is also secretary-general of the Ba'ath Regional (Iraqi) Command and deputy secretary-general of the Ba'ath National Command. The president of the republic has the authority to appoint ministers to the cabinet, to transfer them, and to dismiss them at his discretion. Technically, all ministers are answerable to the president, but in reality the ministers who concurrently hold membership in the RCC are not as subservient to him as the technocrats who hold no executive position in the Ba'ath party hierarchy. The president also has the authority to dismiss the vice-presidents of the republic. The president is elected by a two-thirds majority of the RCC, to which he is responsible.

Executive powers are shared by the RCC and the national government, with ultimate authority formally residing in the RCC. The RCC not only enacts all legislation, but it also supervises all foreign and domestic policies. The national government is subordinate to the RCC since the former, as already mentioned, selects the president and vice-president. However, as the chairman of the RCC is also president of the republic, Hussein in reality controls both the RCC and the government.

The council members, including the chairman and vice-chairman, are answerable only to the RCC, which may dismiss any of its members by a majority vote of two-thirds. The RCC may also charge with wrongdoing and send to trial any of its own members, any deputy, the president, or any cabinet member. When the Ba'ath seized power in 1968, new members of the RCC were drawn from the party's Regional Command. However, a constitutional amendment issued in September 1977 stipulated that all members of the Regional Command should be considered as members of the RCC. This amendment had the effect of expanding the RCC's membership from five to twenty-two until July 1979, when several RCC members were purged and later executed for alleged involvement in a plot against the government. After that the RCC's membership was reduced from 22 to 16.

The RCC's constitutional powers are very broad. It assumed legislative functions pending the establishment of a National Assembly. It approves government recommendations concerning national defense and internal security. It is empowered to declare war, order general mobilization, conduct peace agreements, as well as ratify treaties and agreements. The council approves the state budget, defines the rules for the impeachment of its members, and establishes a special court to try individuals so impeached. The RCC can delegate some of the council's powers to the chairman or vice-chairman, excluding legislative powers.

While the formal governmental structure includes a Council of Ministers (see Figure 4.1), this council is not a decision-making body and has no autonomous power. It is little more than a collection of heads of specialized departments that may influence those policy decisions that are directly related to their particular departments.

As mentioned earlier, actual political power is concentrated in the person of the president. This has been accomplished by overlapping membership in and leadership of Iraq's three most influential political institutions: the RCC, the Ba'ath Regional Command, and the executive authority of the cabinet, and through these, control of the armed forces. The current president's power is reinforced by the appointment of trusted relatives to key positions. In the wake of the purge of alleged conspirators in July and August 1979, Saddam Hussein created a new position, that of deputy commander-in-chief of the armed forces, to which he appointed a close relative, Adnan Khayrallah Talfah, who also held the key post of minister of defense. Talfah is the son-in-law of former president Hassan al-Bakr and Hussein's foster brother's brother-in-law and cousin. Hussein also created a new post of deputy prime minister, to which he appointed six leading Ba'athist officials, including Talfah. The sensitive post of minister of interior (which is responsible for internal security) was filled by Sa'dun Shakir, the chief of Iraqi intelligence and a close associate of Saddam Hussein. Saddam's brother, Barzan Hussein, replaced Shakir as head of intelligence. Saddam also replaced eight cabinet ministers appointed by the former president with his own lieutenants. The six deputy prime ministers and most of the key ministers are members of the RCC and/or the Ba'ath Regional Command.[18] This overlapping membership does not end at the RCC Regional Command-cabinet level. It extends into the party bureaus, many of whose chairmen and vice-chairmen hold dual or even triple memberships in the RCC, the Regional Command, and the cabinet.

The constitution provides for a parliament called the National Assembly. It was not formed, however, until 1980. Elections for the 250-seat National Assembly were held June 20, 1980. Contesting the seats were 840 candidates, including a number of women. While the Iraqi Communist Party and Muslim fundamentalist groups such as *al-Da'wah al-Islāmiyah* (the Islamic Call) boycotted the elections, the elections themselves were remarkably free. Arabic-speaking Americans, visiting several randomly selected polling sites on election day and interviewing party members, election officials, and voters, reported little government interference in the elections.[19] It is also significant that a large number of independent (non-Ba'athist) candidates were elected. While membership in the Ba'ath Party is not a requirement to stand for election, one of the requirements for eligibility according to the election bylaws is that the candidate must "be a believer in the principles and aims of the July 17-30 progressive and socialist revolution of 1968" that put the Ba'athists in power. Similarly, the bylaws state that any candidate who receives funds from opponents of the 1968 revolution or from "foreign quarters with the aim of influencing the election results," will be liable to the death penalty. Such restrictions certainly narrow the scope and intensity of the opposition forces in the assembly.

Technically, the National Assembly elects the president. However, the RCC nominates the president and submits its choice to the assembly for a vote of confidence. If the RCC's choice for president fails to win this vote of confidence, the RCC must make another nomination. Thus, the RCC continues to wield effective supreme executive and legislative authority, even though the president is now chosen "by representatives of the people." Sessions of the National Assembly are convened and concluded by a resolution issued by the RCC.[20]

In addition to voting on the RCC's nomination for president, the National Assembly is empowered to draft legislation on any matters apart from those that are expressly the prerogatives of the RCC, such as national defense and security matters. The National Assembly ratifies the budget, development plans, treaties, and agreements presented to it by the RCC. It can deliberate these and other bills prepared by the RCC or by the president through the Council of Ministers and approve or reject them within 15 days of receiving them. The assembly can summon any cabinet minister for explanations and can propose the removal of a minister, subject to prior presidential consent. The assembly, however, does not have a veto power. If its amendment or rejection of a bill is unacceptable to the RCC, the disagreement is to be resolved by a two-thirds' majority of both bodies in a joint session.

Appended to the government structure at the national level is the structure for the Kurdish Autonomous Region (see Figure 4.2). The implementation of the Kurdish autonomy plan began in March 1974. This plan provides the Kurds with a modicum of self-rule in the northern part of the country, where they have a local majority. There are the three governorates of Dahuk, Irbil, and Sulaimaniyah. The city of Irbil is the administrative center of the autonomous region. Kurdish is the language used in all official communications. However, the government in Baghdad maintains effective control over the administrative affairs of the region. Article 10 of the autonomy plan provides for an elected legislative council in the region and defines its powers of legislation and the procedural aspects of the meetings. Among the powers given to the council are legislative authority to make decisions "to develop the region and promote its social, cultural, constructional and economic utilities within the bounds of the state's general policy, to suggest a budget for the region, and to cast or withhold votes of confidence in the Executive Committee or in one or more of its members. "Anyone in [sic] whom confidence is withheld shall be relieved of his duty."[21]

The Kurdish autonomy law further provides for an Executive Council to administer the region. It consists of a chairman, a deputy chairman, and 10 to 12 members (see Figure 4.2). The president of the republic appoints the chairman from among the elected members of the Legislative Council. This appointed chairman chooses his team from among the council's members. The president has the authority to dismiss the chairman of the Executive Council and, in such a case, the entire Executive Council is dissolved. Until 1980 the members of the Legislative Council were also nominated by the Baghdad government. However, elections for the 50 members of the council were held September 20, 1980, where 701,000 voters elected 50 deputies from among 794 candidates. Most

FIGURE 4.2
Structure of the Kurdish Autonomy Plan

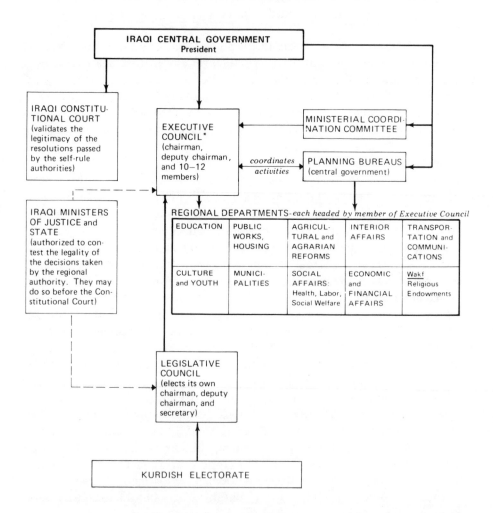

*Chairman is appointed by the president of the republic from among the members of the Legislative Council. The chairman in turn chooses members for the Executive Committee from among the Legislative Council. The chairman and members of the Executive Council hold the rank of minister. The president has the power to dismiss the chairman; in such a case, the Executive Committee is dissolved.

Source: Compiled by the authors.

of the deputies came from such occupational groups as teachers, lawyers, engineers, and farmers.

Even from this brief and incomplete treatment of the Kurdish autonomy plan, it is evident that although the Kurds have obtained some authority over their own affairs, the financial, executive, and judicial powers are still in the hands of the Ba'athist government in Baghdad. Expressly exempt from local jurisdiction are justice, police, internal security, and the administration of the frontier areas. The sweeping powers of the central government became particularly evident in the frontier areas when relations between Iraq and Iran became more hostile in 1979 and 1980. Government security then acted, sometimes hostilely and indiscriminantly, in evacuating Kurdish villagers to new locations in the lowlands.

INTEREST GROUPS IN THE IRAQI POLITICAL SYSTEM

The concept of interest groups in the context of Iraqi politics does not connote the same characteristics that the term does in the West. Moreover, the identification of a particular interest group does not necessarily imply its legitimacy in the Iraqi political system. Interest groups are defined as self-differentiating sectional groups, ad hoc collectivities or organizations bound by vocational or associational interests who seek to influence policies and decisions. A further distinction must be made between interest groups lawfully sanctioned by the regime and those that are not. "Lawfully sanctioned" refers to groups who are committed to the goals of the socialist revolution of 1968. This criterion implies recognition of the legitimacy of the current political and social institutions and the party that created them. A shorthand reference for such groups is "progressive forces."

The Progressive National Front

The vehicle for institutionalizing the role of "progressive" interest groups in Iraqi politics is the Progressive National Front (PNF). This body maintains a semblance of pluralism under strict Ba'ath guidance. Formed in 1973, the PNF represents a Ba'athist attempt at coalition building. It is a device for reversing the vicious cycle that had plagued every regime since the overthrow of the monarchy in 1958: regimes seizing power by a coup d'etat, based on narrow groups of personalities, ruling by decree and repression, generating frustration and alienation, and, eventually, a countercoup. A coalition of progressive forces was viewed as an expedient means of minimizing conflict and rivalry among contending political groups, of ensuring a modicum of political stability, and of attracting a much larger segment of the population to the regime than could otherwise be achieved.

The PNF initially included the Iraqi Communist Party (ICP), several Kurdish parties and Nasserite splinter groups such as the Independent Democrats and the Progressive Nationalists. Non-Ba'athist groups have had a few representatives in the Council of Ministers, which is not a policymaking body.

The Progressive National Front derives its ideological basis from the Charter of National Action, proclaimed by then-president Ahmed Hassan al-Bakr in November 1977.[22] The charter is basically an elaboration of the Ba'athist charter of the Iraqi polity as laid down in the Provisional Constitution of 1970. It remains the embodiment of the Ba'ath regime's goals and principles concerning the nature of the political system envisaged for Iraq and the roles of the Ba'ath party, the armed forces, the bureaucracy, and the Kurdish people in that system. The charter further develops the Ba'ath's view of the economy, society, culture, art, and foreign policy within an Iraqi and a broader Arab context. Two unmistakable themes emerge from the charter: the Ba'ath's commitment to setting Iraq on an uncompromising pan-Arab course both domestically and regionally; and the Ba'ath's right to lead the Arab revolutionary struggle inside Iraq and in the Arab world beyond. According to the charter, the Ba'ath party "represents the interests of the broadest masses from among the workers, peasants, and other hardtoiling groups." Implicitly, there is no need for these forces to be represented by another political party. A cornerstone of the new revolutionary society is the organization of workers, peasants, students, intellectuals, women's associations, unions and federations, and youth organizations. Thus, "interest groups" are defined along vocational and social lines as part of the broad coalition of progressive forces represented by the Ba'ath. In this regard, one interest group conspicuously absent from this list is the armed forces. The political role of the armed forces is discussed below.

The PNF, which represents various shades of progressive opinion, is a mobilizational agency that provides a channel of indirect popular support for the regime. The ruling Ba'ath Party, however, holds the predominant position in the PNF's activities. The internal regulations of the PNF provide for the establishment of a central executive committee, the High Committee (HC) of the Progressive National Front. This is the principal executive organ of the PNF. It was originally composed of 16 members, half of whom were reserved for the Ba'ath Party. The Ba'ath is entrusted with carrying out the Front's decisions through official channels. The Iraqi Communist Party was given three seats, the Kurdish Democratic Party three seats, with the remaining two reserved for other progressive groups.

However, initial overtures to the Kurds in 1973 were unsuccessful. The Kurds apparently viewed the Ba'athist-ICP coalition as an attempt to isolate or neutralize them. It was not until after March 1975, with the collapse of the Kurdish revolt, that the PNF expanded beyond a Ba'athist-ICP partnership. The HC was enlarged from 16 to 18 members to accommodate the factionally split Kurds.[23] Two other progressive groups joined the PNF in 1975. These were the Independent Democrats led by Mazhir al-Azzawi, and the Progressive

Nationalists, a collection of nationalists of various persuasions, led by Hisham al-Shawi.

Officially, the regime maintains that the PNF is vital so long as Arab revolutionary movements are threatened in Iraq and other parts of the Arab homeland. However, by the end of 1981, the PNF was beginning to look more and more superfluous as a device for interest aggregation among progressive groups and as a vehicle for channeling popular support indirectly to the regime. The partnership between the ICP and the Ba'athist government was terminated for all practical purposes in March and April of 1979. Nevertheless, the composition of the PNF is an accurate guide to the principal interest groups in Iraqi politics as far as foreign policy is concerned. These are the civilian and military wings of the Ba'ath Party, the Iraqi Communist Party, and the Kurdish nationalists.

The Arab Socialist Resurrection (Ba'ath) Party

The Iraqi branch of the *Ba'ath al-Arabi al-ishtirāki* was founded in 1952 when Fuad al-Rikabi, a Shi'a student who had just graduated from the Baghdad Engineering College, began to create secret cells of members and sympathizers inside the country.[24] Gradually, the Ba'ath began to attract adherents from a variety of social, economic, and professional groups, including the armed forces. Recognizing the decisive role the military could play in seizing power, the Ba'ath actively recruited a number of army officers who, along with other nationalist and progressive groups in the military, took part in the overthrow of the monarchy in July 1958 that brought Abd al-Karim Qassem to power.

Qassem, however, began to concentrate power into his own hands while becoming more tolerant of the Communist Party. Since the Ba'ath was committed to the interpretation of Arab nationalism as full acceptance of Abdel Nasser's leadership of one Arab nation, a break with Qassem was inevitable. Having failed to outmaneuver him politically, the Ba'ath attempted to assassinate him in October 1959. One of the participants in the assassination attempt was Saddam Hussein.[25] After this incident, many Ba'athists had to live in exile until the party returned to power in 1963. While out of power the party expanded its contacts with both civilian and military groups. It was the military that returned the Ba'ath to power. In February 1963 a group of Ba'athist and Nasserite officers overthrew the Qassem regime and established a coalition government under Abdel Salam Arif. Arif became president and Brigadier Ahmad Hassan al-Bakr, a Ba'athist leader, was made prime minister. The coalition governed through the National Council for the Revolutionary Command (NCRC).

Arif was a popular figure in pan-Arab circles, a devout Muslim, and pragmatic in his approach to politics. Arif was also pro-Nasser and favored a union with Egypt. The Ba'ath was divided into two factions, one favoring a pro-Nasser line and union with Egypt, the other strongly opposed to such a union and preferring closer ties with Syria. Ba'ath leaders were young and inexperienced. Their political tactics were conditioned by their long opposition against former regimes. When at last they gained power, they had to cooperate with other groups in order to make the government function. Rifts and misunderstandings developed between Ba'athists who held government posts and had to make decisions on the spot with no time to consult the party leaderships and the Regional and National Commands of the party. The applications of party principles and doctrine to existing conditions in Iraq had not been studied or thought out. One result was that the practical problems that had arisen were not resolved according to party principles. The lack of coordination among Ba'ath members who held government positions was an important cause of disagreement within the Iraqi Regional Command.

Another serious problem was lack of coordination with Ba'athist cells in the armed forces. Ba'ath officers who had been instrumental in overthrowing the Qassem regime remained out of touch with the Ba'ath civilian leadership. They were not invited to attend meetings of the Regional Command, mainly because the Regional Command no longer held regular meetings after the February coup. The support of these officers was critical, and not just because they were party members. Since the Ba'ath had not yet consolidated its position, these officers were essential to ensure the continuation of the party in power. Left uninformed of what the civilian leaders were doing, the Ba'ath officers became suspicious of the civilian leadership's activities and intentions.

During this period, the Ba'ath leaders were divided into three groups. The right-wing group was composed of Talib Shibib, a member of the NCRC and minister of foreign affairs; Tahir Yahya, also a member of the NCRC and chief of the General Staff; Hazzim Jawad, minister of state and member of the NCRC; Hardin Takriti, NCRC member and commander of the air force; and Abdal Suttar Abd al-Hatif, member of the NCRC and minister of communications. This group advocated cooperation with other nationalist forces, particularly those in the army who might eventually become party members and so strengthen its position in Iraq. They favored postponing the implementation of radical principles, especially the implementation of socialism in Iraq, until the country was ready for them. This group could legitimize its position by referring to the statement by the Ba'ath National Command leader, Michel Aflaq, that declared the party should not try to implement socialism until Arab unity was achieved.

The left-wing group consisted of Ali Saleh al-Sa'di, deputy premier, minister of interior, and member of the NCRC; Muhsin al-Shaykh Radi, Hamdi Abd al-Majid, and Hani al-Fuhayhi, all members of the NCRC; and Abu Talib al-Hashim. This group, which was composed mainly of civilians and was not as engaged in governing the country, insisted on implementing the Ba'ath's basic socialist principles. They argued that the establishment of socialism would accelerate the redistribution of wealth to the people whose support was necessary to gain control of the country. This group was opposed to cooperation with the nationalist (pro-Nasser) army officers in the NCRC, especially those who rejected the Ba'ath's ideology.

Between these two factions was a center group composed of Ahmad Hassan al-Bakr, the prime minister and later vice-president, and Salih Mehdi Ammash, minister of defense. This group tried to reconcile the other two wings, but failed. An intense power struggle erupted between Ali Salem al-Sa'di, the leader of the left wing, and Hazzim Jawad and Talib Shabib, who led the right wing. Jawad and Shabib tried to enlist the support of the nationalist army officers. The latter, however, turned out to be more interested in ousting the entire party from power. Sa'di, whose forces constituted a majority in the Regional (Iraqi) Command, used the Ba'athist national guard to strengthen his position. This party army, however, was a military organization without military discipline; its cruel and wanton acts had aroused hatred among the population and suspicion and resentment among the officers in the army.

The intensity of this intraparty struggle resulted in each camp concentrating its efforts on reducing the other's influence, rather than trying to win support of the broader membership and other political groups for its activities. Consequently, the Ba'ath government became unable to initiate or implement any constructive policies.

This rift in the Ba'ath provided Arif with an opportunity to weaken the opposition to his regime. Arif, who was conservative in his political and economic views, favored the center and rightist camps of the Ba'ath although he himself was not a party member. In early November 1963, Hassan al-Bakr, the leader of the Ba'athist officers who opposed the civilian extremists, engineered al-Sa'di's ousting with Arif's support. This was accomplished on November 10 by a special session of the Iraqi Ba'ath, which elected a new regional leadership — without al-Sa'di who was arrested and exiled to Spain the next day. At this meeting an important change was made in the traditional ratio of civilian to military members in the Regional Command. Instead of keeping the civilians in the majority, the November 10 session elected an equal number of civilians and military members to the Regional Command.[26] At this point real political power passed to the military, who by then had little sympathy for the Ba'ath.

The loss of power was partly due to the split between the Syrian Ba'ath National Command, which had seized power in Syria in 1963, and the Iraqi Regional Command. In Syria, the military wing of the party consolidated its power at the expense of the civilian wing. Consequently, the civilian-dominated Iraqi centrist and rightist factions did not receive any support from the Syrian Ba'athists who disagreed with Bakr and Ammash on cooperation with the nationalist officers. The Syrian Ba'athists advocated an "ideological army" that would defend not only the country's territorial integrity, but also the political and social values imposed by the party. Because of these sorts of disagreements between the Syrian and Iraqi Ba'athists, the position of the Iraqi Ba'athists vis-a-vis the nationalist and Ba'athist officers was further weakened. As a result of these weaknesses and internal divisions, Arif rallied the military to his side. On November 18 Arif launched a coup against the party itself and was able to expel the Ba'athists without any serious challenge to his authority.[27]

Basically, what happened in November 1963 was that the Iraqi officer-politicians were confronted with the question of to whom they owed their primary allegiance and obedience — the party or the army. When they could no longer vacillate, the overwhelming majority, including the members of the Ba'ath Party's military bureau, chose the army and the officer corps. The few who decided in favor of the party were immediately eliminated. Hassan al-Bakr and Hardin Takriti, whose positions were either equivocal or hesitant, were ousted from power after a brief transition period.[28] To be sure, the recruitment of officers by the party, which began in the summer of 1963, did increase the party's influence in the military but not party discipline. Recruitment had not increased party influence in the military nearly as much as it had strengthened the officers' positions in the party. Since the military was more completely institutionalized than the party or the government apparatus it established, military dominance of the party weakened party authority. In the absence of decisive, stable leadership, the military leaders felt that they alone were capable of providing stable, effective government.

After nearly five years, the Ba'ath reemerged as the dominant political force in Iraq. While it was out of power the party analyzed and reflected on the causes of its failure to maintain power in the country. The Ba'ath appears to have learned two important lessons from its experiences in Syria and Iraq. First, while it may be necessary at times to gain the cooperation of other groups, sharing political power with any group or political party does not serve the Ba'ath's political interests. Second, while support of the military is critical to gaining and keeping political power, the military should not be allowed to dominate the party, where civilian leadership must retain strict control over the armed forces and the party apparatus.

That these two cardinal principles have influenced the party's approach to government can be seen in the policies the Ba'ath has followed since it regained power in July 1968. Although Communists and non-Ba'athist Kurds have been appointed to the cabinet and to the vice-presidency, the Ba'ath has been unwilling to share at the level where political power is concentrated and wielded — the RCC. Despite pressure from its Communist allies (when they still were allies) and from the progovernment factions of the Kurds as well as various nationalist groups, the Ba'ath has persistently refused to appoint any non-Ba'athist to the RCC. Similarly, the Ba'ath has monopolized the political activities of the armed forces. The Ba'athists are adamant in their refusal to allow any other organization or group to engage in any form of political activity within the armed forces, which are the mainstay of Ba'athist control of the country. Political activity by any non-Ba'athist organization in the armed forces is illegal. Even retired officers are barred from non-Ba'athist affiliation. The legal sanctions combined with continual purges within the upper ranks of the military since 1968 have decreased the possibility of a non-Ba'athist military intervention against Ba'ath political leadership. If a coup were to occur, most likely it will be initiated by dissident elements within the Ba'ath.

The foregoing discussion does not mean that the military has become apolitical. Ultimately, no civilian regime can be expected to survive unless it receives the blessing of the military. What the Ba'ath apparently has succeeded in doing is to discourage military intervention in politics and in relieving the political process from military pressures. Until 1973 all key offices in the state — the presidency, the premiership, command of the armed forces, and control of the ministries of defense and interior — were all held by officers. By 1978 the RCC had been expanded to 22 members, only three of whom were active-duty line officers. These were President Hassan al-Bakr, Minister of Defense Adnan Khayrallah Talfah, and Minister of Communications Sa'dun Ghaydan Takriti. By 1977 most command positions were filled by party members, and promotion of officers depended upon loyalty to the Ba'ath regime, if not active party membership. The fact that the plot against Saddam Hussein that was uncovered in July 1979 involved mainly civilian members of the RCC and only a small military element is further evidence of the party's success in imposing its control on the military.[29] Speculation concerning the objectives and grievances of the conspirators ranged from a move by Hussein to consolidate his power and remove elements in the party and the RCC who were becoming critical of his authoritarian rule, to a preemptive move to stave off what Hussein perceived as an attempt by forces representing Iraq's Shi'a majority to oust him from power. While it is not possible to determine exactly what took place, it should be noted that absent from the speculation were indications of unrest within the military.[30]

While the civilian wing of the Ba'ath appears to have succeeded in imposing its authority over the military wing, it does not mean that disagreement between them has not occurred. Actually, the two wings have disagreed on several issues facing Iraq: the conflict between Arabs and Kurds, relations with Arab states, economic development, relations with Iran and the superpowers, and problems related to Palestine and Camp David. Since the Ba'ath seized power in July 1968, these disagreements have caused a number of political casualties within the RCC and its auxiliary governing bodies, the cabinet, and the Regional Command. These disagreements have included two attempted coups — one in 1970 by two retired senior officers, neither of whom was a Ba'athist; and a more serious attempt in 1973 by Nazim Kazzar, chief of the Security Police under the Ba'athist regime. Kazzar, a Ba'athist, was in accord with the party's leadership on principles and major issues, but strongly disagreed with the party on the methods of handling the Kurdish problem and the Communists.[31] Of the individuals arrested in July for an alleged conspiracy against Saddam Hussein, only two serving military officers were implicated (and executed). Most of those arrested and tried were centered in the ministries of planning, foreign affairs, and information. By a process of elimination, the civilian wing of the Ba'ath under Saddam Hussein has so far emerged as the stronger faction in the ruling institutions. This is a pragmatic centrist group that has removed, by a variety of legal and extralegal means, the opposition posed by right-wing and left-wing extremists, civilian and military alike.

The goal of the Ba'ath is to build a government and party apparatus that ensures that its tenure in office will depend on civilian rather than military support. Yet, efforts by the civilian rulers to retain military support are clearly evident. Saddam Hussein's acceptance of an honorary degree from the Military College and honorary rank of general in the military hierarchy reflects his concern about support for his leadership in military circles. Similarly, Hussein's conduct of the war with Iran in a way that minimizes Iraqi casualties suggests deference to the sensibilities of the military. These gestures provide a clear indication that the support of the armed forces remains essential to the survival of the government despite the reduced active political participation by military officers during the 1970s and early 1980s.

Moreover, the gradual increase since 1973 in the role of the civilian wing of the party in government does not, by itself, demonstrate the assertion of civilian primacy over the military. One must also take into account the effects of kinship and locality and the fact that the party has become more homogeneous (that is, more predominantly Sunni) in its sectarian composition over the last 20 years.

Parallel to the rising ratio of civilian-to-military in the party hierarchy and government has been the advance of the Takritis in the party's military branch, going back to the first Ba'ath regime in 1963. For example, at the time of the November 18 coup, all of the following leaders were members of the Ba'ath Party's Military Bureau and all were, by birth or origin, from the town of Takrit: Hardin al-Takriti, head of the military Ba'athists, deputy commander-in-chief of the armed forces, and minister of defense; Tahar Yahya, the premier; Brigadier General Rashid Musleh, minister of interior and military governor general; and Ahmed Hassan al-Bakr, the vice-president of the republic. All of these men except Bakr participated in the November 18 coup that ousted the Ba'ath from power. In fact, Hardin Takriti is reported to have personally commanded the aircraft that strafed the Ba'ath national guard into submission.[32]

The influence of the Takritis, already evident in 1963, was subsequently expanded by the transfer of the leadership of the Iraqi Ba'ath to Ahmad Hassan al-Bakr and Saddam Hussein. As both men are from Takrit, they tended to attract into the party those individuals with whom they had close social and personal ties. These were often men who by birth or descent were from their own town. Hussein and Bakr were united by more than common ideological commitment and locality. Both belonged to the *al-Begāt* section of the Albū Nāsir tribe. They were also related by family ties. Saddam Hussein is the foster son, nephew, and son-in-law of Khayrallah Talfah, the governor of Baghdad when Bakr was president, and a first cousin of Bakr.[33] As mentioned earlier, Talfah's son, Adnan, is Bakr's son-in-law and Hussein's brother-in-law and is now in charge of the army. Thus, it is not so much on the strength of the civilian component of the party that Hussein's political position rests, as it is on his family connections with Bakr plus his control of the party's National Security Bureau.

Equally important has been the representation of the Takritis on the RCC. In 1968-69 Takritis occupied three out of five seats. When the RCC was reduced to nine members, Takritis held four of them. They have held not only all of the top posts in the party, the army, and the government, but also, among other positions, the defense portfolio, the governorship and Security Department of Baghdad, as well as the commands of the air force, the Baghdad army garrison, the Habaniyyah air base, and the tank regiment of the Republican Guard. Hanna Batatu, who has written the definitive study on social classes and politics in Iraq, concludes: "Their role continues to be so critical that it would not be going too far to say that the Takritis rule through the Ba'ath party, rather than the Ba'ath party through the Takritis."[34]

Similarly, the Iraqi Ba'ath Party has undergone an important transformation in terms of confessional composition. Until the coup of November 6, the party's membership reflected a genuine partnership between young Sunnis and Shi'as committed to pan-Arab goals. Out of the leadership in the party's top command that ran the party from 1952 to November 1963, 38.5 percent were Sunni Arabs, 53.8 percent were Shi'a Arabs, and 7.7 percent were Kurds. However, between 1963 and 1970, out of a total of 53 party leaders, 84.9 percent were Sunni Arabs, 5.7 percent were Shi'a Arabs, and 7.5 percent were Kurds.[35] A similar change apparently took place in the lower levels of the party's active membership. Thus, the party cannot claim to be nearly as representative of the population as a whole as it once could, but it is more homogeneous and presumably more cohesive. This may be one reason the regime has sought the cooperation of other political groups in implementing the party's policies through the Progressive National Front.

Obviously the leadership has not relied exclusively on the strength of the Takriti clan to consolidate its political position. However, the ties of clan and locality have been critically important in bridging differences between the dominant civilian and military wings of the party. This, in turn, has bought the party more time to effectively institutionalize its leadership in the army; to base its tenure in office increasingly on civilian rather than military support; and to build ties with other political forces.

The Kurds

Apart from the Ba'ath, the most clearly recognizable major interest groups engaged in political activities in Iraq are the Kurds and the Iraqi Communist Party (ICP). Of these two groups the Kurds have fared better than the Communists. Apart from the Ba'ath itself, the Kurds are certainly the most important interest group in terms of impact on Iraq's foreign policy.

In a sense the Kurds are a political casualty of the post-World War I settlement that eventually recognized (after World War II) the principle of self-determination for states, but not for nations or peoples. The Kurds have never formed an independent political entity. Before World War I the Kurdish population lived under two Middle Eastern governments: the Ottoman Empire and the Qajar dynasty in Iran. The fall of the Ottoman Empire brought into independent existence a number of Arab states, two of which — Iraq and Syria — inherited a sizable portion of the Kurdish population. Of the two, Iraq incorporated by far the larger number of Kurds, who by this time had been stirred by the Western concept of nationalism. Like many other ethnic and linguistic groups, the Kurds were very receptive to the Wilsonian concept of self-determination.

As a result of their cordial relations with the victorious European powers (particularly the British, who used the Kurds and other Ottoman ethnic minorities to break up the Ottoman Empire), the Kurds were promised, under the Treaty of Sèvres, an autonomous Kurdistan and, "if they should show that they wanted it, the right to independence."[36] Although the area promised the Kurds was for the most part in eastern Turkey, Kurdish aspirations ignored the artificial boundary that separated the Kurds in eastern Anatolia from their ethnic kinsmen in Iran, Iraq, and Syria. Since the end of World War I the Kurds have struggled on numerous occasions to gain autonomy or independence in one or more of the areas in the states where they constitute a local majority. The closest they have come is the establishment of the short-lived independent Mahabad Republic in Iran in 1946, but their drive for autonomy or independence has persisted intermittently in Iraq and Iran since then.

Because the Kurds have basically been in opposition to the societies in which they are a minority, those majority populations have reacted violently to Kurdish actions that appeared to threaten or undermine "national" interests of the states. Rejecting pan-Turanianism and pan-Arabism, the Kurds have resisted Turkification, Arabization, and Iranization, and have sought to preserve their own culture in isolation — except when they have been provided with an opportunity to seize the initiative and their ultimate goal, independence.

None of the states with Kurdish minorities would be comfortable with the establishment of an independent Kurdish state, which almost certainly would attract their own Kurdish populations. Consequently, even though each of these countries has supported Kurdish unrest across its borders to achieve short-term objectives, ultimately they have worked in tandem to crush any attempted separatism that appeared to be near success.

The Kurdish rebellion began in 1919 against the British mandatory authority in an effort to establish an independent Kurdish state. The rebellion has persisted since 1932 as a struggle against successive Iraqi regimes for autonomy within an independent Iraq. In Iraq, Mulla Mustafa Barzani was the spearhead of the Kurdish rebellion from 1943 to 1975. The military capabilities of the large Kurdish populations in Turkey, Iran, and Iraq have frequently been neutralized but never crushed.

Between 1945 and 1959 there were no major disturbances in the Kurdish area of Iraq despite daily "provocation" in the Kurdish-language broadcasts by a Soviet-sponsored clandestine radio operated by Kurdish expatriates in the

Russian Caucasus. One reason for this apparent Kurdish docility was that the Kurds were once again hemmed in by the cooperation of the three Middle East governments most directly concerned with them — Turkey, Iran, and Iraq. Under the Baghdad Pact these governments had agreed to cooperate in strengthening and protecting one another's territorial integrity. With such an arrangement, there was hardly any possibility for a foreign power to provide large-scale military aid to the Kurds without creating a serious international dispute that would involve not only the three Middle East powers, but possibly Britain and the United States as well. With the overthrow of the Hashemite monarchy in Iraq and the installation in Baghdad of a "revolutionary" regime in July 1958, this international cooperation began to weaken, thereby destroying the *cordon sanitaire* that had prevented foreign powers from interfering in the domestic affairs of these countries.

At first the postrevolutionary regime of Abdel Karim Qassem was sympathetic to Kurdish demands for direct participation in the governing of the areas where the Kurds constituted a local majority. Indeed, prior to the July coup, a few Kurdish officers supported Qassem's Free Officers Movement, believing it would be sympathetic to Kurdish national aspirations.[37]

The initial policies of Qassem's regime seemed to justify the Kurdish officers' assessments. One of the members of the new government's presidency council was a Kurdish officer, Colonel Khalid al-Nagshband. Another Kurd, Sheikh Baba Ali, was made a member of the cabinet. Further, the provisional constitution, promulgated in July 1958, specifically mentioned the Kurds as partners within the framework of Iraqi unity: "Arabs and Kurds are considered partners in this fatherland, and their national rights within the unity of Iraq are acknowledged by this Constitution (Article 3)."[38] The Kurdish leader, Mustafa Barzani, was allowed to return from exile in 1958 by the Qassem government.

In January 1960, under the government's new authorization to form political parties, Barzani's Kurdistan Democratic Party (DKP), founded in 1945, was legalized with a leftist program aimed at radical land reform and coordination of Iraq's foreign and economic policies with those of the Soviet Union and other socialist states.[39] In the first year after the overthrow of the monarchy, the Kurds were among the strongest supporters of the new Iraqi republic.

Kurdish interests converged with Qassem's in a variety of areas. One was opposition to the Baghdad Pact, which to the Kurds meant the collaboration of Turkey, Iran, and Iraq in suppressing the Kurds. Another was opposition to the union of Iraq with Nasser's United Arab Republic. A third area was friendly relations with the Soviet Union (which had given sanctuary to Kurdish leaders prior to the July 14 revolution) and the Communists. The KDP and the Iraqi Communist Party became two major links between the Qassem regime and the Soviet Union. Domestically, Qassem used the Kurds against the regime's opponents. These ranged from large landlords and monarchists to Nasserite and pro-union officers. The Qassem regime generally armed the Kurds and often used them against "rebellious" tribes or officers who opposed Qassem's policies. On at least one crucial occasion in March 1959, the Kurds and the Communists (some of whom were also Kurds) saved the Qassem regime by containing a revolt in Mosul led by a pro-union officer, Colonel Abdal-Wahhab Shawwaf, and by preventing the pro-Nasser Arabs of the Shammar tribe from joining the rebellious military units.[40]

As Qassem's loyal allies during the March uprising, the Kurds expected several significant material and political changes in Kurdistan: administrative autonomy, a Kurdish university and schools, and economic development of the region. None of these changes was forthcoming, partly because Qassem's relations with the Communists had begun to deteriorate. Since the Kurds were allies of the Communists, Qassem had no interest in strengthening any group considered pro-Communist. Furthermore, the Kurds themselves were disunited – a condition that Qassem tried to exploit by extending government support to the Zibori tribes, who are traditional enemies of the Barzanis. Thus, most of Mulla Mustafa's energies were directed toward consolidating and expanding his leadership position in the Kurdish provinces at the expense of his Kurdish adversaries. Apart from the Kurdish link with the Communist left, Qassem apparently became alarmed at Barzani's growing political influence and leadership, which appeared to challenge Qassem's own authority in the Kurdish provinces.

In addition, the KDP was weakened by a long-standing internal division between leftist urban elements who dominated the politburo, on the one hand, and older tribal-feudal leaders, like Barzani, on the other. This division had a negative impact on the development of the party and its attitude toward the Iraqi government. Modern concepts of nationalism and socialism were largely confined to a small number of educated young men in the cities whose ideas seldom extended to the masses in the rural areas. The KDP often lacked a clear national following owing to the predominance of the tribal elements and tribal loyalties that often frustrated nationalist activities.[41]

Consequently, it was not until July 1961 that the KDP and Barzani were able to draw up a memorandum outlining the Kurdish demands in Iraq. The petition officially asked for wide Kurdish autonomy within the framework of the Iraqi state. Functions such as foreign policy, defense, and finance would continue to be the prerogatives of the central government. What the Kurds wanted for their autonomous area was that Kurdish become the principal language in the Kurdish autonomous region; that the police and army units in the region be composed entirely of Kurds; that educational facilities there be placed under the Kurdish provincial government; that a substantial share of the oil industry in the Mosul-Kirkuk region be spent in Kurdistan; that the vice-premier, assistant chief of staff, and assistant ministers of all ministries be Kurds; and that outside Kurdistan, the deployment of Kurdish army units be made only with the consent of the Kurdish leaders, except in the case of an external threat.[42]

The rejection of these demands by the Qassem regime precipitated the Kurdish revolt that continued intermittently, with temporary cease-fires, armistices, and extended negotiations during the 1960s. It was finally settled in April-May 1975. The scope and intensity of the revolt was more serious and threatening to regional peace than any previous Kurdish uprising. The main reason was that the rebellion spilled over onto a struggle between Iraq and Iran for influence in the Persian Gulf. This power struggle prompted Baghdad and Tehran to agitate the centrifugal forces among the ethnic minorities across each other's national boundaries. Iraq supported the Baluchis and the Arab tribes in Iran, and Iran aided the Kurds in Iraq. Iran, however, did not encourage the Iraqi Shi'as to create problems for the Baghdad regime.

The first attempt at a cease-fire occurred soon after the Ba'athist coup of February 1963. On March 9, 1963, the new regime issued a proclamation which reaffirmed the government's recognition of the "natural rights" of the Kurds, based on the concept of "administrative decentralization." Neither this declaration nor the negotiations that followed, however, produced a mutually acceptable solution to the conflict. Once again fighting resumed, followed by another cease-fire and more negotiations without agreement.

These first attempts to reach a settlement were complicated by a successful Ba'ath coup in Syria, which raised the hopes of the pan-Arabists for a union of Egypt, Iraq, and Syria. The Kurds' aversion to such a union was reflected in a memorandum in April that the Kurds presented to the Iraqi delegation that was going to Cairo for Arab unity talks. In it the Kurds said that they would be willing to accept "decentralization," as proposed by the Iraqi government, provided Iraq remained as presently constituted. If, however, Iraq joined other Arab states in a federation, the Kurds would demand autonomy "in the widest meaning of the term." Finally, if Iraq became part of an Arab unitary state, the Kurds would demand a "separate region within that state."[43]

It has already been pointed out that the fall of the first Ba'ath government was brought about mainly by internal dissension and government paralysis. A contributing cause, however, was undoubtedly the divergent views among various party factions on how to deal with the Kurdish problem and the resumption of the Kurdish war.

After another period of protracted hostilities, the Kurds and the Iraqi government under Premier Abdur Rahman al-Bazzaz reached an agreement in June 1966. Under this agreement, the Kurds were promised wider political, cultural, and economic rights. Although they were not fully satisfied with the provisions of this agreement, it was the most they could extract from a government that was under constant counterpressure from anti-Kurdish hardliners.

The new agreement provided, inter alia, that "Kurdish nationality" would be recognized in the permanent constitution; that wider administrative powers would be given to locally elected councils; that in Kurdistan, the Kurdish language would be used for administrative and educational purposes; that parliamentary elections would be held at an early date and the Kurds would be represented in the National Assembly and all branches of the public service in proportion to their numbers in the total population; that generous government grants would be given to Kurdish students for study abroad; that a faculty of Kurdish studies would be established at Baghdad University; that Kurdish officials would be appointed in Kurdistan; that permission would be granted for political association and for literary and political publications; a general amnesty would be granted to political prisoners "when violence ended"; that a special ministry would be established for reconstruction and to coordinate administration of various Kurdish districts; and that evicted Kurds either would be resettled in their previous homes or would be compensated for their property losses.[44]

Before the agreement could be implemented, the Bazzaz government was replaced by another. This was headed by an army officer, Naji Talib, who was known to be opposed to the agreement. Nevertheless, the provisions themselves were a clear victory for the Kurds, who apparently negotiated with the government from a position of strength. Moreover, the agreement did maintain a truce between the Kurds and the government for almost two years. Whether or not the Iraqi government intended to implement the agreement in full, succeeding governments under the Arif regimes declared their respect for the agreement. However, none was either willing or able to implement it in full or to impose an alternative solution prior to the coup that returned the Ba'ath to power in July 1968.

The next serious effort to resolve the Kurdish problem was made soon after the Ba'ath regained power. On August 3, 1968, President Bakr, speaking on behalf of the RCC, announced that the new government would abide by the June 1966 agreement and that it would negotiate with the Kurds on the basis of that agreement. In this regard, the ideological orientation of each side was more conducive to an agreement than was formally the case. On the one hand, one of the principles adopted by the Iraqi Ba'ath called for an equitable resolution of the Kurdish problem as a means of national unity, which was considered a prerequisite for an effective Iraqi role in the Arab revolution and the Arab movement toward unity. On the other hand, the KDP has traditionally sought to achieve Kurdish national aspirations within the framework of Iraqi national unity. It has also stressed the brotherhood between the Kurds and Arabs, and called for a common struggle by the Arabs and Kurds against foreign domination, especially by the Western powers. The KDP has generally advocated social programs that converge with the socialist orientation of the Ba'ath party. Meanwhile, the new Ba'ath government, particularly Saddam Hussein, apparently recognized that the Kurdish problem had been a source of domestic friction and a contributing cause of coups by dissatisfied military officers, and so was determined to achieve an amicable solution. For their part, the urban leftist faction of the KDP, led by Ibrahim Ahmad and Jalal Talibani, found it relatively easy to cooperate with the Ba'ath, since this group viewed the Ba'ath as the "first ruling Arab political party . . . to extend its hand to the Kurdish people directly, sincerely and hopefully . . . making every effort to solve the problem peacefully and justly and in a spirit of brotherhood."[45]

Despite this positive point of departure, the Kurdish problem was incredibly complex. No amount of goodwill and sincerity by small groups of decision makers could change, within a brief period, the mutually hostile attitudes and perceptions of the Kurdish and Arab peoples. The problem was complicated by the hostility between rival Kurdish factions, one led by Barzani, the other by Ahmad and Talabani. In 1968 and 1969, these factions were fighting each other as well as the Iraqi government forces. To complicate matters further, the Iraqi Communist Party had also split into two factions, both of which supported the Barzani forces. One faction, the ICP Central Committee, was hostile to the Ba'ath party and refused cooperation with it. The other group, the ICP Central Command, was less hostile to the Ba'ath but continued to oppose it on the Kurdish issue.

In addition, the Kurdish problem was no longer a domestic issue. The covert involvement of Iran and Israel[46] made the resolution of the conflict even less likely, though the very fact of external interference made its resolution more urgent than ever. Furthermore, the generous military aid provided by Iran made the Kurds less yielding in their demands for regional autonomy and for sharing the oil revenues from Iraqi oil fields in Kurdish areas. Thus, in the mind of some Iraqis, the Kurdish dispute became closely associated with the shah's "megalomania," which was manifested by Iranian seizure of three islands belonging to the United Arab Emirates at the head of the Strait of Oman and by his declared policy of making Iran the dominant military power in the region.[47] Further, the rumored presence of Israeli instructors among Barzani's forces, subsequently confirmed by Israeli Prime Minister Menachem Begin,[48] helped persuade many Iraqis that the Kurds under Barzani (not all Kurds, of course) had become an instrument of Iranian imperialism and Zionism. The Nixon administration reportedly encouraged Iraqi-Kurdish hostilities to keep Iraq "off balance."[49] Presumably, the United States pursued this policy partly because of Iraq's close ties with the Soviet Union (the USSR was the principal supplier of arms to Iraq) and partly in support of Iran's effort to become the dominant power in the Gulf. The principal effect of the external aid to Barzani was that it intensified Iraqi fears, prompting the Ba'ath regime to become even more dependent upon Soviet military aid and to prepare for another round of fighting with Barzani. Under these circumstances, it was extremely difficult for Saddam Hussein to make any new major concessions to the Kurds.

Despite these obstacles and after nearly two years of negotiations and armed hostilities, the Baghdad government announced a 15-point program for ending the Kurdish rebellion. The program, known as the March 1970 agreement, promised the Kurds much of what Barzani had demanded from the Iraqi government in 1961. It was essentially a restatement of the Bazzaz-Kurdish agreement of June 1963. Under the 1970 plan, the government promised to take the following measures:

- Recognition of the existence of Kurdish nationality in the new provisional constitution;

- Establishment of a university in Sulaimaniya and a Kurdish educational academy;

- Teaching of Kurdish in all schools, institutes, universities, teacher's schools, the military college, and the police academy;

- Establishment of a Kurdish printing house that would publish cultural and scientific papers and be backed by Kurdish men of letters and scientists;

- Declaration of *Nowruz* (the Kurdish New Year) as a national holiday;

- Creation of a new government of Dohuk (Dihok) to be separated from the *liwa* of Mosul, near the Turkish border;

- Decentralization of local government;

- Granting of a general amnesty to all civilians and soldiers involved in the Kurdish war.[50]

The program provided for the appointment of five Kurdish cabinet ministers, and Barzani was permitted to retain 15,000 Kurdish troops, which under the agreement became part of an official Iraqi frontier force named the *Pesh Merga* (those who face death). The program, however, did not make any specific commitments about the sharing of oil revenues or the inclusion of Kurdish representatives in the RCC. The agreement made only vague, noncommittal references to ending job discrimination against the Kurds.

A year after the accord was announced there were few signs of its full implementation. Barzani demanded that a minimum of 10 percent of the Iraqi national budget be devoted to development in Kurdish areas. Thousands of Arabs had been encouraged to move into the Kurdish region to dilute the population, while some Kurds were bribed or threatened to move elsewhere. Barzani also pressed for Kurdish representation in the RCC since it was in this body and not the cabinet that political power was vested. In addition, Barzani rejected the premise, stated in the Iraqi constitution, that Iraq was part of the Arab world. This had been a constant irritant between Kurds and Arabs at least since the promulgation of the 1958 constitution. In August 1970 Barzani raised the same issue again, which became the signal for the resumption of rhetorical and military battles.[51] Between March 1970 and March 1974 the Kurds and the Iraqi government tried to resolve their differences and to reduce mutual suspicion. Over those four years it became increasingly clear that the Ba'ath government's concept of Kurdish autonomy differed significantly from that of Barzani and his followers. Differences were unbridgeable on at least two points — Barzani's control over the Kurdish military force, the *Pesh Merga*, and Kurdish fiscal control over the oil-rich Kirkuk region. Finally, on March 11, 1974, just a day or two before the expiration of a deadline set in March 1970, Bakr announced a law enacted by the RCC proclaiming self-rule for the Kurdish people with the pertinent constitutional amendments. The terms fell far short of Kurdish demands and expectations. Briefly, the government declaration reiterated that Kurdish would be one of two official languages in the region; that Kurdish would be the language of education (but the teaching of Arabic would be compulsory at all stages); that a special regional budget would exist; and that a legislative council and an executive council for the Kurdish region would be set up. The president of the republic, however, retained strong executive powers over the Kurdish institutions, which could be dissolved at his discretion. To discourage any thought of the government's relinquishing power over Kurdish affairs, the declaration emphasized that the Kurdish region was an integral part of Iraq.[52] Kurds who viewed this law as acceptable were invited to cooperate in its enforcement.

In their negotiations with the government, the Kurds had demanded all but veto power over legislation in Baghdad pertaining to the Kurdish regions. They also asked the government to define clearly the boundaries of the autonomous region. The Kurds wanted to be assured that the oil-rich district of Kirkuk would be an integral part of the Kurdish region. None of these demands proved acceptable to the government. The Baghdad regime did, nonetheless, promise to define the region's boundaries in accordance with a census that would be conducted within the framework of an earlier one taken in 1957. These conditions were immediately rejected by the Kurds, who, two days after the government announcement of autonomy, resumed hostilities against Iraqi forces in the northern region.[53]

Even prior to the resumption of hostilities, a rift had been developing among the Kurds — between those who accepted the government's autonomy plan and those who rejected it. Those who favored it were mainly the younger urban elements who defected from the KDP, including Barzani's own son, Ubaidullah Mustafa Barzani; Taha Muhi ad-Din Maaruf, who later became vice-president of Iraq; Hashim Aqrawi, a member of the KDP's Central Committee, governor of Duhok province, and later president of the executive council of the Kurdish region; and Aziz Aqrawi (no relation to Hashim), a member of the KDP's politburo and a former Iraqi army colonel who had defected to the Kurdish movement in 1961 and became a leading military commander in the Kurdish armed forces. This group formed a separate KDP.[54] Another Kurdish group, led by Tahir Abd al-Sharif, split from the KDP and formed the Kurdish Revolutionary Party. In addition to accepting the autonomy law, this group favored cooperation with the Progressive National Front. Mustafa Barzani's leadership became dependent by default upon the tribal sections. He thus appeared to represent an older generation fighting to perpetuate tribal and feudal traditions, not a broad cross-section of his people. To these younger Kurdish leaders and the Iraqi government, Mulla Mustafa had to be removed before negotiations between Kurds and Arabs could be resumed. The government's position was further reinforced by the support of powerful tribal elements traditionally opposed to Barzani.

Between March 1974 and April 1975 Kurdish and Iraqi military units fought several pitched battles. Both sides were well equipped with modern weapons supplied by their external patrons – Iran and Israel training and equipping the Kurds, the Soviet Union providing supplies to the Iraqi forces. Since concluding a treaty of friendship with Iraq in 1972, Moscow had stopped expressing any sympathy for antigovernment Kurds. Occasionally, Moscow "urged" the two disputants to resolve their differences in the spirit of "socialist brotherhood," but the Soviet Union did not put effective pressure on either side to move toward a peaceful settlement. The United States, however, had its own reasons for supporting Barzani. The ideology of the Ba'ath government – which advocated the Arabization of the Gulf and the rejection of any Western-sponsored security system – was inimical to U.S. clients such as Israel, Iran, and the oil-rich conservative states. Moreover, Nixon and Kissinger may have viewed Iraq as a Soviet client and wished to achieve a cold war victory by contributing to the collapse of the Soviet-supported Ba'ath regime.[55]

The Iraqi government was determined to follow through with its autonomy plan and to terminate the Kurdish-Arab conflict without making embarrassing territorial concessions to either Iran or the Kurds that would appear to be a sacrifice of Arab interests within the country. In this regard, two factors worked to the government's advantage. One was the phenomenal increase in oil prices that provided Iraq with the means to meet the economic demands of the Kurds without sacrificing Arab interests. The other was Iran's policy of rapprochement with the Arabs, especially with Egypt, which proved helpful to the Iraqi government. With the help of the Egyptian and Algerian presidents, Iraq managed to settle its lingering dispute with Iran. As a consequence of this detente between Iraq and Iran, the shah's government terminated its financial and military assistance to the Kurds. The agreement was announced in Algiers on March 6, 1975. Lacking Iranian support, the Kurdish revolt ground to a halt two weeks later.

The Kurdish struggle for autonomy has revealed that the Kurds as an interest group exhibit the same divisions that characterize Iraqi society as a whole: urban versus rural, tribal versus settled, and, to a far lesser extent, Shi'a versus Sunni. The most important division seems to be rural-urban. These cleavages worked in favor of the government in its efforts to implement the March 1970 agreement, but they can also work against it. There is no one group or leadership that can speak on behalf of all Kurds and commit the Kurds, as a group, to an agreement. The two legal political parties purporting to represent Kurdish nationalism and interest are the KDP and the Kurdistan Revolutionary Party.

The main sources of opposition are a faction of the KDP Provisional Command (KDP/PC), led by Barzani's sons, Massud and Idris, the Patriotic Union of Kurdistan (PUK), led by Jalal Talibani (supported by Syria), and the KDP Preparatory Committee, led by Mahmoud Uthman. These three opposition groups often appear to be more opposed to each other than to the Iraqi government. However, since the overthrow of the monarchy in Iran, the KDP/PC and the PUK have expressed their solidarity and support for the Islamic regime in Tehran.

The threat these groups pose to the government may have become more serious since the war between Iraq and Iran entered its second year,[56] but several factors work to the Ba'athist regime's advantage. First, large segments of the Kurdish population and elite favor self-rule as proposed and implemented by the Baghdad regime. In this regard the government kept very careful check on the army's behavior in recaptured Kurdish areas.[57] Second, the government has undertaken major development programs in the areas under its control and thus fulfilled most of its promises in implementing the March 11 manifesto. Third, the Kurdish dissidents are supported by foreign elements, notably Syria, Iran, and possibly Israel once again, whose interests are best served by prolonged conflict, not by Kurdish victory. The limited convergence of interest between the Kurdish dissidents and their external patrons can be seen when talks of rapprochement between Iraq and Syria were held in December 1977-January 1978. The Syrian-based PUK was reportedly told by the Syrian government to stop all anti-Iraqi operations and to open negotiations with the Iraqi government.[58] Fourth, Iraqi-Kurdish dissidents are operating at cross purposes with their kindred ethnic dissidents in Iran, who are fighting against the Islamic regime in Tehran and who receive supplies from Iraq. For example, in the autumn of 1981 the Syrian-backed Kurdish insurgents led by Jalal Talibani incurred the wrath of the chief Iranian Kurdish leader, Abdol-Rahman Ghasemlu, because the unrest in the Iraqi border areas caused by Talibani's forces disrupted clandestine Iraqi supply lines to Ghasemlu's anti-Iranian forces. The death on March 1, 1979, of Mullah Mustafa Barzani, the leader and symbol of the Kurdish rebellion since the 1940s, meant the disappearance of an important potential unifying influence on the opposition forces.

The Iraqi government's policy continues to be one of placating the Kurdish population by sharing governance with Kurdish leaders, but not by dividing either political power (since no Kurds have been admitted to the RCC) or the country's wealth with the Kurdish populace.

The Iraqi Communist Party

The Iraqi Communist Party was founded as a clandestine organization by Yusif Salman Yusuf (known as Comrade Fahd) in 1934. During the next quarter century the Iraqi Communists remained underground and generally operated out of neighboring countries such as Lebanon. The overthrow of the monarchy in July 1958 and the subsequent split between Qassem and pan-Arab officers (Nasserites) led by Abdul Salam Arif provided the Communists with an opportunity to function more openly. Although there is widespread belief among Iraqis that Communism is contrary to the basic tenets of Islam and Arab nationalism, the persecution of the Communists under the monarchy raised the party to a status of near-martyrs in the eyes of the avidly antimonarchist postrevolutionary leaders. Although the ICP remained technically illegal, the Qassem regime used it (especially the ICP militia) to consolidate power and brutally suppress its opponents. During the Shawwaf revolt, Qassem used the Communists and the Kurds to fight against the rebellious military units and against the Shammar tribe that supported the Nasserite officers. Qassem's growing ties with the Communists alarmed the Ba'ath, which withdrew its support of the regime. This action reopened an ideological rift between the Ba'ath and the Communists that dates back to the early days of the establishment of the Ba'ath. Although Qassem had lost all his former political allies except for the ICP by 1968, he had succeeded in preventing the Communists from broadening their political base and so becoming a threat to his position.

When Qassem was overthrown in February 1963, the new Ba'athist leaders undertook a policy of persecution and vengeance against the ICP. The first Ba'athist government was very short-lived. Ba'athists and Communists remained bitter rivals despite the fact that both were suppressed during the regimes of Abdul Salam Arif (1963 to 1966) and his brother, Abdel Rahman Arif (1966 to 1968). After the Ba'ath returned to power in 1968, both the Ba'athist and ICP leaders called for a reconciliation.

From the very beginning of its return to power, the Ba'ath sought to form a united front of the various progressive political factions in Iraq. Nevertheless, the ICP remained outside the power structure until December 1969, as the Ba'ath was unwilling to share power with non-Ba'athist groups. After that, however, the ICP rose to new public prominence. The Ba'ath government's close cooperation with the ICP in 1972 coincided with both the signing of the Iraqi-Soviet treaty of friendship and cooperation and with Iraq's growing sense of isolation resulting from its frontier dispute with Iran, misunderstandings with various Arab neighbors, and a renewed threat of a foreign-supported Kurdish insurgency. Thus, the Ba'ath appeared to be seeking Soviet support in the foreign-policy arena and ICP cooperation in domestic affairs, particularly with regard to Kurdish problems. As a result of closer collaboration between the Ba'athists and the Communists in Iraq, two Communists, Makharam Talabani (a Kurd) and Amir Abdullah, were added to the cabinet in 1972. The ICP was also permitted to publish its own newspaper, *Tariq al-Sha'ab* (*The People's Way*). The high point occurred in 1973 when the ICP became legal for the first time since its inception in 1934 and joined with the Ba'ath in the creation of the Progressive National Front. The ICP thus became a legitimate, albeit secondary, voice in government decision making. The conditions for joining the PNF were contained in the National Action Charter. In signing the charter, the ICP agreed that only the Ba'ath Party would control the RCC, the armed forces, and the internal security services. The ICP in turn was allotted some minor cabinet posts and was allowed to carry on its activities openly so long as it did not involve itself with the armed forces and its actions did not contravene the letter and spirit of the National Action Charter.

Two issues have made collaboration between the Ba'ath and the ICP uneasy. One was the traditional support of the Communist Party for the Kurds in their struggle for autonomy. Indeed, one incentive the Ba'ath had for collaboration with the Communists was to neutralize this support, both from the ICP and the Soviet Union. The other issue was the position of the ICP on Palestine. The ICP generally had followed the Moscow line, which called for a peaceful solution to the conflict. The Communist position on Palestine has been vague out of necessity, since the Soviet Union on more than one occasion has declared its recognition of the existence of Israel as a state, but not Israel's continued occupation of Arab territories since 1967.

Despite these differences in policy positions, the Ba'ath alliance with the ICP continued until early 1979 with no apparent differences on foreign policy. However, with the settlement of the frontier dispute with Iran and the Kurdish revolt in 1975, the Ba'ath was undoubtedly less dependent on ICP support than before. Moreover, between 1975 and 1979 Iraq began to turn increasingly to the West for goods and technology for its ambitious development programs as Soviet equivalents proved inadequate by comparison. The government also began to shift increasingly away from Soviet weapons to Western sources, especially France.

Indications of strain in the Ba'ath-ICP alliance on domestic issues began to surface in 1978. Particularly significant was an attack in May 1978 by the Ba'ath party newspaper, *al-Thawra*, upon the non-Ba'athist partners in the PNF. The front's partners, especially the Communists, were attacked for not accepting the leadership role of the Ba'ath. They were reminded that the PNF formula could not be extended to the armed forces, and that the PNF partners had accepted these conditions prior to joining the front. Therefore, any attempt to challenge this formula was tantamount to plotting against the revolution.[59] In June the government announced the execution of 21 members of the ICP on the charge of forming secret cells in the army and plotting a coup. Despite attempts to patch up the differences, the break between the Ba'ath and the ICP appeared to be complete by 1979. In March *al-Thawra* published a statement by the PNF accusing the ICP, among other things, of forming secret cells in the armed forces, of inflaming sectarian (Shi'a) and nationalist (Kurdish) sensitivities, and of conducting a "defamation campaign against the revolution."[60] In April the ICP newspaper *Tariq al-Sha'ab* was suspended, and in May the ICP ministers were dismissed from the cabinet.

Although many questions concerning the Ba'ath-ICP break remain to be answered, the growing tensions between the Ba'athists and the Communists coincided with both a 1978 coup in Afghanistan that brought a pro-Soviet government to power and with the growing Soviet influence in South Yemen. These events contributed to a shift in Ba'ath perceptions to the view that Iraq had more to fear from the Soviets than from the United States.

It is only fair to point out, however, that the first visible signs of strain in 1978 may have occurred through no fault of the Ba'ath. The Communists were evidently frustrated by their failure to make any appreciable headway in winning over peasants, workers, and other toiling groups to their banner.

In this regard, the primordial loyalties of clan, sect, and locality, which still influence a majority of Iraqis, rendered politics based on the ICP ideology of class struggle somewhat irrelevant. This is evidenced by reports that the ICP had lost its seats on a number of trade union councils, including the Press Syndicate, after the holding of new elections to these bodies.[61] Compounding the ICP's difficulty was that in the eyes of many Iraqis, the party was still identified as being alien and associated with the Soviet Union.

ISSUE AREAS

The issue areas in Iraqi foreign policy are best understood when viewed in the context of the government's two main foreign-policy objectives: to make Iraq the dominant power center in the Arab Middle East and, in pursuit of that broad objective, to replace non-Arab Iran as the dominant power in the Gulf. In this respect the most salient issue area is the continuing Shatt al-Arab dispute with Iran, which led to open warfare between the two countries in September 1980. This dispute undoubtedly has become intensified by the overthrow of the shah and the replacement of the Iranian monarchy with a hostile, revolutionary, fundamentalist Islamic regime in Tehran. However, some conflict is likely to have developed between the two countries on this issue even if the shah remained in power given Iraq's foreign-policy objectives, the nature of the issue itself, and the circumstances surrounding the settlement of the issue the two countries reached in March 1975.

The Shatt al-Arab Issue

The origin of the Shatt al-Arab dispute goes back to the Ottoman Empire, which prior to World War I controlled both sides of the river.[62] As a successor state to the Ottoman Empire, Iraq claimed the same rights after it became independent in 1932. Iran finally conceded Iraq's position (under British pressure) in 1937 when the two countries signed a treaty that confirmed Iraqi sovereignty over that 100-mile stretch of Shatt al-Arab (the estuary of the Tigris and Euphrates rivers) that divides the two countries before emptying into the Arabian or Persian Gulf. Unlike most other international river treaties, the 1937 treaty gave Iraq exclusive navigational rights up to the low-water mark on the Iranian shore, rather than to the midstream point of the river. The exceptions were the anchorage areas at the Iranian ports of Abadan, Khorramshahr, and Khosrowabad, about ten miles below Abadan where the boundary was fixed in the mid-channel or the *Thalweg* (see Figure 4.3).

After the Qassem coup that overthrew the Iraqi monarchy and took Iraq out of the Baghdad Pact, relations between Iraq and Iran began to deteriorate. Iran was never satisfied with the terms of the 1937 agreement, but the two

FIGURE 4.3
Iraq's Access to the Arabian/Persian Gulf

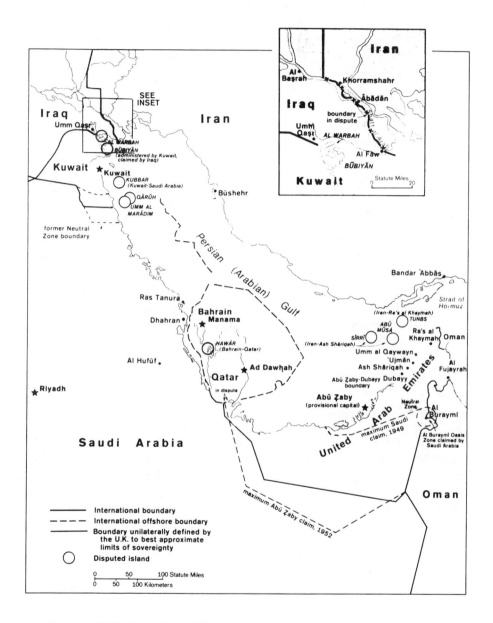

Source: U.S. Central Intelligence Agency, *Atlas: Issues in the Middle East* (Washington, D.C.: U.S. Government Printing Office, 1973), p. 37.

countries' participation in the Baghdad Pact prompted both to subordinate their boundary dispute to their broader purpose of the common defense of the two royal houses against radical nationalism and an impending Soviet threat. Following minor border skirmishes, the Iranian government issued a statement in January 1960 in which Tehran charged Iraq with violating the treaty. On the basis of these alleged treaty violations, the Iranian government declared that henceforth the Iraqi-Iranian border would be marked by the *Thalweg*.[63]

Although Baghdad attempted to negotiate a settlement of the dispute soon after regaining power in 1968, the talks proved fruitless. On April 19, 1969, Iran denounced the 1937 agreement, alleging that Iraq had been violating its provisions for many years. The Iranian announcement declared that Iraq had for years unilaterally collected river tolls on the Shatt without giving Iran its share as stipulated in the 1937 treaty. Therefore, Iranian ships plying the Shatt al-Arab would no longer pay Iraqi tolls and would not fly the Iraqi flag as required by Iraqi law. Baghdad reiterated its claim to the entire Shatt al-Arab.[64] Furthermore, Iraq warned that ships not complying with Iraqi regulations would be prevented from entering the Shatt al-Arab. To assert its claim on part of the Shatt, the Iranian government dispatched a cargo ship with naval and air escort through the estuary to the Persian Gulf. The ship arrived unmolested by the Iraqis, who took no action despite their previous threats. Iraq's inability to take effective action against Iran was a source of humiliation. Iraq's retaliation was limited to expelling thousands of Iranians living in Iraq, to boycotting Iranian goods, and to giving asylum to leftist and religious enemies of the shah. Iraq later severed diplomatic relations with Iran because of alleged Iranian support for subversive activities within Iraq. A series of border clashes began in 1972.

These border incidents and Iraqi charges of Iranian subversion coincided with expanded Iranian aid to Mulla Mustafa Barzani and the introduction of American and Israeli aid to Barzani's forces. The Iranian government may have increased its aid to Barzani for a variety of reasons, all of which were related to the continuing struggle between Baghdad and Tehran for influence in the Gulf. Part of Iran's motivation by 1973 was to force Iraq to make border concessions in the Shatt al-Arab region and in other areas as well.[65] The border clashes increased in 1974 when scores of soldiers from each side were killed in each of several rounds of fighting. Finally, in 1975 Iraq was forced to concede half the sovereignty over the Shatt al-Arab estuary in exchange for the cessation of Iranian support for the Kurds. In addition, under this agreement Iraq and Iran promised to delineate, on the basis of the 1913 Protocol of Constantinople, approximately 670 positions, some in contention, on the Iran-Iraq border.[66] By implication, the agreement symbolized Iraq's conceding primacy in the Gulf to Iran. Further, Iraq implicitly recognized Iran's claims to the three islands at the western end of the Strait of Hormuz.

The 1975 settlement conceded primacy to Iran not only symbolically, but in fact as well. An Iraq trying to assert its influence in the Gulf is inhibited by the fact that access by water to its only Gulf outlet at Basra is at the mercy of a sovereignty shared with neighboring and traditionally hostile Iran. Iraq is confined to 38 miles of coastline on the Gulf and shallow-water ports. Consequently, Iraq's economic security as well as any pretension to being the dominant Gulf power were vulnerable to the growing might of Iran.

Iran's regional primacy lasted only so long as the shah was on the throne. The overthrow of the monarchy and the ensuing revolutionary upheaval undercut Iran's unquestioned military superiority and its position as the Gulf's second leading oil exporter after Saudi Arabia. With the fall of the shah, Iraq moved up into that position.

Following the deposition of the shah, the relative power positions of Iran and Iraq appeared to be the opposite of what they had been in 1975. At that time Iran was on the offensive. Now, it was Iran that was weakened by internal turmoil (including growing separatist tendencies by ethnic minorities such as the Kurds and Baluchis), diplomatic isolation, and military weakness, and was on the defensive. Iraq has sought to reverse the humiliating conditions of the 1975 treaty and to put a definitive end to Iranian pretensions to primacy in the Gulf. Thus in 1980 Saddam Hussein revived the issue of continued Iranian control over three islands near the Strait of Hormuz that were seized by the shah in 1971 — Abu Musa and the Tunb Islands. The revolutionary government in Tehran refused to cede control over the islands. On September 17, 1980, Hussein abrogated the 1975 agreement with Iran, claiming the Shatt al-Arab estuary as "Iraqi and Arab."[67] In this regard, the Iraqi decision to go to war with Iran can be seen as an attempt to undo on the ground what Hussein abrogated on paper.

The Kuwait Issue

The current status of Iraqi territorial pressures on Kuwait can also be understood in terms of Iraq's effort to strengthen its control over access to its two ports on the Gulf, Basra and Umm Qasr. The two Kuwaiti islands of Bubiyan and Warbah virtually block the access to Umm Qasr (see Figure 4.3). It was because of the island's strategic location that Iraq has demanded from Kuwait that they be leased to Iraq for a 99-year period, in return for Iraqi concessions on the land border with Kuwait.

The issue, however, is clouded with suspicion owing mainly to a history of Iraqi claims on Kuwaiti territory. Shortly after Iraq gained formal independence in 1932, King Ghazi called for the annexation of Kuwait, but this claim was largely forgotten until 1961. That year President Abdul Karim Qassem reasserted it on the grounds that Kuwait was integrated into Iraqi Basra Governorate during Ottoman rule. Furthermore, this fact had been recognized by Britain in the treaty of 1899, even though it was British imperial interests that had arbitrarily separated Kuwait from Iraq.[68] The Iraqi claim was firmly rejected by the British, the Kuwaitis, and the other Arab states. The issue was again submerged, and Iraq recognized Kuwait in 1963 after Qassem was overthrown. However, in 1969 relations between Iran and Iraq deteriorated over the Shatt al-Arab issue to the point where war appeared imminent. In April 1969 Kuwait reluctantly acquiesced in an Iraqi request to station Iraqi troops on Kuwait's side of the border in order to protect Umm Qasr from possible Iranian attack.

Although the conflict between Iraq and Iran never reached the point of open warfare, Iraq maintained a force on Kuwaiti territory on the ground that Umm Qasr was still threatened as long as the dispute with Iran over the Shatt remained unsettled. In fact, Iraq even tried to reinforce its garrison and expand its defense perimeter in 1973. On March 20 of that year, a firefight broke out between Iraqi and Kuwaiti forces when the latter tried to prevent the Iraqis from erecting a forward defense outpost at a place called al-Samita. In April, Iraq demanded that Kuwait either surrender or lease the islands of Bubiyan and Warbah to Iraq. Under Arab pressure and through various mediation attempts, Iraq agreed to withdraw its troops from around al-Samita, but insisted the issue was one of direct negotiations between the two countries.[69]

With the settlement of the Shatt al-Arab conflict with Iran in March 1975, Iraq's justification for territorial adjustments to protect Umm Qasr began to lose credence. Iraq was willing to concede that the threat of war was no longer imminent, but Baghdad maintained that Umm Qasr had to be defended against future threats. Finally, in July 1977 Iraq and Kuwait agreed to carry out a mutual withdrawal of troops from the border to a distance of one to two kilometers. This agreement was duly implemented and so put relations between the two countries on a more harmonious footing than they had been for years.

Iran

The overthrow of the Iranian monarchy and the postrevolutionary decline in the military capabilities of the Iranian armed forces have presented Iraq with an opportunity to redress on the ground the terms of the Algiers agreement of March 1975, and to assert Iraqi primacy in the Gulf. However, even without the issue of the 1975 agreement, Baghdad is still confronted with the problem of how to deal with a hostile regime in Tehran that has repeatedly called for the overthrow of the Iraqi government. In addition, despite the untold misery and destruction the war has visited upon Iran, Ayatollah Khomeini himself reportedly has admitted that the war with Iraq is a "blessing" in the sense that without it, his fundamentalist regime would be in greater danger from internal dissent or coup.[70]

From the Iraqi point of view, Saddam Hussein's decision to attack Iran was prompted by an issue far more fundamental than regaining total control of the Shatt al-Arab estuary or compelling Iran to return to Arab control three small islands. The attack was the culmination of some four months of artillery exchanges along the Iran-Iraq frontier, terrorist bombings within Iraq carried out by sympathizers with the Islamic revolution in Iran, and repeated appeals to Iraq's Shi'a population by Khomeini and other Iranian leaders to overthrow "the infidel Saddam."

What must be understood is that even when relations between the Iraqi government and the shah's regime were extremely hostile, both sides apparently shared a mutual concern about the latent antiregime potential of the Shi'as in their respective countries, a potential neither side attempted to encourage. Indeed, after the eruption of some very severe Shi'a riots in early 1977 at the cities of Najaf and Karbala in the heartland of Iraqi Shi'ism, the shah sent a number of influential people, including then-Empress Farah Diba, to the two holy cities.[71] Their visits represented assurances directed at two groups: to reassure Iraqi Shi'as that they had little to fear from the Iraqi government in Baghdad, and to reaffirm Iran's support for President Bakr's leadership and policies.

Iraq reciprocated the gesture in October 1978 by expelling Ayatollah Khomeini from Iraq after he had begun to escalate his activities against the shah's regime in the spring of 1978. Khomeini was reportedly proselytizing his version of Islamic revolution not only among Iranians, but also among devout Iraqi Shi'as who made the pilgrimage to Najaf every year. Thus, in accordance with the Algiers agreement of 1975, Saddam Hussein (then second-in-command) ordered Khomeini to cease his activities or leave the country after Iran conveyed its concern about his antishah agitation.

While the shah was still in power, Iraq made an effort to coordinate policy with him. However, once the shah's position appeared hopeless, Iraq muted its public support for him and made cautious overtures to the emerging opposition figures including Khomeini, who was still in Paris at the time. Iraq moved quickly to establish good relations with the Khomeini regime, officially recognizing it the day after it seized power (February 12, 1979). Iraq praised the new regime for its support of the Arab cause in Palestine and for relinquishing its role as the West's policeman in the Gulf.

Despite these initial Iraqi efforts, by April 1980 relations with Iran had deteriorated to the most hostile level in years. Khomeini, perhaps seeking revenge for his expulsion from Iraq, publicly vowed that the next victim of the Islamic revolution would be the "infidel Saddam."[72] Iranian leaders such as then-President Bani-Sadr, Foreign Minister Ghotzbadeh, and Khomeini himself, were labeling Iraq's leaders "evil and atheistic," and were explicitly urging Iraq's Shi'a community to overthrow the regime.[73]

One Iraqi response to the Iranian threat was the expulsion of over 20,000 of the most suspect Iranian-born Iraqis in April 1980, and the arrest and summary execution of the most militant of Iraq's three Shi'a ayatollahs, Mohammed Baqr-Sadr. Meanwhile, Iran had accused Iraq of supporting antiregime groups in Iran including Iranian Kurds and the Arab minority in Khuzistan province, which Iraq referred to as Arabistan.[74] Iraq accused Iran of complicity in an assassination attempt (April 1, 1980) against the second most powerful leader in Iran, Tariq Aziz. This was one of the incidents that prompted the large-scale deportation of Iranian-born Iraqis.

A detailed description and analysis of the accusations by both sides is beyond the scope and purpose of this chapter.[75] It is sufficient here to note that Iran's incitement of Iraq's Shi'a population was perceived by the Iraqi government as posing a very serious threat to the regime's legitimacy and its very existence. Failure to successfully end the war with Iran, however, has weakened Saddam Hussein's government in several ways.

First, the fact that the war dragged on for so long served to underscore the limits on Iraq's military prowess and so diminish the credibility of the Iraqi government's drive to be accepted as the preeminent power in the Gulf. Second, the protracted conflict has undoubtedly weakened the civilian leadership vis-a-vis the military wing of the party. Saddam Hussein's rapport and influence with the military are due largely to his personal ties with former President Bakr. At issue is not a dispute over objectives, the principal goal being the disappearance of Khomeini from the helm of Iran. However, some senior party members questioned whether the war was the most effective way of unseating the Khomeini regime.[76] If the Iraqi military suffers a series of humiliating defeats or is blamed for serious setbacks, a coup d'etat cannot be excluded. Since the Hussein government remains essentially a one-man show, Saddam ultimately will receive credit or blame for what happens to Iraq. Third, the protracted war has weakened popular support for the government, and has provided an opportunity to dissident Kurdish and other groups to renew their military operations.[77] In addition, one of the first casualties of the protracted war has been the embryonic liberalization of Iraqi society. Apart from growing signs of demoralization in the populations that had expected a quick victory, wartime concern about subversion and conspiracies has led the government to return to more repressive policies. This may lead to considerable discontent and disaffection among Iraq's middle class, many of whom are returned emigres who left Iraq originally in reaction to the political instability and repression of earlier years.[78] While the government does not appear to be faced with any imminent fall from power, the indecisiveness of the war threatens to undo the social and economic progress the country has made in recent years.

The psychological and political repercussions of the military situation could be more damaging than the military situation itself. If Iran is able to depict "miraculous" victories against "overwhelming odds"[79] as proof that the fundamentalist revolution is indeed following the right path, Tehran's resurgent confidence is likely to be expressed in renewed attempts at subversion of the regimes all along the Arab side of the Gulf.[80] This situation in turn can only further weaken Iraq's claim to preeminence there.

Palestine

The Palestinian cause has also been used by the Iraqi government to achieve a leadership position in inter-Arab politics. Iraqi support for a just solution to the Palestine problem is popular at home and is a useful instrument to the government in its power struggles with other Arab countries. The adoption of an unequivocal stand on behalf of the Palestinians and against the Camp David accords enables Iraq to capitalize on its other assets – its geographic location, ideological orientation, and economic strength – to reinforce its claim to a position of leadership in the Arab world. Notwithstanding support of the Palestinian cause at the international level, relations with various Palestinian groups have not always been friendly.

Both domestic conflicts in Iraq and the government's isolation in the Arab world contributed to the tensions with various Palestinian resistance groups. During the early 1970s the government was engaged in an intermittent military conflict with the Kurds, and its relations with the ICP had not yet improved. Externally, Iraq's relations with Syria and Egypt were anything but cordial. Consequently, Baghdad felt extremely insecure in its dealings with Palestinian resistance organizations because of their contact with Iraq's internal and external enemies. The most recent example of this conundrum is the close and sympathetic relations several Palestinian groups developed with the Khomeini regime in Iran for a period. This sense of insecurity is undoubtedly heightened by the fact that Iraq's geographical location – to the rear of the "confrontation states" bordering on Israel – and its interests – oriented increasingly toward the Gulf – have permitted Iraq relatively little influence over the Palestinian movement as a whole. An exception to this condition is a situation where broader pan-Arab issues and the question of Palestine converge. The most recent instance is the Egyptian-Israeli peace agreement and the Camp David accords and the effects they may have on the political fortunes of the Palestinians and other Arab states alike. Egypt's negotiation of a separate peace with Israel provided Iraq with an opportunity to assert its leadership in the Arab world.

Prior to 1972 the only Palestinian resistance group favored by Baghdad was the Arab Liberation Front (ALF), founded in April 1969 by the Ba'athists themselves. The motive behind the creation of the ALF was to have an Iraqi counterpart to the Syrian-sponsored Sa'iqa. Although a number of other Palestinian guerrilla groups welcomed the ALF, that organization's policy of allowing non-Palestinian members caused serious disagreements with the other groups. The ALF's position was that only through general Arab participation and mobilization would the Palestinians be able to achieve their political goals. By contrast, the other guerrilla organizations rejected the principle of general Arab participation in their activities on the ground that this would bring the resistance movement under the tutelage of Arab regimes.[81] As a result of this policy, the ALF at times has had more non-Palestinians than Palestinians among its rank and file. Consequently, it has had less influence in the Palestinian resistance movement than its main competition, Sa'iqa.

After mending its fences with the Kurds and the Communists, Iraq moved to effect a rapprochement with the Palestinians. To that end the RCC announced that Iraqi citizens employed by public and private institutions would be allowed to join the resistance without losing their rights and salaries as employees. Moreover, Palestinians would be given equal treatment in employment, and Palestinian students would enjoy equal opportunities for scholarships.[82] Such changes created a positive rapport between Iraq and the resistance movement. The nationalization of the Iraq Petroleum Company in June 1972 vastly improved the government's status with the Palestinians, who regarded the takeover as "a revolutionary act to be supported without reservation."[83]

This broad-based support evaporated at the end of the October War over an issue that illustrates what happens when Palestinian interests do not coincide with Iraq's pan-Arab policy framework. It was Iraq's rejection of the U.S.-sponsored peace initiatives that caused a split between Baghdad and the Palestinians' largest representative organization, Fatah. This time Iraq was supported by the more radical Palestinian groups, the Popular Front for the Liberation of Palestine (PFLP) and the Popular Front for the Liberation of Palestine-General Command (PFLP-GC), which opposed the formation of a Palestinian state only in Gaza and the West Bank. However, in April 1980 Saddam Hussein expelled the PFLP and another radical organization, the Democratic Popular Front for the Liberation of Palestine (DPFLP). Both groups have long had offices, training bases, and sanctuaries in Iraq. Among the reasons for the expulsion was the groups' support for the Iranian revolution.

The Palestine issue has never been as critical on a day-to-day basis for Iraq as it has been for the confrontation states, Egypt, Syria, and Jordan. Geographically, Iraq is too far from Israel and the majority of Palestinians to serve as a major base of operations. Iraq has exploited the issue and various Palestinian groups, and has also been exploited by these groups from time to time.

Foreign Relations

Given its geographic location, population, resource base, and industrial development, Iraq has long possessed the potential for regional leadership. However, Iraq's leadership ambitions have been undermined by internal political rivalries within the ruling elites and the intermittent war with the Kurds. The current leadership, however, has been in power for nearly 15 years, and has been largely successful in ending the domestic political turmoil (including four coups d'etat, counting the one in 1968 that returned the Ba'ath to power) that has plagued the country since the overthrow of the monarchy in 1958. Moreover, the Algiers agreement of 1975 largely ended the Kurdish problem (eliminating an opportunity for external subversion), which has permitted Iraq to play a more active role in inter-Arab and Gulf affairs based on a policy of rapprochement and pragmatism within an ideological framework of Arab nationalism.

Consolidation of the Iraqi internal position has coincided with a number of regional and systemic factors that have favored a more assertive foreign policy. The most important extraregional or systemic factors were:

- Britain's withdrawal from the Gulf in 1971 and U.S. efforts to build up Iran and Saudi Arabia to fill the vacuum supposedly created by Britain's departure. In particular, American attempts to make Iran the principal guardian of Gulf security created Iraqi fears of a Western-supported power structure in the Gulf dominated by a non-Arab power (Iran), which the Iraqis suspected would lead to a tightening of Western political, economic, and military control of the region;
- The growing importance of oil in the mid-1970s, which not only enhanced the strategic importance of the Gulf, but also provided Iraq with the cash to purchase technology, capital goods, and weapons from the United States and Western Europe rather than relying almost exclusively on the Soviet bloc. This enabled Iraq to pursue a more independent foreign policy, particularly in Arab affairs. Equally important, Iraq's oil has acted like a magnet powerful enough to attract political allies. These include buyers such as Japan or France (now an important source of arms) and recipients of Iraqi economic aid such as Jordan and other Arab and third world countries;
- The pro-Soviet coup in Afghanistan in April 1978 followed by outright Soviet invasion of that country in December 1979 prompted Iraq to improve its relations with the conservative Gulf states. Iraq's support for the Popular Front for the Liberation of Oman (PFLO) terminated, and Iraq broke with Georges Habbash and the PFLP;
- The U.S. response to the Soviet invasion of Afghanistan — a pledge to defend the Gulf against Soviet aggression, the formation of a rapid-deployment force, and, later, a drive to develop an anti-Soviet "strategic consensus" among the Arab countries and Israel — had the effect of nudging the Saudis closer to Iraq's position that the major powers must be kept out of the Gulf.[84]

The principal regional factors that favored the assertion of Iraqi leadership included:

- The establishment of a pro-Soviet government in South Yemen and the retrenchment of the Marxist government in Ethiopia;
- The gradual decline of Egypt's leadership position in the Arab world, particularly in the aftermath of the Sinai disengagement agreements with Israel in 1974 and 1975 and Sadat's historic trip to Jerusalem in November 1977;
- The signing of the Camp David accords in September 1978 followed by the conclusion of an Egyptian-Israeli peace agreement in March 1979;

- The revolution in Iran, which soon appeared to pose a serious threat to both Iraq and the traditional governments on the Peninsula. The need to prevent Iran from exporting its revolution to the Arab side of the Gulf created a new set of common interests between Iraq and the other Gulf states.

These are forces over which Iraq has had very little control but to which Iraqi foreign policy has had to respond. On the whole, they have provided Iraq with opportunities to achieve its basic foreign-policy objectives.

IRAQI OBJECTIVES AND POLICIES

Apart from the paramount imperatives of any nation-state — national self-preservation, maintenance of the integrity of the national territory, and independence — Iraq's principal policy objectives are:

- To promote Arab unity of political action and purpose, if not the political unification of several Arab states. This policy is a prerequisite for a broader objective, which is:
  - To establish Iraq's leadership in the Eastern Arab world;
  - To neutralize or eliminate the Iranian threat to Iraq and other regimes on the Arab side of the Gulf;
  - To maintain cordial relations with at least one superpower while endeavoring to reduce superpower influence in the Gulf;
  - To establish Iraq as the dominant power in the Persian Gulf.

Political Policies

Supremacy in the Gulf, if achieved, would undoubtedly bolster Iraq's claim to pan-Arab leadership, even if Egypt were to reassert its own claim to such leadership. The principal obstacle to achieving this goal in the early 1970s was not Iran, but rather the Ba'ath's left-leaning, doctrinaire ideological line that often aroused fears and suspicions among the more moderate regimes in the Arab world. This was particularly true in Iraq's relations with the conservative monarchies of the Gulf. Consequently, Iraq was extremely isolated.

By mid-1975 the Iraqi government initiated a policy shift based on pragmatism and moderation in order to end Iraq's isolation. The Gulf was also the logical place to begin, given the vulnerability of Iraq's northwest flank — no outlet to the Mediterranean, bad relations with Syria, and cool relations with Syria's ally, Jordan. The principal architect of this policy was then-Vice-President Saddam Hussein. The first step was the agreement with Iran signed in Algiers in March 1975. In addition to settling the Shatt al-Arab dispute and effectively ending the Kurdish rebellion, the two countries agreed on a common policy to keep the superpowers out of the Gulf. Progress toward resolving the territorial dispute with Kuwait was also achieved. Only a month after the Algiers agreement, Iraq agreed with Saudi Arabia in a similar initiative to define their long-disputed border in the area of the Iraqi-Saudi neutral zone. In the same month the two countries agreed to reconstruct the road between an-Najaf and Medina. This route was considered very important for pilgrims traveling from Iraq and Iran to the Islamic holy places in Saudi Arabia.

Iraqi-Saudi relations had for a long time been strained. Saudi suspicions of Iraqi subversion and Baghdad's close relationship to and support by the Soviet Union were matched by Iraq's distaste for the Saudi defense of traditionalism and monarchic regimes, and by the Iraqi perception that Saudi Arabia was a tool of U.S. policy. In this regard the rapprochement was encouraged by the growing concern in Baghdad and Riyadh about the expanding Soviet presence in South Asia, the Gulf, and the Horn of Africa, and by the hostile reaction in both countries to the aggressive nature of Iran's new regime.

The Iraqi government demonstrated its willingness to cooperate with Saudi Arabia in Gulf security matters in 1979 during a conflict between the Yemens in which South Yemeni forces, supported by Soviet and Cuban advisors, occupied part of North Yemen's territory. North Yemen was a Saudi ally while the pro-Soviet People's Democratic Republic of Yemen had been Iraq's traditional ally and Saudi Arabia's traditional adversary. Iraq's effective mediation of this dispute defused the situation, particularly after Saddam Hussein, in front of all 20 ambassadors to the Arab League, told South Yemen's representative: "I called you in to express my strong concern about your attitudes toward North Yemen. Unless you withdraw you will be facing the Iraqi army."[85] The PDRY withdrew its forces.

Iraq's influence in ending the fighting between the two Yemens was more effective than U.S. or Saudi efforts had been. Such a demonstration may also have helped to persuade the Saudis that the combined Iraqi and Saudi naval forces would be at least as dependable and effective as the U.S. navy and without the political liability of making the Saudis look like an American protectorate. Further, in February 1979 Iraq and Saudi Arabia worked out a mutual internal security agreement, which in effect meant working together against the terrorists that Iraq had once supported.

Iraq's new relationship with Jordan and Saudi Arabia not only enabled Baghdad to break out of isolation. The three formed an entente that fundamentally altered the alignment structure of the Middle East and the Gulf. In effect, Iraq, Jordan, and Saudi Arabia were allied against Syria, Iran, and Libya. The role of other regional actors complicated this alignment structure, however.[86]

Egyptian President Anwar Sadat's visit to Jerusalem in November 1977 provided Iraq with an opportunity to assume a leading role in the Arab world as a whole. The initial Arab summit that was held in Tripoli in December 1977 to work out a common response to Sadat's initiative was unable to hammer out a unanimous position. Although the so-called Tripoli Declaration[87] condemning Sadat's visit was issued, the summit conferees were split between moderate and hard-line positions on dealing with Egypt. Iraq had been among the hard-liners, but had not joined the Front for Steadfastness and Confrontation established at the conference, because this front was led by Syria, with whom Iraq at the time was on very bad terms.

The Camp David accords created shock waves throughout the Arab world, leaving the anti-Sadat leadership in disarray, and provided Iraq with the chance to make its own bid for Arab leadership. Iraq suddenly showed a newfound willingness to make minimal ideological adjustments in its declared stand on the Arab-Israeli conflict for the sake of tactical gains in the inter-Arab arena. An important prerequisite for a successful Iraqi initiative was healing the long-standing rift with Syria. Against the backdrop of Camp David, Iraq decided to refrain from criticizing Syria's acceptance of the principle of a negotiated peace in the Middle East. On October 1 Iraq proposed to send troops to Syria to confront Israel and expressed its readiness to host an Arab summit conference for consultation and agreement on "serious joint Arab steps" needed to overcome the "dangers of division and disintegration" within the Arab world.[88] On October 26 Presidents Bakr and Assad signed the Charter for Joint National Action, thereby restoring Iraqi-Syrian amity on the eve of the Baghdad summit conference. A rapprochement was also made between Jordan and the PLO.

Iraq's central role in convening, hosting, and steering two Baghdad summit conferences (the second one held in March 1979 on the heels of the Egyptian-Israeli peace treaty), as well as Iraq's energetic promotion of its position in the Arab League and its affiliated organizations, elevated it to a position of unparalleled prominence in the Arab world. The attendance of Saudi Arabia and the other conservative Arab states revealed both the extent to which political circumstances in the Arab world had changed since the early 1970s and the growing acceptance of Iraq's leadership role. Particularly significant was Iraq's ability at the second conference to persuade Saudi Arabia and the other conservative peninsular states to accept what was basically the Iraqi position on a common stand against Egypt. The Saudis and other Gulf states at first opposed the application and severity of sanctions against Egypt, as favored by Iraq and some of the other Arab states. However, confronted with the choice of joining the Iraqi-sponsored Arab consensus or the American-sponsored Camp David process, the Saudis sided with Iraq (which at the time was still on relatively good terms with the Soviet Union). By March 1979 the name "Baghdad" had come to symbolize Arab opposition to Sadat and, by implication, to U.S. pressures to gain Arab acceptance of Israel. Thus, by a combination of fortuitous circumstances and a pragmatic, conciliatory policy, the Iraqi government had largely succeeded in guiding itself out of a long period of isolation and into the political mainstream of the Arab world. Despite various setbacks such as renewed tensions with Syria, Iraq continues to be identified with the Arab consensus, not with revolution. Belated U.S. recognition of this fact was finally expressed in February 1982 when the U.S. Department of Commerce announced it would remove Iraq from the list of countries formally regarded as supporters of international terrorism. By contrast, Libya, South Yemen, and Syria remain on the list.

A serious policy problem confronting the government is how to harness the strength of this Arab consensus, if it can be held together at all, to consolidate Iraq's leadership position in Arab politics. One answer appears to be President Hussein's Pan-Arab Charter, presented on February 8, 1980.[89]

Apart from helping to consolidate Iraq's leadership position, the charter embodies Iraq's view of its own place in the Arab world and the foundation upon which Arab politics ought to be based. The principles of the charter are grounded in the premise that Iraq must not only be responsible for the defense of its own territory, but must also assume responsibility for the defense of the "Arab Nation's honor, principles, and pan-Arab struggle."[90] The Arabs have discovered that they were "counting on soapsuds – the Soviets who crossed their border and intervened militarily in Afghanistan, and the Americans, who are threatening to occupy the oil sources." Therefore, Iraq must be willing to work with any Arab country in order to prevent the division of the Arab homeland by the superpowers.[91]

The main tenets of the charter, which is intended to "regulate relations among the Arab countries," are:

- The rejection of any foreign bases or armed forces on Arab soil;
- Prohibition against the resort by any Arab state to armed force to solve a dispute with another Arab state or with the states bordering on the Arab homeland, except in the case of self-defense;[92]
- Affirmation of the Arab countries' commitment to the international laws and norms pertaining to the use of international waters, air space, and zones by any state not at war with any Arab country;
- Arab neutrality in wars occurring outside the perimeters of the Arab homeland.

The themes of noninterference in each other's internal affairs and the need to keep the superpowers at bay doubtlessly fell on responsive ears in the more moderate Arab capitals. The first countries to respond favorably to the charter were the moderates, led by King Hussein of Jordan, who publicly endorsed the charter three days after it was proclaimed.[93] Endorsements from Saudi Arabia and Kuwait quickly followed. On March 4 it was announced in Baghdad that 12 Arab countries plus the PLO had agreed to the holding of a special Arab summit conference to approve the Pan-Arab Charter.[94]

The charter was not a plan of action against any Middle East country, including Iran. It was a very useful instrument for easing Saudi Arabia and Jordan away from the United States' embrace, particularly as both Saudi Arabia and Iraq believe that U.S. attempts to acquire bases and facilities in the Gulf will only invite Soviet penetration in the region. If Iraq is successful in this endeavor, it will have effectively undermined the U.S. emphasis on Saudi Arabia as the cornerstone for attaining American policy objectives in the Arabian Peninsula.

So far, Iraq has been able to operate in the Arab political arena without any competition from Egypt. Egypt's own Arabism is bound to reassert itself, and there were some indications that this was beginning to happen even before Israel was scheduled to return the remainder of the Sinai to Egypt.[95] A "rehabilitated" and resurgent Egypt could offer the moderate Arab states an alternative source of leadership, particularly in light of Iraq's indifferent battlefield performance in its war with Iran.

Military Policies

Both the growth and structuring of the Iraqi armed forces reflect the dominant themes in Iraq's foreign policy. Apart from the self-evident goal of national defense, Iraq's putative military capabilities are presumably intended to buttress the government's bid for pan-Arab leadership, supremacy in the Gulf, and independence from major power hegemony. In this regard, the armed forces must be prepared to defend the Arab nation beyond the country's own borders.

Despite Iraq's hard line concerning a settlement with Israel (Iraq still does not accept U.N. Resolution 242), the country's military role in the Arab-Israeli conflict has been limited due to some very real constraints. One of the most important is logistical: Iraq is far from the potential battlefields, and Arab-Israeli wars have generally ended quickly. The logistical factor has been complicated by the reluctance of front-line states like Jordan and Syria to have large formations of Iraqi troops stationed on their territories due to the vagaries of Arab politics. Similarly, Iraq has been reluctant to send large numbers of troops out of the country to face Israel as long as it was confronted with more imminent threats from Iran and the Kurds.

In keeping with Iraq's overriding foreign-policy goals and the country's emergence from isolation, Iraqi training and maneuvers since 1973 have concentrated on, and were reportedly successful in developing, a highly mobile armed and mechanized force that could overcome some of the military's logistical problems.[96] The purchase in 1977 of long-range transports from the Soviet Union, augmented in 1979 by the acquisition of C-160 Transall troop transports from France, provided additional mobility to the Iraqi armed forces and so enhanced the government's power-projection capabilities.

In keeping with its growing emphasis on nonalignment with either superpower, Iraq has shifted away from the Soviet Union as an almost exclusive source of major weapons systems toward Western sources, mainly France, Italy, and Brazil. The French in particular have become an important alternate source for combat aircraft (including helicopters) and armored personnel carriers. Given the pragmatic nature of Iraq's foreign and defense policy, Egypt has become an important source for the acquisition of Soviet-made weapons and spare parts since the beginning of the war with Iran.[97]

As for Iraq's performance in the war itself, several factors help to explain why the Iraqi armed forces failed to achieve a quick, decisive victory over Iran, despite the weakness of Iran's military machine resulting from post-revolutionary turmoil. First, Iraqi planners counted on widespread uprisings in Iran by estranged ethnic groups. These did not materialize,[98] and indeed the attack (or, as Iraq perceives it, "counterattack") in some ways restored at least a small part of Iranian unity. Second, while the Iraqi armed forces are the only ones on the Arab side of the Gulf with recent military experience, it was experience gained from the years of counterinsurgency operations against the Kurds in Iraq. This was a very different type of military situation from the more conventional type of war Iraq has been waging against Iran. Third, the timing of the war caught the Iraqi military establishment in an awkward situation of transition from Soviet- to Western-supplied equipment. In some instances, conversion from older to new equipment was not completed. This was particularly troublesome for the air force, some squadrons of which were converting from old Soviet aircraft to the newer MiG-23A. In other instances, much of the new equipment on order, such as the Mirage F1C, had not yet arrived. Fourth, Israel, through the use of electronic surveillance techniques, has been providing Iran with intelligence concerning the Iraqi order of battle. This information has helped Iranian forces to strike at Iraqi weak spots.

Iraq's determination not to rely exclusively on one foreign supplier may also have detracted from its combat effectiveness. The air force, for example, simply suffered from too many diverse types of aircraft for effective sustained training and maintenance support.[99]

These tactical problems have been complicated by two significant political factors. One, alluded to earlier, involves the "Ba'athization" of the Iraqi army by continuous promotions, based on party loyalty, in order to ensure government control of the armed forces. While this may have made the armed forces more responsive to the civilian regime, the politicization has severely weakened cohesion at the high command and planning levels. Thus, the internal politicization and internal maneuvering for positions weakened the Iraqi armed forces invisibly almost as much as the highly visible convulsions in postshah Iran decimated the Iranian armed forces, also at the senior command levels. A second political consideration alluded to above is that an all-out offensive to end the war will involve sustaining a high rate of casualties and is by no means certain to bring victory. The combination of high casualty rates without decisive victory could seriously jeopardize the staying power of Saddam Hussein's government.

However, all of the Peninsula countries and Jordan have almost as vital an interest in preventing an Iranian victory as Iraq itself. In this sense Iraq can be said to be fighting to preserve the stability of the entire Arab Gulf against the threat of subversion and revolution from Khomeini's Iran, and doubtlessly can continue to count on support from a large number of Arab countries in its war effort.

NOTES

1. Reliable, precise figures on the Shi'a proportion of the population are difficult to obtain. One of the more reliable breakdowns of the Iraqi population by ethnic, linguistic, and confessional affiliations is found in R. D. McLaurin, ed., *The Political Role of Minority Groups in the Middle East* (New York: Praeger, 1979), p. 272.

2. Although Shi'as occasionally achieved cabinet rank under the Hashemite monarchy, only one prime minister, Fadhel Jamali, belonged to the sect. A similar pattern is evident in the cabinets and revolutionary command councils since 1958. While it is difficult to identify the religious affiliation of the current ruling elite in Iraq, it is certain that no more than two or three members of the 13-member Ba'ath Regional Command are Shi'as, and that none of the present Revolutionary Command Council, the highest ruling authority in the country, is of that denomination.

3. Albert H. Hourani, *Minorities in the Arab World* (New York: Oxford University Press, 1947), pp. 94-95.

4. Jonathan C. Randal, "Iraq Expelling 20,000 Iranians Following Border Clashes," *Washington Post*, April 11, 1980, p. A18, and Jonathan C. Randal, "Iraq Shelves Area Ambitions to Focus on Internal Strife," ibid., May 4, 1980, p. A32.

5. David Adamson, *The Kurdish War* (London: Allen Unwin, 1964); Hasan Arfa, *The Kurds: An Historical and Political Study* (London: Oxford University Press, 1966); Cecil J. Edmonds, *Kurds, Turks, and Arabs: Politics, Travel, and Research in North-Eastern Iraq* (London: Oxford University Press, 1957); Edmund Ghareeb, *The Kurdish Question in Iraq* (Syracuse: Syracuse University Press, 1981); William E. Hazen, "The Kurds of Iran, Iraq, Syria, and Turkey," in McLaurin, ed., *The Political Role*; and Dana Adams Schmidt, *Journey Among Brave Men* (Boston: Little, Brown, 1964).

6. *New York Times*, October 2, 1980, p. 16.

7. Randal, "Iraq Shelves."

8. For an excellent analysis of the social, regional, and educational backgrounds of the Iraqi leadership, see Phebe Marr, "Iraq's Leadership Dilemma: A Study in Leadership Trends, 1948-1968," *Middle East Journal*, vol. 24, no. 3 (Summer 1970), pp. 283-301; and Marr, "The Political Elite in Iraq," in George Lenczowski, ed., *Political Elites in the Middle East* (Washington, D.C.: American Enterprise Institute, 1975).

9. Edith and E. F. Penrose, *Iraq: International Relations and National Development* (London and Boulder: Benn and Westview, 1978), p. 486; and Richard F. Nyrop et al., *Iraq: A Country Study* (Washington, D.C.: U.S. Government Printing Office, 1979), pp. 108-9.

10. David Paul, "From Elite to Class: The Transformation of the Iraqi Political Leadership," in Abbas Kelidar, ed., *The Integration of Modern Iraq* (New York: St. Martin's Press, 1979), pp. 78-79.

11. See Hanna Batatu, "Iraq's Underground Shi'a Movements: Characteristics, Causes and Prospects," *Middle East Journal*, vol. 35, no. 4 (Autumn, 1981), pp. 586-87.

12. Hanna Batatu, *The Old Social Classes and the Revolutionary Movements of Iraq* (Princeton: Princeton University Press, 1978), p. 1088.

13. Abbas Kelidar, "Iraq: the Search for Stability," *Conflict Studies* no. 59, (London, July 1975), p. 5.

14. Batatu, "Iraq's Underground Shi'a Movements," p. 586.

15. See Michael C. Hudson, *Arab Politics: The Search for Legitimacy* (New Haven and London: Yale University Press, 1975), pp. 277, 279.

16. For two excellent analyses of Iraqi domestic politics, see Majid Khadduri, *Republican Iraq: A Study in Iraq's Politics Since the Revolution of 1958* (London: Oxford University Press, 1969); and Majid Khadduri, *Socialist Iraq: A Study in Iraqi Politics Since 1968* (Washington, D.C.: Middle East Institute, 1978). For equally penetrating analyses of intra-Arab rivalries, see Malcolm H. Kerr, *The Arab Cold War, 1958-1967: A Study of Ideology in Politics*, 3d ed. (London: Oxford University Press, 1972), and Fouad Ajami, *The Arab Predicament: Arab Political Thought Since 1967* (London: Cambridge University Press, 1981).

17. Text in Khadduri, *Socialist Iraq*, Appendix A.

18. For a list of cabinet members and RCC members appointed after Saddam Hussein became president, see *Middle East Contemporary Survey, 1978-79*, pp. 562-63, 566.

19. Eric Davis, "The War's Economic, Political Damage to Iraq," *New York Times*, October 7, 1980, p. 16.

20. According to Article 48 of the Interim Constitution. Text in Khadduri, *Socialist Iraq*, p. 192.

21. Arts. 10, 11, and 12, as reported in *FBIS*, March 12, 1974, pp. C14-C15.

22. Text of the Charter of National Action is in Khadduri, *Socialist Iraq*, Appendix B., pp. 199-229. All references and citations of the charter are taken from this source.

23. The factions included the Kurdish Democratic Party (KDP), led by Aziz Aqrawi (after the KDP's longtime leader Mulla Mustafa Barzani left the country), the Kurdish Revolutionary Party, a splinter group from the KDP, and other "independent" or "progressive" Kurds. Another branch of the KDP led by Barzani's son, Massoud, is in opposition to the Ba'athist government.

24. For a discussion on the Ba'ath Party in Iraq, see Khadduri, *Republican Iraq*, pp. 115-16.

25. Phebe Marr, "How Ba'athists Keep Lid on Turbulence in Iraq," *Christian Science Monitor*, June 8, 1971, p. 5. See also *An-Nahar Arab Report*, vol. 5, no. 44 (November 4, 1974); Khadduri, *Republican Iraq*, p. 128, fn. 34; and Hanna Batatu, *The Old Social Classes and the Revolutionary Movements of Iraq*, p. 1084.

26. See Eliezer Be'eri, *Army Officers in Arab Politics and Society* (New York: Praeger, 1967), pp. 198-201; and Khadduri, *Republican Iraq*, pp. 202, 209-10.

27. An example of how family and clan relations count in maintaining political leadership is illustrated by the fact that the Iraqi fifth division was commanded by the president's brother, Brigadier Abel al-Rahman Arif, whose forces seized key positions in Baghdad during the coup.

28. Both men were eventually made ambassadors, the political equivalent of being exiled to Siberia, under Arif's new government.

29. Although a number of army officers were reportedly arrested in connection with the alleged plot, only two of the 21 convicted conspirators executed were military. See Marvine Howe, "Baghdad Executes 21 Officials for Alleged Plot," *New York Times*, August 9, 1979, p. 4.

30. See, for example, Marvine Howe, "Baghdad Executes"; William Casey, "Iraq Executes 21 Convicted in Coup Trial," *Washington Post*, August 9, 1979, pp. A1, A16; Jim Hoagland, "Iraqi Leader Moves to Strengthen Rule," ibid., July 31, 1979, p. A23; and *Middle East Contemporary Survey 1978-79*, p. 561. The sectarian motives for the plot seem particularly suspect as the seven-member court that handed down the death sentences for the accused conspirators included three Shi'a members.

31. For an authoritative and detailed account of these two incidents, see Khadduri, *Socialist Iraq*, pp. 53-55, 63-67.

32. Batatu, *The Old Social Classes*, p. 1028.

33. Ibid., p. 1086.

34. Ibid., p. 27.

35. See ibid., pp. 1078, 1086-88. The explanation for this change lies more in discriminatory practices of the police and locality than on sectarian prejudices. The Shi'as lost much of their representation in the party because many of them backed the leader of the left-wing faction, Ali Salih al-Sa'di, who after the November 18 coup challenged the authority of Michel Aflaq, blaming him for the party's defeat in Iraq. When al-Sa'di was read out of the Ba'ath the following year he formed his own group, eventually known as the Revolutionary Workers' Party, which suffered from a terminal case of factionalism. The main reason for the decline of the Shi'as, however, was the discriminatory practices of the police under the Arif regime. After the November 18 coup Shi'a Ba'athists were generally hunted down more systematically than their Sunni counterparts and, when caught, punished much more severely. The reason was that the Sunni Ba'athists were usually from the same town, province, or tribe as the members of the police. For this reason, the Sunni Ba'athists often escaped with light sentences.

36. Schmidt, *Journey*, p. 53.

37. Khadduri, *Independent Iraq*, p. 19.

38. Text of the provisional constitution is in Muhammed Khalil, *The Arab States and the Arab League: A Documentary Record* (Beirut: Khayats, 1962), I, 30-32.

39. Arfa, *The Kurds*, pp. 75, 106, 120-26, 129-30.

40. Col. Abdal-Wahhab Shawwaf, commander of the 5th Brigade of the 2nd Division, was stationed at Mosul in the spring of 1959. A son of the Grand Mufti of Baghdad, Shawwaf was an advocate of Arab unity. There is some disagreement among scholars. concerning the role the Shammar tribe played in the Shawwaf revolt. Arfa contends that the Kurds prevented their arrival from the outskirts of the Syrian desert (p. 132); Beeri, *Army Officers*, claims that the

Shammar tribe participated in what their leader called a war against "the Kurds and infidels" (p. 184). Whatever the extent of the tribe's participation, the fact of their participation clearly reflects the Kurdish-Arab antagonism referred to earlier.

41. Ghareeb, *The Kurdish Question*, p. 37.

42. Arfa, *The Kurds*, p. 134.

43. Khadduri, *Republican Iraq*, pp. 270-71.

44. Text, Khadduri, *Republican Iraq*, pp. 274-76.

45. As cited in Ghareeb, *The Kurdish Question*, p. 75.

46. According to Edmund Ghareeb, who interviewed Aziz Aqrawi, one of the top leaders of the Kurdish movement since 1961, Barzani's contacts with Israel go back as far as 1965. This has been corroborated by Luba Elias, a member of the Israeli Knesset. Ibid., p. 142. Israeli military aid to the Kurds is also reported by John Cooley, "Journey to Kallala," *Christian Science Monitor*, July 15, 1970, p. 18. According to Lee Dinsmore, a former U.S. consul in Kirkuk, Israel trained Kurdish insurgents on Iranian territory. Lee Dinsmore, "The Forgotten Kurds," *Progressive*, no. 4 (April 1977), p. 39.

47. Despite Iranian support and sympathy for the Iraqi Kurds, it is very doubtful that the Shah wished to see an autonomous Kurdish region established in territory contiguous to the area where Iranian Kurds live.

48. Jason Morris, "Begin Airs Secret Israeli Aid to Kurds as Reminder for Iraqis," *Christian Science Monitor*, October 6, 1980, p. 11.

49. Ghareeb, *The Kurdish Question*, p. 144.

50. As reported in *FBIS*, March 12, 1970, pp. C-3 to C-4. The full text is also in Khadduri, *Socialist Iraq*, Appendix C.

51. See John K. Cooley, "New Attack Breaches Iraqi-Kurdish Accord," *Christian Science Monitor*, October 5, 1971, p. 2. The "attack" Cooley refers to is the assassination attempt on Mulla Mustafa Barzani by nine religious sheikhs who came to visit the Kurdish leader in his stronghold at Nawbirdon. For a detailed account of this event, see David Hirst, "Ba'ath-Kurdish Pact Breached in Iraq," *Washington Post*, December 2, 1971, p. F-1. Hirst predicted that hostilities between Kurdish and Iraqi forces would break out in the spring of 1972.

52. Text of President Bakr's speech giving details of the autonomy framework is in *FBIS*, March 12, 1974, pp. C-11 to C-18. Also see Raymond Andersen, "Limited Local Autonomy Granted to Kurds in Iraq," *New York Times*, March 12, 1974, p. 5.

53. Commenting on the Kurdish demand that the Kirkuk Province be included in the autonomous region, Saddam Hussein pointed out that this province was populated by a number of ethnic groups, including Kurds, Turkomans, and Arabs. Therefore, it would not be right to include it in the region. He said that the RCC had suggested a joint administration for the province, but that this proposal was rejected by the Kurds, who demanded either an outright inclusion of the province in the region or, if that was not acceptable to the government, a joint administration for Kirkuk and attachment of it to the self-rule region. Both proposals were rejected by the government. *FBIS*, March 15, 1974, pp. C-1 to C-4.

54. The Aqrawis and Ubaidullah Barzani defended their defection from the Barzani faction partly on the ground that Mulla Mustafa had become totally "beholden" to the imperialists, Israel and Iran. See "Split Reported Within Kurdish Democratic Party: Barzani Accused of Dictatorship," *Arab World*, February 12, 1974, p. 7; and Ghareeb, *The Kurdish Question*, p. 155.

55. See Ghareeb, *The Kurdish Question*, pp. 138-42 for a well-documented discussion and analysis of the U.S. role in supporting dissident Kurdish forces in Iraq. See also Dinsmore, "The Forgotten Kurds," p. 39.

56. See Edward Cody, "Kurds Join Other Rebels in Effort to Overthrow Iraqi Rulers," *Washington Post*, January 7, 1982, p. A17. For an assessment of the threat of the Kurdish resistance in the context of the Iran-Iraq War, see Edgar O'Ballance, "The Kurdish Factor in the Gulf War," *Military Review*, vol. 61, no. 6 (June 1981), pp. 13-20.

57. See Ghareeb, *The Kurdish Question*, pp. 125-80. Ghareeb's information is based on interviews with several Kurdish leaders.

58. *Middle East Contemporary Survey, 1977-78*, p. 522.

59. As reported in *FBIS*, May 30, 1978, pp. E-1 to E-2.

60. Text in *FBIS*, March 15, 1979, pp. E-1 to E-7. Passages cited are on p. E-6.

61. *Middle East Contemporary Survey, 1978-79*, p. 568.

62. Under a 1913 treaty between the Ottoman Empire and Persia, the latter recognized Turkish sovereignty over the estuary up to the low-water mark on the Persian shore.

63. *Keesings Contemporary Archives*, April 9-16, 1960, p. 17,357.

64. *Keesings*, August 30-September 6, 1969, p. 23,544.

65. See Ghareeb, *The Kurdish Question*, p. 147. Ghareeb, citing interviews with Kurdish leaders and documentary evidence from the KDP preparatory committee, reports that in mid-1973 Saddam Hussein sent a message to Barzani asking him not to adopt stands that would eventually force the Iraqi government to make border concessions to Iran in the Shatt al-Arab and other areas in order to end the Kurdish problems.

66. Text of the 1975 agreement between Iraq and Iran in Khadduri, *Socialist Iraq*, Appendix E.

67. *FBIS*, September 18, 1980, pp. E-5.

68. *Keesings*, July 8-15, 1961, p. 18,187.

69. For details on this dispute, see Khadduri, *Socialist Iraq*, pp. 153-59.

70. Ralph Joseph, "Iran, Iraq Struggle for Territorial (and Propaganda) Gains," *Christian Science Monitor*, January 20, 1982, p. 8.

71. Nyrop et al., p. 215.

72. Doyle McManus, "Iraq's Shi'a Muslims Pose Threat of Fifth Column," *Los Angeles Times*, October 17, 1980, pp. 1, 6.

73. *FBIS*, April 8, 1980, pp. I-10 to I-B; *FBIS*, April 9, 1980, pp. I-14 to I-16, I-21 to I-22; and *FBIS*, April 14, 1980, pp. I-31 to I-33.

74. How much support Iraq was giving to Iranian Kurds before the war broke out in September 1980 is open to question. First, the Iraqi government could not have been unmindful that Kurdish unrest in Iran could spill across the frontier into Iraq. Second, one reporter who spent five days in the Kurdish region of northwestern Iran monitoring several routes into Iraq and interviewing

countless refugees from the battle zones as well as rebel officers, concluded that neither Iraq nor the U.S. Central Intelligence Agency "nor any other foreign power arms and finances the Kurds." See Tim McGirk, "Iranian Kurds: A Continuing Revolt Against the Revolution," *Christian Science Monitor*, June 13, 1980, pp. 12-13.

75. A detailed account is found in Edmond Ghareeb, "Iraq: Emergent Gulf Power," in Hossein Amirsadeghi, ed., *The Security of the Persian Gulf* (New York: St. Martin's Press, 1981), pp. 213-17.

76. See Helena Cobban, "Internal Dissension Hampers Iraq's Hussein in Gulf War," *Christian Science Monitor*, December 24, 1980, p. 7.

77. See Edward Cody, "Kurds Join Other Rebels to Overthrow Iraqi Rulers," *Washington Post*, January 7, 1982, p. A17.

78. Eric Davis, "The War's Economic, Political Damage," p. 16.

79. Iranian "victories" in 1981 consisted of the breaking of the siege of Abadan in September and some minor advances in northern Khuzistan near Bustan. Most of these victories were won through virtual "human wave" attacks by revolutionary guards, not through conventional military operations by the regular Iranian army. See Michael Getter, "Iran Winning the Battles Against Iraq," *Washington Post*, January 16, 1982, pp. A, A6; and Robert C. Toth, "Iran May Be Re-emerging as Gulf Power," *Los Angeles Times*, January 25, 1982, pp. 1, 18.

80. Iran is widely believed to be responsible for an attempted coup in Bahrain in December 1981.

81. Riad N. el-Rayyes and Dunia Nahas, eds., *Guerrillas for Palestine* (Beirut: An-Nahar Press Services S.A.R.L., 1974), pp. 55-56.

82. Ibid., p. 105.

83. Ibid., p. 106.

84. See Abdul Kassim Mansur, "The American Threat to Saudi Arabia," *Armed Forces Journal* (September 1980), p. 47.

85. Georgie Ann Geyer, "War in Iran: The View from Baghdad," *Washington Star*, December 24, 1980, p. A5.

86. The rapprochement with Jordan is described in Paul A. Jureidini and R. D. McLaurin, *Beyond Camp David: Emerging Alignments and Leaders in the Middle East* (Syracuse: Syracuse University Press, 1981), pp. 70-72. In terms of other regional powers, Israel was secretly allied with Iran against Iraq, yet remained at odds with Syria, Iran's ally. Egypt, whose principal foe was Libya, supported Iraq secretly. Although Egypt's support was limited, Cairo was a quiet ally of the Saudi-Iraqi entente despite the harsh rhetoric exchanged between Egypt and the other Arab governments. *Middle East Contemporary Survey, 1978-1979*, p. 240.

87. Text in *Middle East Contemporary Survey, 1977-78*, p. 278.

88. *FBIS*, October 2, 1978, p. E-1.

89. Text in *FBIS*, February 11, 1980, pp. E-1 to E-4.

90. Baghdad Voice of the Masses (February 8, 1980), as reported in *FBIS*, February 11, 1980, p. E-2.

91. *FBIS*, February 11, 1980, p. E-4.

92. This does not apply to Israel since Iraq does not consider the "Zionist Entity" a state.

93. *Jordan Times*, February 12, 1980, p. 1.

94. *FBIS*, March 5, 1980, p. E-5. The countries approving the special summit (and by implication the charter itself) were Algeria, Morocco, Tunisia, Mauritania, Libya (!), Jordan, Kuwait, Saudi Arabia, the UAE, Bahrain, North Yemen, and Qatar, as well as the PLO.

95. For example, in January 1982 Saudi Arabia agreed to finance Egypt's purchase of 20 Mirage 2000 fighter aircraft, and Egypt's new president Husni Mubarak was already beginning to put some distance between himself and Washington.

96. Nyrop et al., *Iraq*, p. 233.

97. Nathaniel Harrison, "Iraq Gets Arms for Iran War — from Sadat with Love," *Christian Science Monitor*, April 1, 1981, p. 10. Arab sources insist Egypt has been providing aid to Iraq since the beginning of the war. China has also provided large quantities of military stocks.

98. The fact that they did not rise up cannot be attributed to a lack of covert Iraqi assistance. According to Arab sources, former Iranian prime minister Shakpour Bakhtiari assured the Iraqis that the Bakhtiari tribes around Kermonshak would be among the first to rebel. Anti-Khomeini Bakhtiari tribesmen had been receiving military training in 1980 in Oman, Egypt, and Iraq. The degree to which Egypt and Iraq actually coordinated their activities in this effort could not be ascertained. However, since Egypt was reportedly supplying Iraq with Soviet-built arms to cover Iraqi losses, it is possible that, despite the two countries' differences over relations with Israel and Camp David, Iraq and Egypt did overcome these differences enough to join forces where their interests converged.

99. For a more detailed analysis of Iraq's equipment problems, see Abdul Kasim Mansur, "Iraq: When in Doubt Murder," *Armed Forces Journal* (November 1980), pp. 55-58.

ISRAELI FOREIGN POLICYMAKING

ENVIRONMENT

Israel, the newest of the Middle East nations discussed in this volume, differs from its neighbors in several respects that affect its foreign policy. It is the only country of the region without a large Muslim population. More than 80 percent of its inhabitants are Jewish, nearly half of them immigrants from Europe, the Americas, North Africa, and Asia. The Arab minority is a remnant of the indigenous Muslim and Christian populations who were the majority in Palestine until establishment of Israel in 1948.

The Jewish state of Israel was carved out of mandatory Palestine after 30 years under British control, following almost four centuries of Ottoman Turkish rule. Like its Arab neighbors, Palestine had been part of the Ottoman Empire until the end of World War I. Because Palestine had special religious and historical significance to Jews, Christians, and Muslims, it also acquired a unique political character; during the nineteenth century various European powers used Palestine's religious significance as a way of gaining a foothold in the Ottoman Empire. Jerusalem, for example, became one of the focal points in the Middle East for intervention by, and a center of controversy among, European powers seeking to establish influence in the region.[1]

Palestine also became the focus of an emergent Jewish nationalism during the nineteenth century, although the movement and most of its initial followers were European rather than Middle Eastern. When the Jewish national movement, or Zionism, began at the end of the century,[2] less than 10 percent of Palestine's population was Jewish.[3] During World War I the Zionists won support for their movement from Great Britain, which was given the mandate for Palestine by the League of Nations in 1922.

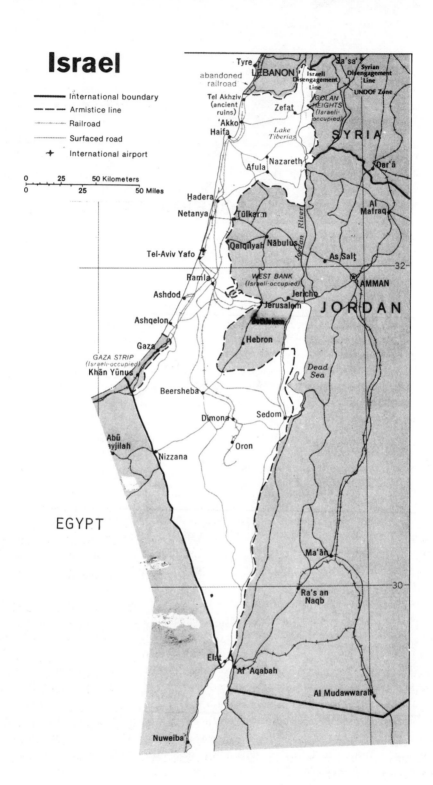

Israel

- —— International boundary
- – – – Armistice line
- ···· Railroad
- ···· Surfaced road
- ✈ International airport

0   25   50 Kilometers
0   25   50 Miles

Tyre
Ja'sa'
LEBANON
abandoned railroad
Israeli Disengagement Line
Syrian Disengagement Line
UNDOF Zone
Tel Akhziv (ancient ruins)
GOLAN HEIGHTS (Israeli-occupied)
Zefat
'Akko
Haifa
Lake Tiberias
SYRIA
Afula
Nazareth
Dar'ā
Hadera
Al Mafraq
Netanya
Tūlkarm
Qalqīlyah
Nābulus
Tel-Aviv Yafo
As Salt
32
Ramla
WEST BANK (Israeli-occupied)
AMMAN
Ashdod
Jericho
Jerusalem
JORDAN
Ashqelon
Bethlehem
Gaza
Hebron
GAZA STRIP (Israeli-occupied)
Khān Yūnus
Dead Sea
Beersheba
Dimona
Sedom
Abū 'ayjilah
Oron
Nizzana

EGYPT

Jordan River

Ma'ān

30
Ra's an Naqb

Elat
Al 'Aqabah
Al Mudawwarah

Nuweiba'

Between World War I and World War II the Jewish population grew from about 10 percent to a third of Palestine, and the foundations of a Jewish state were established against the will of the country's Arab majority.[4] Zionism also became a significant international force so that by the end of World War II, when the full impact of Nazi atrocities against Europe's Jews was revealed, there was widespread support for a Jewish state among the nations of Europe and among world Jewry. Arab opposition to Zionism, British ambivalence about policy in Palestine, and Jewish anxiety to bring the remnants of Hitler's death camps to the country produced a violent three-way conflict. Finally, in 1946 Great Britain turned the problem over to the United Nations, which recommended in 1947 that the country be partitioned into a Jewish state, an Arab state, and an international area to include Jerusalem and Bethlehem.[5]

The country's Arab population, supported by the Arab League, opposed the U.N. partition plan, at first by guerrilla activity, and later, after British evacuation from Palestine in May 1948, with the armed forces of Egypt, Jordan, Syria, Lebanon, and Iraq.[6] Defeated in the first Arab-Israeli war (1948-49), called by Israelis the "War of Liberation," the Arab states refused to recognize Israel or to enter peace negotiations with it until 1977, when Egypt's president, Anwar Sadat, initiated unilateral talks with leaders of the Jewish state. There were three other major wars with Israel, in 1956, 1967, and 1973, in which the Arabs were unable to defeat the Jewish state. A major result of the 1948 and 1967 wars was the exodus of several hundred thousand Arab refugees from territories occupied by Israel.

Arab hostility to Zionism from the early days of the movement, repeated clashes between Jews and Arabs during the British mandate, and the four major wars have been the most decisive factors in shaping Israel's foreign policy. Refusal by all Arab states, except Egypt since 1977, to recognize Israel or to enter direct peace negotiations with its representatives, has colored the perceptions of policymakers and shaped their military, strategic, and foreign-policy doctrines. National security has been the paramount consideration in both internal and foreign policy.

Continued hostilities with the Arab states have made it impossible to resolve such fundamental questions as internationally recognized borders, the status of Israel's capital, Jerusalem, and the fate of the Palestine Arab refugees. Israel's economy, too, is dominated by its security needs. It devotes more of its GNP to military expenditures, and receives more per capita foreign aid than any other nation. Defense expenditures force sacrifices in other areas of vital national development such as education, health, social welfare, and establishment of new Jewish settlements. All Israeli youth, both men and women with few exceptions, must serve in the armed forces, and most males are required to remain in the reserves until their mid-fifties. Thus, relations with the neighboring Arab states affect the daily lives of all the country's inhabitants.

Since 1948 the number of nations interested and involved in the Arab-Israeli conflict has increased greatly, from the Arab countries immediately surrounding

Israel, to Arab North Africa, the nations of sub-Saharan Africa, the third world, and Western Europe. As the number of nations critical of Israel's foreign policies has increased, Israelis feel a growing sense of isolation. Often it seems to them that only the United States is sympathetic to their security requirements and international policies, but there are also frequent disagreements with America.

This sense of isolation has been exacerbated by the resurgence of the Palestine Arab national movement, international recognition of the Palestine Liberation Organization (PLO) as the sole legitimate representative of Palestine Arab nationalism, and the growing importance of Arab oil to the international economy. Although Israel has successfully maintained its powerful military posture, the importance of military considerations has diminished as a result of the rapid escalation in importance of the huge capital surpluses from Arab oil.[7]

Israel's feelings of international isolation are further intensified by memories of the Holocaust in Europe when six million Jews were liquidated by Hitler, by the history of Jewish persecution in many Western countries, and by recent difficulties experienced by Jews in the Soviet Union and in several Arab countries. These historical memories and the more recent pressures we have noted often result in attitudes and policies perceived by other countries as stubborn or provocative. Many Israelis believe that compromise will undermine their security, even their existence, and that there is no alternative to a foreign policy backed by powerful armed forces prepared to engage in direct action against border intrusions and internal terrorism. This configuration of circumstances and Israel's reaction has created what some call a "Masada complex," referring to the last-ditch resistance of Jews against the Romans in an isolated desert fortress overlooking the Dead Sea.

There is a national consensus that security considerations are paramount in nearly all aspects of Israeli policy, both domestic and foreign.[8] Major parties in the various government coalitions and in the opposition have agreed on the principal outlines of policy for relations with the world powers, with the neighboring Arab states, and with the third world. Security rather than economic or political considerations determines policy on what borders Israel will accept; and security is the prime consideration in determining whether to permit return of Arab refugees. There is also a national consensus on establishment of Jerusalem as the capital, despite numerous U.N. resolutions censuring Israel for continued occupation of the city's eastern Arab areas.[9] After the 1967 war when Israel occupied the West Bank area of Jordan, including Jerusalem, the Syrian Golan Heights, the Gaza Strip, and the Sinai peninsula, resistance to territorial compromise became even more intense.[10]

Israeli political life was dominated during the first 30 years by parties affiliated with the Labor movement, but they never were able to form a government without inviting non-Labor groups into their coalition. Politics was a continuation of the system established by the World Zionist Organization and by the Jewish community that developed in Palestine during the first half of the century.[11] Most parties originated as Zionist groups established in Europe; they reflected the diverse political, social, and philosophic currents of thought within the Jewish communities of the diaspora. The orthodox religious Zionists believed that the Jewish state should be guided by the principles of the Old Testament. Some Zionists were anti- or nonreligious with attachments to the Holy Land growing from historical connections. Many Jews in Eastern Europe were socialists and hoped to establish an ideal workers' society in Palestine. From these diverse trends there emerged more than a score of political parties, most of them established before Israel achieved independence.

During the mandatory era the Labor movement acquired the largest following. Its influence was widespread not only among urban workers, but in the agricultural sector, in cultural life, and by virtue of its acquisition and control of much of the Jewish community's industry and commerce. The Histadrut, or General Federation of Jewish Workers, was the large organization in which most of the Labor groups had a common interest. Several Labor parties belonged to the Histadrut, the largest of which, Mapai, was the cornerstone of the Labor coalition.

Mapai's leader, David Ben-Gurion, became Israel's first prime minister and first minister of defense. He led the country through the first two wars and established many precedents that have become part of the country's unwritten constitution. Initially, Israel attempted to follow a nonaligned or neutral foreign policy. Within the Labor movement, opinion was divided between advocates of closer ties with the Soviet Union and those who favored a Western orientation. Ben-Gurion's analysis of Israel's international situation soon led to close ties with the United States, which provided the new state with large-scale economic aid.[12] American Jewry also supplied extensive financial assistance and invaluable political and moral support.[13]

Under Ben-Gurion's guidance, Israel developed a powerful military machine that became the backbone of the country's foreign policy. In contrast to Israel's first foreign minister, Moshe Sharett, Ben-Gurion believed that what Israel did was more important than what the world thought. He placed much greater emphasis on effective military deterrence of the Arab world than on the diplomacy of compromise.[14]

Political differences among major parties have been over ideological issues, social and economic questions, and the tactics rather than the objectives of security and foreign policies. Three blocs of Zionist parties dominate the political system: Labor, religious, and center-nationalist. The blocs and the parties that comprise them have undergone periodic mergers, splits, fragmentations, and reunions. It often seems that the number of parties rises or falls with the political winds. On the eve of independence in 1948 when the Jewish population was a fifth of what it is today, there were more than 30 parties or political groups. Twenty-four participated in the first election in 1949; 16 were represented in the first Knesset or parliament. Twenty-one participated in the 1973 election with ten winning Knesset seats. In 1977, 23 entered the election and 13 won Knesset seats.

Ideologies tend to harden at the peripheries of each major bloc. Mapam, for example, represents the left wing of the Labor Alignment, which was the largest bloc until its defeat in the 1977 elections. Although changes in international politics and Israel's increasing isolation have modified many of Mapam's policies, it still represents those within the Labor movement more inclined toward compromise with the Arab world, nonidentification of Israel with any power bloc, and a preference for the use of diplomacy rather than military strength in achieving foreign-policy objectives. Because of its stand on these questions and its inclination toward a more staunchly socialist position in domestic affairs, Mapam has maintained its separate identity with the Labor Alignment.

The broad outlines of foreign and security policy were determined by the Labor Alignment in accord with basic principles established by Ben-Gurion. Security was the foundation on which most foreign policies were constructed, although Labor was willing to make certain concessions for a peace settlement with the Arab states. The Labor movement considers all of Palestine as part of the Land of Israel, but it was willing to accept partition as a basis for establishment of recognized and secure boundaries. Within the Labor movement there were various interpretations of the partition principle, ranging from those willing to give up only a small part of the territories conquered in 1967, to those who would exchange most of the territories for a genuine peace settlement.[15] Jerusalem was designated as Israel's capital in 1950 by a Labor government, and after the rest of the city was captured, a Labor government declared all Jerusalem Israel's "indivisible" capital.[16] Since the early 1950s, when Ben-Gurion decided that there would be no large-scale return of Arabs to the homes from which they had fled in Israel-held territory, the government has insisted on resettlement of the refugees in Arab countries rather than their repatriation to Israel.[17]

Despite criticism from Mapam and the Communist movement, Labor forged close ties with the United States during its 30 years in office. Frequent sharp differences in policy between Jerusalem and Washington failed to break the ties. Israel's economic and military dependence on the United States became so great that it has often been regarded as an American client state. After the 1973 war Israel became the largest recipient of military and economic assitance from the United States.[18] This increasing dependence, the close ties with American Jewry, and the shifting political orientations of the surrounding Arab states resulted in rapid deterioration of relations with the Soviet Union; by the mid-1950s Moscow and most of its friends perceived Israel as an "agent of American imperialist expansion" in the Middle East.

After 30 years of Labor rule, the Alignment was shaken from power in the 1977 election. The "earthquake," as Labor's defeat was called by many in Israel, resulted from widespread public disillusionment with the governing party. The old idealism of the Labor movement had dissipated as it attempted to become all things to all voters. As its urban base expanded and the country industrialized, there was less emphasis on establishing new kibbutzim (collective settlements) and on pioneering the unsettled regions of the country. Demands of the powerful labor unions had to be balanced against the rising middle-class voters whom the party wanted to attract. Disputes between hawks and doves over the future of the occupied territories and the terms of a peace settlement also divided Labor. Although Israel was not defeated in the 1973 war, the cost in casualties and to the economy was so great that the conflict was regarded as a setback rather than as a victory for the Labor government. The country's economy was in severe straits: escalating defense costs created an inflation of over 30 percent (the highest rate until 1977), traditionally high taxes seemed more oppressive than ever, and unemployment was increasing. Government's failure to cope with these problems occurred against a background of spreading corruption involving the highest officials. Prime Minister Rabin had to withdraw appointment of his designee for director of the Bank of Israel, and a Labor cabinet minister committed suicide when charged with misuse of funds. Finally, during 1977 it was revealed that Rabin and his wife failed to declare ownership of bank accounts in the United States, a serious financial misdemeanor, and he withdrew from the prime ministry.

The 1977 electoral "earthquake" was less an election victory for the Likud Party than an expression of widespread discontent with Labor. The Likud bloc gained only 3.2 percent more votes than it won in the previous (1973) election, while Labor lost 15 percent of its votes and 40 percent of its Knesset seats. Likud emerged as the strongest bloc with 33.4 percent of the votes, and 43 of the 120 Knesset seats.

Decline of the Labor Alignment was caused mostly by appearance of the Democratic Movement for Change (DMC), established as a protest party a few months before the 1977 election. It was led by a former general, Yigal Yadin, who had been an academician since 1948. DMC was a coalition of hawks and doves, zealous and moderate nationalists, conservatives and liberals, all demanding change in the political environment and alterations in the system they believed responsible for the deplorable state of the country.[19] The DMC electoral list included former generals, high-ranking government officials, professors, and intellectuals of diverse political and social orientations. Some were formerly associated with the right-wing Likud, and others came from the Labor movement. Most of the 11.6 percent of the votes it won in the 1977 election came from former supporters of Labor, and its 15 Knesset seats deprived Labor of its leading position.

Likud, like Labor and the DMC, was also formed from a wide spectrum of factions with diverse perspectives. It became Israel's major political opposition in the 1973 elections and its largest party (although a minority) when it won 43 Knesset seats in 1977. Likud was formed in 1973 under Menachem Begin's leadership as a national movement whose goal was to keep all territories acquired by Israel in the 1967 war.[20] Its followers adamantly opposed surrender of the

West Bank and Gaza to Arab control, as much for historical and sentimental reasons as for security reasons. These areas were considered integral parts of historic Eretz Israel and the patrimony of the entire Jewish people. While the Likud Knesset list included factions that had split from the Labor movement, its social and economic programs were antisocialist, favoring free enterprise and economic development unrestricted by government controls. Indicative of the party's social orientation was its request that the conservative American economist Milton Friedman become an economic advisor to the new government.

Israel's new prime minister, Menachem Begin, was the leader and founder of the Herut (Freedom) Party established in 1948, the largest faction within Likud. Herut was heir to the militant nationalist opposition wing of the Zionist movement called the Revisionists. Its founder, Vladimir Jabotinsky, sought to establish a Jewish state on both sides of the Jordan River in the territory that comprised Palestine and Transjordan during the British mandate. Until Herut fused with the Liberal Party in 1965 to form the Gahal bloc, Begin's territorial aspirations remained those of his mentor, Jabotinsky. However, after joining the more moderate Liberals, Begin modified his goals, calling for Israeli sovereignty "between the Jordan and the [Mediterranean] Sea."[21] Sharp differences in social orientation and political methods led to years of acrimonious debate between Begin and Ben-Gurion. The two leaders were reconciled on the eve of the 1967 war when Begin was invited to become a minister without portfolio in a national unity cabinet. He remained a cabinet member for three years until he resigned in protest against compromises made with Egypt and the United States in 1970.[22] In 1973 Gahal (Herut plus the Liberals) joined several other opposition groups to form the Likud.

Like his predecessors, Prime Minister Begin also had to form a coalition government with support from several parliamentary factions if he was to carry a majority of the Knesset on important issues. Thus, he invited the orthodox National Religious Party (NRP) and the DMC to join the cabinet. With their support, he obtained a bloc of 77 Knesset votes, more than enough to insure establishment of a strong government.

At first Begin's style reminded many observers of Ben-Gurion. He seemed assertive, innovative, and personal. It seemed that the prime minister was in the driver's seat. Begin's appointment of former general and defense minister Moshe Dayan (elected to the Knesset as a member of the Labor Alignment) as foreign minister underscored his emphasis on national rather than party considerations. It was unheard of to give such a post to a member of the opposition.

During the election Likud had promised to reduce inflation by one-half, to 15 percent a year, then to 10 percent by 1979. It also promised to boost Israel's GNP by at least 40 percent within five years through encouragement of investment, reduction of the trade deficit, and curtailment of the large bureaucracy. Promises were made to transfer several state corporations and those of the Histadrut to the private sector; public lands would also be sold to raise funds for the government.[23]

Likud's 1977 foreign-policy platform called for direct peace talks with the Arab states leading to signed peace treaties, without conceding territory in the West Bank or Gaza. Jewish settlement would be encouraged in all parts of the Land of Israel without uprooting anyone from his property; Israeli law would be enacted over all Eretz Israel, and Arabs who desired citizenship and promised to be loyal would be granted equal rights.[24]

Soon after Begin became prime minister his cabinet coalition began to crumble. The DMC split, with more than half its Knesset members abandoning support for the government. By 1980 the factions that had comprised the DMC lost most of their public backing, and the remnants of the movement fell to the bottom in public opinion polls. Within the cabinet there was dissension among members of Begin's Likud over economic policy and foreign affairs. Two of the most important cabinet members, Foreign Minister Dayan and Defense Minister Ezer Weizman, resigned in protest against the government's hard-line policies in the peace negotiations with Egypt and with the United States. The minister of finance was replaced because of his inability to stem the tide of economic deterioration, and the justice minister also quit. The new finance minister suggested draconic economies, including termination or cuts in government subsidies for basic food commodities and major cuts in the government payroll. Despite these efforts, he was unable to halt the record inflation, which reached an all-time high of 124 percent for 1979-80.[25]

Begin's major success lay in the conclusion of an Egyptian-Israeli peace treaty (March 1979) following the visit to Jerusalem of Egyptian President Anwar Sadat in November 1977. The treaty terminated three decades of war between the two countries, led to normalization of relations, and restored the Sinai to Egypt. But the treaty alienated the most militant nationalists in Begin's own Herut movement. Two Herut Knesset members quit the party to form their own Tehiya (Renaissance) faction in opposition to the government. Seven of the eighteen Knesset votes against the treaty were from Begin's Herut movement.

Even the 1979 treaty failed to resolve all issues between Egypt and Israel. The most difficult outstanding controversy was over the future of Gaza, Jerusalem, and the West Bank. Differing Egyptian and Israeli interpretations of the clauses calling for autonomy in the Israeli-occupied parts of Palestine led to protracted and acrimonious relations. At times the autonomy controversy seemed to jeopardize the whole peace process; it was complicated by the Jerusalem question. Few Israelis were willing to contemplate surrendering sovereignty over any part of their capital, while Egypt interpreted autonomy as a first step toward Arab self-determination and eventual self-government in Palestine, including East Jerusalem.[26] The dispute only increased Israel's international isolation, for most nations of the third world, the Soviet bloc, and Western

Europe supported Egypt's interpretation. Even the United States, Israel's only consistent ally, tended toward the Egyptian position.[27]

By the end of 1980 Begin's public opinion poll ratings fell to their lowest point since 1977. The continued severity of Israel's economic plight and the bickering over the autonomy negotiations overshadowed success in negotiating the peace treaty.[28] The aura of strength and decisiveness with which Begin came to power disappeared among the squabbles within the cabinet, in the Likud movement, and in the prime minister's own Herut.

STRUCTURE OF THE GOVERNMENT

Although Israel has no written constitution, it is a parliamentary democracy with features of the British, French, and U.S. systems. The 120-member Knesset, or parliament, is legally supreme; it may enact any law and its decisions cannot be overridden by the executive or the judiciary. Instead of a written permanent constitution the Knesset passed a Transition Law in 1949, which with subsequent amendments became the legal basis of government operations. The law established the principal organs and offices of government, and defined their powers and responsibilities (see Figure 5.1). Israel never adopted a permanent written constitution because of differences among its various political groupings. Ben-Gurion also opposed adoption of a final written document, arguing that while the Jewish state was in its formative stages it would be better to encourage a process of constitutional development during which governmental practices and conventions would slowly evolve.[29]

The President

Israel's president is legally its highest official, but under Ben-Gurion's powerful influence, the prime minister emerged as the dominant political personality. The president is elected by the Knesset for a five-year term that may be renewed once in succession. Most of the president's functions are ceremonial, including the signing of laws, accepting credentials of foreign emissaries, and appointment of Israeli ambassadors and other high officials. Perhaps the president's most important task is to consult leaders of various parties prior to formation of a new government. But even that responsibility is so circumscribed by constitutional convention that it too has become merely symbolic, resembling the appointment of a prime minister by the British monarch.

The Prime Minister

The prime minister must be a Knesset member, the leader of the party with the largest number of seats. After being invited by the president to form

FIGURE 5.1
Structure of the Israeli Government

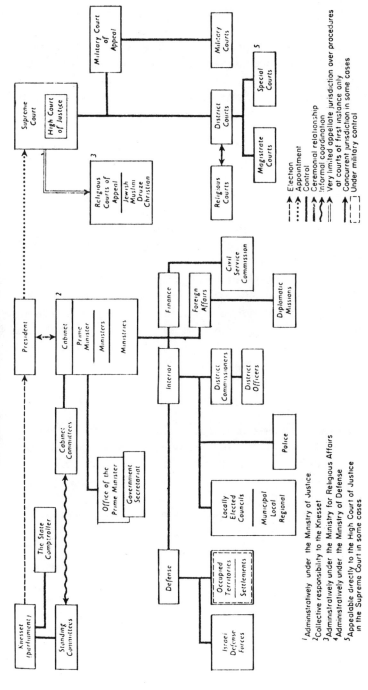

Legend:

- Election
- Appointment
- Control
- Ceremonial relationship
- Informal coordination
- Very limited appellate jurisdiction over procedures at courts of first instance only
- Concurrent jurisdiction in some cases
- Under military control

[1] Administratively under the Ministry of Justice

[2] Collective responsibility to the Knesset

[3] Administratively under the Ministry for Religious Affairs

[4] Administratively under the Ministry of Defense

[5] Appealable directly to the High Court of Justice in the Supreme Court in some cases

Chart labels: President; Cabinet — Prime Minister, Ministers, Ministries; Cabinet Committees; Office of the Prime Minister; Government Secretariat; The State Comptroller; Knesset (parliament); Standing Committees; Defense; Occupied Territories — Settlements; Israel Defense Forces; Interior; District Commissioners; District Officers; Police; Locally Elected Councils — Municipal, Local, Regional; Finance; Foreign Affairs; Civil Service Commission; Diplomatic Missions; Supreme Court — High Court of Justice; Military Court of Appeal; Military Courts; District Courts; Special Courts; Magistrate Courts; Religious Courts; Religious Courts of Appeal — Jewish, Muslim, Druze, Christian.

Source: Richard F. Nyrop, ed., *Israel: A Country Study* (Washington, D.C.: Foreign Area Studies Div., American University, 1979), p. 121. Reprinted with the permission of the copyright holder, the American University.

a government, the prime minister and the cabinet are approved by the Knesset. When they fail to win a vote of confidence, they resign to become an interim government until national elections reconstitute the next Knesset. Elections for the Knesset are usually held every four years unless the government fails to win a vote of confidence. Most governments have been able to sustain power for their full terms.

Keeping control of the government for a full four-year term is a tricky business. Because no party has ever won a majority of votes in a national election, all of Israel's prime ministers have had to form coalition governments composed of two or more parties, which often have different and at times contradictory political goals. Unless a coalition is formed, the party in power will be defeated in the Knesset. Thus, during most of its tenure in government, the Labor coalition included members of the orthodox religious parties whose views on education, sabbath observance, and maintenance of Jewish tradition differed from those of most Labor Party members. Rabin's government collapsed in 1977 when the NRP cabinet ministers failed to support him on a vote of confidence. To remain in power the dominant party usually has to make continuous political concessions to its coalition partners. Begin's dependence on the NRP has led to a substantial increase of orthodox Jewish influence in education and in interpretation of nationality legislation. NRP pressures are also significant in support of Begin's policies for the West Bank and Gaza. Unlike President Sadat, who was often able to make on-the-spot decisions in the peace negotiations, Begin had to consult the members of his coalition, especially those who were members of other parties, before making decisive commitments.

In the Transition Law the prime minister is called "head of the government," with unspecified powers. Real power depends on the prime minister's conduct in office and personality. A strong prime minister like Ben-Gurion dominates his cabinet, holding out the threat of resignation as a pressure for support. Other prime ministers have been less persuasive. On many occasions they were outvoted by their cabinet colleagues and forced to give in to the ministerial majority. Since the cabinet is collectively responsible for policy, if the prime minister resigns in protest against a cabinet decision, the whole cabinet must also resign. Once a member of the cabinet, a minister cannot be forced to resign unless the rest of the government also leaves. However, many ministers have resigned voluntarily because of differences with the prime minister or the rest of the cabinet.

Knesset members (MK) serve a full term unless they give up membership voluntarily. Even if an MK breaks with his party, he may keep his seat; this results in many new factions or parties forming between elections when MKs leave their party. After appointment by Begin as foreign minister in 1977, the late Moshe Dayan left the Labor Party, but retained his Knesset seat. The Tehiya faction was formed in 1979 by two militants who broke with Herut in opposition to Begin's concessions to Egypt.

While the Knesset is supreme, most of its members, especially those in the larger parties, hew to the party line and follow its directives for fear of not being included in a safe position on the party electoral list during the next election. Only individuals with strong ideological motivation, or those who feel that they can carry enough votes to return them in the next Knesset without support of their former party, dare challenge the party whip. Many colorful personalities on both right and left have emerged from this system to create their own Knesset factions. Arie Eliav, one of the founders of Shelli, a dovish, socialist-oriented party, was once the secretary-general of the Labor Party. Disagreement over policy toward a peace settlement led him to form his own Knesset faction. At the other end of the spectrum, Yigal Hurvitz, a Likud member who refused to support the peace treaty with Egypt, also came from the Labor movement.

Most legislation is introduced in the Knesset by the government; its supporters are required to vote with the party leaders in favor of government proposals. Amendments and revisions may be introduced to government bills in the appropriate Knesset committee or at one of the bill's hearings. Only occasionally does a bill introduced by a private Knesset member without government authorization become law. The main functions of the Israeli Knesset, as in most parliamentary democracies, are to debate and discuss legislation proposed by the cabinet, to air public concerns and grievances, and to expose incidents of government mismanagement or malfeasance. In Israel the Knesset fulfills these functions admirably. This is especially true in matters of foreign policy, when nearly every segment of public opinion is heard from before the parliament approves any significant government decision. The Knesset held the longest debate in its history before approving the peace treaty in March 1979.

OPERATION OF THE ISRAELI POLITICAL SYSTEM

Most aspects of Israel's political system are a heritage of the prestate era. The major political parties grew out of the diverse ideological factions that developed among European Jewish members of the Zionist movement. Government ministries and agencies were organized during the mandate as departments of the mandatory government, as offices of the Jewish community in Palestine, or as branches of the World Zionist Organization and the Jewish Agency for Palestine. Since 1948 a melange of practices, customs, perceptions, and perspectives on government has developed. Some institutions are characterized by British efficiency and regularity. In others there are Eastern European attitudes toward the superior prerogatives of officialdom, or Middle Eastern nepotistic preferences for family members and those with whom an official may have long friendships.[30]

Day-to-day administration is carried out by the various ministries. Since the state was established in 1948 their number has varied, sometimes more, and at times fewer than 20. The number depends on the policies and commitments of each government coalition, since many cabinet posts are awarded as inducements to minority factions to join the government. When Begin assumed power in 1977, the ministry of police, often given to a leading Oriental Jewish leader in the past, was absorbed by the ministry of interior. Health and social welfare were united in a new ministry of social betterment.

Two of the most important ministries, foreign affairs and defense, were continuations of the Jewish Agency's Political Department and the Haganah defense organization established by the prestate Jewish community. The ministries of social welfare and education and culture also developed from departments established by the Jewish community during the mandate. Several other government departments and agencies, like posts and telegraph or transportation, were inherited from the British-controlled government of Palestine.[31]

Until 1977 the most important ministries were given to the closest intimates of the prime minister, who were loyal members of his party. The Labor Alignment would never have given the second and third most important cabinet positions, defense and foreign affairs, to anyone but a member of its ruling elite. Only lesser posts, like religion or social welfare, were turned over to coalition partners as part of the bargain to establish a new government. Personnel in the various ministries often were from the minister's party, and bureaucratic practices and policies tended to reflect those of the party that controlled them.[32]

Emergence of the Public Sector

The Israeli government vastly extended the governmental functions for which the British mandatory authorities had been responsible, and the number of official agencies involved in trade, commerce, business, and financial activity increased many times. Israel's social welfare orientation, the encouragement of and responsibility for massive immigration, forced the new state to greatly expand the public sector. As the government attempted to speed up the pace of development, it assumed responsibilities that had been left to the private sector, and it became one of the country's largest entrepreneurs, acquiring a network of government-owned industries including the Electricity Corporation and Israel Chemicals, a conglomerate with shares in the largest chemical works, mining companies, and research institutes.[33]

Because national security was the country's central concern, cutting across all domestic and foreign policies, the ministry of defense emerged as one of the largest agencies. In recent years the defense ministry absorbed as much as 40 percent of the state budget and 20 percent of GNP. Its investments in industry, science, and technology influence the country's total economy. Military equipment exported through the defense ministry has become a major source of Israel's hard-earned foreign exchange, providing as much as 20 percent of foreign income from manufactured items. Military industries supervised by the defense ministry have also become one of the country's largest employers, and they are in the vanguard of scientific and technological development.[34]

Role of the Labor Establishment

Centralization of power and dominant influence of the public sector were enhanced during the 30-year reign of Labor by the intimate relationship with the Histadrut. It was not merely a trade union, but the country's largest social organization, its largest economic entrepreneur, and its largest employer, aside from government. By the 1970s more than half of all Israelis were members, participating with their families in some aspect of Histadrut activities. Ninety percent of the country's organized workers belonged to one or another of its affiliated trade unions. More than two-thirds of Israelis were insured by the federation's health fund. Nearly one in four laborers was employed by one of the Histadrut's economic enterprises. It owned and operated one of the major daily newspapers, and published several other leading periodicals. The cooperative sector of the economy, including the largest kibbutzim (collective settlements) and moshavim (cooperative settlements), were Histadrut affiliated. It owned the largest supermarket chain, the country's two major transportation companies, the largest construction company, a string of industries, banks, and Israel's largest insurance company.[35]

The power of the labor establishment was not only extensive, but also centralized through the interlocking directorate of Histadrut and party. There was frequent leadership interchange among Histadrut, the Labor Party, and government. During the first years several people rotated posts through the three establishments, which were really one. Secretaries-general of the Histadrut headed the Labor Party, and later were prime ministers or cabinet members.[36]

Likud promised to break up the centralization of political power and economic control. It planned to sell many of the large enterprises controlled by government and the Histadrut to the private sector and to foster competition with Histadrut services such as the health fund. Although Histadrut lost its quasiofficial status and has been relegated to one of many competing interest groups (still the largest by far), Begin's government has failed to break its hold on the most vital sectors of the economy. Nor has Likud been able to carry out promises to denationalize government-controlled enterprises like those operated by the ministries of development and defense. There were second thoughts about giving up government control of such vital companies as Israel Aircraft Industries, and insufficient concentrations of capital to take over others like Israel Chemicals.[37] If Likud should be defeated and the Labor establishment returned to power, a crucial question is, will the Alignment revitalize its traditional economic policies and will the Histadrut again attain a commanding role in the governing establishment?

The powerful role of government is derived from the country's Zionist credo, which assigns special responsibilities to the public sector. A major platform of every Zionist party is to encourage large-scale Jewish immigration. This requires strongly directive policies that lead to centralization of authority, extensive economic planning, and larger-than-normal public responsibility for social and economic welfare. A government that attempted to divest itself of these responsibilities would be unable to carry out the Zionist credo. When faced with responsibilities of power, the Begin government had to abandon many of its free enterprise concepts. In the words of one observer, its economic policies were Milton without Friedman.[38]

Centralization of policy often places management of diverse activities in a single ministry. Ministers run their establishments as fiefs, at times independently of what may be happening in other government departments, or even at cross-purposes with the prime minister. An unusually strong personality such as Ariel Sharon, minister of agriculture and later minister of defense in the Begin government, may extend his authority beyond the normal domain. As agriculture minister Sharon frequently made pronouncements about vast Jewish settlement schemes in the West Bank, although the proposals were not yet government policy. He often clashed with Defense Minister Weizman, who controlled the West Bank. Weizman was far more cautious about extending the network of Jewish outposts in heavily Arab-populated areas. Later when Sharon became defense minister, he continued to encourage settlements. Personality clashes in Begin's cabinet became so intense that the prime minister often played the role of peacemaker rather than policymaker among his ministers.

The minister of finance has traditionally been one of the most influential cabinet members because he controls the government's purse strings.[39] A strong finance minister can play a directive role by forcing other ministries to alter major programs or to modify their policies. Significant policy decisions are theoretically collective, with all cabinet ministers participating on an equal footing. However, a strong finance minister in collaboration with a powerful prime minister can use the power of the purse to direct national policy. All cabinet ministers must consult with the finance minister in preparing their budgets, even though they may fail to consult each other in determining policies of their departments. National defense has always had priority, receiving as much as 40 percent of the budget without discussion. Other ministries have had to struggle for the remaining 60 percent.

Role of the Public

The average Israeli participates in the system by voting in national and local elections for one of the many political parties. The voter has a much larger slate to select from than in most parliamentary democracies, and the system of proportional representation gives even the smallest faction (with at least

1 percent of the vote) a voice in the Knesset. Israel's press, one of the most diverse in the world, pays close attention to Knesset debates, so that even parties with one or two representatives receive coverage. Voters who are dissatisfied with the ruling establishment or the major political groupings can have the satisfaction of seeing their dissent recorded publicly in the Knesset or in the press. Most political groups have their own newspaper or other periodical, so that it is not difficult to determine the pulse of public opinion or to uncover dissent.[40] Military censorship still exists, and on occasion journalists have complained that the censors reached beyond their authority to excise political reportage that may cause embarrassment to the government.[41] However, it is not at all difficult to find the most critical commentary or reportage on events that embarrass the government in nearly every issue of the opposition press, and even in journals that support the establishment. After initial indecision, following the 1967 conquest the government permitted publication of several Arabic newspapers that had been anti-Israel in East Jerusalem. These newspapers continue to criticize the government.[42]

Under proportional representation, 13 parties won Knesset seats in the 1977 election. Only four won more than ten seats. The other parties were minority groups that were significant because they represented small but important segments of public opinion.

Political Parties

The four large blocs elected in 1977 — the Labor Alignment, Likud, DMC, and NRP — represented the three main trends of Israeli political orientation — Labor, center-nationalist, and religious. Labor, as we have seen, was traditionally the largest bloc. The current Labor Alignment is a coalition of the Israel Labor Party and Mapam. The Labor Party is itself an amalgam of several factions within the Labor movement, dominated by Mapai (Israel Workers' Party), the party of Ben-Gurion, Golda Meir, and Moshe Dayan.

Mapai was established in 1929 from socialist groups that founded the Histadrut nine years earlier. Until well after the establishment of Israel, Mapai's rhetoric was leftist, its flag — the red banner of the Socialist International — and its identification of Jewish national interests, with those of the working class. Control of the Histadrut gave Mapai an advantage over other parties. Other groups were later represented in the Labor federation, but most top offices were dominated by Mapai. Control of the Histadrut enabled Mapai to capture a large share of the vote through the Labor exchanges and by directing immigrant absorption. Mapai also became one of the strongest international Jewish groups through its command of influential posts in the World Zionist Organization and the Jewish Agency. For example, Mapai party leader Ben-Gurion was for many years chairman of the Jewish Agency, while Moshe Sharett (formerly Shertok) directed the agency's political department before he became

Israel's first foreign minister. From their key positions in the Jewish Agency, the World Zionist Organization, the Jewish National Council in Palestine, Histadrut, its affiliated trade unions, and the Haganah, Mapai leaders continued to control most of the top positions in the Jewish state.[43]

Many early Mapai leaders were Russian and Polish immigrants. A large number were members of the collective and cooperative agricultural settlements established during the prestate era. Until the mid-1960s Ben-Gurion was the uncontested leader of Mapai, a leader who might be compared to the patriarchial figure of de Gaulle in France, Nehru in India, or Nasser in Egypt.

Between 1965 and 1968 Ben-Gurion led a number of influential, younger Mapai leaders out of the party in protest against trends that they believed were corrupting the original ideology and undermining national development. The new faction, Rafi (Israel Labor List), included former chief of staff Moshe Dayan, and Shimon Peres, later to become prime minister. Rafi members believed that the Labor movement was compromising the welfare and security of the nation for short-term gains for the Israeli worker. They also took a more militant position on foreign policy and security issues. In 1969 Rafi rejoined the parent Mapai party, along with two other Labor groups, to form the Alignment for Unity of Israel's Workers. Later they all reunited into the Israel Labor Party.[44]

The second most influential group in the Labor party is Ahdut Ha'avoda (Unity of Labor). While traditionally more leftist in social and economic doctrines than Mapai, it also advocated a more activist and nationalist-oriented foreign policy. A higher percentage of its members were affiliated with the left wing of the socialist kibbutz movement. Many were active in the Palmach before and during the 1948 war. The Palmach won fame as an elite commando force, part of the Haganah, which was fully integrated into the new army of Israel in 1948. Ahdut Ha'avoda favored a policy of nonidentification in foreign affairs during the 1950s, active reprisals against Arab infiltration, and incorporation of all Palestine in a Jewish state. Yigal Allon, commander of the Palmach during the 1948 war, foreign minister and deputy prime minister under Rabin, was one of its leaders. Ahdut Ha'avoda was part of Mapam between 1948 and 1953.[45]

Mapam (United Workers Party), the most left-oriented faction in the Labor Alignment, still maintains a separate identity. Although it joined the alignment, its leaders have refused to become part of the Labor Party because of continued differences over domestic and foreign affairs. The core of Mapam is the Hashomer Hatzair (Young Guard) movement, founded in Eastern Europe as a revolutionary socialist group in 1927. It still maintains much of the original Marxist social doctrine, although its relations with the Soviet Union cooled considerably after Moscow shifted toward support for Arab regimes during the 1950s. Before 1948 Hashomer Hatzair was primarily a kibbutz movement. Opposed to partition, it advocated establishment of a binational Jewish-Arab state in which neither party would dominate the other. Hashomer Hatzair fused with Ahdut Ha'avoda and another small Marxist faction in 1948 to form the

Mapam Party, but differences over foreign policy led to the 1953 split when Ahdut Ha'avoda left Mapam.

After the first Knesset election, Mapam was the second largest party with 19 seats and 15 percent of the vote. Since then it has declined greatly as it passed through ideological, tactical, and political change. By 1965 it held only eight seats and 6.6 percent of the vote, forcing its leaders to join the Labor Alignment. The party lost strength because it was considered too doctrinaire by the growing middle class and insufficiently nationalist by the increasing number of Oriental Jewish voters. Long association with the Communist International and close ties with Moscow made it suspect in the eyes of many Israelis, especially after the break in relations between the Soviet Union and Israel.

Mapam has supported more conciliatory policies toward Israel's Arab citizens and toward a peace settlement with the surrounding Arab states. It opposed establishment of army control in Israel's Arab sectors before the military government was abolished in 1966. After 1967 it favored territorial concessions on the West Bank as part of an overall peace settlement. Many members of the Peace Now Movement established in 1977 came from Mapam; although it opposes recognition of the PLO as the sole representative of the Palestinians, it accepts the right of Palestinians to participate in determination of their political future.[46]

Shelli and Rakkah, the two parties in the Knesset to the left of Mapam, are not considered part of the Labor bloc, although both are represented in the Histadrut. Rakkah (Israel Communist List) represents the far-left opposition in parliament and is the most outspoken Knesset voice of Israeli Arab dissatisfaction.[47] Established in 1965 as a dissident faction of the Israel Communist party (Maki), it soon became the dominant Communist movement. The 1965 split was precipitated by disagreements among Communists over Soviet policy in the Middle East. Several Jewish leaders of Maki were disenchanted with increasing Soviet support for Arab policies, in contrast to Arab Communists who identified with Moscow. The Arab leadership, joined by a Jewish minority, left the party to form the New Communist List with a strong nationalist orientation. Rakkah labeled the 1967 war an act of Israeli aggression and advocated return of all captured territory. It has also supported establishment of a Palestinian state in Gaza and the West Bank. Its five Knesset members voted against the 1979 peace treaty because it neglected Palestinian rights.

Maki, the parent Communist organization, finally disintegrated into several factions. One joined non-Communist segments from Mapam to form the Moked (Focus) Party led by ex-army colonel, Meir Pail; it had one seat in the eighth Knesset. Pail joined several non-Communist groups to form the Shelli (Peace for Israel — Equality for Israel) Party, which won two seats in the 1977 election. Shelli calls for Israel's evacuation of all territories occupied in 1967 as part of a peace settlement, and for qualified negotiations with the PLO leading to establishment of a Palestinian state in Gaza and the West Bank. The party represents a cross-section of the independent left, including students, intellectuals, and kibbutz members disillusioned with the Labor movement. Several leaders of Shelli have met with PLO representatives in Europe, engaging the Palestinian organization in its first open dialogue with Zionists.[48]

There are a number of tiny leftist factions unrepresented in the Knesset. They include Maoists, Guevarists, and Trotskyites, many of them splinters from the Communists. The Israeli Socialist movement or Matzpen (Compass) calls itself revolutionary and anti-Zionist, in contrast to Rakkah, which is "non-Zionist." Matzpen's revolutionary socialists have splintered into at least five factions with a few dozen members in each. They were the first Jewish political groups in Israel to dialogue with the militant radicals of the Palestinian movement. During the 1960s and 1970s a few Jewish members of the revolutionary socialist factions were charged by Israeli intelligence with espionage on behalf of Syria.

During the late 1960s a number of Oriental Jewish youths attempted to form a movement to improve their status. Emulating American black militants, they called their movement the Israeli Black Panthers. Initially, they were apolitical, but as they gained visibility and support among many Orientals, the Panthers became politicized, and were regarded with some apprehension by many establishment figures. Quarrels among the leadership so disrupted the Panthers that by the 1973 elections one group split off to establish the Blue and White Panthers (based on the colors of the Israeli flag), assuming a more patriotic stance than their competitors. By 1977 the Panthers were divided among at least four parties: Zionist Panthers, Hofesh (Freedom), Shelli, and the Rakkah-supported Democratic Front for Peace and Equality.

The short-lived DMC emerged from the 1977 election as Israel's third largest political party. As noted earlier, the DMC represented dissatisfaction with the Labor movement by many middle-class voters. Its emphasis on electoral reform was not a high priority among voters according to public opinion polls, but DMC leaders believed that concentration of power by the governing Labor establishment could be broken if the electoral system, based on proportional representation, was changed. They argued that Knesset members chosen in an American-type electoral system would be less dependent on their party organizations, and more responsive to the constituents who elected them. Direct election of MKs by their constituents would break the throttlehold on political power of the entrenched parties and their leaders.

There were few major differences between the DMC and the large non-religious Zionist parties on other issues. Its program for a peace settlement and the future of the occupied territories resembled the Labor Party's approach. The domestic platform was even more ambiguous, borrowing proposals from both Labor and Begin's Likud. DMC was most decisive in its sharp criticism of the Histadrut.

Although the DMC emerged from the 1977 election as a significant political force, with almost 12 percent of the vote and 15 Knesset seats, it rapidly lost cohesiveness and influence. Its wide spectrum of leadership, from former Labor

Party leaders to Likud nationalists, soon were fighting among themselves about whether to support Begin. By 1980 there were at least five different Knesset factions that proliferated from the parent DMC, none of them strong enough to command a large public following. The founder of the party remained in Begin's cabinet but maintained loyalty from only three MKs in parliament. Another faction joined the opposition, and others shifted from issue to issue. The DMC lost its standing as a credible threat to the major parties; its ratings in public opinion polls almost fell to the vanishing point by 1980.

As we have indicated, the 1977 "earthquake" catapulted the Likud into power without substantially increasing its popular support. Immediately after the election, Begin's popularity soared as his image captured the public imagination. But Likud was also an amalgam of political groups with diverse social and economic orientations. Even the unifying plank of retaining Israel's 1967 conquests was insufficient to prevent bitter internal squabbles.

Likud's backbone was the Gahal bloc (Begin's Herut party plus the Liberals), an alliance forged in 1965 to strengthen the Liberals and to legitimize Herut, the largest party in the Likud bloc. Begin, often called "the commander" by his followers, established Herut in 1948 to replace his former Irgun Zvai Leumi (IZL – National Military Organization) when it was forced to integrate with Israel's defense forces by Ben-Gurion. An offshoot of Haganah, IZL was formed by Jewish dissidents who disagreed with Haganah's policies of restraint in the battles between the Yishuv and Palestine Arabs during the 1936-39 Arab revolt. Begin considered himself the political heir of Zeev Jabotinsky, founder and leader of the Revisionist movement established during the 1930s in opposition to the Zionist mainstream.[49]

The sharp disagreements between Begin and Ben-Gurion over tactics and strategy during the 1948 war caused nearly 20 years of bitterness during which the two men refused to make peace. Begin, considered by some Israelis a "terrorist" because of IZL actions during the 1948 war, was perceived by most of the Labor movement as "reactionary," and unacceptable as a partner in a coalition government until the 1970s. By joining the Liberals in 1965, Herut removed much of his political stigma; Herut was legitimized when Begin joined the wall-to-wall coalition on the eve of the 1967 war. The Liberals represented Israel's private business elite (Israel Manufacturers Association), independent farmers, and many middle-class voters concerned about the strong centralization of economic control under Labor. By joining Herut in 1965 the Liberals were probably rescued from obscurity.

Likud also included remnants of Ben-Gurion's old Rafi party and the Land of Israel or Greater Israel Movement, whose objective was to prevent return of any territories captured in 1967. However, by 1980 the Likud bloc was also disintegrating. It seemed that Begin had lost control of the diverse strands in the party; he even had difficulty with the militant nationalists in his own Herut organization, some of whom charged that he had betrayed Israel by signing the peace treaty.[50]

Support for the religious bloc has remained remarkably consistent, at between 12 and 15 percent of the electorate. Not all orthodox Jews support the religious parties. Many vote Labor, others back Likud, and a handful voted for Shelli. About a third of the Jewish population is considered orthodox, meaning that they strictly observe the sabbath, eat only kosher food, and maintain other orthodox religious customs and practices.

At times the four religious parties have been united in a parliamentary bloc – the United Religious Front. But more often the Zionist religious movement (Mizrachi) has its own candidates and the non-Zionist (formerly anti-Zionist) Aguda Israel parties keep their separate identity. The Mizrachi movement, from the Hebrew, *Mercaz Ruhani* (Spiritual Center), was one of the first Zionist factions formed to resist the secular tendencies of the Labor movement and the mainstream of Zionism early in the century. On issues other than religion the Mizrachi parties, later called the National Religious Party, compromised with Labor and joined most Labor cabinets since 1948. With 9 or 10 percent of the vote, the NRP is now the third largest political grouping. By joining government coalitions, the religious parties have maintained their control over Jewish religious observance in Israel. They control the administration of laws related to marriage and divorce, public observance of the sabbath, and maintenance of strict kashrut in public institutions such as the army. They perceive themselves as the bulwark against secularist trends in Israel, as the link between traditional Judaism and the state, and the defenders of Israel's Jewish character.

During the era of Labor-controlled coalitions, the religious parties usually followed the prime minister's lead on foreign policy. After 1967, the NRP adopted a harder line. The leaders, supported by the chief rabbinate, took the position that no part of biblical Israel under government control should be surrendered, even in exchange for peace. Some rabbis maintained that it would be a sin to return Jewish-held parts of the Holy Land to non-Jews. In exchange for NRP support, Begin intensified official implementation of legislation imposing orthodox interpretations on such matters as citizenship, education, definition of "who is a Jew," and marriage and divorce. Despite the very cordial relationship that developed between Begin and the NRP, by 1980 there were reports in the Israeli press that the orthodox leaders were sounding out the Labor Party about possibilities of collaboration in a new Labor coalition.[51]

INTEREST GROUPS

Interest groups in Israel express themselves mainly through the party system. There are no powerful lobbies with large amounts of money like those in Washington. Citizen groups that desire to influence legislation or government policy usually attempt to exert pressure through political parties. Orthodox Jews are represented not only in the religious parties, but also as a faction within the Labor movement. Retired military officers have their own lobbying groups in both Labor and Likud. Private farmers and industrialists are represented by the Israel Citrus Growers Association and by the Manufacturers Association, with input through the Liberal wing of the Gahal bloc in Likud. Many parties have associations of new immigrants, veterans, educators, women, and youth.

Two groups organized since the 1967 war have attempted to influence foreign policy outside the usual party route, although both also have a following that cuts across the political spectrum. Gush Emunim (Bloc of the Faithful) is a group of Israeli Jews who oppose surrender of territory acquired during the 1967 war. They pursue an activist policy of Jewish settlement in the West Bank, at times in opposition to the government. Shalom Acshav (Peace Now), at the other end of the hawk-dove spectrum, opposed Jewish settlement in the occupied territories and favors territorial compromise as part of a peace settlement.

Gush Emunim

Gush Emunim was established by a group of young activists within the NRP who opposed the wavering policies of the Labor party between 1967 and 1977.[52] They believed that Labor's ambivalence toward Jewish settlement in the West Bank would end in loss of the territory. Therefore, they decided to establish new settlements in areas largely inhabited by West Bank Arabs to preempt the region before a peace settlement. Several of their West Bank settlements were established without approval of the Labor government, leading to skirmishes between Gush Emunim and the Israel army. Gush Emunim's leaders asserted that the settlements were established, not primarily for security reasons, but because God gave the land to the Jews.

When Begin assumed office, relations between Gush Emunim and the government improved. Later, some cabinet ministers deplored Gush Emunim's unilateral actions in the West Bank, charging that they undermined government authority.[53] By 1979, however, several cabinet members and a number of Likud MKs were converted to the Gush Emunim philosophy, and the Begin government moved closer to the group's program for annexation of the West Bank. While overt annexation was not Begin's stated policy (except for Arab Jerusalem, which was officially annexed in 1980),[54] most of his pronouncements and policies pointed toward that ultimate objective.

Kach (Thus), led by Meir Kahane, an American rabbi, leader of the Jewish Defense League in the United States, and advocate of forceful retaliation against the enemies of Israel, was a militant faction to the right of Gush Emunim. Although Kahane commanded only a few hundred followers and was unable to win enough votes in the 1973 or 1977 elections for a single Knesset seat, he attracted wide public attention and caused much concern among officials. Kahane urged all Jews to settle in Israel, and encouraged the Arabs to leave. His concept of greater Israel extended from the Sinai in Egypt to the Euphrates in Syria. This was the land bestowed upon the people of Israel by God, according to the Bible, thus it all belonged to the Jewish state. While small in numbers with negligible political support, Kach became a significant pressure group; its radical stance made less militant groups like Gush Emunim seem relatively moderate.

Peace Now

Peace Now emerged from the protest movements formed by veterans after the 1973 war. Most of the leaders were young reserve officers who were disillusioned with the government's failure to attain a comprehensive peace settlement. They charged that Israel's leaders were squandering opportunities for a settlement by their refusal to recognize changes occurring in Arab society after 1967, by the adamant refusal of government to make territorial concessions in exchange for peace, and by refusal to recognize the significance of the Palestinian nationalist revival.

Peace Now supported the Egyptian-Israeli peace treaty, but saw it as "only the beginning of a process and not the end."[55] Without resolving the Palestinian dilemma, it would be impossible to achieve peace, they asserted. Initially, the movement was cautious; its program was based on broad principles rather than specifics. As it gained a wider following and increased political momentum, it began to focus on several definite objectives and criticisms of the government. Peace Now called for an end to Jewish settlement on the West Bank and in Gaza, and more rapid termination of the occupation, perceived as

> a corrupting influence on our society. It is a disgrace to Zionism. We cannot feel free while we rule another people, especially because we are Jews. . . . "Peace Now" . . . stands for *sane* Zionism, for the Zionism that bases itself on the ethical right of every people to national self-expression . . . [it] believes that the peace process is not just for peace, but also necessary for the maintenance of the democratic character of Israeli society.[56]

Peace Now had a following among youth, army veterans, university students, intellectuals, and many members of Hashomer Hatzair kibbutzim. On a number of issues there was a convergence of views between Peace Now and Shelli. While not a membership organization, it was able to rally some of the largest public protest meetings ever organized in Israel, numbering tens of thousands.[57]

Peace Now considered itself Gush Emunim's "most powerful enemy," and a major obstacle to seizure of Arab lands and to Jewish settlement on the West Bank.[58] Strong opposition to Gush Emunim won it followers from several political parties. Therefore, it sought to avoid close identification with any single Knesset faction. Its supporters even included a small faction from NRP called Shalom v'Oz (Peace and Strength), whose followers argued that the militant nationalist orientation of Gush Emunim was a perversion of Judaism.

Histadrut

By far the largest and most influential interest group is the Histadrut. Until 1977 its quasiofficial status, achieved by virtue of an interlocking directorate with the Labor Party, gave it direct access to government. At times the trade union leaders in the Histadrut differed with the Labor government's domestic policies, but there were seldom disagreements on foreign affairs. Indeed, the Labor government saw the Histadrut as a useful adjunct in furthering certain foreign-policy objectives. The Histadrut served the government by offering training courses and seminars to Labor leaders, women's groups, and other such organizations from Africa, Latin America, and Asia. It also sent many experienced Jewish technicians on official missions to developing countries with which Israel was attempting to create closer ties. The construction companies of the Histadrut accepted contracts from developing countries, not only for their economic benefit, but also to assist the Labor government in building bridges to the third world.[59]

With the defeat of Labor and Likud's ascent to power, the Histadrut lost its quasiofficial status. It became part of the opposition, with a status similar to that of trade union movements in Western countries where labor is not part of the government. Despite Begin's turn toward the right, the Histadrut still serves the government in foreign affairs by maintaining contact with labor movements in the United States and Western Europe.

The Press

Until a few years ago, much of the press in Israel represented the viewpoints of the major political parties. Nearly every party had its own daily newspaper or periodical. In recent years, a strong independent press has emerged to challenge the party publications.[60] The country has one of the highest rates of newspaper and book readership in the world.[61] There are some two dozen dailies, about half of them published in Hebrew, the others in more than a half dozen European languages and in Arabic. The English-language daily, *Jerusalem Post*, is influential in the diplomatic community and among English-speaking immigrants. It has a large clientele abroad, especially in the United States and in Great Britain. Until 1977 the *Jerusalem Post* had a semiofficial status, often presenting the Labor government's perspective on events.

Israel's most prestigious daily is the independent *Ha-Aretz*. It has an international reputation for high journalistic standards, extensive coverage, and a large staff of excellent writers, editors, and columnists. *Ha-Aretz* prints lengthy discussions by columnists of all opinions, and its debates are frequently influential in government.

Although the two mass-circulation dailies, *Ma'ariv* and *Yediot Aharonot*, are independent, the publishers and chief editors tend toward conservative domestic and hawkish foreign policies. However, both papers open their columns to dissenting viewpoints. Many of Israel's most dovish writers, political dissidents, and satirists can be found in the pages of these two papers.

One of the most persistent critics of the political and social scene has been the weekly magazine *Ha'Olam Ha-Zeh* ("This World"), published by Israel's political maverick, Uri Avnery. The journal combines sex and sensationalism with political muckraking that has led to exposure of many a scandal. Its brazen independence made it the target of official pressures, with the result that the editor decided to run for the Knesset to avoid government interference. Avneri has been a vocal opposition voice in parliament, and his magazine has successfully weathered censorship, physical attacks on the editor, and bombing of its offices.

The Arabic press in Israel, especially the East Jerusalem dailies that were formerly in Jordan, persistently criticize the government for policies in the West Bank. The East Jerusalem press now is the only overt expression of Palestinian nationalism published in Israel and is read by the country's Arab population. It plays an important role in galvanizing Arab sentiment in Israel and in the occupied areas.[62]

All dispatches of Israeli and foreign correspondents are subject to military censorship, officially confined to security matters.[63] The army censor's ruling can be appealed before a three-person committee representing the military, the association of newspaper editors, and the public. Journalists have collectively protested that on occasion army censors interpret "security" too broadly, excising politically sensitive items. After Begin assumed office in 1977, his new advisor on overseas information asked the press to adopt a set of "semantic corrections" in terminology related to the occupied territories. He requested that the term "West Bank" be replaced by the biblical designations "Judea and Samaria," and that "annexation" be called "incorporation." Israeli journalists as well as the government radio and television editors resented the interference and disdainfully rejected the proposed "corrections."[64]

Israel's political leaders follow the press closely. They regard it as a useful barometer of influential public opinion. From following the press, it is possible to determine positions of the various parties, to sound out dissident criticism, and to find innovative propositions for dealing with difficult problems. Press revelations of bureaucratic mismanagement and corruption put government officials and political leaders on their guard. Along with the court system and the official ombudsman, the press is a vital defender of the public interest and the rights of the individual citizen, Jewish or non-Jewish.

The Military

Officially, the military in Israel is subordinate to civil authority; the civilian minister of defense has the final word on military affairs. Major decisions affecting foreign policy are made by the cabinet, whose ministerial committee on security and defense gives detailed consideration to foreign-policy matters. The army chief of staff has on occasion participated in cabinet meetings, but under Likud Defense Minister Ezer Weizman the practice was ended. In times of crisis the chief of staff is likely to have more input in decision making, but his influence is not always dominant. There have been many occasions, such as on the eve of the Six-Day War in 1967, when eagerness of the military to initiate a campaign was overruled by the civilian cabinet ministers.[65]

There is no entrenched bureaucracy in the upper ranks of the military, thanks to the policy of rapid upward promotion for gifted officers and a relatively short tenure in senior ranks before retirement at an early age. A strong affinity exists between the military and the civil population; universal conscription has exposed most men and a large number of women to military service. A high percentage of the most important cabinet posts have been held by former officers or generals. Prime Minister Rabin was chief of staff during the 1967 war, and Begin was commander to the IZL, although their civil decisions seem to have been influenced less by former military associations than by political considerations.

Since 1948 there has been little evidence of a "military mentality" influencing Israeli foreign policies. Of course, the top command always attempts to acquire sufficient resources and a substantial share of the budget to provide the forces with the latest weapons and infrastructure to carry out its mission. Politically, the army and the general staff have represented a wide spectrum of views. An exceptionally high percentage of officers, between a fourth and a third, have come from the kibbutzim and moshavim, although their population is less than 8 percent of Israel's total.[66]

A survey of 75 senior officers (colonel and above) who retired between 1950 and 1973 showed that about a third became senior executives in industrial and economic institutions, a fourth worked for the defense ministry and defense-related institutions, over 10 percent became senior officials in government or in public institutions, 10 percent worked for political parties, and the rest were involved in university teaching, research, administration, or work in the foreign service.[67]

Surveys also showed that Israeli officers hardly constitute a distinctive ideological bloc. More than half voted for the Labor Alignment in 1965. Nearly two-thirds were either liberal or moderate in attitudes related to nationalism, economics, state and religion, and democracy.[68] In a 1972 survey, retired senior officers expressed a greater willingness to make territorial concessions for peace than the civilian population.[69] The diversity is reflected in the hawk/dove spectrum of views on foreign and security policies. Relative moderation of top officers was demonstrated during Begin's tenure as prime minister. Three former generals in his first cabinet — Yadin, the deputy prime minister, Foreign Minister Dayan, and Minister of Defense Weizman — were willing to make concessions for a comprehensive peace settlement. Their moderate views often placed them at odds with militant nationalists in the cabinet who never held top military commands. Disputes over the government's tough stand in the autonomy negotiations with Egypt led to resignation of Dayan and Weizman in 1979 and 1980. On the other hand, former General Ariel Sharon was the prototype of the nationalist hard-liner who insisted that the government intensify Jewish settlement in the occupied territories even though it seemed to threaten the peace negotiations.

Ethnic Interest Groups

Attempts to establish Jewish political groups on the basis of national ethnicity have been singularly unsuccessful in Israel. Only in the first Knesset did four Sephardim and one Yemenite win seats as representatives of ethnic parties. Since then, attempts to rally support for political groups or leaders on the basis of ethnic separation have failed.[70] Even the Black Panther movement disintegrated after a few years, not only because of divisiveness among its leaders, but also because ethnicity was an inadequate basis for capturing Jewish votes in Israel.[71] Most political parties make ethnic appeals for votes, and several of them have ethnic sections; perhaps in election campaigns they neutralize each other. Associations representing Jews from Arab countries and of Sephardic origin attempt to influence all the major parties, rather than supporting only one.[72] When Jews from Arab countries demanded reparations for the property they left behind, they won support from all the Zionist parties.

The Sephardic Community Council in Jerusalem has been an active proponent of minority rights and has often taken liberal positions on foreign policy. It supported efforts to encourage Jewish immigration from Muslim lands, demanded compensation for Jewish property left behind, and urged diplomatic relations with Spain. After the 1967 war some of the Jerusalem Sephardic leaders became identified with "dovish" views on political compromise with the Arab states; a few called for recognition of Palestinian Arab national rights and negotiations with the Palestinians to attain peace.[73]

The Arab minority in Israel is a distinctive ethnic interest group with its own foreign-policy orientation and outlook. Even Arab representatives in the Knesset, who for years were controlled by the Labor Party, occasionally spoke out to support payment of compensation for Arab lands requisitioned by the Israel government or to urge reunion of Arab families separated by the 1948 war. The Israel Communist movement has been outspoken in its support of Arab claims and interests, and to a large extent was the surrogate of Arab nationalism in Israel. After 1967, as Israeli Arabs established closer direct ties with Arabs in the West Bank, they became increasingly radicalized on national issues. Arab citizens began to identify with aspirations and goals of Palestinians elsewhere, and Arabs elsewhere have now included Israel's Arabs as members of the larger Palestinian community. International events also strengthened ties between Israel's Arabs and Palestinians outside the country. Growing recognition of the PLO by the third world, the United Nations, and Western Europe, the spate of U.N. resolutions recognizing the PLO as the legitimate representative of the Palestinian people, PLO leader Yasser Arafat's appearance before the international organization, and the General Assembly resolution condemning Zionism as racist, all helped to create an aura of legitimacy around the Palestinian cause.[74]

Observations by Israeli sociologists have indicated that there is growing polarization between the political attitudes of Israeli Arabs and Jews. A recent survey showed that nearly 60 percent of the Israeli Arabs questioned believed that the term "Palestinian" described them best; some 70 percent felt that there was a distinct contradiction between being identified as Israeli and as Palestinian. Even Arabs who considered themselves Israeli had ambivalent feelings about Israel's role as a Jewish Zionist state. Nearly two-thirds of those questioned in the sample perceived Zionism as racist and attacked Israeli legislation such as the Law of Return, which gives Jewish immigrants preference over others. These differences in perception have created sharp clashes in attitudes toward foreign policy. Whereas the Arab minority strongly supports the Palestinian nationalist movement, with many backing the PLO, whereas they urge repatriation of Arab refugees who left the country in 1948, and whereas they favor partition of the country, most Israeli Jews have diametrically opposed views − they regard the PLO as a subversive terrorist group, oppose partition, and adamantly resist return of the refugees.[75]

These opposing viewpoints have embittered relations between the Arab minority and the Jewish majority. The differences tend to become ideologized so that sympathizers of one view become anathema to their ideological opponents. Issues such as Jerusalem, the return of the refugees, and the Palestinians are regarded as touchstones of loyalty to the state by many Jewish Israelis; for Israeli Arabs, however, they are often questions of the most intimate family concern.

Diaspora Jewry

Diaspora Jewry has intimate ties with Israel; it is at times the object of foreign policy, and at other times the subject. This relationship was expressed by Ben-Gurion when he told the twenty-fifth World Zionist Congress in 1960 that "the state of Israel was not established for its citizens alone. It is the foremost bulwark for the survival of the Jewish people in our generation."[76] World

Jewry has an important stake in Israel, so much so that many Jews in the diaspora consider Israel's ambassadors their ambassadors, Israel's diplomatic missions their representatives, and Israel's struggle for survival their own struggle. Jewish contributions and financial support through organizations such as the American United Jewish Appeal and the sale of Israel's bonds have been invaluable assets in development of the country. The political clout of large Jewish communities in the United States and in Great Britain has raised the importance of Israel to the highest priority among Western governments. Not only are the Jews of the diaspora considered part of Israel's constituency, but in some cases Israel is considered a constituency of diaspora communities. Government policy toward Israel thus figures as an important issue in U.S. presidential elections and in many local campaigns.[77]

The assistance of American Jews has been critical in making it possible for Israel to receive more economic and military aid from the U.S. government than any other country does. The concentration of Jews in certain strategic electoral districts in the United States is instrumental in influencing policy in Washington on the Palestinians, on peace negotiations between Israel and the Arab states, on the U.S. position regarding Jerusalem, and on other key Middle East issues.[78]

Diaspora Jewry has input into Israel's foreign and domestic policies through the World Zionist Organization and through the Jewish Agency. Representatives to the periodic congresses of the World Zionist Organization are elected by members of Zionist groups in many different countries, most of them affiliated with political parties in Israel. In the United States the Israel Labor Party is affiliated with the Zionist Labor movement, Likud is affiliated with the Zionist Organization of America, Mapam with Americans for Progressive Israel, and the National Religious Party with the American Mizrachi movement. The various Israeli parties make their needs known to diaspora Jewry through these affiliates, and the Israeli government informs world Jewry of its requirements for funds, for Jewish immigrants, and for political support.[79]

While Zionists in the diaspora can influence the Israeli political system, in practice the Israeli government usually determines the nature of the contacts. The dominant role of Israel in this relationship is facilitated by the large numbers of Israelis on the executive and in the administrative apparatus of the World Zionist Organization and in the Jewish Agency.

Size, extensive organizational apparatus, positions of influence, and affluence have given American Jewry a unique relationship with Israel. Dozens of American organizations, both Jewish and other, have special ties, from those emphasizing religious or cultural themes to general fund-raising organizations. Many ties are informal, others are institutionalized in written agreements. Some are Zionist, others are non-Zionist. Several American labor unions have direct links with the Histadrut, and at the same time are in a strong position to influence positions of politicians in the United States on issures related to Israel.[80]

The American Israel Public Affairs Committee (AIPAC) in Washington, D.C. is one of the capital's more influential lobbies. Financed and supported by diverse American Jewish groups, it has access to and frequently influences members of the U.S. Senate and House of Representatives on matters related not only to Israel, but also to the whole Middle East.[81]

ISSUE AREAS

Until Sadat's visit to Jerusalem in November 1977, Israel's foreign policy was based on the assumption that "the Arabs won't make peace." All foreign and many domestic policies were derived from this fundamental perception. The common Israeli belief that the Arab states were seeking to destroy them led to the all-pervasive preoccupation with national security. Most political leaders argued that concessions on key issues such as territory, the Arab refugees, Jerusalem, and military retaliation would undermine security; therefore, maintenance of the status quo was Israel's only alternative in the face of Arab intransigence. Sadat's visit and the subsequent Camp David peace process modified some of these perceptions and altered policies.[82]

Territory

Because Israel has been at war with its Arab neighbors since independence, its borders have never received formal international recognition. The territorial concept of Israel differs not only in the international community, but even among Israelis themselves.

According to the 1947 United Nations partition proposal, accepted by Israel and the majority of U.N. members at the time but rejected by the Arab states and several of their sympathizers, the territory of Israel was to have been approximately 6,000 square miles. The rest of mandatory Palestine was to be divided into an Arab state and an international enclave including Jerusalem and Bethlehem. The U.N. plan also called for economic union between the partitioned parts of the former mandate.

The plan was never implemented. Before the British departed in May 1948, civil war erupted between the country's Jewish and Arab populations. After Israel declared its independence in May, the surrounding Arab states declared war on the Jewish state, joining Palestinian guerrilla forces in opposing partition. Israeli forces extended territory under their control by some 2,000 square miles beyond the partition frontiers. The armistice demarcation lines separating Israel from Lebanon, Syria, Jordan, and Egypt were based on territory held by the respective combatants at the end of the fighting in 1948-49.

Jerusalem never became an international enclave. Instead, it was divided by the Israeli-Jordanian armistice agreement into a Jewish and a Jordanian Arab sector. The West Bank also remained under Jordanian control. According to the Israeli-Egyptian armistice agreement, the Gaza Strip remained under Cairo, although it was never annexed by Egypt. The Israeli-Syrian armistice agreement fixed the frontier at approximately the border separating mandatory Palestine from Syria. Small enclaves in Palestine held by the Syrian army at the end of the war remained disputed, becoming the subject of continual quarreling over the next two decades. The border with Lebanon was fixed by the Israeli-Lebanese armistice agreement along the old frontier between mandatory Palestine and Lebanon.

For the next 20 years Israel accepted the armistice frontiers as the basis for territorial settlement. Although these borders were considered strategically difficult to manage, they were significantly larger than those in the 1947 partition plan. The Arab states, however, refused to recognize the armistice frontiers; they demanded that Israel return to the partition borders. All Arab states refused to accept Israel's hold on West Jerusalem. With the exception of Jordan, which declared the city, along with the rest of the West Bank, to be part of the Hashemite Kingdom, most Arabs insisted on internationalization of Jerusalem according to the partition plan. No other nation recognized Israel's armistice frontiers as definitive, and the question of territory remained in limbo. Various proposals were made by Western countries for a settlement to include territorial concessions by Israel. At one time Anthony Eden, the British foreign secretary, suggested a peace in which Israel would surrender the Negev, which would have meant the loss of about half its territory and access to the Gulf of Aqaba.

The situation changed dramatically as a result of the 1967 war when Israel seized all Arab-held Palestine, including the West Bank, Jerusalem and Gaza, the Egyptian Sinai peninsula, the Saudi islands of Sinafir and Tiran, and the Syrian Golan Heights. Between 1967 and 1973 the Labor government emphasized security in its approach to the territorial question. Prime Minister Rabin asserted that Israel would return nearly all Sinai in exchange for a genuine peace, although he insisted that Israel should be allowed to control Sharm el-Sheikh, the strategic point at the entrance to the Gulf of Aqaba. It was also assumed that Sharm el-Sheikh would be linked by a road to the Negev.[83]

Most major political groups also insisted on control of the Golan Heights for security reasons. Return of the area to Syria, it was argued, would give the Syrians a vantage point to attack Jewish settlements in the valley below. Jewish settlers in the north were a vocal pressure group, insisting that the Golan Heights remain with Israel lest the settlers again be exposed to Syrian attack. The Heights also were important because they controlled the headwaters of the Jordan River system from which Israel draws most of its scarce water supplies. Conquest of the Golan aborted an Arab League plan to diminish the flow of streams into the upper Jordan; it was meant to deprive Israel of a major economic asset. From 1967 to 1973 Labor preempted the future of Golan by establishing several Jewish settlements there and by encouraging the remnant of the Syrian Druze community to cut its ties with Damascus.[84]

Policy toward Gaza was somewhat more ambivalent. Although the area was not annexed, the Labor government stated that Gaza would never be returned to Egypt because of its strategic location. The Strip reached up the coast to within a few miles of Israel's most thickly populated and most heavily industrialized areas. However, Gaza's Arab population, especially the large number of unemployed refugees, caused many in the Labor movement to hesitate about incorporating the region into Israel.

The future of the West Bank and Jerusalem caused the greatest controversy, however. Arab Jerusalem was incorporated into Israel by the Labor government a few weeks after the 1967 victory, although there were legal ambiguities about the status of the city that have not yet been totally resolved.[85] The future of the West Bank caused anxiety among Labor Party leaders. Its large population, combined with the Arabs of Gaza and Israel's own Arab minority, made a total of 1.5 million Palestinians under Israeli control. Their unusually high birth rate would lead to an Arab majority in less than a century.[86]

But policymakers were reluctant to give up control of the whole West Bank, or even a major part, because of security. While the Labor Party opposed outright annexation, it insisted that the area remain under Israeli security control, meaning that there would be free movement for the armed forces in the area.[87] While not adopted as formal policy, the "Allon Plan" seemed to become the basis of Labor's approach. The plan foresaw a string of Jewish settlements in the lightly populated Jordan Valley, close to the banks of the river. Establishment of these settlements would not interfere with the indigenous population, nor would it make Israel responsible for the day-to-day governance of the West Bank Arabs. Allon proposed restoration of some self-government to West Bank Arabs concentrated in towns and villages between the Jordan River and the 1967 Israeli-Jordanian armistice frontier. Some politicians described the Jordan River as Israel's "security border" in contrast to the 1967 "political border."[88] Another version was proposed by Labor Party leader Shimon Peres, who advocated a federation or common market among Israel, the West Bank, and any other adjoining Arab entity, especially Jordan.[89]

None of the major Israeli political parties would countenance establishment of an independent Palestinian state on the West Bank or in Gaza. They all argued that a separate Palestinian state would be dominated by the PLO and would fall under control of the Soviet Union.[90] Only Rakkah and Shelli supported establishment of a Palestinian state in the occupied territories; a few dovish members of the Labor Alignment also were amenable to the idea.[91]

After Likud took power in 1977, the emphasis on Israel's historic connections with the West Bank increased. While security was still the paramount consideration, an intense campaign was developed to demonstrate that Jerusalem and the West Bank were integral parts of Israel's historical heritage. The Allon Plan was jettisoned, and Jewish settlement in such heavily Arab-populated areas as Hebron and Nablus was encouraged.[92] A law was passed in the Knesset that formally declared that Jerusalem was Israel's eternal and indivisible capital.

Begin's government was subjected to pressures from the militant nationalists of his Herut Party to also annex the entire West Bank, Gaza, and the Golan Heights. Annexation would have been consistent with Begin's own Revisionist ideology, based on incorporation of all mandatory Palestine into the Jewish state, but international objections to unilateral territorial decisions by Israel deterred him.

The Egyptian-Israeli Peace Treaty signed in March 1979 made no specific reference to the territorial issue in the West Bank and Gaza, but in a joint letter (accompanying the treaty) to President Carter from Sadat and Begin, the Israeli and Egyptian governments agreed to open negotiations on the subject. The autonomy negotiations were to be concluded "within one year so that elections will be held as expeditiously as possible after agreement has been reached between the parties."[93] By May 1980 it was clear that the differences separating Egypt and Israel over the future of the West Bank and Gaza were so great that agreement was unlikely.

Egypt's objective was to attain self-determination for the Palestinian population in Gaza and the West Bank, leading to either an independent state or an entity governed by Palestinians in cooperation with Jordan.[94] Israel interpreted autonomy quite narrowly to mean some form of local government in which the Arabs would manage their own schools, sanitation, municipal traffic, and street lighting. The proposed autonomous entity would have no say in foreign affairs, security, or in allocation of water and land on the West Bank. Jewish settlements would remain under Israeli control rather than under authority of the autonomous government.[95]

Jerusalem

The Jerusalem dilemma is closely related to the territorial issue. The international status of the city has been ambiguous since 1948, when the United Nations was unable to implement the partition resolution that called for internationalization. Within the walled sector of Jerusalem's Old City are sites sacred to the three monotheistic faiths — Judaism, Christianity, and Islam. The Church of the Holy Sepulchre is believed to contain the tomb of Jesus. The Dome of the Rock, al-Aksa Mosque, and Harem ash-Sherif constitute Islam's third most holy site after Mecca and Medina. They are linked with Muhammad's mystical night journey mentioned in the Qur'an. The Wailing Wall adjoins the mosques; it is believed to be a remnant of the Jewish temple destroyed by the Romans during their conquest of Palestine, and is considered by many Jews as the most holy site of Judaism.

During the mandate, many of the quarrels between Jews and Arabs erupted over incidents related to these sites. Thus, the United Nations sought to place Jerusalem under an international authority rather than give it to a Jewish or Arab state. But the U.N. plan was frustrated by the 1948 war that divided

Jerusalem between Israeli and Jordanian control. The Old City with its important relics remained in Arab hands. The Jordanians evicted all Jews from the Old City, and it remained off limits for them until Israel captured it in 1967.

Since 1967 the United Nations has adopted numerous resolutions disapproving Israeli annexation and efforts to change the status of the city. Israeli archaeological work, construction of new Jewish housing, evacuation of Arab residents and destruction of Arab houses, and Jewish settlement in the city have all been condemned. Most nations that have diplomatic relations with Israel refused to recognize Jerusalem as the capital, and maintained their embassies in Tel Aviv, the country's first capital. The United States refused to recognize either East Jerusalem, the Arab sector captured in 1967, or West Jerusalem, the Jewish sector taken in 1948, as definitively Israeli. The American consulate general in Jerusalem, with offices in both Jewish and Arab sectors, has never been under jurisdiction of the embassy in Tel Aviv, but reports directly to the State Department in Washington.

Israel's position is that Jerusalem is the heart of Zion. To be deprived of the Holy City would subvert the morale and raison d'être of the Jewish state. The Labor government accepted the partition plan, but by 1950 Ben-Gurion decided to move the capital from Tel Aviv to West Jerusalem. At first many governments refused to recognize the move, and forbade their envoys from conducting official business in Jerusalem. Gradually resistance was softened, so that by 1967 many ambassadors were commuting between their embassies in Tel Aviv and the Israeli foreign office in Jerusalem.

After 1967, the entire city was declared an integral part of Israel. However, the status of the 70,000 Arab inhabitants of East Jerusalem remained ambiguous. A few accepted the offer to become Israeli citizens, but the overwhelming majority refused to acknowledge the conquest. Only a small number of East Jerusalem Arabs participated in municipal elections when they voted as residents rather than as Israeli citizens. No country has recognized Israel's annexation, and moves to integrate it into the Jewish state were regarded as a violation of international law.

After 1977 the Begin government increased the pace of integration and stepped up the rhetoric that asserted that Jerusalem would remain forever the capital of the Jewish state. Begin stated Israel's position during the Camp David discussions in a letter to President Carter, declaring that "the government of Israel decreed in July 1967 that Jerusalem is one city indivisible, the capital of the state of Israel." Although Sadat was willing to accept unification of the East and West sectors, he insisted, in a similar letter to Carter, that "Arab Jerusalem is an integral part of the West Bank . . . [and that] Arab Jerusalem should be under Arab sovereignty."[96] Discussion about the future of Jerusalem was avoided in the peace treaty, but it became a focal point of the autonomy negotiations because the Egyptians regarded it as part of the West Bank territory under discussion.[97]

Begin attempted to circumvent a head-on collision with Egypt over Jerusalem, but was pushed toward confrontation by militants in his Herut Party.

They insisted that Israel assert its claims to the city and that there be no ambiguity about the future. In an attempt to force Begin's hand, a bill was introduced in the Knesset during 1980 declaring all Jerusalem (both East and West) the capital, although for all practical purposes this had been government policy since July 1967. Public sentiment forced even critics of Begin's policies to support the bill, and it was overwhelmingly passed. The law merely reiterated already-existing policy. Whereas the July 1967 Knesset legislation authorized the appropriate minister to include Jerusalem within the law, jurisdiction, and administration of the state, the 1980 law explicitly stated that "complete and united Jerusalem is the capital of Israel."

The new legislation changed nothing, but it elicited an outburst of criticism from nearly every member of the United Nations. The Muslim nations urged punitive measures against Israel, and called on Turkey, the last Muslim state to maintain diplomatic ties with Israel, to sever its connections. A U.N. Security Council resolution called on the 13 nations with embassies in the city to remove them. To express its disapproval of the Jerusalem law, the United States abstained on the Security Council vote rather than vote against it. However, Secretary of State Edmund Muskie demonstrated an evenhanded approach by decrying the spate of "unbalanced and unrealistic" resolutions that damaged prospects for Middle East peace. The new law further inflamed relations between Egypt and Israel, which were already aggravated by Begin's West Bank policies.

The Palestinians

The Palestinian issue was belatedly recognized in Israel as important for achieving peace. But Israelis were not alone in overlooking the significance of the Palestinians. Until 1967 the issue was labeled by most governments as a refugee problem, and as such it was on the annual agenda of the U.N. General Assembly at every session since 1948. About half the Palestinians were refugees in the countries surrounding Israel — Jordan, Egypt, Syria, and Lebanon.

Israel's position after 1948 was that the refugee flight was instigated by Arab leaders, that Israel bore no responsibility for them, and that the solution for their plight could be found in resettlement in underdeveloped areas of the surrounding countries. The whole problem was a consequences of Arab aggression in 1948, Israel argued, and therefore full responsibility for their fate fell on the aggressors. Except for a token number, the refugees could not be permitted to return because they were a security threat, a foreign element in the body politic, and their assets had been absorbed into the Jewish economy. Israel stated willingness to pay compensation for lands and property left behind during the flight in 1948, but payments would have to be balanced against claims of Jewish refugees from Arab countries and war reparations paid to Israel. Additional tens of thousands of refugees fled from the West Bank during the 1967 war; most were not permitted to return to their homes or refugee camps because they too were perceived as a threat to security; their future would also await a peace settlement.

Reorganization of the PLO, increased activity by Arab guerrillas, and the growing international importance of the Palestinian nationalist movement after 1967 focused attention on the problem and thrust it into the forefront of issues facing Israel. At the international level, the Palestinian refugee question was transformed into a political-national problem. The number of non-Arab nations recognizing the PLO as spokesman for the Palestinians increased until the large majority of U.N. members invited the organization to participate in deliberations of the General Assembly. In November 1974 the General Assembly granted the PLO observer status and invited it to participate in sessions and work of all international conferences convened under General Assembly auspices, or the auspices of other U.N. organs. By 1980 the cause of Palestinian nationalism was espoused by nearly every member of the United Nations, with the exceptions of the United States and Israel. The PLO had acquired international legitimacy as the sole representative of the Palestinians, and had the status of a government-in-exile.

The initial reaction of the Israel government was to reject all PLO claims and to disavow its legitimacy. In an often-quoted statement, ex-Prime Minister Golda Meir exclaimed that "there are no Palestinians,"[98] meaning that Arabs of the country had no special rights to self-determination. The prevailing view was that the Arabs from Palestine were the same as other Arabs, that those who were refugees in Syria, Lebanon, Jordan, Gaza, or elsewhere in the Arab world should assimilate with their hosts who had the same language and culture.

After 1973 there were nuances of change in many Israeli perceptions. Most continued to reject negotiations with the PLO, but even in the establishment there was growing recognition that Palestinian revival was more than a propaganda ploy directed at Israel. The PLO was anathema to all the major political groups because of its guerrilla activities inside Israel and against Jews abroad. Palestinian guerrilla acts aroused particular opprobrium because many of the victims were women and children, and most of the targets were not military but were public institutions such as schools, markets, or civilian transport facilities. Furthermore, the national charter of the PLO expressed a fervent determination to eliminate the Jewish state and to deprive most of its Jewish inhabitants of the right to live in the country.

Changes also occurred after 1973 in PLO attitudes toward Israel, resulting in a series of bilateral meetings between a group of nonofficial Israelis who were close to the establishment and Palestinian representatives. There were approximately 25 meetings held under the auspices of ex-French Premier Pierre Mendes-France at his home in France. The discussions led to agreement that a Palestinian state should be established alongside Israel rather than in its place. The contacts were broken off after 1977 when the PLO objected to the peace treaty between Egypt and Israel.

The Camp David Framework for Peace in the Middle East, signed in September 1978, signaled a significant change in Israel's position on Palestinian nationalism. For the first time, Israel officially recognized the Palestinian people as a political entity that "should participate in negotiations on the resolution of the Palestinian problem in all its aspects."[99] The agreement stipulated that the solution emerging from autonomy talks "must also recognize the legitimate rights of the Palestinian people and their just requirements. In this way the Palestinians will participate in the determination of their own future."[100]

This formulation was notable because it was accepted by Begin; especially surprising was acceptance of the term, "legitimate rights of the Palestinian people," long considered by many Israelis as a code expression for negation of Israeli rights. Before Camp David, even the Labor Party refrained from using the term. Only Israeli "doves" recognized Palestinian "legitimate rights," and even then with many qualifications and reservations. Since Camp David and the peace treaty, disagreement between the Begin government and Egypt over an acceptable definition of these "legitimate rights" has been the major obstacle to successful conclusion of the autonomy negotiations.

Israel's Status and Security

The uncertainty of Israel's borders, its precarious situation among a group of nations that refuse to recognize it, and its struggle to win international recognition have made Israelis extremely sensitive to achieving status among the nations. Between 1948 and 1977 no Arab country recognized Israel's right to exist or the legitimacy of its Zionist ideology. The barrage of radio broadcasts and newspaper commentary from the Arab world declaring Zionism a cancerous growth fed Israeli insecurity and fear. The average Israeli believed his country besieged by a multitudinous host seeking to drive the Jews into the sea. This perception, against the background of the holocaust during World War II when the Germans exterminated six million Jews, strengthened resistance to concessions on territory, the refugees, and security. Only a handful of Jews believed that concessions to the Arabs would lead toward a peace settlement; to most, concessions meant giving the enemy the upper hand or surrender of national security.[101]

Arab refusal to enter direct negotiations was regarded as an insult and denial of the country's right to exist.[102] Attempts were made to compensate for Arab policy by developing a network of relationships with other third world countries through a series of economic, trade, technical assistance, and cultural agreements. An "international cooperation" program was begun in the early 1950s with assistance to Burma as a way to redress Israel's exclusion from the newly formed Third World Bloc created at the 1955 Bandung Conference. Israel's exclusion from Bandung and from the New Delhi Asian Socialist Conference in 1956 impressed Israeli leaders with the effectiveness of Arab pressure and the importance of creating third world ties to prevent political and economic isolation. Initial assistance to Burma was in defense, but it was later extended to nonmilitary fields. Similar assistance was given to Ghana, followed by establishment of diplomatic ties in 1957. Several other African countries were included in the plan, and later cooperation efforts were extended to Latin America, the Caribbean, Oceania, and other Asian countries. When these efforts reached their peak, some 7,000 Israeli experts had been sent to developing countries on official bilateral and multilateral missions, and more than 20,000 people came from these countries to Israel for training.[103]

Until the mid-1960s most Israeli assistance programs were in Africa. The Israeli style — low costs and lack of political pressures associated with great power assistance — appealed to the Africans. By the late 1960s African and Arab political interests began to converge when Arab countries started to play a more active role in the pan-African movement, especially in the Organization for African Unity (OAU). Israel's victory in the 1967 war alienated a large number of third world countries that tended to identify with the defeated Arabs, leading to increased Israeli political isolation. By the end of the 1973 war all African states except Malawi, Lesotho, Botswana, and Swaziland severed relations with Israel, terminating most of the bilateral cooperation agreements.[104]

Since 1973 the PLO, backed by the OAU and the Arab League, has captured the diplomatic offensive against Israel. Not only the third world, but an increasing number of Western European countries, formerly friendly to Israel, have supported a series of U.N. General Assembly and Security Council resolutions backing Palestinian self-determination and condemning Israel for a variety of acts — from establishing Jewish settlements in the occupied territories to mistreating Arab political prisoners. Arab success in isolating Israel has only increased fears and apprehensions about security, strengthened Israeli resistance to concessions for a peace settlement, and intensified resentment against the United Nations, which is regarded as an obstacle to stability in the region.

Relations with the United States

Relations between Israel and the United States often seem like a love-hate affair. Israelis are torn between insistence on their own independent Middle East policies and a close affinity with the United States, so close that some have described the country as the fifty-first state. Despite the large, affluent, and influential Jewish community in the United States, relations have not always been cordial. There have been periods of coolness, even antagonism, when Israel pursued policies regarded by the U.S. government as provocative or reckless, while U.S. policies often seem ambivalent or inconsistent to Israelis.

American ambivalence began when Israel declared its independence in 1948 contrary to advice from the State Department. Immediately after the declaration, President Truman became the first head of state to grant de facto recognition, a gesture the Soviet Union attempted to undercut with de jure recognition.

Close links with the United States are a result of ideological and cultural affinities. Many Americans perceive Israel as an outpost of Western democracy, a last stronghold against Communist attempts to subvert the Middle East, and a model of progress and development for the third world. Israelis seem "more like us" to most Americans than the Arabs, Iranians, or Turks who are unpredictable and whose governments are unstable. Israel benefits from the centuries old animosity between the Christian West and the Muslim East associated with the Crusades.

On the other hand, the security importance of the Middle East, American dependence on its oil, and Soviet attempts to establish close political and military links with the Arabs counterbalance the ties of sentiment. Interplay between sentiment and practical diplomacy often results in American Middle East policies that seem ambivalent or weak to Israelis.

Most presidential candidates usually campaign on platforms that include planks declaring strong political support and large economic assistance for Israel. Presidential policy seems to cool toward Israel between elections when there are pressures for concessions on territory, the refugees, or Jerusalem. Many Israelis believe there is a cabal of State Department "Arabists" seeking to undermine Israel's interests in the Whilte House.[105]

Attempts during President Eisenhower's administration to enlist Arab participation in the Baghdad Pact, the close relations between Washington and Cairo that developed after the 1952 Eygptian revolution, and Secretary of State Dulles's visit to Egypt in 1954 caused apprehension among Israeli policymakers who feared that their country would lose its special relationship with the United States. Both Arabs and Israelis perceived President Kennedy as a friend genuinely interested in a peaceful settlement of their conflict based on agreements considering the vital interests of both. President Johnson faced several crucial decisions resulting from the 1967 war. Through the use of the hotline between Washington and Moscow, he successfully prevented the war from escalating into a major conflict. Israel began to receive its first large-scale military assistance from the United States during Johnson's administration, and the pattern of dependence on military imports shifted from France to the United States.

Initial relationships with the Nixon administration were soured by a call for an "evenhanded approach" issued by the new president's special envoy to the Middle East, William Scranton.[106] The so-called Roger's Plan devised by Nixon's first secretary of state, calling for Israel's return to the 1967 frontiers with Egypt, Jordan, and Syria, aroused great skepticism in Israel, where it was regarded as pro-Arab.[107] Henry Kissinger, Nixon's national security advisor and international troubleshooter, kept out of Middle Eastern affairs until he was secretary of state. Then his role in bringing a halt to the 1973 war and in negotiating the disengagement agreements between Israel, Egypt, and Syria from

1973 to 1975, made him a hero for many Israelis and a villain for others. While most welcomed the halt in hostilities, many believed that Kissinger extracted too high a price for the agreements.[108] But Nixon and his successor, Gerald Ford, benefited greatly from the era of good feeling resulting from Kissinger's shuttle diplomacy.

President Carter was an enigma to Israeli policymakers. During his administration Israel received more economic and military assistance than from any other president, and more than was ever given by the United States to any other country.[109] Through Carter's efforts Israel signed its first peace treaty with an Arab state, a goal considered impossible by many Israelis before Sadat's visit to Jerusalem in 1977. Yet, Carter's public call for a Palestinian homeland[110] antagonized many Israelis, and the occasional disagreements on Middle East policy were regarded almost as an American betrayal.

Israel's growing isolation and the increased acceptance of the PLO have made ties with the United States crucial since 1973. Israel has no other source of foreign economic or military assistance and no other ally. As military expenditures skyrocket, even the private contributions of world Jewry have been dwarfed by U.S. government assistance.[111] The dimensions of aid have increased in geometrical progression, from millions to billions of dollars. The hope of economic and military independence has been frustrated as Israel finds itself unable to compete with the vast funds available to the Arab world from oil.[112] There are frequent disappointments in the American connection, and at times acrimonious diplomatic exchanges, but in the final analysis this issue is the most crucial for Israel.

OBJECTIVES AND POLICIES

Israel's major objectives have been to expand development of a Jewish state within secure and recognized borders, to "ingather" as many Jews from the diaspora as possible, to achieve a high standard of living based on modern agriculture and industry using high-level scientific and technological know-how, and to create a world center for the cultural and intellectual genius of the Jewish people.

Zionist visionaries like Ben-Gurion had messianic aspirations for the future. According to him, Israel

is not the outcome of any local or temporary conditions; it was created by the prophetic concept of the universe, the destiny of man on earth and the millenial era. It does not recognize idols of gold and silver; it does not accept the robbery of the poor, the oppression of peoples; the lifting up of swords by nation against nation or the study of war; it foretells the coming of the Redeemer whose loins are girt with righteousness; it looks forward to the day when the nations will cease to do evil, which will assume two forms: the ingathering of the exiles and the creation of a model nation.[113]

Political Policies

Israel's establishment in a hostile environment has necessitated the subordination of nearly all other goals to the primary one of security. How to survive has been the chief question faced by all governments. National security intersects with any other goal or policy, whether "ingathering of the exiles," attainment of social and economic justice, expansion of commerce, industry and agriculture, achieving a high level of education and culture, or urban development.

For years, immigration was the raison d'être of Zionism: its major goal was to establish a Jewish majority in Palestine. As a result of the Arab flight during the 1947-48 war, the new state acquired a Jewish majority inside Israel, although Israel's Jews were less than 10 percent of the world Jewish population when the state was established. A major, but unrealized, goal of all governments has been to bring most Jews from the diaspora to Israel. Initially the motive was not only Zionist idealism, but also to establish a large enough Jewish population to ward off attack from the surrounding Arab world.

One of the first acts of the new Knesset in 1950 was to pass the Law of Return, one of Israel's basic constitutional documents. It confirms provisions of the Declaration of Independence by guaranteeing that "every Jew has the right to immigrate to the country." Any Jew who desires to settle is guaranteed an immigrant visa, with the exception of one who "acts against the Jewish nation" or who "may threaten the public health or state security."

When the law was presented to the Knesset, Prime Minister Ben-Gurion noted, "This law lays down not that the state accords the right of settlement to Jews abroad but that this right is inherent in every Jew by virtue of his being a Jew if it but be his will to take part in settling the land. This right preceded the state of Israel; it is that which built the state."[114]

The volume of immigration has varied from 240,000 in 1949 to a low of about 11,000 in 1953. The largest immigration period was during the first four years, when the Jewish population nearly doubled as a result of the tidal wave of newcomers, many from the displaced persons camps of Europe. Since 1948 the Jewish population has increased nearly five times, mostly from immigration. From 1948 until the mid-1950s most immigrants were European Jews from Poland, Russia, Bulgaria, and other Eastern European countries. Between the mid-1950s and early 1960s most came from Mulsim countries. By the 1970s there began to be an influx from the Communist bloc, especially from the Soviet Union.[115]

Jews from Asia and North Africa, usually called Oriental Jews, and their offspring, now outnumber the Europeans. Many Oriental Jews came without skills, with low levels of education, and without the Zionist nationalist orientation of the Europeans. Integrating them into the Western life-style and political culture of the European-dominated elite became one of the government's chief objectives. Leaders such as Ben-Gurion believed that it was necessary to "Westernize" the Orientals lest the country's technological and scientific superiority over its Arab neighbors be undermined.[116]

Despite efforts to close the gap in education, housing, living standards, and nationalist orientation between Europeans and Orientals, great differences persist. There is some intermarriage but not enough to eliminate the distinctive social and economic patterns of each group. After the 1967 war many Western members of the establishment believed that there were significant qualitative changes among the Orientals. The youth had performed well in combat, they seemed to have accepted Western values and adapted to modern technology. Oriental Jewish leaders and intellectuals were hardly flattered by the compliment. Many regarded it as an affront to non-Western Jewish culture. One Oriental Jewish intellectual, Nissim Rejwan, a native of Iraq, charged that the Ashkenazi establishment was seeking to absorb the Oriental community into its own European culture, based "on the asumption that there exists in Israel a fairly well-defined 'native' culture to which these immigrants have to adapt and into which they can and have to be fused."[117] He observed that

> the declared goal of "remoulding the Oriental" . . . was pursued with a vigor and a self-assurance that in retrospect seems truly staggering. . . . Using a variety of threadbare excuses and rationalizations, the dominant group practiced a systematic policy of exclusion and incapacitation, a policy which did not leave unaffected even the country's institutions of higher learning.[118]

Rejwan recalled that in an interview former Prime Minister Ben-Gurion had stated: "We do not want Israelis to become Arabs. We are duty bound to fight against the spirit of the Levant, which corrupted individuals and societies, and preserve the authentic Jewish values as they crystalized in the Diaspora."[119] "Our suspicion," Rejwan commented, "is that the authentic Jewish values which Mr. Ben-Gurion is so eager to preserve have just about nothing to do with Jewish values and Jewish culture as, say, a Yemenite, Moroccan, Persian, or Iraqi Jew would understand the term."[120]

Fusion of ethnic and class differences is evident in concentrations of Oriental Jews in certain development towns and in the slums of Israel's larger cities. At first the Jewish Agency, responsible for Jewish immigration, attempted to obliterate ethnic distinctions by establishing new settlements from mixed ethnic groups. But sociologists and anthropologists advised that there were advantages to preserving already existing communal structures. This often reinforced ethnic separateness and concentrated the less affluent newcomers in ethnic neighborhoods. The result is that Oriental Jews often perceive themselves as a disadvantaged group, without political power, controlled by an elite European minority.[121]

Constituting more than half the Jewish population, with a larger number of children per family, Orientals provide the largest number of recruits to the armed forces. True, many of the Oriental youth acquire technical skills, an Israeli nationalist orientation, and familiarity with aspects of Western material culture in the armed forces. However, when leaving the services it is often more difficult for them to find a place in civilian society than it is for Westerners.

The disparities in economic and social status are evident in the country's political leadership. As of 1973 there were only 19 Oriental Jews in the 120-member Knesset. Similar patterns exist in the upper ranks of the party leadership and among heads of the civil service. Of the 64 Israeli cabinet ministers who served during Israel's first quarter century, only three were of Oriental background. In 1978 Israel acquired its first Oriental head of state when Yitzhak Navon, a Sephardic Jew born in Jerusalem, was elected by the Knesset as president. There are substantially larger number of Orientals in the lower ranks of the civil service; the police force, for example, includes many Oriental Jews.[122]

As they became more "Israelized," the Orientals played a more active role in local politics, assuming leadership positions in municipalities, local councils, and trade union organizations. Many of them abandoned their traditional support for the Labor Party in 1977 to vote Likud. Public opinion polls show that Oriental Jews are more hawkish in their attitudes toward Arabs and toward terms of a peace settlement. Attempts by radical Palestinian guerrilla organizations to create divisiveness between Orientals and Ashkenazi Jews in Israel are therefore in vain.[123]

The original objective of absorbing indigent immigrants without skills, vocations, or loyalty to the nation-state concept forced the government to adopt unique economic and social policies. The country became a welfare state par excellence, with a wide array of services for new immigrants to facilitate their absorption. Initial efforts to speed up immigration also required sacrifices by the Yishuv (the Jewish community in Israel) and by the world Jewish communities.

A large network of schools, hospitals, clinics, and health services was developed with assistance from diaspora contributions. Much of the social service apparatus, such as the Kupat Holim (Sick Fund), which provided medical insurance and care to most of the country's inhabitants, was dominated by the Histadrut. Health, education, and welfare services were available to most Israelis through the public sector, either through government, the Histadrut, or one of the various Zionist agencies.

The public sector was also important in economic development. Most land in Israel is in the public sector, owned either by the state or by the Jewish National Fund, an arm of the World Zionist Organization. Most produce is marketed and distributed through cooperatives or other public sector organizations.

The country's largest industrial enterprises are also in the public sector, owned by the state or the Histadrut. Most military industry, which now accounts for a large share of industrial exports, is owned by the state; the largest chemical plants are affiliated with the ministry of development; and a variety of industrial organizations from housing and construction to iron and steel is dominated by the Histadrut.[124]

As a result, the public sector in Israel employs a larger number of people than in most countries outside the Communist world. Productivity in Israel is lower than in most of Western Europe and only 25 percent of workers are in industry.

Although the Labor governments were socialist oriented, a mixed economy developed. Ben-Gurion was not a doctrinaire socialist. In keeping with his principle of state above party, he frequently compromised in economic and social policy, a necessity required to obtain nonsocialist partners in government coalitions, to attract large amounts of foreign capital, and to win American political as well as economic support. Welfarism was an accepted credo, but other socialist policies such as central planning and income redistribution were diluted in deference to nonsocialist domestic and foreign alliances.

The immense weight of security costs also influenced economic development. Israel allocates more of its resources to the military than do most other nations. About 30 percent of total output is expended on defense. It accounts for almost half the government budget. Nearly 15 percent of industrial production and a fifth of the labor force are consumed by the military. As the scale of military operations has escalated from war to war, the cost of security reached about $1,000 per capita in 1978.[125]

The goal of becoming less dependent on foreign military imports, if not self-sufficient, has vanished as quantities and sophistication of weapons have grown, especially after the 1973 war. During its first 19 years, U.S. government aid to Israel totaled nearly $1.5 billion. After 1967 U.S. aid escalated rapidly, from an annual level of under $100 million to about $500 million per year. In the five-year period after the 1973 war, U.S. assistance was over $10 billion, more than half in outright grants.[126] As a result of agreements ancillary to the Egyptian-Israeli peace treaty, total U.S. economic and military aid reached a record $2.8 billion. In addition, Israel will receive about $1 billion a year for the next three years as part of the peace package.[127]

Private contributions and the sale of Israeli bonds once provided the largest source of foreign aid, but they have been dwarfed by U.S. government contributions. From 1951 to 1978 over $4 billion in Israeli bonds were purchased abroad; about half that amount is held by private American institutions and individuals. Bond sales provide more than a third of Israel's development budget, which is essential for building the country's infrastructure in industry, agriculture, energy, communications, and transportation. Total private American assistance, including bonds and United Jewish Appeal contributions, is now estimated at about $600 million per year. The total of private and official U.S.

government assistance equals more than $1,000 per person in Israel, an amount equivalent to the per capita expenditures on defense.[128]

During 1979 several factors converged to increase the drain on Israel's foreign currency expenditures. As a result of the revolution in Iran, a major source of Israel's oil supply was cut off. Israel also lost another large oil source when it turned over the Sinai oil fields to Egypt. The escalating increase of world oil prices resulted in an annual energy import bill of over $2 billion by 1980, nearly 10 percent of GNP.[129] The oil import crisis added to tensions between Israel and the United States because of disagreement over American promises to provide oil to Israel should other sources be cut.

Without American private and official aid, Israel would be unable to maintain its high security costs while at the same time sustaining the highest standard of living in the Middle East. Many Israelis see a contradiction in attempts by the state to reconcile the two goals — high-level security and a high standard of living. These economic contradictions — high living standards, geometrically increasing defense costs, low economic productivity of the industrial worker, a vast social welfare system, and a huge debt repayment obligation — have conspired to produce triple-digit inflation. The central bank has been forced to print money to meet the constantly growing government deficits, and in 1978 the money supply was increased by 45 percent.

Despite the burdens of security and the influx of hundreds of thousands of unskilled and untrained immigrants, Israel has achieved many remarkable feats of economic and social development. An agricultural revolution brought by irrigation and scientific farming increased production tenfold during its first quarter century. At the same time, the number of people employed in agriculture decreased from 17.6 to 8 percent of the labor force. After the economic boom of the late 1960s, labor shortages in Israel required the employment of Arab laborers, many of them from the occupied territories.

Income from the industrial sector grew thirtyfold between 1952 and 1972, and there was a 350 percent increase in industrial investment. Industrial exports increased by 1,100 percent with a rise of almost 500 percent in the value of industrial output. Although the percentage of the labor force employed in industry remained about the same, the absolute number of industrial workers nearly doubled between 1955 and 1972. In certain areas Israel has developed specializations that make its products competitive on world markets: these include weapons, electronic equipment, textiles and clothing, medications, and quality fruits and vegetables. Israeli innovations in housing and road construction established a demand for services of its large construction firms such as those of the Histadrut, especially in developing countries. Several Histadrut subsidiaries still have contracts for construction in Asia and Africa.

Transition of the economy from pioneer agricultural settlement to urban industry caused reorientation of early Zionist objectives and policies. The ideal of socialist egalitarianism, rooted on the land in small collective or cooperative settlements, has all but vanished except among a handful of Mapam zealots. Long before Begin's Likud government assumed power, the country's socialist leaders had to reorient the goals and plans for an ideal society. Major ideological transition began in the Labor Party during the 1960s when a group of younger leaders, led by "the Old Man," Ben-Gurion, urged greater emphasis on science, technology, and development of the country's industrial infrastructure. To the new young technocrats, pioneering no longer meant exclusively establishment of agricultural outposts, but also opening new electronics plants, aircraft factories, and steel-rolling mills. They also placed loyalty to the state above loyalty to the party or the Labor government. Internal clashes between the "young guard" and the old Labor establishment split the party during the 1960s, when Ben-Gurion and his followers left Labor to form the Rafi Party (reintegrated into Labor before the 1969 elections).[130]

After the 1967 war the pace of industrial expansion accelerated sharply. There was an influx of foreign capital and a further shift away from the original socialist orientation. A British Zionist writer, Jon Kimche, has described the effect of these developments:

> The combination of this massive domestic investment and the interests of large foreign concerns linked to the large inflow of capital — donations, the sale of bonds, foreign loans and aid — created a new Israeli elite, a new establishment that to a considerable extent displaced the old, or embraced part of it into its amply financed New Deal. This resulted in a new parallel power-structure to that which had dominated Israel for the previous 30 years, even in the days before the state was established. Thus, alongside the old establishment — the political parties, the Jewish Agency, the Histadrut, the Kibuttz organizations and the armed forces — there grew up the new elite, which was no longer dependent on the restrictive patronage of the old establishment but was strong enough and had the financial resources to exercise its own form of patronage and influence.[131]

Changing economic and social orientations redirected Israel's foreign policy also. Aspirations of the state's founders to remain unaligned with any power bloc and to maintain an independent course through the thicket of international and regional problems was impossible. It was not only the Soviet Union's rejection that drove Israel into an American alliance, but the need for American aid, American export markets, American imports, American managerial and technological skills, and the development of an economic infrastructure that was dependent on the United States. There was not only an identity of American and Israeli political interests, but emergence of an Israeli economy intimately linked with that of the United States. After 1967 this was evident in the number of American multinational companies with interests in Israel. These included

ITT, RCA, IBM, Allied Chemicals, Coca-Cola, Ford, ITEK, Motorola, Bethlehem Steel, and Monsanto. By 1970 these and other foreign firms were investing about $150 million a year in Israel.

Abandonment of nonalignment and the close links with the United States have been manifest in the convergence of U.S. and Israeli positions on most issues in the United Nations, other than those related to the Middle East. There have also been more direct relations between the U.S. and Israeli military and intelligence communities since 1967.

During the 1977 election, Begin's Likud Party ran on a platform that promised to terminate or to reverse the socialist policies of its Labor predecessors. Once in power, however, Likud found it difficult, if not impossible, to rearrange the pattern of the economy. Institutionalization of the large Histadrut and government-owned enterprises over a third of a century was a major obstacle. Israel's economy was also the victim of world forces — the escalation of oil prices, the trend of inflation in the West, and a general unease and lack of confidence. All these forces, added to the unique circumstances of Israel's situation — its unusually high immigration rate and the high cost of security — conspired to undermine the promises of Likud to adopt the economic programs of Milton Friedman. Instead, under Likud, inflation is greater than ever, the number of public sector employees has increased, and attempts to loosen the economic structure have been to no avail.

Despite the close ideological affinity between Likud and the United States on economic and social questions, on containment of Communism in the Middle East, and on relations with the Soviet Union, there have been several sharp clashes over Middle East policy. The difference between Begin's perspectives on Middle East questions and those of the Labor movement is the difference between a policy motivated by territorial acquisition for ideological reasons and acquisition for security. Lack of sympathy for Begin's interpretation has not only created tense Israeli-U.S. relations, but has also driven Israel into greater international isolation than it has ever experienced.

Military Policies

Israel's military objectives are a corollary of its political goals and aspirations: to assure territorial integrity of the Jewish state; to prevent formation of any Arab military combination that could threaten the country; to establish internationally recognized, militarily secure borders; to block both Soviet penetration of the Middle East and establishment of bases that could be used to threaten or pressure Israel; to become self-sufficient in development and production of military technology; to maintain U.S. guarantees of Israel's security through acquiring long-term commitments of military and other aid required until the country can become self-sufficient; to develop a military strategy based on the use of high-level technology rather than large manpower; and to assure instant readiness, mobility, and flexibility of all defense units.

Until Begin became prime minister in 1977, security rather than historic destiny determined the government's policy on borders. Before Israel was established, the Jewish Agency was prepared to accept as a compromise the borders defined in the 1947 U.N. partition resolution. It was not until several months later, when it became clear that there would be a prolonged war with the surrounding countries, that the government redefined its minimum territorial demands. Between 1949 and 1967 the frontiers fixed by the 1949 armistice agreements with Egypt, Lebanon, Syria, and Jordan were declared by the government as acceptable for a final arrangement with the Arab states, although even the Labor Party recognized them as only part of historical Eretz Israel. After 1967 the concept of a secure territorial base was again extended to include substantial parts of, if not all of, the areas seized in the Six-Day War. Within Israel, disagreements have not only been among politicians, but have also divided military and former military leaders over the new concept of secure borders. There are those, including former generals, who would accept a much smaller area than that conquered in 1967 as a secure base for the country.

Israel's military machine is based on a concept of readiness for immediate use; it maintains only a small regular army rather than a large conscript force. Other Middle East countries with large populations, like Egypt and Turkey, have two or three times the number of men in their armed forces. Israel compensates for the difference in manpower by keeping its civilian reserves in constant training and immediately available through a unique mobilization system. The quality of manpower education and training, the level of technical competence of the forces, the availability of the most sophisticated weaponry and support systems, and the morale and individual adaptability of the Israeli soldier help to redress the imbalance in manpower.[132]

In 30 years, Israel's armed forces developed from small, semivolunteer defense units equipped with not much more than small arms (22,000 rifles of various calibers), 1,550 machine guns (light and medium, 11,000 mostly home-made submachine guns), 195 infantry mortars, 682 two-inch mortars, 86 PIAT projectors and antitank rifles, and 5 very old 65mm field guns. The Haganah also owned a few tanks and fighter aircraft that were waiting in Europe for shipment to the new state.[133] From this meager collection, Israel's military forces, called the Israel Defense Forces (IDF), have developed into one of the most respected military machines in the world. Today, the armed forces compare in equipment and readiness with the forces of several NATO members. They include over 3,000 of the most modern tanks, several thousand armored vehicles and personnel carriers, and about the same number of aircraft as Great Britain or France.[134]

Initial military tactics were based on the use of small, independently operated units. The high morale and strong motivation, the concept of volunteerism, and the lack of class relationships between officers and enlisted men were strengths that could not be overcome by quantitative superiority of opposing forces.

As the armed forces grew larger and more routinized in their tactics, and as they lost the motivation of volunteerism, operations and tactics became more conventional. Field officers still retained much discretion in their operations, but individual units were organized in more conventional operational patterns. The influx into the armed forces of conscripts without the motivation of the first recruits required adoption of more conventional military distinctions between officers and their men, disciplinary methods, and training techniques.[135]

After the 1956 Sinai war, greater emphasis was placed on mechanized war, on building up the armored forces. Technology became as important in waging successful operations as highly motivated manpower. From the growing emphasis on technology emerged a doctrine in which the following elements were important: exploitation of a covenient international situation as a precondition for large-scale military operations; the central importance attributed to speed in military operations; and deception and surprise.[136] Related to this doctrine was Chief-of-Staff Dayan's motto, "When in doubt, always attack."[137]

Another aspect of military doctrine has been the emphasis on deterrence. At the tactical level, a major manifestation of deterrence is massive retaliation against enemy forces seeking to probe Israel's frontiers. Special commando striking forces were organized to seek out and destroy Palestinian guerrillas attempting to infiltrate from Egypt, Jordan, and Syria. The air force was also trained in tactics of aggressive pursuit of enemy planes that overflew or seemed about to penetrate Israel's skies.[138]

Development of a nuclear option is another level of deterrence. From the early 1960s there have been rumors, still unverified, that Israel is not only capable of producing atomic weapons but possesses several. The Israeli government never confirmed or denied its nuclear capabilities, and its atomic reactor at Dimona has been kept off limits to international inspectors. Official policy is based on the public assertion that "Israel will not be the first one to introduce atomic weapons in the region." Even if Israel possessed a nuclear option, there is little comfort in knowing that it could be used since Israel itself would be obliterated with one or two such devices, and the perils of use by Israel are such that its own population would be exposed to fallout if it used nuclear weapons against a neighbor in either a first or second strike.[139]

The Israeli air force (IAF) played a major role in tactics of the 1967 war by totally destroying the effectiveness of potential Arab air strikes during the first hours of combat. During May and the first days of June 1967, the armed forces of Egypt, Syria, Jordan, and Iraq appeared ready for a massive thrust. Israel responded by mobilizing its forces, but at the same time gave the appearance of readiness for continued negotiations. In the meantime, the general staff prepared a preemptive response that successfully undermined Arab military credibility for the next few years and turned the balance in Israel's favor until the 1973 war.

During the 1960s the IAF enjoyed priority in allocation of resources and in development. Israel was able to compete with Soviet planes provided to Egypt and Syria by acquiring the best French aircraft. By June 5, 1967, its French equipment neutralized the threat of Arab airpower. The results were clearly evident during the next week when Israeli ground units swept the Egyptians out of Gaza and Sinai, the Syrians from the Golan Heights, and Jordan from the West Bank.[140]

The strategy based on deterrence of Arab attacks has in the long run not been effective. Arab policy is determined less by analyses of battlefield results than by expectations of achieving political victory as part of a scenario in which military defeat is the price of political victory. In each war, although IDF leaders believed they had achieved military success, they failed to achieve Israel's larger political objectives. While military victory gave most Israelis a sense of physical security and fortified the concept that "Israel is here to stay," it has not deterred further Arab attacks. Israel's victories have not ended the country's isolation or Arab hatred. On the contrary, military victory has often appeared to motivate most Arab leaders to ultimately redress the balance in their own favor.

The 1973 war illustrated how reversible were Israel's previous military achievements. During the first week of combat, Egypt and Syria adopted several elements of Israel's own military doctrine: they exploited the international situation, they successfully deceived and surprised Israel, and they used speed in initiating operations. Both Arab states were able to penetrate Israel's lines, causing consternation and fear. Although Syrian and Egyptian forces were checked and forced into defensive positions, their initial success and the high costs in casualties and war expenditures extracted from Israel paid off politically. Combat ended after three weeks with Israel again on the offensive, but many Egyptian and Syrian political objectives were realized. In relative terms, the war was far more costly to Israel, for it lost a much higher proportion of its youth and expended a greater share of its 1973 GNP than either of the enemy states.[141]

In the disengagement agreements negotiated with Egypt and Syria, and in the peace treaty signed with Egypt, Israel made territorial concessions that ended the post-1967 status quo. Israel's strategic planners were forced to abandon the assumption that all occupied territories would remain under their military, if not political, control indefinitely. While they continued to argue that the extended frontiers were essential to national security, they realized after 1973 that long-term alternative strategies would have to be devised.

Public opinion in Israel turned against the government for its conduct of the 1973 war, leading to establishment of a high-level commission chaired by Dr. Shimon Agranat, American-born president of the supreme court, to investigate the military's lack of preparedness and intelligence failures. The investigation took a year and a half, but in a preliminary report submitted to the government in April 1974, the commission castigated the army intelligence chief for misevaluating the likelihood of attack by Egypt and Syria.[142] The army's misreadings were based on a doctrinaire "conception" that Egypt's airpower was insufficient to initiate a full-scale war and that Syria would not attack without Egypt. No defense plans had been devised to ward off surprise attacks, and the armored corps was not properly deployed at the outbreak of war. The report recommended dismissal of the intelligence chief, and resulted also in the resignation of Chief-of-Staff Elazar.[143] The major effect of the report was resignation within the next few weeks of Defense Minister Moshe Dayan and Prime Minister Golda Meir. In the long run, the report added to public disaffection from the Labor Alignment, and led to the 1977 election victory of Menachem Begin.

In the euphoria generated by Sadat's visit to Jerusalem during 1977 and by subsequent events leading up to the peace treaty in 1979, hopes were raised that Israel would become less dependent on its military forces. The actual results of the peace treaty belied those hopes, however. Accompanying the treaty was a memorandum of understanding in which the United States promised to "take into account and . . . to be responsive to military and economic requirements of Israel," with counterbalancing promises to Egypt. The payoff included U.S. assistance totaling $4.8 billion over three years, in addition to "regular" financial aid to Egypt and Israel. The bulk of this amount, according to Secretary of State Cyrus Vance, was to help Egypt and Israel "meet urgent security requirements." Some $800 million of the amount for Israel was a grant to help finance reconstruction of two military airfields transferred from Sinai to the Negev. The remaining sum for Israel was to finance foreign military sales. By the end of 1979, both Egypt and Israel submitted additional requests for even larger amounts of American aid to "meet urgent security requirements."

After the 1973 war and peace treaty, Israeli military dependence on the United States substantially increased. The IDF received certain weapons systems before they were used by frontline American forces,[144] increasing Israel's ability to influence political events and to alter the military balance in the Middle East. The peace treaty with Egypt almost assures that there will be no combination of Arab military forces offering a credible threat to Israel.[145] However, the treaty also has temporarily isolated Egypt in the Arab world, forcing it to escalate its own military development, as well as stimulating internal divisiveness. While the treaty diminishes the immediate prospect of war, it contributes to long-term regional unrest that jeopardizes Israel's security. Threats of Soviet penetration are not diminished by the escalation of Israeli military might. On the contrary, some Arab states now perceive the need for Soviet military assistance as more urgent. Israel's borders are no more acceptable nor have they become more impervious. The number of nations with ambivalent policies toward Israel has increased and Palestinian consciousness and confidence have grown. The agreements derived from the peace treaty have demonstrated how elusive is the goal of military self-sufficiency. While the objectives of mobility, high-level technology, and flexibility are being realized, the question is, will the price in economic, military, and political dependence on the United States be worth the achievement of superior force as an instrument of foreign policy?

NOTES

1. Disagreements between Latin Catholic clergy (supported by France) and Greek Orthodox clergy (backed by Czarist Russia) over their respective rights in the Church of the Holy Sepulchre, supposed burial place of Jesus in Jerusalem, fueled the tensions between the two European powers, leading to the Crimean War. See J. A. R. Marriott, *The Eastern Question* (Oxford: Clarendon Press, 1917).

2. The movement was established at the first World Zionist Congress convened by the founder, Theodore Herzl, at Basel, Switzerland, in 1897. See Walter Laqueur, *A History of Zionism* (New York: Holt, Rinehart and Winston, 1972).

3. The number of Jews in Palestine during the nineteenth century increased from about 12,000 in 1845 to some 47,000 in 1895.

4. In 1914 Palestine's Jewish population was nearly 85,000, but declined by 1919 to an estimated 65,000 due to conditions during World War I. By the end of World War I Palestine's total population was about 580,000, and by the end of the British mandate, two million. See J. C. Hurewitz, *The Struggle for Palestine* (New York: Norton, 1950).

5. The United Nations General Assembly voted to recommend partition on November 29, 1947, in Resolution 181(II). Thirty-three states voted for the plan, 13 voted against, and 10 abstained. The United States, the Soviet Union, and France supported partition; Great Britain, China, Argentina, Chile, Colombia, El Salvador, Ethiopia, Honduras, Mexico, and Yugoslavia abstained; Egypt, Iraq, Lebanon, Saudi Arabia, Syria, Yemen, Afghanistan, Cuba, Greece, India, Iran, Pakistan, and Turkey voted against. See Fred J. Khouri, *The Arab-Israeli Dilemma*, 2d ed. (Syracuse: Syracuse University Press, 1976), Chap. III.

6. Although the Arab forces were considerably larger than those of Israel, they were uncoordinated, poorly equipped, and led by militarily incompetent officers, thus never developing a unified plan of action or a common front against Israel in the first war. See Edgar O'Ballance, *The Arab-Israeli War, 1948* (New York: Praeger, 1957), and Trevor N. Dupuy, *Elusive Victory: The Arab-Israeli Wars, 1947-1974* (New York: Harper, 1978).

7. The capital surpluses derived from oil income, especially those of Saudi Arabia and Kuwait, have made it possible for them to extend grants of several hundred million dollars a year to the Arab "confrontation states," Egypt, Jordan, and Syria. The oil income of the producers facilitated acquisition of large amounts of the most sophisticated weapons, and helped to finance the 1973 war against Israel. Furthermore, Saudi investments of surplus oil income in Western countries and Arab oil exports to the industrialized nations have given the producers significant international influence. See Russell A. Stone, ed., *OPEC and the Middle East: The Impact of Oil on Societal Development* (New York: Praeger, 1977), but cf. also the analysis of R. D. McLaurin and James M. Price, "OPEC Current Account Surpluses and Assistance to the Arab Front-Line States," *Oriente Moderno*, LVIII, no. 11 (November 1978), pp. 533-46.

8. In 1979 Israel's defense expenditure was some $5.2 billion of its estimated GDP of $16.4 billion. Defense expenditures contributed to an inflation rate that reached 135 percent by the end of 1980, necessitating economies in

domestic programs such as education, health, and social welfare. International Institute for Strategic Studies, *The Military Balance, 1980-1981* (London, 1980).

9. Despite United Nations censure, the Knesset passed the "Basic Law: Jerusalem the Capital of Israel" in July 1980 by a vote of 69 to 15 with three abstentions. Most members of the opposition Labor Alignment supported the law. *Jerusalem Post* (international edition), August 3-9, 1980.

10. Before the 1967 war, Israel's official peace proposals included a settlement based on the 1949 armistice frontiers. After the 1967 war territorial demands were extended to include parts of the newly occupied lands. Begin's Likud wanted to acquire all occupied territories; there was disagreement within the Labor Alignment over how much territory to return to the Arab states. See discussion of these different perspectives in Rael Jean Isaac, *Israel Divided: Ideological Policies in the Jewish State* (Baltimore: Johns Hopkins University Press, 1976).

11. Most Israeli political parties were established as affiliates of the world Zionist movement during the first half of the twentieth century in Europe. After World War I many of these movements were organized in Palestine as political parties participating in the self-governing institutions of the Jewish community. For a good discussion of development of political life and culture, see Amos Eon, *The Israelis: Founders and Sons* (New York: Holt, Rinehart and Winston, 1971).

12. American economic assistance to Israel began shortly after the state was established, with $135 million in loans from the Export-Import Bank and $1.2 million under Public Law 480, extended in 1950. Between 1950 and 1961 total U.S. aid reached $831.09 million. Between 1978 and 1981 total U.S. aid to Israel reached over $11 billion, a large part of this in military assistance related to the Camp David peace agreements.

13. Between 1949 and 1959 world Jewry, mostly American Jews, provided more than 47 percent of Israel's $3.1 billion in capital imports through contributions to the United Jewish Appeal and other similar organizations and through the sale of Israel Bonds. As U.S. government assistance has escalated, the proportion of private Jewish assistance from abroad has been dwarfed. According to the Bank of Israel, U.S. aid in 1970-79 was $13.135 billion. During the same period, world Jewry provided $5.089 billion. *Jerusalem Post* (international edition), August 17-23, 1980, p. 5.

14. "The difference between Sharett and Ben-Gurion was, however, in their long-range views. Sharett did not share Ben-Gurion's fatalistic views of the necessity of conflict with an implacable Arab foe who would only relent from trying to destroy a Jewish state out of utter despair at complete military defeat. Sharett was aware of Arab hostility but he did not ignore the existence of factors and interests working for an accommodation." Simha Flapan, *Zionism and the Palestinians* (London: Croom Helm, 1979), p. 160.

15. The Achdut Haavoda wing of the Labor Party led by Israel Galili and Yigal Allon, who died in 1980, tended toward annexationist views (their kibbutzim have called for Israel's annexation of the Golan Heights), while other leaders represented by former foreign minister Abba Eban are more prone to make territorial compromises for a genuine peace settlement.

16. On June 27, 1967, the Knesset passed without debate a law enabling the minister of interior to apply Israeli law in all parts of Jerusalem. The next

day the government declared unification of both Jewish and Arab sectors of Jerusalem and extended the borders of the city to include Kallandia Airport, Mount Scopus, the Mount of Olives, and several Arab villages south of the city. See Joel L. Kraemer, *Jerusalem: Problems and Prospects* (New York: Praeger, 1980).

17. Until 1950 Israel was willing to consider repatriation of a limited number of Arab refugees to Israel as part of an overall peace settlement. At one time it offered to take back as many as 100,000 refugees. See Don Peretz, *Israel and the Palestine Arabs* (Washington, D.C.: Middle East Institute, 1958).

18. Total U.S. aid to Israel between 1973 and 1975 was $3.680 billion; between 1976 and 1980, $9.690 billion. *MERIP Reports*, no. 92 (November-December 1980), p. 8. These amounts were not only the highest per capita, but were also the largest amounts of aid extended to any country, reaching an amount of over $1,000 per capita.

19. See Don Peretz, "The Earthquake: Israel's Ninth Knesset Elections," *Middle East Journal*, XXXI, no. 3 (Summer 1977), pp. 251-66; and Howard R. Penniman, ed., *Israel at the Polls* (Washington, D.C.: American Enterprise Institute, 1979), Chap. 6.

20. Penniman, *Israel*, Chap. 6; Rael Jean Isaac, *Party and Politics in Israel: Three Visions of a Jewish State* (London: Longman, 1981).

21. *New Outlook*, XX, no. 3 (April-May 1977), p. 22.

22. Begin's principal protest was against the so-called Rogers Plan, a proposal by then-Secretary of State William Rogers based on Israel's return to pre-1967 frontiers with the exception of minor border rectifications.

23. The Likud's economic program was shaped largely by the leaders of the former Liberal wing of Gahal, who represented private farmers and industrialists advocating as little state direction of the economy as possible. See Isaac, *Party and Politics*, pp. 161-62.

24. See note 21. Likud's foreign policy plank was influenced most by Begin's Herut movement.

25. By the end of 1980, inflation had reached 135 percent, and the International Monetary Fund indicated that Israel's inflation rate was the world's highest in 1980. (*New York Times*, January 3, 1981.) For an informed discussion of Begin's economic policies, see Ann Crittenden, "Israel's Economic Plight," *Foreign Affairs*, LVII, no. 5 (Summer 1979), pp. 1005-16.

26. According to Egyptian Foreign Minister Butros Butros-Ghali, "Israel wants a kind of administrative autonomy. . . . We seek the autonomy as a framework offering the Palestinians self-determination. If they want a Palestinian state they can have a Palestinian state. If they want a federation with Jordan they can have a federation with Jordan. If they want a federation with Israel they can have a federation with Israel. But it is essential that one million people say what they want." *New York Times*, August 9, 1979.

27. In summing up his work as President Carter's special envoy in the Middle East, Sol M. Linowitz outlined five critical areas of disagreement between Egypt and Israel in the autonomy negotiations. They included assuring Israel's security; ensuring fair and equitable distribution of water among Israelis, Palestinians, and Jordanians; disposition of publicly owned lands in the West Bank that had been owned by the Jordanian government; solution of the nature

of administrative and legislative powers of the self-governing authority; and a decision on whether Arab Palestinians in East Jerusalem would be permitted to vote in elections for the self-governing authority. *New York Times*, December 20, 1980.

28. A poll ordered by the *Jerusalem Post* in August 1980 showed 17.8 percent of voters expressed a preference for Likud in contrast to 48.5 percent who preferred Labor. Begin was the second-preferred candidate for prime minister after Rabin. (International edition, August 31-September 6, September 7-13, 1980.)

29. Although Israel's Declaration of Independence called for a Constituent Assembly that met in 1949, the Assembly became the First Knesset and deferred the task of drafting a formal constitution. Instead, the Transition Law, called the "small constitution," provided the foundations of government and laid out the respective roles of the Knesset, cabinet, president, and other institutions of government. See Don Peretz, *The Government and Politics of Israel* (Boulder: Westview, 1979), Chap. 5.

30. Initially, the ministry of foreign affairs was run by Israelis with a Western European background, defense was under the close supervision of Ben-Gurion, while social welfare was managed by the orthodox parties. Ibid., Chap. 6; see also Marver H. Bernstein, *The Politics of Israel: The First Decade of Statehood* (Princeton: Princeton University Press, 1957), as well as the memoirs of various Israeli leaders including David Ben-Gurion, Moshe Dayan, Golda Meir, Shimon Peres, Yitzhak Rabin, Ezer Weizman, Abba Eban, and Yigal Allon.

31. The government of Palestine was headed by the high commissioner for Palestine, who was responsible to the Colonial Office in London. Great Britain acquired its authority through the League of Nations Mandate for Palestine in 1922. See Royal Institute of International Affairs, *Great Britain and Palestine, 1915-1945* (London, 1946).

32. Peretz, *The Government*, ar.d Bernstein, *The Politics*.

33. For a list of government agencies and their functions, see the Israel *Government Year-Book*, published annually.

34. For a brief description of Israel's military industries, see Edward Luttwak and Dan Horowitz, *The Israeli Army* (New York: Harper and Row, 1975).

35. For a description of various Histadrut activities and interests, see the *Israel Pocket Library* volumes of "History − from 1880," "Zionism," "Immigration and Settlement," and other relevant subjects.

36. David Ben-Gurion, Israel's first prime minister, was secretary-general of the Histadrut from 1921 to 1935. Golda Meir also headed the labor organization and several cabinet members were leaders of the Histadrut.

37. See Peretz, *The Government*, Chap. 6.

38. Crittenden, "Israel's Economic Plight."

39. Peretz, *The Government*, and Bernstein, *The Politics*. Finance ministers under Ben-Gurion, such as Eliezer Kaplan and Pinhas Sapir, were adept in using the power of the purse in collaboration with the prime minister.

40. Peretz, *The Government*, p. 39.

41. In 1980 there were several instances of censorship: CBS correspondent Dan Raviv was expelled from Israel for reporting detonation of an Israeli nuclear

device; former Prime Minister Rabin's report in his autobiography about expulsion of Arabs from two towns in the 1948 war was excised; and three Arab editors of Jerusalem papers were banned from leaving their villages. *New York Times*, February 23, March 2, December 17, 1980.

42. Among these publications are the communist weekly, *at-Talia* (The Vanguard), and the dailies *al-Fajr* (The Dawn) and *ash-Shaab* (The People). They became increasingly nationalist and critical of the government, until in 1980 action was taken against their publishers or editors. A third East Jerusalem Arabic daily, *al-Quds* (Jerusalem), takes more moderate positions. The three dailies were published as Jordanian newspapers before the Israeli occupation.

43. Useful books about the background of the Labor Party include Peter Y. Medding, *Mapai in Israel* (London: Cambridge University Press, 1972); Yonathan Shapiro, *The Israeli Labor Party, 1919-1930* (Beverly Hills: Sage Publications, 1976); Amos Perlmutter, "Ideology and Organization: The Politics of Socialistic Parties in Israel, 1897-1957" (Ph.D. diss., University of California-Berkeley, 1957); and Walter Preuss, *The Labour Movement in Israel* (Jerusalem: Rubin Mass, 1965).

44. Medding, *Mapai*.

45. Ibid.

46. Mapam's affiliate in the United States, Americans for Progressive Israel (Hashomer Hatzair), has two publications in English giving Mapam perspectives, *Israel Horizons* and *Progressive Israel*. Its daily newspaper in Israel is *Ha-mishmar* (On Guard).

47. For an early study of Israel's Communist movement, see Moshe M. Czudnowski and Jacob M. Landau, *The Israel Communist Party and the Elections for the Fifth Knesset* (Stanford: Hoover Institution Press, 1965). Cf. Dunia Nahas, *The Israeli Communist Party* (London: Croom Helm, 1976).

48. The Israeli monthly magazine, *New Outlook*, published in Tel Aviv, frequently represents perspectives of Shelli.

49. Sympathetic interpretations of Likud and its background can be found in Rael Jean Isaac's books, *Party and Politics* and *Israel Divided*. A personal perspective of Begin by one of his former associates can be found in Samuel Merlin, "The Rise of Menachem Begin," *National Jewish Monthly*, XCII, 7 (July-August 1977). See also Laqueur, *A History*, Chap. 7.

50. Only 29 of Begin's 45-member Likud bloc in the Knesset voted for the Camp David accords in 1978. In 1979, 13 Likud members voted against the Egyptian-Israeli peace treaty, and in October 1979 two members of Begin's Herut party left to form their own Knesset faction because of opposition to the treaty and disagreements on other "national" issues.

51. For a discussion of religious Zionism, see Basil J. Vlavianos and Feliks Gross, eds., *Struggle for Tomorrow* (New York: Arts Press, 1954), Chaps. 4, 9. A critique is offered in Israel T. Naamani and David Rudavsky, eds., *Israel: Its Politics and Philosophy* (New York: Behrman House, 1974), Part III.

52. See Isaac, *Israel Divided*; a critique in Yigal Elam, "*Gush Emunim* — A False Messianism," *Jerusalem Quarterly*, I (Fall 1976).

53. *Jerusalem Post*, May-July 1977, passim.

54. The "Basic Law: Jerusalem the Capital of Israel," passed by a Knesset vote of 69 to 15 with three abstentions on July 30, 1980. It states:

1. Jerusalem, complete and united, is the capital of Israel.

2. Jerusalem is the seat of the President of the State, the Knesset, the government, and the Supreme Court.

3. The holy places will be protected against desecration and any other offense, and against anything liable to infringe on the free access of adherents of religions to their holy places or on their sentiments towards those places.

4. (a) The government will look after the development and prosperity of Jerusalem and the well-being of its inhabitants. . . .

55. Orly Lubin, "For Peace and a 'Sane' Zionism," *New Outlook*, XXII, no. 8 (November-December 1979); also "Peace Greater than Greater Israel," Peace Now pamphlet, October 1979.

56. Lubin, "For Peace," p. 34.

57. *Jerusalem Post*, 1978-79, passim.

58. Lubin, "For Peace."

59. See notes 35 and 43.

60. See *Facts About Israel 1973* (Jerusalem: Ministry of Foreign Affairs, 1973), pp. 163-64 and "Democracy," *Israel Pocket Library* (Jerusalem: Keter, 1974), pp. 158-63.

61. For readership figures, see Arthur S. Banks and William Overstreet, eds., *Political Handbook of the World 1980* (New York: McGraw-Hill, 1980), p. 241.

62. See note 42.

63. See note 41 and Hirsh Goodman, "The Sense of Censorship," *Jerusalem Post* (international edition), July 12, 1977, p. 8.

64. *Jerusalem Post*, international edition, October 18, 1977, p. 4.

65. For a discussion of the role of the military in state and society, see Amos Perlmutter, *Military and Politics in Israel: Nation-Building and Role Expansion* (London: Frank Cass, 1969) and "The Israeli Army in Politics," *World Politics*, XX, 4 (July 1968), pp. 606-43.

66. Peretz, *The Government*, pp. 126-30.

67. Ibid.

68. Yoram Peri, "Ideological Portrait of the Israeli Military Elite," *Jerusalem Quarterly*, no. 3 (Spring 1977), pp. 28-41.

69. Ibid.

70. For a discussion of Oriental Jews in politics, see Shlomo Avineri, "Israel: Two Nations?" *Israel: Social Structure and Change*, ed. Michael Curtis and Mordechai S. Chertoff (New Brunswick: Transaction, 1977), pp. 281-306.

71. For a discussion of the Black Panthers, see Sammy Smooha, *Israel: Pluralism and Conflict* (Berkeley: University of California Press, 1978), passim.

72. See sources identified in notes 70 and 71. For a discussion and analysis of election returns and ethnic patterns, see Alan Arian, ed., *The Elections in Israel – 1969* (Jerusalem: Jerusalem Academic Press, 1972) and *The Elections in Israel – 1973* (Jerusalem: Jerusalem Academic Press, 1975).

73. A number of leaflets authored by the former leader of the Jerusalem Sephardic Council, Eliahu Eliachar, and that advocated these views, were circulated.

74. Extensive discussion of the Arab minority in Israel is found in Smooha, *Israel*, in Elia T. Zureik, *The Palestinians in Israel: A Study in Internal Colonialism*

(London: Routledge and Kegan Paul, 1979), and in Ian Lustick's excellent study, *Arabs in the Jewish State: Israel's Control of a National Minority* (Austin: University of Texas Press, 1980).

75. Sammy Smooha, "The Orientation and Politicization of the Arab Minority in Israel," occasional papers on the Middle East (Jewish-Arab Center, Haifa University, n.d.).

76. *New York Times*, January 18, 1961, pp. 52-53.

77. Some books on the subject of Jewish influence in politics include Richard P. Stevens, *American Zionism and U.S. Foreign Policy, 1942-1947* (New York: Pageant Press, 1962); Naomi Cohen, *American Jews and the Zionist Idea* (New York: KFAF, 1975); Melvin Urotsky, *American Zionism from Herzl to the Holocaust* (Garden City: Doubleday-Anchor, 1975); Edwin M. Wright, *The Great Zionist Cover-Up: A Study and Interpretation* (Cleveland: Northeast Ohio Committee on Middle East Understanding, 1975); John Snetsinger, *Truman, the Jewish Vote and the Creation of Israel* (Stanford: Hoover Institution Press, 1974); Evan M. Wilson, *Decision on Palestine: How the U.S. Came to Recognize Israel* (Stanford: Hoover Institution Press, 1979); Stephen D. Isaacs, *Jews and American Politics* (New York: Doubleday, 1974). Isaacs reports that in New York state Jews compose an estimated 14 percent of the population, but cast between 16 and 29 percent of the votes. In New York City where they are one-fifth of the population, they cast half the votes in Democratic primaries. Although they constitute only about 3 percent of the national population, they cast 4 percent or more of votes in elections for president, and, more importantly, cast them in concentrated, high electoral-vote states. Isaacs estimates that Jews constitute between 10 and 20 percent "of all those actively involved on the Democratic side of American politics today" (p. 7).

78. Traditionally, Jewish voters have supported liberal Democrats, but in the last few elections there has been a move toward conservative Republicans. More than half of the American Jewish population lives in the greater New York metropolitan area, with other large concentrations in principal urban centers, including Chicago, Los Angeles, San Francisco, Boston, Washington, D.C., and others. According to Isaacs, Jews are concentrated in the eight states of California, Maryland, Massachusetts, Pennsylvania, New York, Connecticut, New Jersey, and Florida.

79. For a survey of the range and diversity of American Jewish organizations, see the listing of several hundred organizations in the *American Jewish Yearbook*, published annually by the American Jewish Committee.

80. Ibid.

81. AIPAC and other Israel lobbying activities are described in *The Middle East, U.S. Policy, Oil and the Arabs*, 4th ed. (Washington, D.C.: Congressional Quarterly, July 1979), pp. 89-95.

82. Among the very useful volumes on Israeli foreign policy and how perceptions affect policies are Michael Brecher's *The Foreign Policy System of Israel: Setting, Images, Process* (New Haven: Yale University Press, 1972), *Decisions in Israel's Foreign Policy* (New Haven: Yale University Press, 1975), and *Decisions in Crisis: Israel, 1967 and 1973* (Berkeley: University of California Press, 1980).

83. Two useful volumes on the negotiations after 1967 and Israeli perspectives are Shlomo Aronson, *Confict and Bargaining in the Middle East: An Israeli Perspective* (Baltimore: Johns Hopkins University Press, 1980); and William R. Brown, *The Last Crusade: A Negotiator's Middle East Handbook* (Chicago: Nelson-Hall, 1980).

84. An extensive discussion of Israeli settlement policies is found in William Wilson Harris, *Taking Root: Israeli Settlement in the West Bank, the Golan and Gaza-Sinai, 1967-1980* (New York: Research Studies Press, Wiley, 1980).

85. See note 16. As of the beginning of 1981, several Western nations including the United States refrained from recognizing Jerusalem as Israel's capital. In 1980 the 13 countries with embassies in Jerusalem moved them to Tel Aviv in response to the Begin governments's Jerusalem: Basic Law (see note 54 above).

86. In 1978 the yearly rate of Jewish population increase was 2 percent, of which 26.1 thousand was due to immigration. The rate of non-Jewish (Arab) population increase in Israel was 3.5 percent. In the West Bank the yearly rate of increase was 1.4 percent and in Gaza it was 2 percent. Although Palestinian Arabs had a birthrate of over 3 percent, population increase was diminished by emigration. Between 1967 and 1978 West Bank Arab population increased from 585.7 thousand to 690.4 thousand, and in Gaza from 380.9 to 450.2 thousand. Israel, Central Bureau of Statistics, *Statistical Abstract of Israel 1979* (Jerusalem, 1979). See Edward E. Azar and R. D. McLaurin, "Demographic Change and Political Change," *International Interactions*, V, no. 2 (1978), pp. 267-76, which uses the PLATO model to establish population projections for the occupied territories and Israel.

87. A comprehensive and definitive Labor Party pronouncement on policy in the occupied territories was the Galili Document, issued by the party in August 1973, reprinted in the *Jerusalem Post*, August 17, 1973.

88. See Abba Eban, "Talking Sense and Nonsense," *Jerusalem Post*, June 8, 1979, and Yigal Allon, "Anatomy of Autonomy," *Jerusalem Post Magazine*, May 31, 1979.

89. *Jerusalem Post*, 1978-79, passim.

90. Ibid. For a discussion of this perspective, see Moshe Ma'oz, "Soviet and Chinese Relations with the Palestinian Guerrilla Organizations," *Jerusalem Papers on Peace Problems* (Jerusalem: Hebrew University of Jerusalem, 1974).

91. A prominent Labor Party dove was Yossi Sarid, who frequently supported Peace Now and recognition of Palestinian political rights.

92. For a discussion of these views, see Harris, *Taking Root*, and John Edwin Mroz, *Beyond Security: Private Perceptions Among Arabs and Israelis* (New York: International Peace Academy, 1980).

93. United States Department of State, *The Egyptian-Israeli Peace Treaty* (Washington, D.C., April 1979), Selected Documents no. 11, DOS Publication 8976, p. 21.

94. See note 26 above.

95. See "Begin: There Is No Green Line," *Jerusalem Post*, April 30, 1979, and "Begin Airs Autonomy Blueprint," ibid., May 4, 1979. The proposal of autonomy was made by Prime Minister Begin in 1978 and later accepted for discussion by Egypt and the United States.

96. United States Department of State, *The Camp David Summit* (Washington, D.C., September 1978), DOS Publication 8954, p. 14.

97. After the Knesset passed the Jerusalem Basic Law in July 1980, Egypt suspended further negotiations on autonomy in protest against Israel's unilateral action. See "Cairo Voices Concern on Israel's Jerusalem Measure," *New York Times*, July 25, 1980, and both the *New York Times* and the *Jerusalem Post*, July-August 1980.

98. The solution of the Palestine problem, according to Golda Meir, was "inexorably linked to Jordan: 'The Palestinian Arabs are entirely capable of attaining national expression in Jordan. They need Jordan just as Jordan cannot exist without them.' " Brecher, *Decisions in Crisis*, p. 58.

99. *The Camp David Summit*, A1.

100. Ibid., A1(c).

101. See "Israel: Perceptions of Threat," *Beyond Security*, by Mroz; and Brecher, *The Foreign Policy System*, the section on "Ben-Gurion and Sharett."

102. Brecher, *The Foreign Policy System*.

103. Don Peretz, *Regional Cooperation in Education in the Near East* (Washington, D.C.: AMIDEAST, 1978), pp. 6-11.

104. Ibid. and Shimeon Amir, *Israel's Development Cooperation with Africa, Asia and Latin America* (New York: Praeger, 1974); Michael Curtis and Susan A. Gitelson, eds., *Israel in the Third World* (New Brunswick: Transaction, 1976); Susan A. Gitelson, "Israel's African Setback in Perspective," *Jerusalem Papers on Peace Problems*, no. 6, May 1974.

105. Isaacs, *Jews*, writes: "Many Jews regard the State Department as being staffed by a white, Anglo-Saxon, Protestant elite that is all but openly anti-Semitic." Henry Kissinger's post as secretary of state only slightly diminished these perceptions despite State Department attempts in recent years to expand the source of its personnel. To some extent, perceptions of differences on Israel between the executive and State Department are reinforced by observations in the books cited in note 77 above and by presidential memoirs relating experiences having to do with Middle East policy and Israel.

106. Don Peretz, "The United States, the Arabs, and Israel: Peace Efforts of Kennedy, Johnson, and Nixon," *Annals of the American Academy of Political and Social Science*, CDI (May 1972), pp. 116-25.

107. William P. Rogers, "A Lasting Peace in the Middle East: An American View," *United States Foreign Policy, 1969-1970* (Washington, D.C.: U.S. State Department, 1971), pp. 409-12.

108. For an expression of these views see Gil Carl AlRoy, *The Kissinger Experience: American in the Middle East* (New York: Horizon, 1975); Joseph Churba, *The Politics of Defeat: America's Decline in the Middle East* (New York: Cyrco, 1977); and the frequent columns of Shmuel Katz, Begin's former press advisor and now critic, in the *Jerusalem Post*.

109. See "The Jewish Community's Relations with Carter," *The Washington Lobby*, 3d ed. (Washington, D.C.: Congressional Quarterly, 1979), p. 145. According to this report, the Harris poll indicated in October 1977 that 60 percent of Jews interviewed gave Carter a negative rating and that 69.4 percent expressed disapproval of his Middle East policies. Between 1946 and 1981 Israel received a total in loans and grants from the United States of $20.7 billion.

Since then Israel has received some $2 billion a year in aid and additional assistance related to the Camp David agreements.

110. "There has to be a homeland provided for the Palestinian refugees," Carter stated at Clinton, Mass., on March 16, 1977. *The Search for Peace in the Middle East: Documents and Statements, 1967-79*, Committee on Foreign Affairs, U.S. House of Representatives, 1979.

111. Since the 1973 war, annual assistance received by Israel from the U.S. government is several times that received from world Jewry, whose principal contributors and purchasers of bonds are in the United States. The two major sources of private funds in the United States are the United Jewish Appeal, which collects voluntary contributions, mostly from Jews, and the sale of Israel Bonds to both Jews and private banks.

112. Saudi Arabia alone receives more than fifty times the capital imports from the sale of its oil that Israel receives from foreign economic assistance each year.

113. Cited in Peretz, *The Government*, p. 70.

114. *Divrei ha-Knesset* (Parliamentary Records), VI, 2035-37.

115. In 1980, 21, 471 Jews emigrated from the Soviet Union via Vienna, a 58-percent decrease from the 51,320 in 1979. By 1980, some 65 percent of the Jews leaving the Soviet Union, although nominally (according to their visas) headed for Israel, went to other destinations. *New York Times*, January 4, 1981.

116. In an interview with Eric Rouleau of *Le Monde* some years ago, Ben-Gurion observed: "We do not want Israelis to become Arabs. We are duty bound to fight against the spirit of the Levant, which corrupted individuals and societies, and preserve the authentic Jewish values as they crystallized in the Diaspora." Cited in Nissim Rejwan, "The Two Israels: A Study in Europocentrism," *Judaism*, XVI, no. 1 (Winter 1967), pp. 97-108. For an excellent discussion of this problem, see Smooha, *Israel: Pluralism and Conflict*.

117. Rejwan, "The Two Israels."

118. Ibid.

119. Ibid.

120. Ibid.

121. Smooha, *Israel: Pluralism and Conflict*.

122. There are extensive tables in ibid. giving information about distribution of occupations, 1954-75; percentage distribution of education, 1961 and 1975; percentage of Oriental students and graduates by type of school and class standing, 1956-57 to 1975-76; estimates of retention rates in primary and postprimary education, late 1960s; school performance comparisons; political representation in selected positions of power by rank and sector, 1955-73; Knesset, supreme court, Histadrut, military, police, local government, and other political representation.

123. Mina Zemah, *Positions of the Jewish Majority in Israel Toward the Arab Minority* (Jerusalem: Van Leer Institute, 1980), in Hebrew, including 1980 surveys of Jewish attitudes toward Israeli Arabs.

124. A critique of Israel's economy can be found in Abba P. Lerner and Haim Ben-Shahar, *The Economics of Efficiency and Growth: The Case of Israel* (London: Cambridge University Press, 1975).

125. Crittenden, "Israel's Economic Plight," and Joel Beinin, "Challenge from Israel's Military," *MERIP Reports*, no. 92 (November-December 1980). Beinin cites figures from *Ha-Aretz*, February 20, 1980, indicating that in 1980 the military budget was 32.7 percent of government expenditure; in 1979 military consumption was 13.7 percent of total resources (GNP plus value of exports); local military consumption was 16.6 percent of GNP in 1980 (excluding military imports); and the index of local military spending (excluding imports) rose from 100 in 1971 to 148 in 1980.

126. Beinin, "Challenge."

127. Ibid.

128. Crittenden, "Israel's Economic Plight."

129. The country's energy bill rose from $650 million in 1978 to over $2 billion in 1980. *Jerusalem Post* (international edition), July 20-26, 1980, p. 6.

130. Medding, *Mapai*. Good coverage of Israel's political history during the 1950s, 1960s, and early 1970s is found in Howard M. Sachar, *A History of Israel from the Rise of Zionism to Our Time* (New York: Knopf, 1976).

131. Jon Kimche, *There Could Have been Peace* (New York: Dial, 1973), p. 274.

132. Useful discussions of these subjects can be found in Luttwak and Horowitz, *The Israeli Army*; Michael I. Handel, *Israel's Political-Military Doctrine* (Cambridge, Mass.: Harvard University Center for International Affairs, 1973); Louis Williams, ed., *Military Aspects of the Israeli-Arab Conflict* (Tel Aviv: University Publishing Projects, 1975); and in personal memoirs such as Yigal Allon, *The Making of Israel's Army* (New York: Universe Books, 1970); Shimon Peres, *David's Sling* (New York: Random House, 1971); and the autobiographies of Moshe Dayan, Ezer Weizmann, Yitzhak Rabin, and Golda Meir.

133. Luttwak and Horowitz, *The Israeli Army*, p. 36.

134. International Institute for Strategic Studies, *The Military Balance 1980-1981* (London, 1980), pp. 43-44.

135. For a discussion of recently changing attitudes, see Beinin, "Challenge."

136. Handel, *Israel's*, pp. 32-35.

137. Ibid., p. 25.

138. See Major General Binyamin Peled, "The Air Force in the Yom Kippur War: Main Moves and Lessons," *Military Aspects*, ed. by Williams, pp. 238-45; and Ezer Weizman, *On Eagles' Wings* (New York: Macmillan, 1977).

139. William B. Quandt, *Decade of Decisions: American Policy Toward the Arab-Israeli Conflict, 1967-1976* (Berkeley: University of California Press, 1977), observes that when U.S. officials discussed the nuclear nonproliferation treaty with Israel in 1968,

> The most the Israelis would say was that they would not be the first ones to "introduce" nuclear weapons in the Middle East. In trying to clarify what this meant, United States officials discovered that it was understood by Israeli Ambassador Rabin to mean that Israel would not be the first to "test" such weapons or to reveal their existence publicly (p. 67).

For an extensive discussion of this topic, see Paul Jabber, *Israel and Nuclear*

Weapons: Present Option and Future Strategies (London: Chatto and Windus, 1971), and especially Robert E. Harkavy, *Spectre of a Middle Eastern Holocaust: The Strategic and Diplomatic Implications of the Israeli Nuclear Weapons Program* (Denver: University of Denver Monograph Series, 1977).

140. Luttwak and Horowitz, *The Israeli Army*, Chaps. 6-8.

141. According to Israeli Finance Minister Pinhas Saphir, the 1973 war cost Israel more than $2 billion during the first three weeks. Israeli government specialists estimated the total cost at $7.1 billion. Beyond the military expenditures, the war cost Israel some $480 million in losses from reduced productivity in the national economy. Almost 3,000 Israeli youths lost their lives as a result of the war, a total in casualties larger than those of 1956 and 1967 combined. See Don Peretz, "Energy: Israelis, Arabs, and Iranians," *The Energy Crisis and U.S. Foreign Policy*, ed. Joseph S. Szyliowicz and Bard E. O'Neill (New York: Praeger, 1975). Other useful discussions of the 1973 war are legion. Dupuy, *Elusive Victory*, covers this and other Arab-Israeli wars well from a military standpoint, and Avraham (Bren) Adan, *On the Banks of the Suez* (n.p.: Presidio Press, 1980), is an outstanding commander's view of the Sinai campaign. See also S. Z. Abramov, "The Agranat Report and Its Aftermath," *Midstream*, XX, no. 6 (June-July 1974), pp. 16-28.

142. See S. Z. Abramov, "The Agranat Report and Its Aftermath."

143. Ibid.; *Jerusalem Post*, 1974, passim.

144. A similar policy was followed in Iran before the revolution in 1978-79. The U.S. Arms policy in Iran was severely criticized in a U.S. Senate report, *U.S. Military Sales to Iran*, Staff Report of the Senate Committee on Foreign Relations, July 1976. In Max Holland, "The Myth of Arms Restraint," *International Policy Report*, V, no. 1 (May 1979), the author reports that "A 1977 GAO study found that it took the U.S. Army four years to rebuild its depleted inventory of M-113 armored personnel carriers after the 1973 Mideast war because recipients like Morocco were given higher priority. In another instance, TOW missile deployment to 13 Army installations was delayed because of expedited sales abroad" (p. 7).

145. Past experience has shown that Egypt's military contribution is essential in any Arab attack on Israel. Egypt was the only country participating in each of the four major wars against Israel; its casualties outnumbered those of all other Arab countries combined, and its war expenditures exceeded those of any other Arab combatant. In Cairo it used to be said that "The Arabs can't make war without Egypt, nor peace without the Palestinians."

SAUDI FOREIGN POLICYMAKING

ENVIRONMENT

Saudi Arabia and its foreign policy have assumed central importance in the contemporary Middle East even though it is a distinctly weak military power. The country's regional influence — which is substantial — derives not from its military capabilities, but from the kingdom's religious and economic position within the region and from its international leverage. This last element involves perceived influence on the United States, in particular, as well as Saudi Arabia's weighty voice in petroleum and financial circles.

Yet, Saudi Arabia was not until quite recently a major power, and is both the oldest and newest of the states studied in this volume. Although petroleum has been extracted and exported in the kingdom for almost a half-century, the criticality of its oil reserves and production, as well as of its resulting financial strength, emerged definitively only after the October 1973 War. By the early 1970s, petroleum experts foresaw the approach of a period during which rapidly growing demand would outstrip surplus production capacity, creating an apparent oil shortfall.[1] This oil problem was hastened by a selective oil embargo and limited production cutback applied by the members of the Organization of Arab Petroleum Exporting Countries (OAPEC), including Saudi Arabia, following the October War. One of the results of the energy crisis, apart from radically altering the importance attached to energy issues generally and materially affecting the nature and quality of life in the industrialized world, was the emergence of Saudi Arabia as a key country in the world arena.

Saudi production levels made it the world's premier oil exporter. Moreover, staggering Saudi oil reserves (also the world's largest) were seen to allow for production capacity increases that could help meet the projected oil shortfall.

196

While a number of factors intervened in this scenario — unforeseen drops in demand, internal Saudi pressure to limit production, little understood structural limitations on the feasible increases in production capacity[2] — Saudi Arabia was able in the late 1970s to influence, and clearly by 1981 to control, the international petroleum pricing system in large measure, aided by the Iranian revolution and the Gulf war between Iran and Iraq.

By the late 1970s, then, Saudi Arabia was seen by the world's major powers as critical: by Japan and Western Europe as the key supplier to their petroleum-dependent economies; by the United States as an important oil supplier to that country, a critical defender of the dollar, and as a vital element in NATO (for without Saudi oil, NATO's European members would have insufficient petroleum to consider, much less conduct, the defense of Europe); and by the USSR as a major Western vulnerability and diversion.

So much for the kingdom's rapid rise to international power. What is remarkable is that just 60 years ago there was no Saudi Arabia. Egypt, Iraq, Israel, and Syria are all "new" countries in the sense that each has emerged from colonial or quasicolonial status in the last five decades. Each in this sense is "newer" than Saudi Arabia as a wholly independent member of the community of nations. Yet, all are older in terms of traditions. Egypt's history can be traced to the earliest days of recorded history, and Iraq or Mesopotamia has an equally hoary tradition. Modern Iraq clearly traces its antecedents back for centuries. Israel's history can be said to have begun a new phase in the 1930s or 1940s, but Israel's raison d'être is inextricably linked to the unbroken history of Jewish habitation in the Holy Land, which can again be traced to ancient times. Modern Syria, too, is an artificial entity, yet Syrian political culture and a discrete and identifiable political tradition unique to Syria have resided in the general area occupied by the present state for millenia.

By contrast, Saudi Arabia is a totally different and much newer state. The name in English has come to be identified with the country, without reference to its meaning. Yet, Saudi Arabia means "the Arabia of the Sauds" even in English, and it was quite literally as the Sauds' Arabia that the country was unified. Before King Abd al-Aziz (Abd al-Aziz ibn abd ar-Rahman as-Saud), the Peninsula was not united. By the early 1800s, Britain controlled the Gulf littoral (although on a treaty rather than a colonial basis), the Ottomans controlled the Hejaz (the western area including Mecca and Medina) and parts of eastern Arabia, and various leading families vied for control of the interior. Between 1902, when he captured Riyadh, and 1926, when Ali ibn Hussein's forced exile effectively ended Hashemite control of the Hejaz (the Ottomans having been forced out as a result of World War I), Abd al-Aziz succeeded in bringing all of the present-day kingdom under the House of as-Saud, unifying the country officially in 1932.[3]

From the time of the unification of Saudi Arabia until somewhat after the halfway point of the twentieth century, Saudi leadership was particularly suspicious of the Hashemites, who had been displaced to what are now Jordan and Iraq, losing the throne of the latter in a republican revolution in 1958. Since the 1960s, however, this consideration has largely disappeared as a major element in foreign policy, though some residual suspicion remains in each royal family as regards the other.

King Abd al-Aziz remained in power until his death in 1953, by which time the seeds of an eventual close strategic relationship with the United States had been planted. Over the next few years, U.S.-Saudi relations vacillated, but American support for the external security of the kingdom never waned, nor did the magnitude of U.S. interests cease to grow. More and more Saudis were educated in the United States, and the cooperative relationship developed with ARAMCO and the U.S. government left a positive impression in many important circles. United States support of Israel was the major irritant in bilateral relations, and it is safe to say that Saudi elites simply could not understand U.S. policy in the Levant, considering it quite irrational.[4]

Still, the Levant and the Gulf were insulated from each other much more in the 1950s and 1960s than they are today, and Saudi Arabia was a much less visible actor. This low visibility meant that the kingdom was more often the reactor to than the initiator of events, but did at least provide flexibility and leeway during a period in which Saudi Arabia needed to develop greater infrastructure.

To consider the major political issues of the past decade in the Middle East is to conduct a series of case studies of Saudi foreign policy, for, unlike the years until 1973 when the kingdom pursued a low-visibility role, Saudi Arabia has participated very actively in the evolution of virtually every major regional problem. Yet, few claim to understand Saudi policy or even to be able to identify the process by which policy decisions are reached.[5]

STRUCTURE OF THE GOVERNMENT

Unlike the other countries addressed in this book, Saudi Arabia is a monarchy. Its governmental structure thus differs from that of Egypt, Iraq, Israel, and Syria. However, while no Saudi would claim his country is democratic, it does *not* follow that it is more autocratic than soi-disant republican regimes. Egypt, Iraq, and Syria, while "republics," are all governments in which one man's will is the essential determinant of key policy lines. In Saudi Arabia, no single individual enjoys such power at this time, although both King Abd al-Aziz and King Faisal in his later years did have enough prestige and respect to have enormous freedom of action. In important deliberations, their views carried such weight that they were generally able to act with full support where others pursuing the same approach would be questioned.

The governmental structure of Saudi Arabia is unusual in the contemporary world. Most states, new and old, have analogous structures whether they have a ministerial, presidential, or some other form of government. Saudi government reflects compromises in that direction as well, but retains many of its tribal traditions. The monarch combines religious and tribal leadership with his role as head of state: he is imam and guardian of Mecca and Medina; *shaykh al-masha 'ikh* (leader of the tribal shaykhs); and king.

Moreover, ultimate responsibility for all legislative, executive, and judicial functions resides with the king. Since the Qur'an is seen as the constitition of the kingdom, and since the *Shari'a* (Islamic law) is the legal code, there is theoretically virtually no restriction on the king's power.

Until 1958 the Council of Ministers had neither statutory nor customary authority beyond an advisory role, although the views of some individual ministers (for example, Crown Prince Faisal under King Abd al-Aziz) received substantially greater consideration than this statement might suggest. Even today, however, when ministers direct the activities of much larger bureaucracies within the ministries in which they are responsible, all policy and legislation are the provinces of the Council of Ministers as a whole and, therefore, ultimately of the king. Thus, the ministers have both more and less power than their counterparts in other systems: more, in the sense that they represent a unitary branch of government and need not fear restrictions imposed by a legislative or judicial branch; less, in the sense that all directive power derives from and is ever dependent upon the king.

The king is selected by and must retain the support of the royal family council. This council has a flexible membership and is composed of the leading members of the large royal family. It is within this council and among its constituencies that Saudi national politics evolve. The public and private forums of party politics in Western democracies are dissimilar in their media penetrability, but not dissimilar in their function from the council and its formal and informal subgroups. Because the immense royal family has many branches, several of which are clearly dominant, and because these branches are an admixture of matrilineal, tribal, regional, and personal relationships, the council resembles Western party processes in many ways. Decision making requires compromise to achieve the consensus that is at the heart of the Saudi system.

Royal family views are considered on all major questions confronting the kingdom, and these views normally diverge, reflecting the wide range of perspectives and interests one would expect from any large and diverse group so represented. The bringing together into consensus of these differing views is the hallmark of Saudi decision style. Few outside the country can understand how this system has worked so well for so long. The continued tenure of the as-Sauds depends upon family unity, but this can be said of many leadership groups that have disintegrated.

INTEREST GROUPS

Domestic interest groups relevant to Saudi foreign policy and decision making do not serve the same function as similar groups in Egypt, Iraq, Israel, or Syria. There is no formal process by which they articulate or press for specific policy approaches within the highly personalized Saudi system of decision making.[6] Indeed, even the pretense of such consultation is eschewed by the Saudi government.[7] In Saudi Arabia only a small group, ranging from two to perhaps 20, depending upon the issue and its salience, makes important foreign-policy decisions. Why, then, even consider interest groups?

The role and operation of interest groups vary across countries and over time. All that can be said generally is that any government ignores the opinions of powerful interest groups at its peril. ("Power" here is usually issue-specific.) Normally, we think of an interest group as an organized body of individuals, possessing some identifiable commonality of interest or value and able to articulate their views in such a manner as to exert some influence on policy. However, an identifiable and discrete influence on policy, even if it is immeasurable, is really sufficient to establish that a given corpus of persons is an interest group.

As we have indicated, interest groups do not apply direct pressure on policy, as interest groups, in Saudi Arabia. Nevertheless, there are groups, even if they are not cohesive, whose views, interests, or values are taken into account in either the formulation, choice, or articulation of foreign-policy options. These groups include the royal family, the technocracy, the military, Arabian tribes, the 'ulema, the educated, and city dwellers.[8]

Political Interest Groups

The primary interest group in Saudi foreign policymaking is the royal family, which in fact determines both the general guidelines for and specific policies of the country in its international behavior. Key policy decisions are made by the king in consultation with a small number of advisors. While the composition of the primary foreign-policy decision making elite varies to some extent depending upon the issue and its sensitivity, it includes the king, the crown prince, the foreign minister (Prince Saud), the minister of defense (Prince Sultan), and the chief of general intelligence (Prince Turki).[9] More generally, policy responsibility lies with the Committee of Senior Princes.[10] Because foreign policy often overlaps other issues (see below), the committee does play a role. However, key decisions continue to receive policy treatment by a much smaller group.

Lest the reader be led into believing the royal family to be very exclusive, we hasten to note that it encompasses between 3,500 and 4,000 princes, or (with female members of the family included) well over .1 percent of the entire Saudi population. Within the royal family there are a number of factions based upon blood lines. However, the royal family is omnipresent, permeating not only the senior levels of national government, but also the armed forces and provincial governments. The Saudi royal family must be seen as a principal political institution, but one combining tribal, family, national, social, and economic loyalties.

American and some other foreign analysts have seized with alacrity upon reports of divisions within the royal family.[11] Although differences of view do exist — as in any family, and certainly as in any elite of this size — the unity of the royal family is a far more profound characteristic at this time. Throughout the Middle East conflicts or apparent conflicts are emphasized by those in power as a tactic for the preemption and cooption of dissent. But there can be little question that despite differing individual priorities and policy preferences, royal family members almost universally recognize the importance of their fundamental unity to Saudi stability and progress.

One area of discord that may test the bonds of family unity is the succession to the throne. The strength of the royal family as a unifying institution bred — literally — by the founder of Saudi Arabia, King 'abd al-Aziz, is also its potential weakness, because the pretenders to the throne can be numerous. Although Khalid succeeded Feisal and Fahd succeeded Khalid without serious incident, succession after Fahd may become more troublesome. At the same time, the House of Saud has faced and overcome this issue in the past, and detractors often tend to underestimate the survival instincts and political sagacity of the royal family.[12]

Decision processes within the royal family are not well understood outside that institution. The traditional process by which decisions are reached is consensus among the senior royal family members, many of whom are largely unknown beyond the kingdom. (Royal family hierarchy does not coincide with official position in government or other institutions.) Achieving a consensus may prove elusive and thereby complicate and delay decision making on time-sensitive issues. Nevertheless, major questions of strategic direction, and many other salient but less momentous issues, continue to be addressed and resolved within the royal family.

In view of the breadth of authoritative decision making enjoyed by the royal family, much of the national-level decision-making apparatus and bureaucracy often appear irrelevant, so arbitrary seem the outputs. It is clear that the royal family believes it benefits from foreign ignorance concerning the means of reaching foreign-policy decisions, and rather than erecting a façade of democratization or consultation, the family goes to some length to underscore the personal nature of foreign-policy decisions. However, this process is undergoing change.

Choices that were once made unilaterally and without consultation by the royal family are sometimes influenced by public opinion and attitudes. Indirectly, of course, all governments are influenced by anticipated public reaction to policies and actions. Today in Saudi Arabia, the royal family frequently uses a first statement only to elicit a public response. That is, some decisions serve as ballots — they are designed to stimulate the reaction of both mass public and selected elites. The technocrats and 'ulema function as channels of communication to inform their publics of their decision. As a reaction emerges, the royal family assesses it and may revise the initial decision in light of (and not necessarily in accordance with) this reaction. This process, like that of consensus formation within the Saud family, consumes a substantial amount of time.

Another interest group that plays a growing role in Saudi decision making, including — but less markedly — foreign policy, is the technocrats. The technocrats are young men, for the most part, relatively well educated outside Saudi Arabia, who possess either technical or managerial competence. Although some royal family members may overlap this category as well, we exclude them from the appellation for analytical purposes. The technocrats are best exemplified by men such as Ahmed Zaki Yamani and Ghazi al-Qusaibeh. The former, as minister of petroleum, interacted heavily with foreign leaders following the OAPEC oil embargo of 1973-74, and as a result became an internationally known figure even where he had not been heard of before. He secured and retained the complete confidence of the king and crown prince. Al-Qusaibeh, less well known, became the minister of industry and electricity. Despite the nonforeign relations nature of that title, al-Qusaibeh was in fact a principal figure in more than commercial relations with the United States. He took an active role, for example, in encouraging the U.S. Congress to approve the controversial sale of F-15s to the kingdom. When irritated Saudi leaders observed the preoccupation of Americans *and* their government with the prospects of Saudi stability, and when it was revealed that the CIA had reported the Saudi monarchy to be on the verge of collapse, it fell to al-Qusaibeh to publicly decry the former trend and to recall that stability "does not depend on . . . the pronouncements of third-rate bureaucrats reading fourth-rate intelligence reports from fifth-rate spies."[13]

Apart from Yamani and al-Qusaibeh, the other key technocrats involved in the most sensitive deliberations are Hisham Nazer (minister of planning), Muhammad Aba al-Khayl (finance minister), and 'abd Allah al-Qurayshi (Saudi Arabian Monetary Agency director). For their part, in order to play an important role in decision making, senior technocrats in the kingdom must recognize and accept the special situation of the royal family and their own obligations to ensure its security.

The Military

Unlike the armed forces of other Arab countries, the Saudi military is directly administered by the royal family.[14] Considering the size, importance, and wealth of Saudi Arabia, the country's armed forces are relatively small and weak.[15] Army size is slightly over 30,000; navy, between 1,000 and 2,000; air force, about 15,000. Administration and control of operations of the services remain with the Saudi royal family. For example, the minister of defense is Prince Sultan, and his deputy is Prince Turki (both members of the "Sudairi Seven"); the chief of air operations is Prince Fahd ibn 'abd Allah; and for many years the commander of the national guard was Prince 'abd Allah, now the crown prince.[16]

A second unique aspect of the Saudi armed forces involves the role of the national guard. Palace guard units within or even outside the regular armed forces are not uncommon, but they are usually small, elite forces. The Saudi national guard maintains a strength of approximately 20,000, or two-thirds of that of the regular army. Personnel are virtually all of Bedouin background, most from the Nejd (where the Saud family originates). The national guard is entrusted with the security of the royal family, the oil fields, and the holy cities of Mecca and Medina. It is viewed as a counterpoise to the regular armed forces in the event of mutiny, attempted coup, or insurrection.[17]

Thus, the military establishment cannot realistically be considered an interest group separate from the royal family. There is little pretense concerning the political nature of Saudi armed forces. Their influence as a discrete political force is limited largely to questions of resource allocation, but periodic revelations of jealousy between the national guard and the regular armed services[18] indicate typical problems that arise in these types of circumstances. Should the military become an effective force as a result of the major efforts currently being devoted to upgrading all branches, the professional leaders might in turn develop power bases apart from the royal family. Such an eventuality is unlikely for at least the next several years.

The Tribes

Saudi Arabia was originally constituted as and remains a tribal kingdom. The principal tribes have traditionally played a major role in the public and private political life of the monarchy, which has for its part taken care to see that the tribes, both as social institutions and as political constituencies, had a vested interest in the continued security and strength of the royal family and national institutions. There is some question of the extent to which the tribes continue to exert significant control over their members, and even more skepticism of their hold in a country that is urbanizing as rapidly as Saudi Arabia. However, it is important to remember that familial and tribal loyalties are highly salient in Saudi Arabia, even among the "detribalized" (the urbanized). Moreover, tribes (and, again, families) do not operate alone; they are not unsophisticated political actors. Tribal politics shows patterns of coalition and alliance formation (and dissolution) similar to domestic or international politics in industrialized societies. In the aftermath of the Mecca incident,[19] the Saudi royal family has increased its consultation with and support of key tribes.[20]

As a discrete constituency, the tribes remain important even in the face of the complex modernization that is changing the shape of the Saudi social landscape. They continue to serve as the principal recruitment focus of the national guard. They represent the bedrock social conservatism and Wahhabi fundamentalism that are resistant to inroads of Marxist or other revolutionary ideologies. Consequently, the tribes provide fertile soil for the continued health of the Saudi monarchy; but left unattended to, this role may erode. Tribal elders are concerned about the weakening of adherence to Islamic values and to strict standards of moral behavior; about the distribution of financial largesse resulting from oil exports; and about what they believe to be an increasing tendency to take their support of the monarchy and of the monarch for granted.[21]

The 'Ulema

Second only to the royal family, the 'ulema (Muslim religious scholars) have traditionally been the most powerful interest group in Saudi Arabia. They continue to wield substantial weight, although the educated and the technocrats are playing an increasingly prominent role in the articulation of options from which decisions are made. The 'ulema tend to take a less active role in foreign-policy decision making, if only because their concerns are principally domestic in nature.

The Educated

Growth in the number of well-educated Saudis is impressive. Large numbers have been sent abroad for undergraduate, graduate, and technical education beyond the secondary level. However, concern has increased within the kingdom that Saudi students educated in the West may return with political ideas and social values contrary to the interests of the monarchy.[22]

As much as possible, the government has attempted to coopt returned Saudi students into the system to give them a vested interest in its preservation. Yet, many seek a greater role in — and responsiblity for inputs to — decision making than is possible in the current approach to foreign policy.[23] Moreover, as key policy decisions continue to be the prerogative of the royal family, with only a handful of technocrats participating, aspirations to a growing participation cannot be realistically encouraged.[24]

Saudi students abroad are widely believed (within Saudi Arabia) to be violating many of the tenets of Islam. Most Saudis, for example, have heard that Saudi students consume alcohol, smoke, and are lax in their prayers while in the West.[25] Such behavior is viewed as irreligious and deeply offensive in the Wahhabi culture of Saudi Arabia. But it is more than a social act; it is an act pregnant with political meaning because conservative elements in the country, elements on whose support the monarchy rests, blame the government for sending students into unhealthy environments. These elements exhibit hostility toward the principal foreign cultures they perceive as threats to Islamic values both within and outside the country. In recent years, and particularly in the aftermath of the Mecca incident, a substantial effort has been made to enlarge Saudi third-level facilities for education, and thereby to reduce the proportion of Saudi university students who must go overseas for the continuation of their education.

The foreign-policy impact of the educated class of Saudis is still relatively negligible, and a discrete approach to Saudi Arabia's foreign affairs is not discernible. Over time, however, it can be anticipated that pressure will build to transfer responsibility for the handling of less critical issues in foreign policy to the "bureaucracy," which must mean the educated class.

ISSUE AREAS

Saudi foreign-policy issues are highly interdependent. Decisions on national security problems such as force improvement and Gulf security cooperation, for example, interact with such phenomena as the nature and intensity of relations with the United States and oil production decisions. In this section we consider these and other questions. First, the military modernization issue is considered in terms of its foreign-policy aspects. The issue of oil production and the relationship with OPEC is then addressed. Third, we treat the Saudi foreign-policy implications of the Arab-Israeli conflct. Before considering general Saudi foreign relations, subjects such as Gulf security cooperation and foreign-policy impact of alien workers are explored.

Military Security

The preeminent foreign-policy objective is national security[26] — enhancing the security of the government of the kingdom from external attack or subversion. Saudi leaders have been forced to depend upon financial and other resources because of their country's military weakness. Yet, in a region where the use of military force is not uncommon, improvement of the capabilities of the Royal Saudi Armed Forces appears imperative. This view is not seen within the country to be the result of an arms race mentality. Rather, it derives from the abundance and value of Saudi oil reserves in a region characterized by violence and most of whose major countries are much stronger. Saudi Arabia seeks an effective capability to defend itself, not to attack its enemies even if provoked.[27]

Yet, if military security is an undisputed need for the kingdom, the subject has engendered several debates, a few of which are relevant to Saudi foreign policy and relations. There is less hue and cry against arms acquisition expenditures than found in Iran during the 1970s, although some groups, particularly some Saudi students studying overseas, have raised objections to the mounting and already impressive total of budgetary outlays dedicated to weapons spending. However, a steady and growing undercurrent has favored increased democratization in the country, and focuses on the military sector as a classic example of misplaced priorities. Although these controversies are not without importance, we shall bypass them as essentially domestic in nature to concentrate instead on the foreign relations and policy issues — What security strategy should Saudi Arabia adopt? How do the kingdom's allies fit into this military picture? What arms acquisitions and force structure patterns are desirable?

As in other governments, Saudi defense planning begins with an assessment of the external threat.[28] This threat assessment must consider Egypt, Iran, the Yemens, currently friendly Iraq, and, increasingly in recent years, Israel.[29] But beyond the potential attacker, such assessments — particularly in Saudi Arabia's case — must distinguish between alternative targets and conflict scenarios. Successful capture of thousands of square miles of empty desert would generate high costs for few benefits. Yet, for most potential attackers, the major Saudi cities are either inconceivable (for example, Mecca) or unreachable as targets. Thus, the principal target area must be assumed to be the oil fields of the Eastern Province, fields relatively close to both Iran and Iraq.[30]

Deterrence remains the primary Saudi defense objective. But the force that deters more effectively is the one that *appears* more lethal, not necessarily the one that *is* more lethal. Thus, the Saudis have in recent years moved toward the acquisition of prestige aircraft that may have greater deterrent value than combat value in the Saudi environment.[31] Within the national security sector, weapons acquisition decisions have come in for debate. Patterns of acquisition have also been challenged, as we shall see below.

The process of force modernization based on foreign inputs of expertise and equipment is a difficult, conflict-breeding process.[32] Trainer-trainee relations engender complex and often divisive reactions, including jealousy, feelings of inadequacy, arrogance, rejection, resentment, and others. Inevitably, trainees are unequally treated, both because of uneven trainer competence and because of trainee political standing. Costs, especially in a situation where the emphasis is on rapid change rather than economy and efficiency, become the subject of debate. Concern over the penetration of the armed forces community by foreign countries involved in training and equipping that community increases over time.[33]

All of these phenomena are present in Saudi Arabia, but it must be said that the Saudis have so far managed these problems as well as or better than the United States, the principal foreign country involved in the force modernization effort. Yet there is a noticeable growth in concern:

> The development of Saudi Arabia's . . . military forces . . . is almost totally dependent on U.S. equipment . . . advisors, and contractors and

is paced on U.S. advice. . . . [T]he Saudis spent about $19-billion on U.S. military goods and services during 1971 to 1978, and now spend over $1.5-billion a year on U.S. . . . military sales and procurement. . . . The Saudis now feel they have gotten little military capability for such a massive involvement.[34]

There has been little public debate about long-term Saudi defense planning. The royal family recognizes that domestic problems and subversion are more probable threats to security than a military attack.[35] However, the frequency of Middle East war, as well as the proximity — Aden's attack on the Yemen Arab Republic in 1979, the Iraqi attack on Iran in 1980 — preclude an exclusively internal focus. Moreover, the nuclearization of the Middle East[36] has changed from a "peaceful atom" nature to a sophisticated nuclear weapons capability in Israel[37] and a probable nuclear weapons program in Iraq over the next few years. Too, the Pakistani nuclear weapons program and Libya's avowed desire to develop such a program add fuel to the nuclearization process.

Despite the lack of comment within the kingdom, outside observers can hardly fail to note that the country's small population base places severe constraints on potential conventional capability and that cost of individual weapons systems is not a consideration.[38] In addition, because Saudi Arabia is not seen as an offensive military threat by any other major country, nuclear weapons may be considered less proliferative and more deterrent in the Saudi arsenal. They would successfully and substantially raise the price an attacker would have to plan to accept in order to gain control of Saudi resources.

It is in this light that Saudi support of the Pakistani "Islamic bomb" must be seen. The traditionally close relations between Pakistan and Saudi Arabia (see below) may facilitate either the transfer of nuclear weapons technology or an agreement by Pakistan to defend, even with nuclear weapons, the territorial integrity and political independence of Saudi Arabia.

Oil Production

The Saudis have used their influence in OPEC to restrain increases in the price of crude oil. This influence derives from the magnitude of Saudi production and reserves. Through manipulation of production and in conjunction with one or two other producers supporting price moderation, Saudi Arabia can create substantial surpluses of crude oil as long as the output of other major exporters is not interfered with by exogenous factors (for example, the Iran-Iraq war of 1980-81). Such surpluses, together with low prices that the kingdom could maintain, would undercut petroleum sales and revenues of other producers. Most educated Saudis have accepted their government's price moderation as necessary to maintain the stability of the international economy on which the Saudi economy depends.[39]

In contrast to Saudi public support of price moderation, high production levels are widely opposed and are generally believed to be a concession to the United States. Opposition to high production levels predominates in the country, but has so far not prevailed in the royal family, although it is found among some there also. Current Saudi policy is a rallying point for dissident groups, especially students, and irritates some regional governments as well. What makes the policy even more controversial is the belief, widespread in Saudi Arabia, that the country is "getting nothing in return" for this sacrifice.[40] (It is seen as a "sacrifice" in the sense that the kingdom is believed to be undermining its future by marketing more oil than it needs to, at lower prices than it could, and generating consequently unabsorbable revenue.)

The Arab-Israeli Conflict

The Arab-Israeli conflict has not been the principal foreign-policy issue for any of the Gulf states, including Saudi Arabia. However, the problem has been (especially since 1967) and continues to be one of the most important issues confronting Saudi foreign-policy decision makers.

Even before 1967, Saudis, like all Arabs, sympathized with the Palestinian people, and supported the frontline Arab states in their confrontation with Israel. Yet, the conflict was somewhat distant from the Gulf and did not significantly affect Saudi Arabia, the royal family, or the people.[41] However, as a result of the June 1967 War, Israel occupied all of Jerusalem, as well as the rest of the West Bank of the Jordan River, the Sinai, the Gaza Strip, and the Golan Heights. Also undergoing Israeli "occupation" (actually, only "control" in this case) were the Saudi islands of Sanafir and Tiran.

Saudi policy has been to play down Israeli control of Saudi territory.[42] By contrast, the Jerusalem issue has played a prominent role in Saudi pronouncements since 1967, and continues to cast a long shadow over Saudi policy toward the Arab-Israeli conflict. As a former U.S. ambassador to the kingdom has written:

> Jerusalem is *the* important issue. . . . Any Saudi government must have as its cardinal foreign policy aim the liberation of Arab Jerusalem. . . . Their official position, which is repeated in all private conversations, is that the only solution is . . . full, unimpeded Arab sovereignty over the Old City of Jerusalem.[43]

Indeed, Americans have tended to misunderstand Saudi Arabia's position vis-a-vis the Arab-Israeli problem. On the one hand, those who emphasized the irrelevance of Israel to Saudi Arabia simply fail to comprehend the Saudi perception of reality. To Saudi elites, Israel is "the real enemy," more proximate, more realistic, and more threatening than the Soviet Union.[44] Israel has continued to overfly Saudi territory, has made practice bombing runs on Tabuk, Saudi Arabia's northwestern military base, and has used Saudi territory for such activities as its 1981 air attack on Iraq's nuclear reactor in Baghdad. Moreover, events since the U.S. debate over an agreement to sell F-15s to the kingdom have substantially increased Saudi awareness of and sensitivity to the Israeli military threat to Saudi Arabia.[45] Beyond the threat presented, Israel is popularly identified as the enemy by virtue of its perceived usurpation of Arab territory. Across the country, all population groups are profoundly anti-Israeli. Such unanimity cannot be disregarded even in monarchic Saudi Arabia.

On the other hand, those who see Saudi Arabia as a threat to Israel fail to understand the limits on Saudi power. Financial transfers to the confrontation states have been limited, and have not offset IDF force improvements.[46] The concept that a militarily weak Saudi Arabia would simultaneously reduce its capability and increase its risks[47] by retransferring advanced weapons systems (for example, F-15s) is hardly a description of rational behavior. (And, in fact, none of Israel's Arab enemies has pilots trained to operate the F-15.) Since the U.S. proposal to provide Airborne Warning and Control System (AWACS) aircraft to the kingdom, Israel has claimed the AWACS could be used to coordinate an Arab air attack on Israel. For technical reasons, the AWACS provided to Saudi Arabia have negligible offensive capabilities against Israel[48] and, in fact, cannot even provide warning against Israeli attack,[49] although they can be effective against attacks by the other states of the region.[50] Israel is a far more credible threat to Saudi Arabia than the kingdom is to Israel.

The Arab-Israeli conflict has direct and important consequences for other aspects of Saudi foreign policy. Despite the trust the Saudi royal family evinces toward the United States (but see below), popular attitudes are less and less sympathetic to the United States because of its support for Israel. The great and growing gulf between elite and popular attitudes is at least partially recognized by Saudi leaders who refuse to accept U.S. bases, and even applied an oil embargo in 1973-74.[51] Saudi leaders also resent the subjection of what they feel to be their legitimate arms requests to scrutiny and "veto" by pro-Israeli elements in the United States.[52]

In addition, the cost of the Arab-Israeli conflict is staggering. Saudi Arabia, like other Arab oil exporters, has supported the frontline Arab states with assistance for economic development and military expenditure offsets, and has provided substantial subsidies to the Palestine Liberation Organization.[53] To the Saudis, Israel is not only a direct military threat but, even more importantly, an indirect political threat. Saudi leaders believe that it is the presence of Israel that has served as the principal boost to Soviet and radical inroads.[54] Arab countries have been compelled to turn to the USSR, in this view, because of U.S. support for Israel.

Therefore, foreign-policy elites in Saudi Arabia lament the Arab-Israeli problem. However, they are ill-prepared to resolve it because: they have been unable to support a compromise on Jerusalem; Israeli policy has discouraged

Arab compromise; the Arab world and the Palestinians are divided over what the shape of the best deal might be; and no reasonable deal has been put forward for their support. Several of these elements may change, however, and the Saudi leadership is anxious to do away with the Arab-Israeli conflict. Thus, leaving aside the thorny problem of Jerusalem, we believe Saudi Arabia would support a compromise the Arab world could accept. In 1980, the Crown Prince Fahd publicly pledged Saudi efforts to convince other Arab states and the Palestinians to accept a settlement concordant with the provisions of United Nations Security Council Resolution 242. On August 7, 1981, Fahd set forth eight principal points as fundamental to such a settlement. While the so-called Fahd Peace Plan was never more than a series of ideas designed to serve as an agenda for negotiations, the initiative and its importance were not lost on those who recognized that it symbolized a sense of Saudi urgency to restore some momentum to settlement progress.[55]

Gulf Security

One of the principal focuses of Saudi foreign policy has been Gulf security. While the subject first gained currency in the late 1960s and early 1970s, King Faisal pointedly refrained from exclusive claims on the role of Gulf protector,[56] claims such as those advanced by the shah of Iran. One major reason for this modest role was the military weakness of the kingdom vis-a-vis Iran and Iraq. However, other problems were involved as well — hostile relations with Iraq, distrust of the shah, and a number of outstanding border conflicts without the resolution of which any planning for Gulf security appeared chimeric.

In recent years, some of the impediments to security cooperation in the Gulf have diminished. Iraq and Saudi Arabia (with Jordan) have become closely aligned, and the shah has been overthrown. Current border disputes in the Gulf include disagreements between

- Iraq and Iran over the exact location in the Shatt al-'Arab of their common maritime frontier, a dispute which the world was informed had been "settled" when the late Shah was still in power by the terms of the March 1975 Algiers Accord, the provisions of which were declared null and void by Iraqi President Saddam Husayn in September 1980 [preceding the outbreak of full-scale war between the two countries];
- Iraq and Syria over control and use of the Euphrates River;
- Iraq and Kuwait over their common frontier and the question of control over Warbah and Bubiyan, two strategic islands lying in their offshore waters;
- Bahrain and Qatar over the Hawar Islands group located in the Bay of Salwa and over the village of Zubarah on the west coast of the Qatar Peninsula;

- Ra's al-Khaimah and Iran over the islands of Greater and Lesser Tunbs, forcibly seized from the former by the regime of the late Shah on 30 November 1971;
- Sharjah, 'Ajman, Umm al-Qawain, and Iran over offshore waters in which petroleum was discovered in 1972 near Abu Musa Island;
- Sharjah and Iran over the question of whether the ultimate locus of sovereignty with respect to Abu Musa Island itself should reside in the former or the latter state or be apportioned between them;
- Sharjah and Fujairah over their respective land boundaries, a dispute which re-erupted in June 1972 and resulted in the death of some two dozen Sharjan and Fujairan tribesmen and, as the 1980s began, still necessitated the intermediating presence of a United Arab Emirates Defense Force battalion;
- Dubai and Sharjah over territory being considered for commercial development along the border between them;
- Saudi Arabia and Kuwait over their maritime boundary;
- Saudi Arabia and Southern Yemen over the lengthy, undemarcated boundary between them and, specifically, in the al-Wadi'a area where armed clashes (and the capture and subsequent exchange of prisoners by both sides) have occurred;
- Saudi Arabia and Oman over Umm Zamul, a waterhole and surrounding territory in the undemarcated border area at the northernmost reaches of the Rub' al-Khali desert;
- Saudi Arabia and Egypt over the ultimate disposition of the island of Sanafir in the Straits of Tiran which, previously under Egyptian suzerainty, fell to Israeli control in the June 1967 war [see above] but is to revert to Egyptian control under the Camp David Accords of 1979, although sovereignty over Sanafir is claimed by the Kingdom;
- Ra's al-Khaimah and Sharjah over a valley area situated in disputed territory between them which is believed to contain potentially lucrative deposits of phosphate; and
- Ra's al-Khaimah and Oman over their respective land and off-shore boundaries on the Musandam Peninsula.[57]

Since 1973 the Saudi government has placed a high priority on the settlement of border disputes in the Gulf area, with some success.[58]

In place of these hurdles, however, others have appeared, most notably a new Shi'a consciousness in the Gulf area stimulated by the Iranian revolution,[59] the violence of the Iran-Iraq war,[60] and the increasing interest of outside powers in the Gulf.[61]

Although Oman and Iraq both put forward Gulf security plans, the Saudi government was not enthusiastic about either of these approaches. Of these plans, Oman's focused principally upon protection for Gulf navigation. Iraq's proposal was for formal military cooperation, including a joint security force.[62] The realistic Saudi view is that the fragile political structures of the Gulf states are their most vulnerable characteristic, and emphasis on security should therefore address this problem. To this end, Saudi Arabia has worked intensively to upgrade internal security capabilities and intelligence cooperation among the Arab Gulf countries.[63] Moreover, in late 1980 the Saudi government promoted a "collective security plan" for the traditional Gulf monarchies — Saudi Arabia, Bahrain, Kuwait, Oman, Qatar, and the United Arab Emirates. The Saudi approach stressed cooperation against subversion and other internal threats through police cooperation, information exchanges, improved communication channels and technologies, and agreement to deny refuge or access to subversive elements.[64] The Saudi plan led to the formation of a Gulf Cooperation Council in which the smaller Arab Gulf states and Saudi Arabia invested considerable effort beginning in 1981. The council concerned itself with the broadest possible range of security coordination, but residual distrust and paranoia, as well as solid security reasons, continued to limit some exchanges. No Gulf cooperation organization had begun more auspiciously.

Foreign Nationals

The presence of foreign nationals in large numbers is necessitated by the growth in the Saudi economy, which requires a labor force of both skilled and unskilled workers far in excess of what Saudi manpower can provide. Some 60 percent of the work force is foreign — Yemenis, Egyptians, Palestinians, Jordanians, Lebanese, to be sure, but also non-Arab (Koreans, Indians, Pakistanis, Filipinos, Thais, Malaysians, Sri Lankans, and so forth).[65]

Even apart from the social disruption that may be caused by non-Muslims in traditionalist Saudi society, Saudi concern about the security threat posed by the sheer number of aliens present is considerable, and popular attitudes frequently border on xenophobia. That foreign nationals can introduce a subversive element into the country is the more general fear. To reduce that possibility, East Asians (who are not as likely to be able to move freely or be involved in political issues in Saudi society) are being employed increasingly on short-term contracts, after which they must leave the country.[66] Relations with the countries of origin of workers may be affected by problems in the work force.[67]

A second concern is the Palestinians who comprise a large community in Saudi Arabia. Because the role of the kingdom is important in the Arab-Israeli context, the royal family and other Saudi leaders worry that for some reason Palestinians may move to undertake a concerted attack on oil facilities — the fields, conversion plants, pipelines, other installations, or shipping. These facilities are not secure and cannot be completely secured.[68] Nor are Palestinian skills for such an enterprise lacking: PLO personnel have had experience in refinery and many other phases of the petroleum industry. Thus, Saudi-U.S.

relations, as well as the country's support of the PLO and the Palestinian movement generally, may be affected by Palestinian capabilities to disrupt oil supply. Indeed, isolated incidents have occurred, but such problems are of manageable proportions. Certainly, Saudi perception of Palestinian disruption capabilities influences foreign-policy decision making. Yet, it is a systematic policy of disruption that concerns Saudi — and consumer — authorities.

Although it is true that Palestinians in the oil fields possess a capability for some sabotage and disruption, the primary royal family concern about the Palestinians is based on a somewhat different concern. The direct Palestinian threat may, in fact, be marginal except for short-term disruption. What Saudis fear is that the Palestinians, whose cause is supported by the entire population, may either provide the necessary external linkage for the small opposition groups that exist within the country or, as a result of external manipulation, cooperate with and support internal dissidents to foment some sort of upheaval. In other words, the royal family is less concerned about what the Palestinians can do than about what they can help others do.

In this respect, the foreign nationals issue, or at least the Palestinian component of it, is directly related to the Arab-Israeli issue; it is the sympathy of the Saudi population for, and their identification with, the Palestinians that provides the latter with their capacity to cause or aid unrest. Their plight evokes strong support and could possibly be used to mobilize some quarters against the government of its policies, especially policies perceptually related to the United States, which is seen as Israel's primary supporter.

Foreign Relations

Today Saudi Arabia is a very active participant in international relations, but this highly active and visible role is a clear departure from the past. Consequently, in this section we emphasize Saudi Arabia's contemporary foreign relations rather than the country's diplomatic and international history. First, we consider Saudi interaction with nonregional powers; then we turn to a consideration of the kingdom's relations with the countries of the Middle East.

Unlike most states of the Middle East, Saudi Arabia never experienced Western colonialism.[69] It is perhaps for this reason that its xenophobia never reached the apogee noted in most other Muslim states. King 'abd al-Aziz, founder of the kingdom, maintained generally satisfactory relations with the United States, which blossomed toward the end of and after World War II as Saudi petroleum revenues began to grow. From the 1940s to the present, the United States and Saudi Arabia have enjoyed a "special relationship."[70]

In the early and mid-1950s, Saudi foreign policies were often at odds with those of the United States. While the latter sought to erect a Middle East military alliance against the Soviet Union,[71] King 'abd al-Aziz and, after his death, King Sa'ud ibn 'abd al-Aziz, actively opposed this alliance for several reasons, principal among which were dynastic rivalry with the Hashemite rulers of Iraq and Jordan and concern over the potential isolation of the Arabian Peninsula from the rest of the Middle East. For some time, then, the kingdom and Nasser's Egypt cooperated and conspired to block alliance schemes.[72]

Later developments — the sanguinary overthrow of the Iraqi monarchy and the civil war in Yemen, which saw a large Egyptian expeditionary force supporting the republican side against the Saudi-supported royalist forces — made the earlier dynastic rivalries pale into insignificance.[73] Saudi Arabia became a silent but strong leader of the socially conservative forces of the Arab world, using its by then growing wealth for foreign-policy leverage.

Despite the early post-World War II conflicts between the United States and Saudi Arabia over the establishment of an anti-Soviet alliance, despite official Saudi nonalignment, despite continuing and fundamental disagreements between the two countries concerning the Arab-Israeli conflict, and in the face of substantial differences over the production and pricing of petroleum, Riyadh and Washington undeniably place a high priority on the continuation of their special relationship. Constant visits and careful coordination between leaderships of both countries characterize this relationship, which is based tangibly on Saudi value to the United States as a supplier of oil to the West and American value to Saudi Arabia as a protector, and based intangibly on the commonality of a number of values deriving from Islam (as perceived through the lenses of the royal family) and opposition to instability and Soviet influence (as seen by Washington).

At the same time, the U.S.-Saudi special relationship has become a major and very controversial issue in Saudi Arabia. There are increasing doubts that the United States is prepared to or could defend Saudi Arabia;[74] that Washington appreciates the value of its Arabian friend;[75] that the United States can upgrade the quality of the Saudi armed forces.[76] Moreover, the American stance on the Arab-Israeli issue both makes the relationship costly to the royal family and appears to suggest the United States takes Saudi Arabia for granted.[77] Finally, the new United States Rapid Deployment Joint Task Force, too weak to defend the area against the Soviets, is seen as the potential leading edge of a U.S. oilfield seizure.[78] Thus, there is increasing pressure within the leadership of the country — even in the royal family — and particularly from the educated classes, to put some distance between Saudi Arabia and the United States, to act more independently of U.S. interests, and to recognize and behave in accordance with the priority Washington accords the kingdom. The 1980 decision to request additional equipment for U.S.-supplied F-15s during an American election campaign, a time when such a request could not conceivably be approved, was clearly intended to test Saudi status in American eyes and to set the stage for a more "correct" relationship.[79]

Still, cooperation rather than conflict continues to dominate U.S.-Saudi relations. The executive branch of the U.S. government has endeavored to be responsive to Saudi needs and anxieties, sending sophisticated reconnaissance aircraft during the Iran-Iraq war, refraining from filling the strategic petroleum reserve, and working diligently to convince Congress to meet legitimate Saudi defense needs. For their part, the Saudis have exerted Herculean efforts to moderate oil price increases, continue to produce and export far more oil than the optimal level for their economy, and still look to the United States for support and assistance in political and defense areas. Common existential interests and perceptions outweigh growing differences. For now.

As these differences have emerged, as limitations on the American ability to provide desired weapons systems have become more evident, and as the patterns of petroleum and political interaction have changed, Western Europe has assumed a greater and greater role in Saudi Arabia's foreign relations. Never having undergone a colonial relationship with any European country, Saudi society has therefore not experienced the penetrative influence of European cultures. British diplomatic activity in the country antedates the establishment of the kingdom, but what were perceived as broken promises following both world wars and British-Hashemite links minimized the value of this experience to London.

Recently, European dependence upon Saudi Arabia's oil exports has generated a much greater degree of interaction than heretofore, as the Saudis have debated how to exploit that dependence and the Europeans how to ensure the continuity of the oil production. While public attention has focused upon joint and several European policy departures regarding the Arab-Israeli problem, and particularly the Palestinian issue, more fundamental linkages between Saudi Arabia and France, on the one hand, and between the kingdom and Germany, on the other, are evolving on the foundation of Saudi security needs. Both European countries aspire to a greater role in Saudi defense procurement, and Europe is emerging as an alternative to the United States in the minds of some Saudi elite members.[80]

Neither France nor Germany (nor any other European country) is in a position to project sufficient power to block a Soviet military move into the Gulf, but the latter contingency is recognized as unlikely in Riyadh. The French can project sufficient power to affect domestic disturbances and to significantly influence the course (but not necessarily otherwise determine the outcome) of local wars. Moreover, Paris has shown the *willingness* to act, and is believed to be more predictable than the United States with respect to domestic ability to carry out such a foreign-policy decision.[81] Europe's political stance on the Palestinian problem facilitates closer relations from a domestic standpoint, and several European governments have shown themselves capable of much more discretion than their U.S. counterpart. Thus, the Saudi Naval Expansion Program may be coordinated with the U.S. Department of Defense, but Saudi Arabia's naval procurement commitments already include $1.4 billion in systems acquisitions from France.[82]

Relations with the USSR began at an early period in Saudi history, indeed before the creation of the united kingdom under 'abd al-Aziz.[83] Despite an initial flurry of commercial activity, however, the two countries have had no real relationship for many years. That Saudi-Soviet interaction will grow seems clear,[84] but the royal family and Saudis generally harbor distrust of Soviet motives and reject Soviet values.[85] Most believe — whatever their views toward a tactical maneuvering vis-a-vis the USSR — that Moscow will work toward ending the Saudi monarchy and Wahhabi ethic.

Within the Middle East Saudi Arabia was a marginal actor until quite recently, with no significant political relationship with the Maghreb and little with the Levant. Even today, Saudi interaction with the Maghreb is distinctly limited. However, the interplay between the Peninsula and the Levant has grown markedly.

Saudi Arabia dominates the Arabian Peninsula. It is by far the largest and wealthiest country of the Peninsula, and is generally conceded leadership by the small sheikhdoms of the Gulf — Bahrain, Kuwait, Oman, Qatar, and the United Arab Emirates. All are monarchies struggling with the same processes of modernization and social change in conservative societies. The Yemens, by contrast, have experienced greater psychological independence from Saudi indirect influence, though the kingdom's intervention in the Yemen Arab Republic has been more direct. The only countries on the Peninsula approximating nation-states, the Yemens have less difficulty separating their own interests from those of their larger neighbor.

After the formation of Saudi Arabia, the kingdom and Yemen (North Yemen) remained the only two truly independent countries on the Peninsula. Both were conservative, both largely isolated from world affairs, both autocratic monarchies. Following a successful coup in Yemen, the republican regime, close to Nasser and supported by the Soviet Union, was opposed by the deposed royalist forces, supported by Saudi Arabia. However, the June 1967 War brought about the hasty withdrawal of Egypt's expeditionary force, and a subsequent Saudi-sponsored coup ushered in a new, pro-Saudi government. Since 1967, through several violent changes of government and policy in Yemen, the two countries have worked cooperatively most of the time. Yemeni leaders feel the Saudis and the royal family take Yemen for granted; are unappreciative of the key role Yemenis play in Saudi development and the Saudi standard of living; and meddle too openly, too deeply, and too frequently in internal Yemeni affairs. But Saudi Arabia and Yemen share a number of common interests, and, remembering 1962 through 1967, Saudi leaders will continue to view developments in Yemen as vital to the kingdom.

Meanwhile, the colony and protectorate of Yemen (later the Federation of South Arabia, then Southern Yemen, and finally the People's Democratic Republic of Yemen [PDRY]), following a long and bloody struggle, attained its independence from the United Kingdom. Since independence the country's governments have uniformly espoused, propounded, and supported revolution both as an ideology of government and as a program for the "liberation" of the Arabian Peninsula. The republic's three neighbors — North Yemen, Saudi Arabia, and Oman – have all experienced PDRY-supported revolutionary violence.[86] To the Saudis, the PDRY, the region's only avowedly Marxist government, is a Soviet base in the Arab world, a role about which Saudi leaders are very concerned. However, while the Soviet Union has been able to establish air and naval facilities on South Yemeni soil, there is evidence Moscow views the Yemenis, probably because of the inherent weakness of the government, as anything but dependable allies. Notwithstanding these Soviet-Yemeni problems and its isolation in the region, the current leadership of the PDRY will continue its pro-Soviet revolutionary orientation. Thus, as long as the present group of leaders in South Yemen and their supporters remain in power, the republic and the kingdom will behave as enemies.

Saudi Arabia's neighbors to the north, Jordan and Iraq, were previously monarchic rivals of Riyadh. The Hashemite Sherif Hussein was evicted from the Hejaz, abdicating the throne in 1924. 'Abd-Allah, son of Hussein and emir of Transjordan, became the first king of Jordan; Faisal, another son, became king of Syria (1920) for several months, then king of Iraq (1921-33). Thus, from the 1920s until the Iraqi revolution of 1958, the throne of both countries belonged to the House of Hashem, and Saudi interaction with both governments was affected by concern over Hashemite ambitions. Since 1958, however, Jordan's King Hussein, great-grandson of the Sherif Hussein of Mecca and grandson of King 'abd-Allah, has maintained cooperative if not particularly intense relations with Saudi Arabia. As Riyadh's role in regional politics has grown, the two kingdoms' interests have usually been parallel.

By contrast, Iraqi-Saudi relations were generally poor for two decades after the Iraqi revolution, as a succession of coups brought one soi-disant revolutionary regime to power after another. As we note below, the Saudis fear a dominant power in the Fertile Crescent, and continue to experience strategic concern as regards Iraq and Syria, the two principal powers of that subregion. The current government in Baghdad, however, has initiated a period of close cooperation with Saudi leaders in the form of a tripartite entente involving Iraq, Jordan, and Saudi Arabia. Despite the Ba'thist ideology and rhetoric propounded by Baghdad, the pragmatism of all three leadership groups has enabled them to work together effectively toward several common objectives.[87]

As Iraqi-Saudi relations have improved, those between Saudi Arabia and Syria have deteriorated. In part, this change reflects Saudi recognition of the weakness of the 'Alawi government and its likely demise. Damascus' isolation and weakness have pushed the regime toward the Soviet Union, another policy direction disliked in Riyadh. Moreover, Syria's moves in Lebanon were unpopular in Saudi Arabia, though Saudi leaders realized even their subventions were an inadequate tool to control Syrian policy.[88]

We have already discussed Israel in the context of the Arab-Israeli issue. Another non-Arab country, Iran, has played a more prominent role in Saudi policy in recent years, however. When the British left the Gulf area, the question of Gulf security arose in a new and more immediate way. United States policy suggested that the two pillars of Gulf security should be Iran and Saudi Arabia, as if Iraq — which American policymakers saw as too pro-Soviet — were not a major Gulf power.[89] In principle, the Saudis could accept this policy, and as long as they were fully backed by the United States might even believe they could play the role. In reality, however, none of the Gulf countries was "fully backed" by any external power. Closest was Iran, where the shah had a virtual blank check regarding arms transfers from the United States.[90] The size of Iran's population, its relative state of industrial development, the size of its armed forces, and especially the determination of the shah to be the dominant force of the Gulf and a principal third world power — indeed, eventually to become a great power — propelled Iran to the forefront as a political-military force in the Gulf. Yet, as Iran's military strength grew, and even as the shah's ambitions increased, the decline of Iran's oil-production capacity came into focus. Saudis (and other Arabs) became convinced that Iran as self-appointed (and American-anointed) Gulf policeman had an altogether too openly covetous eye turned toward the oil fields on the Arab side of the Gulf.[91]

Lest we overdraw concern about the shah's ambitions, we hasten to point out that Saudi-Iranian relations were on the whole cooperative; more, that the elites of both governments shared common views of the external threat and at times worked together effectively to guard against revolutionary ideologies and movements.[92] On balance, Saudi suspicions were directed more at potential than at actual Iranian behavior.

The deposition of the shah has completely altered the nature of the relations between Iran and Saudi Arabia, and has directly and seriously affected Saudi foreign-policy thinking. Postrevolution Iran is no longer a country that can — or for some years will be able to — project sustained military power across the Gulf. More than the shah's ambitions are gone; so, too, are Iran's military capabilities for a sustained offensive. However, more immediate and pregnant perceived dangers have replaced fears of the shah:

- First, the indecision and inaction of the United States have seriously degraded the value of the many commitments the United States has made to Saudi Arabia over the years. Thus, Saudi leaders feel more vulnerable, less protected, than ever before;[93]
- Second, neither Iraq nor Saudi Arabia is strong enough to replace Iran as guarantor of Gulf stability;
- Third, the fall of the imperial monarchy in Iran has been followed by near anarchy in that country. As much as Saudis feared the shah, they fear the unknown even more. Anarchy is seen as inviting dismemberment and, worse, some form of eventual Soviet presence across the Gulf;[94]
- Fourth, the leaders of the Islamic Republic of Iran have made little secret of their determination to export revolution throughout the Islamic world. They have specifically included Saudi Arabia as a prominent target of this objective;[95]

- Fifth, and finally, Iran's Islamic revolution has awakened the conscious-ness and restiveness of Shi'a communities in the Gulf, including the Saudi Shi'a population.[96] This potential problem is not one Saudi leaders are anxious to address, particularly given the communication linkages between the Iranian leaders and the Palestinians, on the one hand, and the Palestinians and Saudi Shi'as on the other.[97]

Saudi-Egyptian relations have been affected by Egypt's unique role in the Arab world and by Egypt's size. Whether in the domain of politics or in those of economics, military affairs, or society, Egypt's position in the Arab world is strong and independent. It is the size of Egypt's population that guarantees Egypt's role, for even though the country is poor, its labor force and aggregate output are important factors in the Arab world. Its military forces, from sheer size, are central to the Arab-Israeli military balance. Representing almost 40 percent of the total Arab world in population, Egypt's social practices and perceptions are of special significance and impact. Its Muslim centers of learning, such as al-Azhar, are respected and have traditionally enjoyed great deference in the Islamic world. Egypt is more able to act independently of the Arab world than other Arab countries. Egypt is more independent than Saudi Arabia, whose financial assets represent a resource desperately needed by Egypt.

Relations with Egypt were of little significance until the end of World War II, when Saudi Arabia first became deeply involved in regional politics. Between the end of the war and 1956, the governments of Egypt (both before and after the Free Officers' coup) and Saudi Arabia shared common tactical objectives and often coordinated their actions. Initially, this cooperation reflected Riyadh's Hashemite and Cairo's British concerns. Both governments feared the impact of alliance proposals for the Fertile Crescent, and worked together actively to undermine the appeal and potential for realization of these plans.[98]

After 1956, as the "Age of Ideology" settled in upon the Middle East, and in the wake of a Washington-based modus vivendi between the Houses of Hashem and Saud, Riyadh's policies were oriented more toward cooperation with ideologically conservative, administratively royal, and confessionally Islamic governments. After 1956 until Nasser's death in 1970, Saudi policy and that of Egypt generally collided, while cooperation predominated with Iran, Jordan, and the Gulf sheikhdoms. Egypt's support of the Yemeni republicans and dispatch of a large expeditionary force were perceived as a direct threat and challenge to Saudi Arabia in a geographical sector clearly within the Saudi sphere of security concern. The revolutionary rhetoric of Egypt (and Iraq and Syria) was hardly a balm to the royal family, and the growth of Egyptian-Soviet rela-tions deepened Saudi concern.

Anwar Sadat's religious background and commitment, his views on the Soviet Union and the United States, and his understanding of regional realities facilitated the return of the two countries' cooperation. Substantial Saudi assistance to Egypt went well beyond the financial plane; for example, the Arab Military Industries Organization (AMIO) was established in Egypt, directed by Egyptians, and funded principally by the oil-producing states, prominently including Saudi Arabia. The two countries' leaders supported each other in their interactions with their principal extraregional ally, the United States. General political strategy before and after the October 1973 War was discussed extensively among the two leaderships.

The Egyptian initiative of 1977, especially Sadat's visit to Jerusalem, temporarily troubled relations. Although most Saudi leaders understood what Sadat was attempting to accomplish, his uniquely Egyptian approach could not be endorsed or publicly tolerated by Saudi Arabia. Moreover, by 1980 Israeli activities in the occupied territories, and particularly Jerusalem, provided little ground for optimism. On the contrary, the Egyptian approach had the apparent effect of giving away the Arab trump card — for no credible military threat to Israel exists without Egypt — with only negative returns. Saudi leaders understood Egyptian policy, which was discussed with them by both Egypt and the United States. Privately, many Saudis felt that Sadat's approach, as long as it included "full participation" by the United States, held some potential to arrive at an acceptable, full settlement. They all recognized, however, that it entailed a go-it-alone policy. No major Arab country — certainly not Saudi Arabia — was in a position to support the policy.[99]

Despite fundamental differences over Egyptian policy toward Israel, differences that required severance of diplomatic relations as Egyptian-Israeli normalization proceeded, leaders of both countries recognized and accepted the predominance of shared long-term interests. Informal contacts between the two governments remained constructive, except for a brief period when Saudi leaders appear to have misunderstood the importance Egyptians attach to the Sudan. Some Saudi money has continued to move to Egypt, and Saudi leaders, whatever they think of Egypt's policy toward Israel, would certainly prefer a moderate to a pan-Arabist leader like Nasser, a revolutionary or a leader who supports revolutionaries, or to instability that could easily spread quickly. They share Egypt's perspectives on Libya's Muammar Qaddafi, on Soviet intentions and the threat from communism, and to some extent on the United States.

We advert to Saudi relations with Parkistan only because the relationship has important potential ramifications both for Saudi foreign policy generally and for the Middle East. The two countries have traditionally enjoyed cooperative and very friendly relations based upon Pakistan's devout and pervasive Islamic heritage and Saudi Arabia's fundamentalist Muslim ethic and role as custodian of Islam's holiest cities. Many of their international perspectives were compatible, if not shared, including close relations with the United States and distrust of the USSR.

Over the years, the good relations between Pakistan and Saudi Arabia have taken on a more concrete form. Saudis have looked to Pakistan's large Muslim army for added security;[100] in return, Pakistan has received considerable Saudi economic assistance.[101] The recent Iraqi move toward nuclear power has pushed this quid pro quo even further. Although Baghdad and Riyadh are now allied, Saudi leaders realize fully that this new relationship may deteriorate, recognize that Iraq's conventional military power is already immeasurably greater than that of the kingdom, and fear that the Saudi oil fields 150 (nearest land point for offshore wells) to 375 miles to the south may look irresistibly attractive.[102] Consequently, Saudi psychological movement toward a credible deterrent, a nuclear deterrent, is visible in support of the Pakistani nuclear weapons program.[103] Saudi Arabia at the present time has no nuclear infrastructure, and is not known to have enough trained scientific personnel to undertake a nuclear weapons program of its own.[104] However, Saudi leaders are likely to conclude that a U.S. or Pakistani nuclear umbrella is not credible and that their country would be well served by an ability to rapidly deploy nuclear weapons (a bomb-in-the-basement strategy). The development of Pakistani-Saudi relations will probably reflect Iraqi progress in nuclear technology, though Iraq too is less anxious to deliver nuclear weapons than to have a capability to do so.

SAUDI OBJECTIVES AND POLICIES

Until very recently, Saudi foreign-policy decision makers have been able to respond to problems in their domain, and undertake initiatives there as well, with much less regard to domestic problems or opposition than that faced by the other countries studied in this volume. In part, this fact reflects the charisma and leadership of the country's founder, King 'abd al-Aziz ibn 'abd al-Rahman al-Saud, and his son, King Faisal ibn 'abd al-Aziz, who reigned over the kingdom for virtually all of its first half-century. However, the traditionalist nature of Saudi government, where absolute real power has lain with the royal family, is also an important factor. As a result of the foregoing and of other aspects of Saudi political culture already discussed, the foreign policy of the kingdom has been characterized by an abnormally consistent and well-integrated set of interests, objectives, and policies.[105] Although there have been and continue to be some internal disagreements over optimal policies at any specific juncture, the range of agreement generally has been extraordinary.

Compared with the Levant, the Arabian Peninsula as a whole, certainly including Saudi Arabia, has been less frequently and severely upset by political ferment. The security of the monarchy has not really been in question since soon after the unification of the Hejaz-Nejd in 1926 (that is, the conquest of the Hejaz). Thus, the principal Saudi objective — regime security — is easily overlooked in favor of more immediate goals. With the growing number of Saudis exposed to revolutionary thought and foreign education; with changes in both economic and social structures sweeping the peninsula; with the added stresses of being a central rather than a peripheral actor in regional and international politics; and with the fresh spectre of Iran's revolution, Saudi leaders are much more concerned today with the security of their government and stability of their country than at any time in the past. Security is far and away the preeminent national objective.[106] Other objectives are subordinate to or supportive of this goal, and include:

- Prevention of the emergence of a hostile alliance to the north;
- Supporting the security of friendly governments and general stability in the Arabian Peninsula, Gulf, and nearby areas;
- Economic development of Saudi Arabia to improve the quality of life of Saudi subjects;
- Improvement of indigenous capabilities to defend Saudi Arabia against external threats; and
- Settlement of the Arab-Israeli dispute in a manner consonant with the preservation of Islamic and Arab interests.[107]

Saudi foreign policy, then, is increasingly and principally concerned with ensuring the security of the monarchy. The perspectives of the key figures in the country can best be understood as a series of defensive circles. Inside the first circle is Saudi Arabia itself; inside the second, the Peninsula and the southern Gulf; within the third, the remainder of the Gulf, the Red Sea, the northern Indian Ocean, and the Middle East.[108]

Arrayed against Saudi security, the leadership perceives a growing number of threats. Most immediate are hostile regimes and subversive political movements on the Peninsula and in the Gulf. Potential hostile alignments and groups are a second concern, but one of significant magnitude. A third threat consists of more distant foreign powers whose nature or interests are viewed as inherently dangerous to Saudi security.

Any proximate military power, if not counterbalanced by an equally potent enemy, is seen to pose an immediate threat to Saudi Arabia because of the country's extensive petroleum reserves and its limited defensive capabilities. Thus, while Iran enjoyed undoubted military paramountcy in the Gulf, the shah's ambitions were seen as suspect despite the commonality of monarchic self-preservation interests. Tehran's continued weapons acquisitions added to these fears, especially procurement of hydrofoils. Similarly, Syrian hegemony and the Jordano-Syrian alliance to the north from 1975 to 1978 were sources of limited concern for their potential threat. Saudi elite concern about military power is easy to understand because it reflects Saudi military weakness. Today, the threat posed by Iran is of an entirely different nature; Saudis remain worried about the new danger, and this fear is hardly less salient and preemptive than was their earlier concern.

Clearly, political agreements and cooperation between Saudi Arabia and other regional powers — potential threat actors — serve, as in other countries, to reduce the immediacy of the sense of danger. However, Saudi leaders are perhaps more conscious than many of their counterparts of the transience of alliance relationships. The attempt to construct an interdependent relationship with the industrialized countries of the Western world is a logical outgrowth of this recognition.

An important change in Saudi policy is its vigor. Prior to the late 1960s and 1970s, Saudi Arabia was less visible, less powerful, and less determined to act. Since the mid-1970s, the kingdom has gained at least as much in activism as it has in importance. Once concerned with relatively parochial and immediate foreign-policy issues, the Saudi monarchy today manifests both attention and initiative well beyond the confines of the Peninsula, though generally within the geographical area delimited by the three circles described above.[109]

Political Policies

Saudi Arabia is unquestionably one of the more powerful countries in the world, but the configuration of the elements of Saudi power is highly unusual. Moreover, most great powers are domestically, locally (regionally), and internationally powerful for similar reasons, while Saudi domestic, regional, and international power are rather asymmetrical. The government's internal power derives from institutional stability and legitimacy. The institutions of Saudi government have uncommon strength in the developing world, but strength based upon a social order that may undergo very fundamental shifts as a result of the process of social change in which the country now finds itself.[110] (Little wonder Saudi leaders have often been ambivalent about the development process!) Saudi regional power is based upon the country's international role (its ability to significantly influence great powers, and even the United States, to a degree unmatched by other third world governments), its stability, its financial wealth, and by its religious role. The international power of the kingdom derives principally from its role as a major oil supplier with vast reserves, and secondarily from its financial status. Saudi Arabia's political stability has also played a role in its international position.

Saudi leaders understand that the influence conferred by their oil supply role has given them more power internationally than regionally, a highly unusual situation. (None of the Middle East states has a large enough economy to depend upon oil supply as much as the United States, Western Europe, and Japan.) They understand intuitively that an interdependent relationship with the developed world — or some of its leading countries — therefore holds out a much greater prospect of stability in alliances than any accord with other Middle East states can. Yet, this is no idle exercise in philosophy; it is a question of survival. Construction of an enduring interdependent relationship has been a high priority in Saudi policy with a view to securing from the other party — the West, Europe, and the United States — the military wherewithal necessary to defend the regime in return for a stable supply of oil. It is within this overall objective that specific political, economic, and military programs related to foreign policy should be understood.

Saudi political power in bilateral relationships derives principally from the country's mineral and financial wealth, and secondarily from the regional influence this wealth confers (both through actual and potential financial transfers to the other party, and through the regional visibility and leadership the volume of these transactions has conferred). As another result of this wealth, Saudi Arabia is widely believed to have substantial influence over U.S. behavior. Thus, some element of Saudi political power is based on regional beliefs that Saudi Arabia is protected by and can affect the policies and actions of the United States. Also, as the largest and richest of the traditional monarchies of the Arabian Peninsula, Saudi Arabia has long been the acknowledged leader of the smaller Gulf sheikhdoms. Other elements of national power (such as religious leadership) are treated below.

To the north of Saudi Arabia lies the only contiguous area occupied by a more developed country. Among developing countries, military prowess is directly correlated to the achievement of a certain level of advancement. Thus, the only direct military threat to Saudi Arabia from a contiguous state derives from the north, since the Yemens are both smaller in population and much less developed. To the north, then, Saudi leaders have instinctively recognized the potential of an Iraqi-Syrian alliance or entente. Consequently, Saudi behavior has reinforced the differences separating Iraq, Jordan, and Syria. Because Jordan's weakness constrains that country to maintain a protector, the Hashemite kingdom is usually aligned with another important power, most recently Iraq or Syria. The Saudis have therefore aimed at keeping these alliances fluid enough to ensure that Iraq, Jordan, and Syria never joined forces in any meaningful way.

We have already discussed the shifting relationships between these countries over the last few years. Lacking military power, and recognizing the inherent limitations on the effectiveness of economic and social power, Saudi leaders have endeavored to retain some options within their northern neighbors' domestic political arenas. They have been most successful in Syria, where Muslim conservatism and the Muslim Brotherhood have always enjoyed considerable and widespread support. Cooperation with Jordan has precluded the recourse to whatever latent internal resources Saudi Arabia may enjoy there. The Saudis seemingly have even less direct influence in Iraq. Nevertheless, as communication with Syrian opposition elements was never completely severed, similar patterns of behavior can be expected vis-a-vis Iraq.

More elusive than the threat posed by conventional states is that posed by several minority groups — particularly the Palestinians (a nonstate national minority), the Shi'as (a religious minority), aliens as a whole, and the educated (a socioeconomic minority). Because this book concerns foreign policy, we will not spend a great deal of time discussing these issues in detail. However, Saudi concern for security with respect to these groups has a direct bearing on foreign policy, since Saudi leaders believe, with some justification, that one or more of the groups could be exploited by a foreign power.

Palestinians in Saudi Arabia are numerous (over 100,000), playing a key role in oil field labor. They appear to be and act apolitical. However, intragroup communication is excellent, and a sufficient number among them are closely linked with the PLO to carry out such disruptive actions as that organization may direct, should Saudi-PLO relations deteriorate. It is precisely because of the important, constructive role the Palestinians currently play and of the disruption of which they are capable that Saudi leaders have worked so diligently to maintain cooperative relationships with the Palestinian movement. (We do not by this statement mean to call into question Saudi support for the Palestinian cause. Saudis identify completely with the Palestinian position vis-a-vis Israel.)

By contrast with policy foresight directed toward the Palestinians, Saudi elites have neglected, and thereby permitted or encouraged the discrimination against the large number of Shi'as inhabiting the Eastern Province. Previously passive in the face of such discrimination, Saudi Shi'as have in recent years been much more open in their communal consciousness, and even violent in their opposition to the conditions they face in Saudi Arabia. The clearly Shi'a nature of the Iranian revolution and the public statements of Iranian leaders concerning the export of their revolution have undoubtedly breathed life into Saudi Shi'a consciousness.

While not a majority as in some of the Gulf states, foreigners as a group constitute a significant proportion of the Saudi population. Saudis are correctly less concerned about the capabilities of foreigners to form a fifth column than are Westerners. The former feel that they have sufficient intelligence assets located among the alien population as a whole; that most of the foreigners in Saudi Arabia are apolitical and incapable of conspiring against the regime, and in fact have a vested interest in maintaining the regime; and that the foreign population is composed of many groups of diverse nationality and more diverse interests. However, specific nationalities do attract some concern among Saudi elites – the Palestinians and Yemenis, for example.

Educated Saudis do not constitute a threat to the government at this time, perhaps because there is so much opportunity for them in the country. Notwithstanding the dynamism of the economy, however, there is a natural ceiling on the number of Saudis likely to find satisfying positions in the country. If they are not influential – and all cannot be – will their dissatisfaction result in antigovernment plotting? Will the frustration of economic power and political weakness lead them in this direction? What will the effect of Western education, secular and democratic in orientation, be on their political values, objectives, and actions?

Military Policies

The size of Saudi Arabia's skilled manpower base and the nonmilitary demand for technically competent manpower are such that the kingdom's armed forces are not large or sophisticated enough to be considered capable of offensive military operations. Saudi Arabia's defense may be more easily effected by virtue of the deficiencies of potential opposing military forces and of geographical considerations. Yet, military programs do play a role in Saudi foreign policy.

Major long-term programs are currently aimed toward upgrading the quality of the Royal Saudi Air Force and the Royal Saudi Navy. Ground forces equipment modernization and manpower-training programs are also under way. The purpose of these and other military enhancement programs is to significantly increase the likely cost of military operations against Saudi Arabia to any attacker. Defense of all Saudi territory may not be necessary, however, for there are really only three target areas of value in the country — the oil facilities, which are the economic and financial lifeblood of Saudi Arabia and the West; the capital, which symbolizes the government's political control (and to a large extent, that of the royal family); and Mecca and Medina, the holy cities of Islam. (Moreover, it is almost inconceivable that any foreign power would attack Mecca or Medina, so the government needs to guard these cities only or principally against internal threats.) Thus, construction of an effective deterrent may feasibly rely more upon effective tactical defense — almost point defense — than upon deterrence through retaliatory capacity.

In addition to upgrading national defensive capabilities, the general concept of "Gulf security," including regional defense coordination, has been publicly endorsed by several Saudi leaders. In practice, the rivalries and suspicions among the Gulf states have precluded collaborative defense planning on a meaningful level. Moreover, although Saudi Arabia is the primus inter pares on the Peninsula itself, it is highly questionable whether Saudi forces could be projected effectively into the other Gulf states to defend their regimes. Still, the creation of a potent, mobile defense force may at least serve some deterrent effect, and any such contribution to stability in the Gulf would be considered extremely valuable by Saudi decision makers.

Programs of armed forces modernization, including extensive procurement plans, are also intended to retain and expand cooperative relations with Western industrial powers, especially the United States. On the one hand, these programs are designed to increase the willingness of the Western powers to defend Saudi Arabia, if necessary. On the other hand, the programs may spur potential attackers into believing such Western intervention is more likely.

Soviet penetration of the region, as well as communism as an ideology, are viewed with considerable concern by many in the royal family. However, no Saudi seriously contemplates defending the country militarily against a Soviet attack. Protection in such a contingency would of necessity depend upon a

Western response. However, the Saudi leadership believes it can play an effective role in countering the external subversive threat from the Soviet Union and other hostile regimes. The political element of this role is in support of Saudi allies and clients both in terms of domestic institutions and of international affairs. In particular, Saudi influence (and money) is used to reduce the presence of the Soviet Union and its attractiveness as a political option for nearby states. In effect, Saudi foreign policy serves as an adjunct to military defense of the country to deny bases of operations to external forces perceived to be hostile.

Economic Policies

As we have indicated, Saudi leaders depend principally on economic tools to achieve their political and military objectives. Saudi economic resources are of two types — petroleum and petrodollars. These assets can be employed to buy protection, to buy off (dissuade) a threat, and to reward or punish.

The sale of or refusal to sell oil is often less valuable as a policy tool than pledges to provide oil in the event of a tight market or threats to withhold oil or restrict production. (Clearly, the effectiveness of any of these tools is dependent as well upon actual and anticipated market conditions.) Until 1973, Saudi leaders generally eschewed the use of oil as a weapon with few exceptions. In that year, however, some futile attempts were made to secure a privileged position in the American economy in return for certain guarantees as to production and supply.[111] The later October War oil embargo and price increases, followed by production cutbacks and additional increases, have firmly established the utility of the oil weapon.

The most controversial and constant use of oil as a weapon has been in the context of the Arab-Israeli conflict, where Saudi leaders have acted or threatened to act unless U.S. policy reflected greater sympathy to the Arab and Palestinian causes. A threat to act *is* an employment of the oil weapon. However, Saudi leaders have shown themselves anxious to avoid production action contrary to sound economic principles both for economic reasons and in deference to the larger strategy of interdependence described above. That Saudi leaders are torn over the linking of petroleum supply to the Arab-Israeli issue is clear and understandable, because conditions could lead to sacrifice of the most important strategic goal (a strong, interdependent relationship with the West to guarantee Saudi security) for a (possibly transient) tactical objective (good relations with neighboring states and the PLO, support of the Palestinian cause, and so forth).

Capital generated by the petroleum trade has placed a strategic asset of enormous importance in Saudi hands. In the regional environment, these funds are used for economic assistance and "security supporting assistance" (materiel procurement offset). Development loans have been provided through a variety of mechanisms, and in some cases Saudi investment has also been directed to other than official recipients. By "security supporting assistance" we mean financial aid designed to offset or underwrite the costs of weapons acquisition. While such aid is customarily provided for political purposes, it may also be viewed as a military investment, since the country assisted may be more inclined to put its armed forces or its equipment at the disposal of the Saudis.

Saudi Arabia has also used several channels to provide economic assistance to the West. The most important direct form of aid has been large-scale Saudi investment, both public and private. A second type of assistance, critical to the world economy, is the availability of Saudi funds for the major capital markets of the West. International liquidity has become dependent upon the Arab oil producers' capital surpluses and their willingness to allow these surpluses to be used.

Recognizing that collapse of the international economy would destroy the economies of the oil producers as well, Saudi leaders cannot seriously or rationally contemplate capital hoarding to such an extent. However, the availability of, and the ability to transfer or withhold, vast financial resources constitute, within these parameters, considerable potential power at both the bilateral and multilateral levels, power that has been used on a limited basis from time to time.

Thus, petroleum and petrodollars are formidable resources to attain political and military objectives. Aid has been used, for example, to persuade a proximate country to extrude Soviet advisors, end the substantial Soviet presence, and reorient its cooperation toward the West. Similarly, Riyadh subsidizes its enemies' adversaries. These uses of Saudi capital and oil can be seen as both buying protection and buying off the threat.

Social Policies

Given the political objectives of cultural and social policies pursued by the other states studied in this volume, we have concentrated on their political and military policies instead. However, the importance of Islam both as a channel of communication of Saudi power and as policy compels special treatment of the subject in this chapter.

Because the holy cities of Mecca and Medina are in Saudi Arabia, the birthplace of Islam, the Saudi government occupies a singular position in the region as guardian of the holy places and as Islamic leader. Not only are the holy cities sacred to Muslims worldwide; visiting them is the obligation of every Muslim who can, visits that must fall to Saudi Arabia to facilitate and protect. Moreover, Saudi Arabia's role as religious leader derives as well from the fundamentalist nature of Islam in Saudi practice (Wahhabism) and from the intimate relationship between state and faith in the kingdom.[112] Saudi Arabia's religious role has been used to legitimize Saudi foreign policies, and to broaden support for Saudi policy as "Islamic policy."

Even beyond the use of religious leadership, the Saudi royal family believes that a more fervent Islamic consciousness throughout the region is desirable.[113] The reason for this belief may be explained as nationalistic or may be explained simply by reference to the frequent observation that "the constitution of Saudi Arabia is the Qur'an," that is, that which supports Islam supports Saudi Arabia. To this end, economic leverage has been used to fight secular trends or to desecularize Muslim countries:

> In both the domestic and the international arenas, therefore, Islam is far more than a mere rhetorical subject for the ruling elite. It pervades social customs and interactions. It dominates images and attitudes. It motivates policies and is used to justify them. And it embodies the system of values upon which the legitimacy of the regime rests.[114]

NOTES

1. See James E. Akins, "The Oil Crisis: This Time the Wolf Is Here," *Foreign Affairs*, LI, 3 (April 1973), pp. 462-90.

2. See U.S. Congress, Senate, 96th Congress, 1st Session, Committee on Foreign Relations, Subcommittee on International Economic Policy, *The Future of Saudi Arabian Oil Production*, Committee print, Washington, D.C., April 1979.

3. For a more detailed history, see David Holden and Richard Johns, *The House of Saud: The Rise and Rule of the Most Powerful Dynasty in the Arab World* (New York: Holt, Rinehart and Winston, 1981), and sources there cited, as well as the classic H. St. John B. Philby, *Saudi Arabia* (London: Benn, 1955).

4. James E. Akins, "Saudi Arabia, Soviet Activities, and Gulf Security," *The Impact of Iranian Events upon Persian Gulf and United States Security*, ed. Z. Michael Szaz (Washington, D.C.: American Foreign Policy Institute, 1979), p. 90.

5. Exceptions are William B. Quandt's excellent study of *Saudi Arabia in the 1980s: Foreign Policy, Security and Oil* (Washington, D.C.: Brookings, 1981); Enver Khoury's *The Saudi Decision-Making Body: The House of al-Saud* (Hyattsville, Md.: Institute of Middle Eastern and North African Affairs, 1978); and Adeed I. Dawisha, "Saudi Arabia's Search for Security," *Adelphia Papers*, no. 158 (1979). See also Lincoln P. Bloomfield, Jr., "Saudi Arabia Faces the 1980s: Saudi Security Problems and American Interests," *Fletcher Forum*, V, 2 (Summer 1981), pp. 243-77.

6. We should not overlook the fact of institutional developments outside the narrowly defined foreign-policy sector that may someday impinge upon decision making, however. In 1980 the government stated it would move toward the establishment of consultative representation. While such democratic forms were not, and were not described as, powerful institutions of popular will, it is premature to assess their potential or future direction.

7. Some of the Arabian tribal traditions are much more "democratic" than the monarchic traditions of Europe. The Saudi king still requires support by the many tribes of the kingdom, for example. Far and away the most interesting and "democratic" of these traditions, however, is the king's weekly audience with those of his countrymen who wish to speak with him. Indeed, it was in the course of such an audience in 1975 that King Faisal was assassinated.

8. The royal family, the technocracy, the educated, and the 'ulema are groups based on *class* distinctions. To some extent, this is also true of Saudi city dwellers, although the population of Saudi cities is heavily foreign. Collins correctly notes the importance of regional interests within the kingdom, but interest groups based on region are usually irrelevant to foreign-policy issues. Michael Collins, "Riyadh: The Saud Balance," *Washington Quarterly*, IV, 1 (Winter 1981), pp. 200-1.

9. It is interesting to note that King Fahd, Prince Sultan, and Prince Turki are full brothers. This group, with its four other members, constitutes the so-called Sudairi Seven, perhaps the most powerful branch of the royal family. Another group of full brothers, junior to the Sudairis but a force to be reckoned with in the future, includes the sons of the late King Faisal, led by Foreign Minister Saud al-Faisal.

10. The institution of the royal family is very broad, encompassing several major branches such as the Jaluwis and the Thunayans, and is not limited to the immediate family of King 'abd al-Aziz. Indeed, hierarchy within the family depends to a large extent upon seniority on the genealogical basis of the eponymous founder of the House of Sa'ud. Thus, brothers of 'abd al-Aziz (the "uncles") have senior standing within family councils.

11. E.g., Henry L. Trewhitt, "U.S. Fears Unrest in Saudi Arabia," *Baltimore Sun*, January 23, 1979, p. 4; Jim Hoagland, "U.S. Sees Signs Saudi Leadership May Be Shifting," *Washington Post*, April 15, 1979, p. 1; "The Saudi Puzzle," *Newsweek*, April 30, 1979, p. 27.

12. Collins, "Riyadh," provides a good overview of the succession problem (pp. 205-8). The focal point of dispute has always been Crown Prince 'abd-Allah and his rivals rather than King Fahd. How long will the throne remain in the hands of the first generation of 'abd al-Aziz's heirs? What makes the succession problem more dangerous to stability today is the increased pressure on the kingdom as a result of external regional conflicts and threats.

13. Speech before the National Association of Arab Americans, May 3, 1980.

14. Some other Arab governments also directly control their military establishments, but usually on an informal basis. The true role of Rifaat Assad in Syria, for example, substantially exceeds his nominal position in the armed forces.

15. Smaller than those of Algeria, Egypt, Iran, Iraq, Israel, Jordan, Morocco, the Sudan, and Syria; smaller than those of Libya, if only regular armed forces are included. Only Lebanon, Tunisia, the Yemens, and the sheikhdoms of the Gulf have smaller armed forces.

16. But see note 12 above and source cited there.

17. See Adeed Dawisha, "Saudi Arabia's Search for Security," *Adelphia Papers*, no. 158 (Winter 1979-80), p. 16.

18. Collins, "Riyadh," p. 204, discusses the intentionally created rivalry between the National Guard and the regular armed forces.

19. In November 1979 the Great Mosque in Mecca was seized by about 250 persons, allegedly Mahdist zealots. There has been some speculation that the action was part of a planned uprising of much greater proportions, but certainly the most alarming element of the attack was the prevalence of Utaybeh tribe members in the Mahdist group. The Utaybeh are an important tribe stretching from Palestine to the Gulf, who play a major role in Saudi internal security forces. It required two weeks − and the assistance of other countries − to extricate the occupiers.

20. While the purpose of the new emphasis on consultation is not to reinforce tribal loyalties, and, as Collins suggests (p. 202), new consultative institutions are designed to facilitate participation instead by the educated and the technocrats, the royal family is attempting to purchase greater support on the basis of an increased role for their own views. Whether they accept this approach, and whether, indeed, they retain the decisive force they once held in the kingdom, will probably become clear in the naming of a successor to Fahd as king.

21. Leaders of key tribes or tribal alliances believe they should be consulted on the question of succession.

22. One response is, as it did a decade earlier, for the government to attempt to minimize the number of Saudis undertaking undergraduate education overseas. See Hermann Fr. Eilts, "Social Revolution in Saudi Arabia, Part II," *Parameters*, I, 2 (Fall 1971), p. 25.

23. Adeed I. Dawisha, "Internal Values and External Threats: The Making of Saudi Foreign Policy," *Orbis*, XXIII, 1 (Spring 1979), p. 133.

24. See, however, Collins, "Riyadh," p. 202.

25. This has been a constant claim of conservative Sunni elements in Saudi Arabia. Because it is largely true, the credibility of other complaints is increased.

26. See Dawisha, "Saudi Arabia's Search," p. 6.

27. However, effective deterrence may require a counterstrike capability. Acknowledging this fact and preparing for it will still lead to force structuring and equipment acquisition fundamentally different from those required for conquest.

28. But see Abdul Kasim Mansur (pseud.), "The Military Balance in the Persian Gulf: Who Will Guard the Gulf States from Their Guardians?" *Armed Forces Journal International*, CXVIII, 3 (November 1980), on "Saudi Arabia: The Most Oil and the Most Hope," who discusses the lack of clarity of the threat to Saudi planners. No one even vaguely familiar with Saudi defense strategy can contest Mansur's position in this regard. However, instead of systematically analyzing "the threat(s)," Saudi planners are moving against several threat concepts − a dangerous approach that will likely undermine the effectiveness of limited forces against any individual threat.

29. Cf. Lewis W. Snider and R. D. McLaurin, *Saudi Arabia's Air Defense Requirements in the 1980s: A Threat Analysis* (Alexandria: Abbott Associates, 1979) and Dale Tahtinen, *National Security Challenges to Saudi Arabia* (Washington, D.C.: American Enterprise Institute, 1978).

30. Indeed, so close that without round-the-clock patrols interception of an air attack is virtually impossible givèn the launch-delay time of most interceptor aricraft. Snider and McLaurin, *Saudi Arabia's Air Defense*, passim.

31. Abdul Kasim Mansur (pseud.), "The American Threat to Saudi Arabia," *Armed Forces Journal International*, CXVIII, 1 (September 1980), p. 52, points out that Americans have counselled against such purchases and that Saudis consequently increasingly question the realism of American advice. (Of course, from 1973 until the late 1970s, most U.S. administrations believed they would be unable to make such sales due to U.S. congressional resistance; this fact may be directly related to the nature of U.S. advisory inputs.)

32. There is a substantial literature on the subject of international military training. See, e.g., Robert J. Foster, *Examples of Cross-Cultural Problems Encountered by Americans Working Overseas* (Alexandria, George Washington University, Human Resources Research Office, 1965); George M. Guthrie, *Conflicts of Culture and the Military Advisor* (Arlington Institute for Defense Analysis, 1966); and Kenneth and Mary Gergen, "International Assistance in Psychological Perspective," Ronald D. McLaurin et al., eds., *The Art and Science of Psychological Operations: Case Studies of Military Application*, 2 vols. (Washington, D.C.: U.S. Government Printing Office for the Department of the Army, 1976), I, 314-26.

33. Several of these problems had a profound effect on Egyptian military personnel during the period in which Soviet military advisors were present in Egypt in large numbers.

34. Mansur, "The American Threat," pp. 51-52. Mansur also notes that some Saudis believe the United States intends to keep the kingdom vulnerable and dependent upon its American supplier.

35. See Dawisha, "Internal Values," pp. 134-36.

36. See, e.g., Brody and Rowen's contribution to Joseph A. Yager, ed., *National Security Aspects of Nuclear Proliferation* (Washington, D.C.: Brookings, 1978); Paul Jabber, "A Nuclear Middle East: Infrastructure, Likely Military Postures and Prospects for Strategic Stability," ACIS Working Paper, Center for Arms Control and International Security, University of California, Los Angeles, 1977; Geoffrey Kemp, "A Nuclear Middle East," *International Political Effects of the Spread of Nuclear Weapons*, ed. John Kerry King (Washington, D.C.: U.S. Government Printing Office, 1979), pp. 61-78; Theodor H. Winkler, "Nuclear Proliferation in the Third World: Problems and Prospects for the 1980s," *International Defense Review*, 2 (1980), pp. 198-204. Steven J. Rosen argues that nuclearization will conduce to stability in the region: "Nuclearization and Stability in the Middle East," *Nuclear Proliferation and the Near-Nuclear Countries*, ed. Onkar Marwah and Ann Schulz (Cambridge: Ballinger, 1975), Chap. 7.

37. The best analysis of the Israeli nuclear weapons program is Robert E. Harkavy, *Spectre of a Middle Eastern Holocaust: The Strategic and Diplomatic Implications of the Israeli Nuclear Weapons Program* (Denver: University of Denver Monograph Series, 1977).

38. Mansur, "The Military Balance."

39. See Richard D. Erb, "The Gulf Oil Producers: Overview and Oil Policy Implications" and "Saudi Arabia: Economic Developments," *AEI Foreign Policy and Defense Review*, II, 3-4 (1980), pp. 5-13 and 21-30, respectively;

the comments of Petroleum Minister Sheikh Zaki Yamani, cited in *Arab Report and Record*, 1976, p. 762; S. Fred Singer, "Limits to Arab Oil Power," *Foreign Policy*, no. 30 (Spring 1978), p. 55.

40. Mansur, "The American Threat," p. 56; Erb, "Saudi Arabia," pp. 27-30; Ray Vicker, "Oil Pressure: Saudi Arabian Citizens [sic] Urge Slash in Output, But Leadership Resists," *Wall Street Journal*, April 7, 1980, pp. 1, 19.

41. This is only true when viewed from the perspective of an outsider, however. Saudi decision makers were anti-Zionist from the outset and never wavered either in their support of the Palestinians or their opposition to Isarel. Cf., e.g., David E. Long, "King Faisal's World View," *King Faisal and the Modernisation of Saudi Arabia*, ed. Willard A. Beling (London: Crown Helm, 1980), Chap. 10; Abdullah M. Sindi, "King Faisal and Pan-Islamism," ibid., Chap. 11. However, other foreign-policy issues had far greater existential relevance to the kingdom before 1967. Moreover, U.S. policy consciously reinforced a conceptual and actual division between the Eastern Mediterranean and the Arabian Peninsula, a policy that continued to be applied until the October War of 1973 overtook it. Hermann F. Eilts, "Security Considerations in the Persian Gulf," *International Security*, V, 2 (Fall 1980), p. 85. (The wish being the father of the thought, "What we would like to do is separate the Arab-Israeli crises from Gulf politics," a U.S. diplomat recently said. See Andrew Borowiec, "Arab Leaders Doubt Saudis' Military Might," *Atlanta Journal-Constitution*, July 6, 1980, p. 18.)

42. Cf. James E. Noyes, *The Clouded Lens: Persian Gulf Security and U.S. Policy* (Stanford: Hoover Institution Press, 1979), p. 37.

43. James E. Akins, "Saudi Arabia, Soviet Activities, and Gulf Security," *The Impact of the Iranian Events upon Persian Gulf and United States Security*, ed. Z. Micahel Szaz (Washington, D.C.: American Foreign Policy Institute, 1979), p. 91 (italics in original).

44. Ibid., pp. 90-93.

45. Ibid., p. 93. It is the recent Israeli focus on Saudi Arabia as an enemy that has concerned the Saudis, a new emphasis — preposterous to Saudis — on Saudi Arabia as a threat to Israel.

46. See R. D. McLaurin and James M. Price, "OPEC Current Account Surpluses and Assistance to the Arab Front-Line States," *Oriente Moderno*, LVIII, 11 (November 1978), pp. 533-46.

47. Both by inviting Israeli attack and by cutting itself off from future U.S. aid.

48. Anthony H. Cordesman, "The U.S. Search for Strategic Stability in the Persian Gulf," *Armed Forces Journal International*, CXIX, 1 (September 1981), pp. 61-84. This article is adapted from the source in note 49.

49. For a thorough examination of the impact on Israel of the Saudi enhancement program, including AWACS, see Anthony H. Cordesman, "Saudi Arabia, AWACS, and America's Search for Strategic Stability in the Near East," draft working paper, International Security Studies Program, Woodrow Wilson International Center for Scholars, Washington, D.C., July 1981.

50. Mazher Hameed, R. D. McLaurin, and Lewis W. Snider, *An American Imperative: The Defense of Saudi Arabia* (Washington, D.C.: n.p., 1981), passim, esp. Part III.

51. Sindi, "King Faisal," is a detailed study of the embargo decision.

52. See Mansur, "The American Threat," passim.

53. McLaurin and Price, "OPEC"; issues of *An-Nahar Arab Report and Memo*; Bard E. O'Neill, *Armed Struggle in Palestine: A Politico-Military Analysis* (Boulder: Westview, 1978), pp. 186-88.

54. It is in this sense that King Faisal saw Zionism and communism as integrally related.

55. Taken together, Fahd's comments of the spring and summer of 1980 show clearly that the primary Saudi concern was to accelerate movement toward a peace, since Israel "is gradually devouring the Arab territories . . . is annexing all the occupied Arab lands," and "is declaring that Jerusalem is its united and eternal capital." (See *Washington Post*, May 25, 1980, p. A22; Saudi News Agency releases, August 13 and 20, 1980.) It is interesting to note that these last comments were made before Israel's annexation of the Golan Heights.

The Fahd initiative comes from a Saudi Press Agency interview, August 7, 1981, broadcast over Riyadh domestic radio on that date. The eight points were the following:

1. Israel should withdraw from all Arab territory occupied in 1967, including Arab Jerusalem.

2. Israeli settlements built on Arab land after 1967 should be dismantled.

3. There should be a guarantee of freedom of worship for all religions in the holy places.

4. The right of the Palestinian people to return to their homes and to receive compensation if they do not wish to return must be affirmed.

5. The West Bank and Gaza should be administered by the United Nations during a transitional period lasting not more than several months.

6. An independent Palestinian state should be established with Jerusalem as its capital.

7. All states in the region should be entitled to live in peace.

8. The United Nations or its member states should guarantee to execute these principles.

See *FBIS*, Middle East and Africa, no. 153 (August 10, 1981), pp. C3-C6, for the entirety of the interview.

56. See M. S. Agwani, *Politics in the Gulf* (New Delhi: Vikas, 1978), p. 107, who quotes Omar Saqqaf (then Saudi foreign minister) to the effect that "The Gulf is not for us alone, but for all its people."

57. John Duke Anthony, "The Arab States of the Gulf," *Seventh National Security Affairs Conference 1980 Proceedings: Rethinking U.S. Security Policy for the 1980s* (Washington, D.C.: National Defense University Press, 1980), pp. 203-4.

58. See the interview with Crown Prince Fahd, *al-Anwar*, July 30, 1976.

59. James Dorsey, "Saudi Minority Sect Is Restive," *Christian Science Monitor*, February 20, 1980, p. 12; John S. Rossant, "Saudi Shiites Say They Receive Second-Class Treatment," *New York Times*, January 3, 1980, p. 2.

Saudi Foreign Policymaking / 235

60. E.g., Karen Elliott House, "Engulfing Gulf: U.S. Role in Defense of Saudi Oil Fields Revises Relationships," *Wall Street Journal*, October 15, 1980, pp. 1, 29, and "Assertive Arabia: Iran-Iraq War and Win by Reagan Lead Saudis to Eye New U.S. Arms," ibid., November 14, 1980, pp. 1, 17; Youssef M. Ibrahim, "Iran-Iraq War a Setback to Saudi Role in OPEC," *New York Times*, October 16, 1980, pp. D1, D7; Claudia Wright, "Implications of the Iraq-Iran War," *Foreign Affairs*, LIX, 2 (Winter 1980-1981), pp. 275-303.

61. See J. C. Hurewitz, "The Middle East: A Year of Turmoil," *Foreign Affairs*, LIX, 3 (1981), pp. 540-77, passim, and R. D. McLaurin, "Arab Nationalism and Soviet Middle East Strategy," Abbott Associates SR (January 1981), pp. 3-6.

62. The Iraqis also advanced proposals aimed at eliminating U.S. and Soviet politicomilitary influence and military presence or access. See Chap. 4 of this book.

63. Dawisha, "Saudi Arabia's Search," p. 20.

64. "Gulf Security Document," *Middle East*, January 1981, pp. 16-17. See also John Yemma, "Saudis, Gulf States, Pakistan Try to Forge Their Own Security Ties," *Christian Science Monitor*, December 26, 1980, p. 6.

65. Migrant laborers and other foreigners number over 2 million persons, of whom Yemenis constitute about 50 percent.

66. The principal reason for the shift to East Asian workers in the 1970s was, however, economic: the Koreans were more efficient and less costly than the laborers theretofore employed in Saudi Arabia had been. Since the mid-1970s, the other worker groups, especially Thais, have begun to challenge the Koreans.

67. Saudi pride – which foreigners see as "arrogance" – is well known. As Collins puts it, "They have always been exceedingly proud even when they were regarded by their neighbors as nothing more than ignorant nomads. Their present wealth has finally allowed them to command the respect they believe they have always deserved" (p. 202). Unfortunately, however, *hajis* (Muslim pilgrims) and other visitors often return from Saudi Arabia with bad memories of Saudi "arrogance."

68. See "Saudi Internal Stability: A Saudi View," *Armed Forces Journal International*, CXVIII, 1 (September 1980), p. 60.

69. Part of the region was colonized by the Ottomans, but even the Ottoman hold on Arabia was tenuous.

70. The symbols of this "special relationship" to the Saudis are recurrent American pledges by all presidents, since Franklin D. Roosevent, of U.S. support. See, too, Georgie Ann Geyer, "The 'View from Riyadh': What We Must Know about the Saudis," *Washington Star*, January 7, 1981, p. 11.

71. Actually, the United States concentrated on the "northern tier" of non-Arab, Muslim states. However, a Middle East linkage was always foreseen.

72. See below.

73. See below.

74. Mansur, "The American Threat," pp. 47-51.

75. William Tuohy, "Uneasy Saudi Arabia Eyes Its 'Special Relationship' with the U.S.," *Los Angeles Times*, April 20, 1980, pp. 1, 6.

76. Mansur, "The American Threat," passim.

77. Youssef M. Ibrahim, "Saudis Are Trying to Maintain a Safe Distance from the U.S.," *New York Times*, March 9, 1980, p. E3; Walter Taylor, "For Many in the House of Saud, U.S. Diplomacy is Undiplomatic," *Washington Star*, August 22, 1980, p. 1.

78. Mansur, "The American Threat," p. 51. Writes former U.S. Ambassador to Saudi Arabia James Akins, "It must not be forgotten that the only country which has ever threatened invasion of Arabia is the United States itself." ("Saudi Arabia," p. 93.) Cf. Marwan R. Guheiry, "U.S. Threats of Intervention against Arab Oil: 1973-1979," I.P.S. Papers, no. 4 (Institute for Palestine Studies), 1980.

79. "Saudis See Arms Request as Test of U.S. Attitudes," *Washington Post*, December 19, 1980, p. 13.

80. Ibid.

81. For example, France is reported to have played a direct role in assisting Saudi security forces to recapture the *Masjid-al-Haram*, the holy mosque, during the Mecca incident of 1979. See Cord Meyer, "Rumors from Saudi Arabia," *Washington Star*, March 1980, p. 9.

82. Drew Middleton, "Not Just the Superpowers Are Assembling Mideast Armadas," *New York Times*, October 19, 1980, pp. 4-5. In addition to naval purchases, the kingdom has hundreds of tanks, armored cars, and armored personnel carriers, and aircraft from the French. Mansur, "The Military Balance," pp. 72-74. Moreover, Saudi Arabia will participate in the development of a new advanced French fighter aircraft.

83. A good overview of Saudi-Soviet relations in the early part of the century is Stephen Page, *The U.S.S.R. and Saudi Arabia: The Development of Soviet Policies and Attitudes Toward the Countries of the Arabian Peninsula, 1955-1970*, (London: Central Asian Research Centre, 1971).

84. Cf. Tuohy, "Uneasy Saudi Arabia," p. 6; Akins, "Saudi Arabia," p. 99.

85. Dawisha, "Saudi Arabia's Search," p. 20.

86. In fact, the hostility between the two Yemens is the contemporary expression of a rivalry that is as much as 2,000 years old. Action against Saudi Arabia has been limited, and is far less important than the Saudi reaction might suggest. (The Saudi government is more concerned about Yemen's general role in political unrest and as a Soviet surrogate than about specific anti-Saudi initiatives.)

87. For a discussion of the "tripartite entente," see Paul A. Jureidini and R. D. McLaurin, *Beyond Camp David: Emerging Alignments and Leaders in the Middle East* (Syracuse: Syracuse University Press, 1981), Chap. 3 and passim.

88. The most detailed treatment of Saudi policy with respect to the Lebanese civil war is M. Graeme Banneman, "Saudi Arabia," *Lebanon in Crisis: Participants and Issues*, ed. P. Edward Haley and Lewis W. Snider (Syracuse: Syracuse University Press, 1979), Chap. 6.

89. This was the essence of National Security Decision Memorandum (NSDM) 92, issued by President Nixon in 1969. The margin of force inequality between Iran and Saudi Arabia was in any event too great to allow even roughly similar roles for the two countries. American policymakers therefore contented

themselves with an air of cooperation between Iran and Saudi Arabia, but became resigned to Iran's assuming the mantle of Gulf policeman.

90. See Michael T. Klare, "Arms of the Shah," *Progressive*, August 1979, pp. 15-17. Although the tone of the article is alarmist, it is accurate in its essentials.

91. See Jureidini and McLaurin, *Beyond Camp David*, p. 46.

92. Agwani, "Politics," passim; and Eilts, "Security," p. 104.

93. Mansur, "The American Threat," passim.

94. Jureidini and McLaurin, *Beyond Camp David*, discusses Iranian futures, pp. 4-7.

95. For example, in early January 1980, Tehran Radio condemned Saudi handling of the Mecca incident and called for "death to the criminal and mercenary government of the Saudi family."

96. See above.

97. Most Palestinians in Saudi Arabia are in the oil field region, and the eastern province is also the home of most Saudi Shi'as. This latest threat and the linkages between Iran and the PLO have been sources of some worry to Saudis charged with internal security problems. (After the early days of the Iranian revolution, however, Iranian-PLO relations deteriorated, especially after the Gulf war between Iran and Iraq broke out in September 1980. The ties remain, but are much narrower and more ideological than they were initially.)

98. Nyrop et al., *Area Handbook*, Chap. 2, and Agwani, *Politics*, pp. 95-98, discuss this period.

99. This is not to suggest that Saudi leaders privately believed the Sadat approach would prove successful, only that they felt it *might*. Most Saudis do not believe Israel will withdraw from the West Bank peacefully unless "compelled" – presumably by the United States – to do so.

100. In late 1980, for example, the governments of Pakistan and Saudi Arabia were reported to have concluded an agreement by the terms of which a Pakistani brigade would be assigned to defend key Saudi installations. See "Pakistan Ready to Send Troops to Saudi Arabia," *Washington Star*, December 10, 1980, p. 15.

101. Almost a quarter of all Saudi aid in 1976, for example, went to Pakistan – aid equal to about $514.8 million. Dawisha, "Saudi Arabia's Search," p. 18.

102. It is approximately 375 statute miles from the Iraqi frontier to Dammam by the existing road. The area would include the following fields: all Kuwaiti oilfields, Abu Hadriyeh, al-Qatif, al-Fawaris al Janubiyeh, al-Kharsaniyeh, and al-Fadhili. Abaiq, Fazraa, Khurays, Harmaliyeh, and the giant Ghawar fields are all just outside the 375-mile range.

103. "Saudis Reported Aiding in Bomb," *Washington Star*, January 19, 1981, p. 13. The Saudi government has denied that it is assisting Pakistan's nuclear weapons program.

104. Lewis A. Dunn et al., *U.S. Defense Planning for a More Proliferated World* (Croton-on-Hudson, New York: Hudson Institute, 1979), pp. 68-81; Lewis A. Dunn and Herman Kahn, *Trends on Nuclear Proliferation, 1975-1995* (Croton-on-Hudson, New York: Hudson Institute, 1976), passim.

105. Long, "King Faisal," p. 174.

106. Dawisha, "Internal Values," pp. 133-34.

107. This formulation signifies, on the one hand, the importance of obtaining an acceptable status for Jerusalem and the return of most of the occupied territories to Arab control, as well as a solution to the Palestinian problem; and, on the other hand, the recognition that Israel will exist and will, as a result of a settlement, hold accepted title to not less than the territory under Israeli control on June 4, 1967. Saudi leaders recognize that the Palestinian issue, which is in fact intimately related to the question of the West Bank, must be decided by Israel and the Palestinians and, depending upon the nature of accords reached, with such other governments as may be directly affected. They will interpose no objection to these agreements except as regards Jerusalem, where the Saudis themselves feel they must be consulted.

108. To some extent, the image of concentric circles reflects the Saudi elite world view in which the Arab world is the center, surrounded by the remainder of the Islamic world (together, *dar al-Islam*), surrounded in turn by the monotheistic Western world (*abd al-Kitab*), and finally, outside these circles the rest of the world, alien, threatening (*dar al-Harb*). See Long, "King Faisal," passim.

109. Dawisha, "Internal Values," p. 129.

110. Mansur, "The American Threat," passim. Since the fall of the Pahlavis in Iran, attention has focused on Saudi Arabia as a new "Iran." While no one — certainly not the Saudis — would deny the kingdom faces many challenges in the years ahead, there are enough differences between imperial Iran and Saudi Arabia to at least question the analogy. See "Saudi Internal Security: A Saudi view," and Collins, "Riyadh."

111. See, e.g., Sheikh Ahmad Zaki Yamani's speech before the Middle East Institute, Washington, D.C., September 1972.

112. See, e.g., George Rentz, "The Saudi Monarchy," *King Faisal*, Chap. 1, passim.

113. It is often remarked within the kingdom "the constitution of Saudi Arabia is the Qur'an." To the extent this is so, then that which supports Islam also supports Saudi Arabia.

114. Dawisha, "Saudi Arabia's Search," p. 10.

CHAPTER
7

SYRIAN FOREIGN POLICYMAKING

ENVIRONMENT

In what we today call Syria, and in fact throughout much of the Middle East, Western-style institutions of administration ("government") have been superimposed upon traditional social systems. The peoples of Syria have strong loyalties to their family group. Other important focal points of their loyalties differ, although region and ethnic group exert powerful influence as primordial loyalties when challenged. By contrast, Syrian nationalism is a weak concept.

Syria is a political term given to a geographical entity. The reality is that this name, which unites only some Syrians to some degree,[1] covers a bewildering array of groups and ideas. Syria is characterized by heterogeneity and the schisms to which it has given rise — schisms based on political philosophy and support, on sectional rivalries, on economic philosophy, on economic group, on religion, on the urban-rural dichotomy, and on ethnic background, to name only the most important. Although individual scholars have searched for a unifying theme to explain the differences that rend Syrian society,[2] we believe this unnecessary for our purposes. It suffices to understand that Syria in its present form is a result of colonial boundary making.

In 1946 Syria was scarcely more than a name. The French mandate over Syria and Lebanon was characterized by a determination to fractionate these territories, to maintain French control by encouraging the extant social divisions.[3] Not until the 1950s did a feeling of Syrianism develop, and only during the 1958-61 union with Egypt did the feeling begin to take hold. After the advent of the Ba'ath regime in 1963, however, rapid progress toward the establishment of a Syrian personality took place,[4] only to later run aground on the shoals of sectarianism.[5]

239

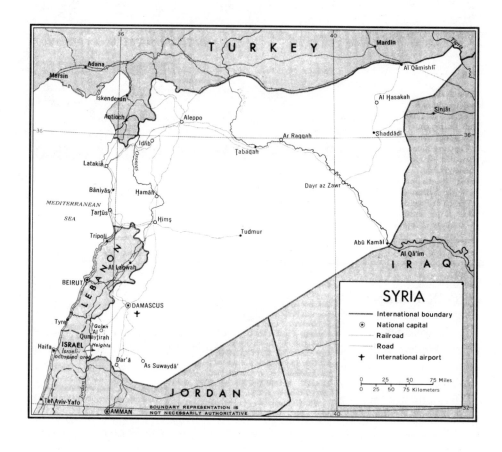

240

Syria was composed of nine agrocities (Aleppo, Dair as Zor, Damascus, Deraa, Hama, Homs, Kuneitrah, Latakia, and Suwayda) that still form the basis of Syrian regionalism. Syrian "political" thought has emphasized Arab nationalism or subnational loyalties rather than (and therefore at the expense of) Syrian nationalism. Political groupings before 1970 sought a personal, regional, or class following instead of a broad national one.[6]

The absence of a body of political belief or behavior that might be called "national" and the unavailability of jobs meant that politics took place on two levels — among the powerful families who constituted the traditional political elites and among the powerless group of politically interested individuals of middle-class and peasant origins. The political training ground of the latter was the government high school. The career destinations of the products of this training were teaching and the military.[7]

We shall not discuss the stormy political history of postwar Syria before 1966 in any detail, for that has been done elsewhere.[8] It is a story of successive coups. For the most part the resulting regimes enjoyed no significant popular constituency. As a result, even though much of the energy of the adult male population has been devoted to political thought,

> this energy has typically been employed to oppose whatever government is in power at the time and to criticize other political forces and even other members of one's own political group. . . . [M]ost politically aware individuals have had limited means of expressing opinion. Often frustrated, they have sought the most direct means available: strikes and demonstrations, personal contacts with influential politicians and, at times, removal of an offending individual through assassination.[9]

Despite revolutionary rhetoric, until 1963 none of the military regimes that succeeded either each other or one of the intermittent civilian administrations ever undertook a true revolution or even major social change.[10] Even after 1963, a concerted and broad-based movement toward social change had to await the advent of the neo-Ba'ath in 1966.

The Ba'ath Party was founded in Syria and recruited members among ex-peasant, lower-middle-class groups. Important elements of Ba'athism included pan-Arabism and secularism (although the special place of Islam as a cultural influence in Arabism was recognized), the latter being particularly attractive to religious minorities such as the Alawis. Indeed, when the Ba'ath began serious recruiting in 1947, one of the first cells was established in the 'Alawi-populated Latakia region. Both the Ba'ath and the Syrian Social Nationalist Party, particularly the latter, were highly successful in recruiting the socially mobilized and downtrodden 'Alawis.[11]

Soon after the union of Egypt and Syria in 1958, Gamal Abdel Nasser disbanded the Ba'ath Party in Syria. In fact, however, the party simply went underground in the Latakia region. In another action to subordinate Syria and preempt any military threat to the union, a number of officers were transferred to Egypt or dismissed from military service. In 1959, several of those officers in Egypt founded a secret Ba'athist military committee. The leadership of this committee consisted of three 'Alawis and two Ismailis (another Islamic minority group). The leaders included Salah Jadid, Hafez Assad, and Abd al-Karim al-Jundi, all of whom were to become major figures. After the secession of Syria from the United Arab Republic in 1961, many military officers with political ties, including much of the membership of the still-secret military committee, were separated from the army. Meanwhile, the Syrian Ba'athists who had remained organized surfaced as Qutriyin ("regionalists," that is, separatists)[12] after the Ba'ath Fifth National Congress (1962) and established a distinct Ba'ath organization. Neither the Qutriyin Ba'ath nor the old-time Ba'ath (now essentially an Iraqi creature) considered the other to be legal.[13]

On March 8, 1963, a military coup toppled the Syrian civilian government. The Ba'ath Party played no real role; indeed, within the military there were very few Ba'athists just before and during the coup. Once the operation was completed, however, Ba'athists were well represented: through careful precoup placement of individuals in personnel jobs, Ba'athist officers were called back and put in crucial positions throughout the army. The Ba'athists dominated the army by virtue of their effective organization (based on the military committee founded in 1959) and sectarian loyalties. As a result of the unity of the Ba'athist military participants and followers (contrasted with the disunity of the other groups that took part in the coup), the Ba'ath gained control of the new regime, holding half the cabinet posts.

There were still two distinct Ba'ath parties, however, and the civilian Ba'athists were unaware of the existence of the secret military committee. Through a variety of maneuvers,[14] the military group infiltrated the civilian organizations while its own committee remained secret. The years following the Ba'ath coup of March 1963 and leading up to the seizure of power by Salah Jadid were marked by the consolidation of the position of the secret military committee, which eliminated one group of rivals after another, and by the division of the army along sectarian lines. The latter development was unintentionally hastened by Amin al-Hafez, the Syrian strongman, and directly benefited Salah Jadid, for the minorities ('Alawis, Druze, Ismailis) tended to consolidate while the Sunnis did not. During these years, the Ba'ath also witnessed a growing schism between the National Command under Michel Aflaq and Salah Bitar and the Regional Command, which was dominated by the military Ba'athists.

The Syrian army has had a tradition of overrepresentation of the ethnic minorities. There are several reasons for this. First, the French consistently recruited military personnel from the minorities in order to prevent Syrian unity. Second, the Sunnis did not cooperate with the French, refusing to enlist. Third, the rural minorities could not afford the fee required for exemption from military service. Fourth, a military career offered one of the few avenues for social advancement. Fifth, 'Alawis used the military academy as a means to further their education. Sixth, military life was more attractive to rural villagers than to urban members of the ethnic majority. Seventh, 'Alawis and Druze recruited among and promoted their friends and relatives. Eighth, the succession of coups in Syria led to the dismissal of many Sunni officers. The result of all these factors was that by December 1965 — on the eve of the neo-Ba'ath coup — 'Alawi and Druze officers were in charge of 70-75 percent of all army units[15] and Sunnis only 25-30 percent. Since Sunnis constitute the vast majority of the population, this pattern of power is remarkable.[16]

Thus, with the army (and the secret Ba'ath military committee) and the Ba'ath Regional Command behind him, Salah Jadid led a coup on February 23, 1966 that removed Amin al-Hafez from the government and party, and the Aflaq-Bitar-led National Command from party leadership.[17] The new Syrian leadership preached a radical doctrine. The novelty was that a serious effort was made to implement the program.[18]

Ba'ath doctrine, radicalized after the Sixth Ba'ath National Congress (1963) as a part of the political process[19] and as a function of minority discontent with the Syrian social status quo, gave rise to more rapid and extensive land reform, nationalization, socialism, and secularism. All economic support was directed to the public sector. The favoritism shown rural districts and the minorities, especially the 'Alawis, was flagrant under the new regime.

The first challenge to Jadid's authority was an abortive coup, led by Salim Hatum, that reflected the growing sectarian divisions in Syria.[20] (Hatum was Druze. After the neo-Ba'ath takeover in 1966, the 'Alawis began consolidating their position and eliminating the other minorities that had been allies.) Although the Hatum coup was foiled, intraparty conflicts began to arise in late 1966. By then, Jadid apparently had recognized Hafez Assad as his major potential rival. Assad's position in the military had been crucial to the success of the Jadid coup.

As the conflict between Jadid and Assad grew more apparent, antigovernment (in fact, anti-'Alawi) demonstrations erupted and the June War began. These episodes may be seen as interludes in the Jadid-Assad confrontation that lasted for four years (1966-70). It is probable that Assad would have initiated a coup sooner or later. His power was increasing,[21] and power lay with the military. Jadid, in order to overcome this fact, tried to establish new forces in Syria. Setting up and arming Sa'iqa and looking to the militia for additional support, Jadid governed through the party and tried to reduce the military's role in Syria. (Indeed, Jadid maintained control from a relatively obscure position in the Ba'ath, preferring low visibility because of the 'Alawi-Sunni division.)

In 1967 Jadid sought to blame Assad's military for Syria's poor showing in the June War. Although public opinion placed blame on both the party and the armed forces, the latter was subject to particularly scathing attacks from both ends of the political spectrum. However, in 1968 the militia's arms were withdrawn, and in 1969 the security forces were taken over by the ministry of defense. Increasingly, Jadid's supporters in the military were removed or changed their allegiance. By 1968 Assad's ascendancy to power was relatively clear. In 1969 he staged a semicoup that was inconclusive, but continued the trend of improving his position vis-a-vis that of Jadid. Assad, a frequent critic of the Soviet role in Syria — and more specifically of Jadid's agreements with Moscow — continued to move against possible opposition groups while trying to smooth his relations with the Soviet Union.[22] Finally, in September 1970, Jadid and others in the party hierarchy decided to send Syrian tanks to participate in the Jordanian civil war. Hafez Assad and some others in the military hierarchy strongly opposed the commitment; and Assad, commander of the air force, refused to send in support for the Syrian armor, on the ground that greater Syrian participation in the Palestinian-Jordanian conflict would result in Israeli, or perhaps American, involvement. The outcome of the Syrian "invasion" was not in doubt, since the tanks had no protection against Hussein's air strikes. Yet the final outcome was even more significant for Syria — the replacement of Jadid by Assad.

Since March 1969, the conflict between the two former military allies, Jadid and Assad, had become open. In the end, the fact that Assad controlled the only armed force in the country proved decisive.[23] Although the Ba'ath Party voted to remove Assad and several of his supporters from their positions, the coup that followed that decision resulted in Assad's assumption of unquestioned political supremacy. Jadid and many of his allies were replaced in mid-November 1970.

Despite a number of attempted coups and frequent rumors of unrest within various sectors of the population (the military, 'Alawis, Sunnis, Damascenes, Ba'ath cadres), Hafez Assad's regime brought Syria its greatest political stability in many years. This is all the more remarkable when it is recalled that the entire Assad tenure has been accompanied by Israeli occupation of the Golan Heights, and that after 1970 Syria experienced one major Middle East war, attained and then lost an important degree of regional leadership, and lived under the domination of a small and unpopular religious minority group.

STRUCTURE OF THE GOVERNMENT

The Syrian constitution, revised in 1973, has remained fundamentally unchanged for many years. The newest revision provides for a very strong executive (with substantial legislative powers as well) directly elected by the populace (see Figure 7.1). The president, however, is nominated by the People's Assembly on recommendation of the Ba'ath Regional Command. Although the judicial system is nominally independent of the executive, the president appoints members of the Supreme (or Higher Constitutional) Court, as well as of the Higher Judicial Council, whose responsibility is to ensure this independence.

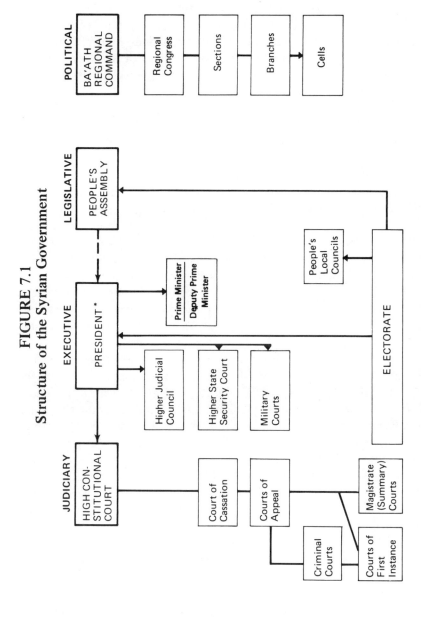

FIGURE 7.1
Structure of the Syrian Government

POLITICAL

BA'ATH REGIONAL COMMAND

Regional Congress

Sections

Branches

Cells

LEGISLATIVE

PEOPLE'S ASSEMBLY

EXECUTIVE

PRESIDENT*

Prime Minister
Deputy Prime Minister

Higher Judicial Council

Higher State Security Court

Military Courts

People's Local Councils

ELECTORATE

JUDICIARY

HIGH CON-STITUTIONAL COURT

Court of Cassation

Courts of Appeal

Criminal Courts

Courts of First Instance

Magistrate (Summary) Courts

*President nominated by People's Assembly on recommendation of the Ba'ath Regional Command.

Source: Compiled by the authors.

Moreover, the constitution provides for military courts, which have played an important role in Syria by circumventing the civil and criminal court systems.

The arenas in which Syrian politics takes place have changed under the Assad regime. The People's Assembly serves as a national legislature and is directly elected. This body and the local councils effect most of the legislation. The president, however, has important legislative functions, principally between sessions of the People's Assembly but also "in cases of absolute need."[24] Moreover, he can "submit important matters concerning higher national interests" to a popular referendum.[25]

OPERATION OF THE SYRIAN POLITICAL SYSTEM

The Ba'ath Party's formal role in governance is indirect but multifaceted: "The vanguard party in the society and state is the Ba'ath Arab Socialist party."[26] In addition, the Ba'ath Regional Command proposes one or more presidential nominees to the People's Assembly, which in turn nominates a presidential candidate.[27]

Yet the primary mission of the Ba'ath in the national leadership is more visible at the local level, where its two main functions are penetration and mobilization. Thus, the Ba'ath must ensure communication of local views upward to the national leadership, and of national programs and concepts downward from the leadership to the masses. Despite many problems and the shortage of resources necessary to fully implement this model, the Ba'ath Party system in Syria has adhered rather closely to it.[28] The party extends down to the smallest villages, and its membership has expanded considerably over the years.[29] Unlike the early years, the Ba'ath is closer to a mass than an elite party. At the same time, it must be said that actual support of and membership in the Ba'ath, while not limited to an intellectual elite, is still confined to a very small proportion of the populace.

The coup that brought Assad to power, even though it was a putsch in many senses, reflected national resentment at Jadid's controls. Assad placed a very high priority on reversing the trend toward a police state, and succeeded for a decade in maintaining order with infrequent (but determined, when used) resort to force and with tight control over communications and intelligence apparatuses.[30]

Symbolic of Assad's approach to governing was his promulgation of provisions leading to direct election of the president. In turn, the Syrian electorate gave Assad a strong vote of confidence in the March 1971 presidential election, when 99 percent of the votes affirmed his nomination and elected him to a seven-year term.[31] After selection by the Ba'ath Party and the People's Assembly, election may appear superfluous, yet the principle is crucial: popular election allows the president to maintain a position above the party, the army, the 'Alawis, or other groups within society.[32]

Similarly, Assad early moved toward the creation of more democratic participation in the Syrian government. Three months after his accession to power, he announced formation of the People's Assembly. Although initially appointed, later People's Assemblies were to be, and have been, elected. Perhaps as important as its election was the composition of the assembly. In the first (appointed) assembly, Ba'athists barely outnumbered the sum of other groups represented, which included, besides Syrian Communists and Nasserites, members of traditionally anti-Ba'ath groups.

From May 1971 until the spring of 1972, negotiations over the terms of the National Progressive Front (NPF) — a bloc of parties and popular groups — took place. The NPF institutionalizes non-Ba'ath popular representation in the government and can be viewed as another indication of Assad's determination to broaden the power base of Syrian government. Assad stated that national unity is the key to Syrian progress. Whether his concern was directed toward national stability or his own regime's stability, he clearly has set out to bring about a greater degree of participation in, identification with, and national unity behind the Syrian government.[33] The NPF includes the Syrian Ba'ath, the Syrian Communist Party, the Arab Socialist Union (a Nasserite group), the Socialist Union, and the Arab Socialist Party. This is also essentially the makeup of the People's Assembly elected in 1973, with 159 of the 195 seats having been won by NPF parties. Similarly, the Syrian cabinet generally has been composed of about 50 percent non-Ba'athists since 1972. Since 1973, one or both Syrian Communist Party factions have been represented, as have the Arab Socialist Union, the Socialist Union, and the Arab Socialist Party. Also like the assembly, the cabinet has a number of independents. The diverse makeup of the assembly, the NPF, and the cabinet can be seen as an effort to broaden Assad's power base.

At the local level, too, the regime took a more relaxed attitude than its predecessor, allowing opponents of the regime to run for election. For example, in 1972 Muslim Brotherhood candidates soundly defeated those of the NPF in Homs, a city of conservative, strong anti-Ba'ath feeling.[34]

The foregoing should not be taken as a suggestion that Assad had less control of Syria than did Jadid or others, nor that the Ba'ath and the military have relinquished their dominance. Assad always made the important decisions in Syria, but was careful to see that "key members of the party and army elite" were present at critical points in the decision process.[35] Decisions, once reached, received unanimous or nearly unanimous backing in the People's Assembly, the NPF, Ba'ath Party Congress, the media, and elsewhere. The decision-making process might be called participatory consensus — that is, a process by which all parties agree at the outset to support the final decision, in return for which the views of each party will be taken into account by the policymakers. That the participants did not necessarily receive any accommodation or compromise on individual issues distinguishes this process from that of consensus in its more widely accepted form. The benefits of participation were significant: the opportunity to function as a political party at the national level, to recruit, to campaign;[36] the chance to advance views on major issues with the knowledge that these positions, constituting the feeling of an important and representative group, were seriously considered by the regime; and the possibility of shaping opinions through communication "down" and in the media. The regime also derived benefits of capital significance: more broad-based support with consequently increased legitimacy; an opportunity to hear a variety of positions (and to deal with public opinion) on crucial issues; greater credibility in domestic communications; and a larger resource base in the communications effort.[37] To some extent, the operations of overt and legal parties are both easier and more difficult to monitor than are those of proscribed groups.

Syria is like most developing countries in that a small power elite governs with little reference to the everyday life of the populace. Notwithstanding the democratic trappings of Syrian government, traditional distrust of national-level politics and politicians is characteristic rather than atypical of most Syrians. In the People's Assembly elections of 1977, an unprecedentedly low turnout of about 5 percent of the electorate participated, for example. It is a testament to the political skill and integrity of Hafez Assad that until 1980 relatively little popular criticism had been personally directed at the president, in spite of his having created an essentially 'Alawi power structure in Syria.

It is true that among the senior civilian and military personnel, many are Sunnis. However, most of these Sunnis are either personally loyal to Assad himself or are without any real power. Control in Syria rests in the hand of security and military personnel, most of whom are 'Alawis.

On the one hand, this description of Syrian politics in the Assad years reflects a remarkable adaptation of Syrian political customs and institutions; on the other hand, it demonstrates an equally unusual sensitivity by Assad and his small group of trusted advisors to the economic and political currents of the country, as well as to his own requirements for the stabilization and development of Syrian politics. The major exception to this insight was the serious miscalculation of the political, economic, and social costs of Syrian intervention in Lebanon. We discuss the objectives and nature of this action below; it suffices here to recognize the catalytic effect of the intervention on Syrian politics.

In many countries of the Middle East, political development has meant increased within-group communication and a resurgence and reassertion of primordial loyalties at the expense of national integrity.[38] While this phenomenon would have taken place in Syria eventually,[39] there can be little question that Syrian actions in Lebanon hastened the process.

A minority group as small and unpopular as the 'Alawis cannot expect to control a large country like Syria indefinitely unless group identifications change so that public feeling does not identify that group as "different." (In a sense, Assad endeavored to blur the 'Alawis' particularist image by stressing their Muslim character and his own devotion to Islam. However, the effort was unsuccessful due to the depth of the social cleavages and to the behavior of the government, which clearly depended upon and exploited sectarian loyalties.[40])

By the late 1970s, under the pressures of a regional Islamic revival,[41] the controversial and unpopular Syrian role in Lebanon, popular concern over corruption, and, principally, the cumulative resentment over minority domination, 'Alawi control began to erode seriously. Assassinations of 'Alawis and Sunni 'Alawi supporters reached epidemic proportions, occurring on an almost daily basis.[42] Major episodes — the massacre of cadets (mostly 'Alawis) at the Syrian artillery school in Aleppo, anti-'Alawi riots in Hama and Latakia, large-scale civil disobedience in Aleppo — grew in frequency and intensity.[43]

The perpetrators or instigators of these problems were rarely apprehended — and little wonder, since the police and security force personnel involved were primarily Sunni. Thus, in several major cities the army was called upon to restore security in early 1980,[44] but with little prospect of success, since there, too, the rank and file sympathize with those behind the violence.

Thus, by 1980 the Syrian government was near paralysis and 'Alawi control of Syria probably near collapse. Only the failure of viable Sunni leadership to emerge and the still rather complete control by the 'Alawis of the security apparatus precluded a non-'Alawi coup or some other violence leading to abrupt political change. However, opposition leadership is beginning to organize within Syria, and also in Jordan and France. A number of personalities are emerging, with none yet able to claim clear-cut predominance. Even the Muslim Brotherhood is now uniting a number of essentially secular opposition leaders, as well as its religious elements.

Although policy levels of the Syrian government have been particularly affected by the country's succession of coups and political purges over the years, most of the civil service has provided some continuity. Indeed, before the 1963 coup that led to Ba'ath rule, "the civil service remained generally outside of politics, and appointments were usually based upon professional background, including education and the results of written examinations. . . . [C]ivil service rolls showed little evidence of prejudice against religious or ethnic minorities." However, after the 1963 coup, the increased emigration of trained personnel adversely affected the civil service. In addition, the new regime and those that followed it politicized civil service recruitment. This was particularly true at higher levels of the bureaucracy. So while the structure of the civil service has been stable, the staffing has not, thus lessening bureaucratic effectiveness. Moreover, the Syrian civil service is hampered by problems facing its counterparts in other developing countries: a shortage of trained personnel, unwillingness to accept or delegate responsibility effectively, and lack of coordination between various parts of the bureaucracy.[45]

As in any regime originating as Assad's did, the difficulty of integrating career civil service and political appointee efforts is considerable. This generic problem has both diminished and increased over time. It has diminished insofar as standard operating procedures and routines of interaction have been established to facilitate the implementation of policy. The relative stability Assad has brought to Syria has meant less extensive and frequent personnel turnover.

As in any large organization, individuals tend to look for and work with and through those who have been effective in other interactions. Time aids this selection process. Individual and organizational learning and change over time have produced results.

Several factors are operating to produce less integration of policy levels and career civil service actions. First, despite unwonted regime stability, the presence of 'Alawis in key decision-making roles has increased. Second, Assad has consistently been concerned to see that no one builds bridges to key constituencies of such strength as to threaten his regime. Third, the administrative requirements of his position atop three bureaucracies (government, party, military), of the determination to shoulder important policy decisions, and of the unwillingness of others to do so have slowly isolated Assad. Time and other constraints limit his extensive contact to other key figures in the regime – Abdel Halim Khaddam (foreign minister), Mustapha Tlas (defense minister), Adnan Dabbagh, 'Ali Haydar, Ahmad Iskander Ahmad, and, of course, the most important individual in the regime after Hafez Assad, his brother Rifaat. Given Assad's determination to isolate potential rivals, his estrangement is reinforced.[46] Finally and paradoxically, the stability of the regime acts as a further hurdle to integration by virtue of the socialization of sectoral organization chiefs to the parochial outlooks and approaches of the groups they manage.[47]

INTEREST GROUPS

Syria, like other countries, has a number of constituencies whose attitudes decision makers ignore at their peril. Although in Western-style democracies we require that groups of people be organized in order for us to consider them as interest groups,[48] this requirement is unrealistic in countries where such organization is proscribed. It would, however, be quite incorrect to conclude that Syrian groups, because some are not organized, are of no consequence in decision-making councils. Indeed, it is precisely the diversity of constituencies – we shall call them interest groups – to which communications are directed and for which specific policies are chosen that confounds outside attempts to explicate those communications and policies.

In Syria, interest groups must be visualized in proper perspective. The complex of issues and cross-cutting interests precludes the facile assumption that because two individuals may subscribe to differing views in one issue area, they will of necessity oppose each other. No single issue has a salience level so high as to dominate all others.[49] Alliances are extremely fluid: groups coalesce and disperse in different patterns, depending upon the issue. Put another way, groups have overlapping membership; few individuals are allied – or opposed – across all issue areas. We shall consider four types of interest groups: political, military, socioeconomic, and nonstate national.

Political Parties

Political interest groups are of two types, ideological and partisan. In fact, of course, the two overlap considerably. Ideological Communists tend to belong to one or another faction of the Syrian Communist Party. Ideological dissent, however, is not the stuff of which political opposition is made in Syria, except in terms of intraparty politics.

The Ba'ath Party is the umbrella of unity under which continual disagreements take place. It is a party now almost totally dominated by Hafez Assad, however. Where the party was previously riven by personality, ideological, ethnic, associational, and other schisms, it has become much more fully subordinated to the Assad brothers and the political apparatus they have created. Rivalries within the Ba'ath — and within the government and country at large — often concern personalities. There is some reason to believe that Hafez Assad has used popular or important leaders loyal to himself as rallying points for dissent in order to maintain surveillance and control over dissidents.[50]

Within the Ba'ath, followers of Salah Jadid posed several early challenges to Assad's control. After surviving these challenges, and to some extent as a result of them, the Syrian president centralized and tightened his grip on the party and government through the careful placement of those on whom he felt he could depend, principally his fellow 'Alawis. At the same time he made a sincere, concerted, and temporarily successful effort to create a broad base for himself throughout the country. In all of this the Ba'ath played a role, but its slavish support for the president ultimately revealed the true nature of the relationship between party and government, a relationship unflattering to the former.

At the national level, the Ba'ath today is largely a legitimization agent for the Assad government. While it would be untrue to suggest Assad fails to consult others, it is no exaggeration to say that Ba'ath support for government policy is automatic. At the same time, Ba'athist doctrine and ideology do have meaning and salience at lower levels, where the party functions with some autonomy, albeit still within the parameters of official policy.[51] Only when Ba'ath leaders achieve some prominence does a conflict arise between policy and ideology — and this is precisely the stage at which key figures in the regime have been able to secure senior Ba'ath leaders' support on an individual basis through appointment to coveted positions or other techniques, frequently including subventions.[52]

In a sense, Rifaat Assad, the second most powerful figure in Syria today, is an example. The younger Assad had a reputation for radicalism and was reputed to be a focal point for leftist thinking and action in the Ba'ath Regional Command to which he was elected in March 1975.[53] Yet the reputation was little more than a façade. His written defense of the regime's corrective movement, his close friendship with Lebanese establishment figures, and his behavior since assuming command of the Defense Units[54] all reveal anything but Ba'ath socialist or even leftist thinking. The younger Assad received a doctorate in the Soviet Union, but like his brother, distrusts and dislikes the Soviets.[55] Rifaat is periodically rumored to be plotting against, or at least at odds with, Hafez; but these apparent differences then seem to evaporate once again. In fact, the Assad brothers have worked together very effectively to channel and limit dissent, to use the Ba'ath Party, and to maintain control of the country.

The extent to which the Ba'ath itself may be considered an interest group has been reduced by President Assad's control. To the degree that it may still be distinguished as an interest group different from the administration, the Ba'ath − or elements of it − frequently is influenced by the Iraqi position on various issues.[56] (This is less true today than it was even five years ago.) Since many of the early Ba'ath leaders and their followers have been purged from the party, Assad has a much more disciplined and less fractionated party.

The Ba'ath Party is therefore employed for communication, administration, and legitimization; its blessing is used to legitimize Assad's regime and decisions. Assad, remembering Jadid's fate, can be expected to retain control of the military, the civilian government, and the party. One of his techniques is to restrict the roles of other individuals to fewer branches of political power. This has the advantage of making it difficult for any individual to have access to several levers of power, while preserving political havens for Assad.

Within the Ba'ath Party, and within the country as a whole, there are various ideological trends. These are never clear-cut, for Ba'athist ideology (especially in Syria) is singularly diffuse. However, the positions of groups are clearer with respect to concrete issues than in terms of ideology, or even ideological justification. Ba'athists have traditionally been pan-Arabists (rather than nationalists), secularists, and, more recently, social reformers. There has been something of an inverse relationship between dedication to social reform and dedication to pan-Arabism. Since a real revolution in social thinking has already taken place under Ba'ath guidance,[57] the ideological question has been lessened to a significant degree. Secularism was important in Ba'ath recruitment, and it has been critical, too, in the subsequent political evolution of internal Ba'ath politics. Thus, while 'Alawis have been specially emplaced and empowered throughout the government, army, and party, charges of 'Alawi particularist favoritism are typically met with counteraccusations that these charges are attempts to sow religious discord.[58]

The other political parties and groups in Syria wield much less political power than the Ba'ath − even the Assad-controlled Ba'ath − but may well represent a larger constituency. Major parties include the Arab Socialist Union, the Syrian Communist Party, the Arab Socialist Party, and the Socialist Union.

The Arab Socialist Union (ASU) is a Nasserite group participating in the NPF. It has perhaps the largest constituency in Syria. Jamal Atassi, head of the Syrian ASU, claims that 80 percent of the population is at least sympathetic to the group.[59] The ASU supports the creation of a single, mass political party in Syria (along the lines of the Egyptian ASU). Although it has been at odds with the Ba'ath — even dropping out of the NPF — Atassi recognizes the necessity of coexisting with the Ba'ath as one of Assad's chosen tools, particularly in view of the restrictions imposed upon the ASU and the other parties.[60]

The Socialist Union (SU) is also a Nasserite party, but is composed of ex-Ba'athists. The party traces its origins to the breakup of the Egyptian-Syrian union in 1961, when Sami Sufan bolted the Ba'ath Party separatist group to create the SU. Its following is smaller than that of the ASU; but taken together, the two major Nasserite parties represent a considerable segment of political opinion in Syria.[61]

A smaller but important party is the Syrian Communist Party (SCP). Led for many years by Khalid Bakdash, the party has suffered a serious schism in recent years. The difference embraces several issues, one of the most important of which is the independence of the party from Soviet policy. After a number of attempts at reconciliation were aborted, several leaders of the anti-Bakdash group, including Daniel Neemeh and Zohair Abdel Samad, rejoined the Bakdash group at the end of 1973. However, the split was formalized when the unreconciled anti-Bakdash Communists formed their own party. Some sources believe the second SCP is larger than the Moscow-oriented party. In early January 1974 the new SCP held the Fourth Congress of the Syrian Communist Party, electing Riad Turk as first secretary. There has been considerable speculation that the Assad government encouraged the split; but although representatives of both factions were in the cabinet and the People's Assembly before the formal secession of the Turk group, none of the new secessionists has been so placed. Syrian Communists are not as numerous as Nasserites; and since their traditional recruiting ground (universities and schools) has been denied them, they pose no real threat to the regime. Soviet support, direct or through the party, can, however, be helpful. Syrian Communists tried to calm near-civil war between the Assad and Jadid factions in 1969, even though Assad criticized Jadid for his concessions to Moscow.[62]

The SCP enjoyed a relatively secure and stable role in the political system under Assad, particularly after its institutionalization in the NPF.

The last of the official participants in the NPF, the Arab socialists, are Hourani socialists — that is, remnants of Akram Hourani's old Arab Socialist Party. While they seek to exploit the popularity of his name and do, in fact, agree with Hourani on virtually everything, Hourani has disavowed the Arab socialists (on the ground of his firm principle not to support the Ba'ath in any way). Hourani, the great reform politician of modern Syria, still commands a considerable following.[63]

The term National *Progressive* Front should indicate that not all currents are represented. None of the traditionally conservative political trends in Syria, for example, is acceptable to the regime. Nevertheless, such views are still current in the public. The Muslim Brotherhood has long had a following in Syria.[64] It continues a relatively high level of activity, especially in the Homs region, where its candidates easily won election in the spring of 1972. It also is active in Aleppo, Hama, and Damascus. As one of the heartlands of Islamic fundamentalism, Syria is a natural base for the *Ikhwan* (from Muslim Brotherhood — *Ikhwan Muslimin*). We shall discuss the role of the Muslim Brotherhood below, but it is important to recognize the political nature of this religious interest group. Because Syrian politics has devolved into a Sunni-'Alawi rivalry for power, but because too the 'Alawis today hold all effective institutions of government, Islamic groups that cannot be openly opposed by the government are a focal point of opposition to the Assad regime. The government in turn has blamed anti-'Alawi (which it defines as anti-Syrian) sentiment in the country upon the Muslim Brotherhood, which the government describes as a fanatical, terrorist organization.[65] Saudi Arabia has sporadically financed Brotherhood activities, and the *Ikhwan* has had a relatively free administrative hand in neighboring (and allied) Jordan.

Finally, Syrian politics has always allowed a great role for political independents. This is in some measure a function of the agrocities discussed earlier — that is, of regional leaders who used no conceptual or ideological appeal, relying instead upon personal status in their region.

Another form of "independent" is the political leader or group linked with foreign interests. The Arab world, particularly in the Levant, is a transnational society — or, at the least, a society of nation-states uniquely subject to regional transnational pressures. Political pressures often are exerted through transnational families or through individuals with personal or (often ephemeral) financial ties to other Arab polities. Because of the relative novelty of Syrian nationalism, these forces are singularly strong in Syrian society. The Assad regime often must prepare itself (and communicate its policies) in the light of expected (or unanticipated but actual) pressures from Iraq, Saudi Arabia (sometimes working through the Muslim Brotherhood), and Egypt.[66]

The Military

Perhaps the most potentially effective interest group in Syria is the military. Although divided by national issues and trends, the military forces — particularly the officer corps — have been homogenized as a result of social factors already discussed and through the long series of political purges. Internal security (intelligence) functions are devoted to identifying antiregime movements, trends, and individuals. 'Alawi solidarity also leads to military unity. This is not to suggest that the armed forces are unified, for they are not. Rather, it suggests that on certain issues — such as budget allocations, disengagement, and other war/peace issues where significant unity does exist — the officer corps is in a uniquely powerful position to influence policy. It also suggests that to the extent differences surface, they must be cast in the framework of policy options, not regime alternatives.[67] Syrian military interests are wide-ranging because "the army's roots . . . preserve its sense of social mission."[68] Thus, the armed forces often have strong feelings concerning social and economic issues. However, the military has been riven with different views on these issues, and therefore is less effective as a single interest group on socioeconomic matters than on military concerns.

The Syrian armed forces are composed of an army, a navy that is administratively part of the army, and an air force. Although manpower levels vary somewhat, the army is by far the largest service. All are Soviet-equipped and Soviet-trained. Thus, Syrian military training is based on partially modified Soviet prenuclear strategic and tactical doctrine.[69] The army is incapable of mounting a sustained offensive beyond Syrian territory against a well-trained and well-equipped adversary. Syrian military forces are overcentralized and poorly led at senior levels. Junior-level officers are considered vastly improved, and enlisted personnel are good, basic fighters. However, the technical level of military personnel is also a handicap. Syrian armed forces are not well educated and come from an environment in which they have not been exposed to sophisticated technology. Moreover, the high rate of turnover has adversely affected overall capability. On the other hand, the Soviet Union has had adequate time to train a large number of officers and enlisted personnel, who have been exposed to increasingly advanced military equipment. All reports from the October War suggested that the Syrian armed forces demonstrated great improvement over 1967. Syrian military preparedness is high, and the Syrian army represents a significant defensive force. The air and naval forces appear to have made less progress than the ground forces, which acquitted themselves very well in 1973.[70]

The Syrian military demonstrates relative solidarity on issues such as the strategy of confrontation with Israel. Generally, Syrian military personnel favor greater military action and fewer concessions in the conflict with Israel. Agreements of any sort with the Zionist state are suspect. It can be presumed, too, that the armed forces' leadership lobbies actively for a large share of the Syrian budget. Assad has tried to upgrade the pay, benefits, and prestige of the officer corps.[71] Decisions of a political or economic nature that might undermine military effectiveness — for instance, by threatening sources of supply — would encounter substantial opposition. As in most developing states, the Syrian military is jealous of its position as the most important (and best-funded) armed force. Thus, despite some fractionation on this issue when it applies to the Palestinians, the services actively oppose the establishment or arming of any group at such a level that it may threaten their position.[72]

The armed forces are also becoming increasingly involved in internal security. Disturbances of an antiregime character in major Syrian cities have resulted in greater use of the army to quell civil disorder since 1979. It is important to recognize the fact that although the officer corps of the army is heavily laden with 'Alawis, the rank and file remains Sunni, which complicates the problem of policing internal disorder that is at base anti-'Alawi. Internal security within the armed forces consists of pervasive intelligence networks directed by persons trusted by Assad and two types of units, the Defense Units and the Struggle Companies, directed by Assad's brother and cousin, respectively.[73] Moreover, the strike forces of the Syrian army, as well as many key combat units, tend to be disproportionately 'Alawi.

The command and control of the Syrian armed forces, particularly the army, are also directly 'Alawi oriented. Even where unit commanders are not 'Alawis, the senior 'Alawi within the unit is directly tied to the higher command structure and quite closely linked to the presidential palace. In effect, then, there is an 'Alawi command structure parallel to and more effective than the formal military command structure. For this reason, a coup is virtually impossible, unless it be an 'Alawi coup.

Ethnic-Religious Groups

The most important of the many divisions of Syrian society is the ethnic-religious. Although Arabs constitute approximately 90 percent of the population (Kurds, Armenians, Turkomans, Circassians, Assyrians, and Jews amount to 6 percent, 3 percent, 1 percent, 1 percent, .5 percent, and a fraction of 1 percent, respectively), homogeneity does not exist. Syrian Arabs include several important religious minority communities, notably the 'Alawis. Muslims constitute over 85 percent of the population, but they include 'Alawis (11-15 percent), Ismailis (1 percent), and other Shiite sects (1 percent), as well as the Sunnis (about 70 percent). Christians — including Greek Orthodox (Melkite), Syrian Orthodox, Armenian Orthodox (Gregorian), Maronites, Syrian Catholics, Greek Catholics, Armenian Catholics, Chaldeans, and Nestorians (Assyrians) — make up about 10 percent of the Syrian population. Remaining religious minorities include the Druzes (3 percent of the population), Yazidis, and Jews.[74]

The 'Alawis make up between 9 and 13 percent of the Syrian population. They are a Shi'a sect similar in some of their beliefs to the Ismailis, but with greater Christian and other elements. Most 'Alawis live in Latakia Province, but they are dispersing as the nation becomes more urbanized. 'Alawis consider themselves Muslims; many Sunnis — but, significantly, not the more conservative — so consider them as well. Traditionally, 'Alawis have been held in contempt and discriminated against as poor, uneducated peasants by the Sunni landowners and by Sunnis in general. The results of this status are visible in anti-'Alawi demonstrations based upon an underlying Sunni resentment of 'Alawi control.[75]

Until the late 1970s the 'Alawis were principally concerned with improving their position in Syrian society. Traditional supporters of secularism, they clustered most homogeneously on any issue that affected 'Alawi advancement. With Syria under 'Alawi control, disproportionate attention was paid to their welfare — internal investment and foreign assistance projects were heavily oriented toward the improvement of the 'Alawi area around Latakia, and a disproportionate number of 'Alawis constituted the bulk of Syrian students permitted to study overseas.[76] 'Alawis continue to follow military careers in large numbers, and under Assad they continue to hold virtually all real power in the country. The special forces, defense companies, and intelligence arms of the military are predominantly 'Alawi, as is the *mukhabarat*. In order to forestall sectarian rivalry, Assad gave publicity to military discharges of 'Alawis who failed to perform satisfactorily in the October War; to the appointment of Sunni and minority, non-'Alawi, officers to senior military posts; and to the deemphasis of Ba'ath preferences in the armed forces.[77] He has distributed high-visibility posts with little real power to Sunnis, retaining 'Alawis in key positions.[78] Moreover, he has taken a number of steps to blur the 'Alawi-Sunni distinction — changing the presidential oath, spotlighting his participation in the activities of the Syrian Islamic community, and encouraging Sunni *'ulama* to portray the 'Alawis as Shi'a Muslims, a highly debatable proposition.[79]

By the late 1970s the Sunni majority of Syria had begun to demonstrate a cohesive determination to rid itself of 'Alawi domination. Sunni resentment was unmistakable. However, it is important to recognize that Sunnis frequently oppose the current regime on nonreligious issues, when, in fact, that opposition is based on their desire to return Syria to Sunni rule. Conservative Sunnis lead the opposition; and in the antiregime demonstrations that have taken place, Sunni sheikhs and the Muslim Brotherhood have played a prominent role.

The Muslim Brotherhood, founded in Egypt in 1928, has long found a deep sympathy among certain Syrian Sunni groups. Since the outset of 'Alawi rule, the Brotherhood has been active, first overtly, later clandestinely.[80] After the Aleppo artillery school massacre, the Assad government decided to make the Brotherhood the scapegoat for rising opposition to 'Alawi rule. Yet, the Brotherhood is not the only anti-'Alawi organization in Syria, nor even the only fundamentalist Sunni opposition.[81] It is allied with a number of like-minded groups, on the one hand, while being split into at least four factions, on the other.[82] Moreover, it may be said that focusing on the *Ikhwan* as the ubiquitous, malevolent force in Syria has at least partially backfired: majority Sunni opposition to 'Alawi rule has resulted in widespread support for the Brotherhood even among secular Syrians now.[83]

The Druzes were, with the 'Alawis, the major beneficiaries of the French divide-and-conquer strategy. Like the 'Alawis, the Druzes came to have a disproportionate representation in Syria's most important political group, the army. Until 1966, they and the 'Alawis worked together to improve their position in the army. Since the abortive Salim Hatum coup, however, the Druze role has decreased considerably.[84] As a group, Druzes and other minorities see secularism as in their interest. On such issues, Druzes will align with 'Alawis.

Syrian Christians are more educated, active, and affluent than their Muslim counterparts. Although they participate in public affairs, Syrian Christians have been noticeable by the secularism of their activities. Collective actions as an interest group have included support for religious equality and opposition to favoritism toward Islam. They have consistently opposed the establishment of an official state religion. In Syria, Christians have played a less pronounced role in the armed forces than 'Alawis and Druzes, but have dominated the Syrian air force (of which Assad is a former commander). They have in recent years been seen by the Sunni majority as linked with the 'Alawi ruling group, and consequently today are concerned about the future of their community in Syria should Assad fall.[85]

Economic Groups

There are several divisions in Syrian society along economic lines: urban-rural, radical-conservative, and merchant-(middle class) peasant. To some extent, analysts tend to merge these conflicts, often combining the categories with groups previously discussed. Certainly, the fact that 'Alawis, for example, have been poor, rural, social reformists is significant: it is not chance that led the 'Alawi-dominated neo-Ba'ath to reforms that aimed at improving the lot of poor, rural Syrian classes. It should be recognized, however, that the coincidence of interests is not complete.

The revolutionaries and reformists composing the "radical" wing of economic thought in Syria are not confined to the Ba'ath Party. On the contrary, they cross party lines and are an important force in today's Syria. They support nationalization of industries, more consistent implementation of land reform measures already enacted, and generally a larger role for the public sector (in some cases, to the virtual exclusion of the private). Although the revolutionaries are not numerous in Syria, they do have a strong base within the Ba'ath and Communist parties and, therefore, exert considerable influence.[86]

Before about 1970, Syrian social structure, although not based upon economic classes, could be divided into an upper class of landowning aristocracy (Damascus and Hama) and wealthy industrialists (Aleppo), paralleled by *ulama*; a professional and clerical middle class that had begun to emerge after World War I; and the lower classes of laborers, peasants, and others. Traditionally, the middle class of merchants aspired to the position of the upper class; but the new middle class, composed of some scions of the upper class and, primarily, of those of lower-class, rural, backgrounds, resented the old upper class. After some years of Ba'ath-led social revolution in Syria, the position of the old upper class had been materially altered, its influence greatly weakened.

The rising new political and professional elite looks with suspicion on the members of the old upper group. The old urban commercial middle class, in which religious minorities are heavily represented and which traditionally admired and emulated the upper class, consequently finds itself in a precarious position and is likely to avoid any public acknowledgement of the formerly wealthy and powerful. The *ulama* have ... made peace with the revolutionary regime.[87]

Prestige now lies in education and management. The new originally rural class of technicians, professionals, bureaucrats, and some merchants has successfully captured symbolic leadership. However, it does not have a class consciousness or a unified value system. In this respect, at least, the old upper class and the merchants just below it retain greater agreement and collective awareness. There remain upper and middle classes, but much of the membership — and capital — of both fled the country beginning in the mid-1960s. The return movement from 1975 to 1979 attested more to the continuity of economic interests than to an affection for the Ba'ath.[88]

The Syrian General Union of Peasants has had limited but important success in organizing and mobilizing Syrian peasants. Although it represents largely the Ba'ath sympathizers among the peasantry — it has scarcely recruited around Hama or in the Jazira because peasants in those areas have had ties to Akram Hourani and the SCP, respectively — a concerted effort has been made to spread regime views through the Union. "Peasant" leadership in the organization is frequently well-to-do. In some areas, the union is unsuccessful because the regime does not care to alter the social status quo; in others, because local leadership is hostile to the regime. The Syrian General Union of Peasants is one of several "popular organizations" widely and correctly viewed as tools of the Assad regime. Given its role and membership, the union does not exert any real pressure on the Syrian government.[89]

The General Federation of Trade Unions is the only "popular organization" to antedate the Ba'ath regime. Moreover, unlike other organizations in Syria, it has consistently permitted the continued membership of many non-Ba'athists. Houranists, Communists, and Nasserites are numerous. On the other hand, since 1964, the federation has been controlled by the regime. All political tendencies are allowed, but Ba'ath predominance is exercised at the national level. About half the industrial labor force is in the General Federation. Labor issues do rise through its pyramidal organization, but union and labor as a whole can scarcely be taken as an autonomous interest group on other matters.[90]

In general, economic issues and groups are much less important in the Syrian foreign policy decision-making equation than they have been in many years.

Transnational Interest Groups

A most unusual feature of the Syrian political system has been the important role played in it by non-Syrians — Palestinians now living in Syria. Palestinian power in Syria is not the result of military force but, rather, a function of the Syrian political self-image. "Most politically-conscious Syrians have held and continue to hold firmly to the conviction that Syria is the throbbing heart of Arab nationalism."[91]

As a result of Syria's self-conscious role as leader in Arab nationalism, the Palestinian cause is a central question, a test (or proof) of Syria's position. Also, Syrians feel a personal link with Palestine as a part of greater, prepartition Syria. Thus, the Palestinian view is accorded great weight in Syria. Palestinians have pushed Syria to lead the "rejection front" — the resistance to any settlement short of the destruction of Israel and re-creation of Palestine — and do not hesitate to use their moral influence. They also were used to buttress the Jadid regime. Jadid consciously created and armed Sa'iqa to reduce the relative monopoly of power in military hands and to increase his own leverage. Hafez Assad, however, replaced the Sa'iqa leadership with Palestinians loyal to him; Sa'iqa has existed under both regimes and will continue to be a creature of Syrian policy.

Syrian policy vis-a-vis the Palestinian resistance as a whole has varied as a function of immediate Syrian foreign-policy goals and domestic needs. The government has not hesitated to restrict the resistance — or even prohibit it from undertaking operations against Israel — when such restriction aided the realization of other objectives. When Syria needed time to install surface-to-air missile (SAM) air defenses, for example, and did not want Israeli retaliatory air strikes, Palestinian operations from Syrian territory were stopped. Both Sa'iqa, which can be considered a Syrian organization, and the Palestine Liberation Army (PLA) brigade stationed in Syria are completely subject to Syrian control. The army supervises the Yarmouk Brigade; the regime, Sa'iqa. Certain elements in the Syrian armed forces are particularly hostile to Palestinian freedom of action.

In addition to the PLA and Sa'iqa, at least two other Palestinian commando groups have enjoyed a close relationship to the Syrian government — the Popular Front for the Liberation of Palestine-General Command (PFLP-GC) and the Democratic Popular Front for the Liberation of Palestine (DPFLP), led by Ahmed Gibril and Nayef Hawatmeh, respectively.[92] Sympathies throughout Syria are extremely pro-Palestinian, and any important Syrian action regarded as anti-Palestinian engenders significant popular opposition, though minor infringements on Palestinian freedom of action are not likely to do so.[93]

The most controversial foreign-policy initiative taken by Assad — certainly far more politically dangerous than the decision to go to war in October 1973 or the more unpopular choice to accept a Golan disengagement agreement with Israel — was his decision to use military force in Lebanon against the Palestine Liberation Organization. Assad's conviction of the solidity of his own power base in 1976 is evidenced by this action, which generated very considerable opposition in Syria.[94]

ISSUE AREAS

The two most important issues until recently in Syria have been the recovery of Syrian territory currently occupied by Israel (the Golan Heights) and the resolution of the Palestinian question. They are much more completely interwoven in Syria than in other Arab countries (even those — except Jordan — whose territory is occupied by Israel). Syrians cannot divorce the Palestinian territorial-political problem from their own for a number of reasons. First, Palestine was part of the greater Syria that is still a more real object of loyalty to many Syrians than the present-day state is. Second, there are many Palestinian refugees living in Syria.[95] Third, Syrians have taken pride in their role as the Arab conscience; they, more than others, have remained loyal to the Palestinian cause to demonstrate this role. Fourth, Syria has laid claim to the title of leader in the fight against Israel, a claim that integrates, or at least has integrated, the Palestinian and Arab (hence, Syrian) conflicts with Israel. Fifth, there are a number of political, economic, and social issues similarly affected by Israeli occupation of Syrian territory and by the Palestine problem. Refugee questions[96] and resultant constraints on the demographic options available to Syria are but two of several such areas.

More recently, the sectarian conflict between 'Alawis and Sunnis has impinged directly and importantly on Syrian foreign policy.

Occupied Territory and the Arab-Israeli Conflict

Syria's own territorial conflict with Israel is limited to the Golan Heights, occupied in June 1967.[97] The public campaign to liberate the Golan has been unremitting. There is no evidence that a Ba'ath government, humiliated by its poor military showing against Israel in 1967, has tried to soft-pedal the issue. Quite the contrary: Syrians were constantly reminded of the Israeli occupation and of the certainty that the occupied Golan would be retaken by Syria.[98]

Thus, the primary issue with respect to the Golan has never been whether to accept its loss or to seek its return. Instead, issues have concerned the means and the timing of its recovery. Virtually all Syrians have accepted the need for force in the effort. How to use force in victory — rather than in a 1967-like defeat — is the problem.

The current set of issues that confronts Syrians on the Golan and Arab-Israeli questions includes the following: Should Syria follow a moderate or a rejectionist line? Should Syria engage in talks with Israel? Should Syria accept any partial approaches, even if linked to an overall settlement?

Individuals and groups within Syria were long divided on the direction the nation's policy should take. Assad abandoned Syria's traditional "irreconcilable" status, and the ensuing debate centered upon the wisdom of this abandonment. For example, one group supported the Golan disengagement agreement negotiated in the spring of 1974 and promoted a compromise overall settlement with Israel, while another felt that Syria should accept nothing less than total and immediate withdrawal.[99] (In some cases, leaders of the second group proved much more flexible when dealing with specific issues and proposals.[100])

The first line of reasoning stressed that Egypt was an undependable ally, Iraq untrustworthy and relatively peripheral to the conflict with Israel. The Soviet Union, helpful as it may always have been, always backed down to the United States, which will never allow Israel to be conquered. Syria's relatively improved showing in the October War also seemed to provide an additional bargaining card for the first years after that war. By contrast, those arguing against a settlement suggest that such a resolution in today's terms (with Saudi prominence) would mean an end to the Arab revolution. Some saw the outcome of the October War as a sign that Israel was on the ropes and could be knocked out eventually, while the oil weapon neutralized the United States.[101] Moreover, Syrians, including Assad, remain convinced that Israel will never surrender the Golan Heights, a sine qua non for a settlement with Syria.

Many of those supporting immediate withdrawal are not prepared to accept any compromise with Israel. Most Syrians probably still oppose negotiations with Israel, and certainly they still fear it.[102] There is a substantial body of opinion in favor of Syria's joining a "rejection front" composed of Iraq, South Yemen, Libya, and certain Palestinian elements.[103] (The latter include the PFLP.)[104] In fact, Assad has used this opinion, sometimes by capitalizing on tactical points of agreement to solidify his position, sometimes to strengthen his bargaining posture vis-a-vis Israel.[105] The disengagement agreement was a focal point of this "hawkish" dissent, and it can be assumed that further agreements with Israel would face similar opposition.[106]

Palestine

The Syrian government has considered itself, and generally has been viewed, as the most consistent supporter of the Palestinian cause. There is also an indissoluble link between the Palestinian issue and the larger Arab-Israeli and Syrian-Israeli problems. The questions Damascus has had to face in this area include the extent to which political support should be furnished to the Palestinian cause; the ends for which this support should be provided; the degree of military and logistical assistance to be provided Palestinian resistance forces and the purposes for which the assistance may be used; and, directly associated with each of these problems, the specific Palestinian groups to be supported.

To date, Syria has consistently supported the Palestinian cause, at first even rejecting U.N. Security Council Resolution 242 of November 1967. Assad came to power, however, over Palestinian resistance and after Sa'iqa and the Syrian-based PLA had been neutralized by the Syrian armed forces. Although Sa'iqa has been taken over by the Assad regime, Palestinian wishes retain some influence. The army continues to jealously safeguard its military role, which the Palestinians have learned to accept. During periodic crackdowns on guerrilla activity, the Palestinians may appeal through sympathetic channels to Syrian opinion; they do not challenge Syrian authority to impose whatever restrictions may be promulgated.

Political support for the Palestinian cause is, then, substantial; but it is unlimited only in the sense that the issue of political goals is scarcely argued. Assad claims he will not become involved in such a debate. (We shall see, however, that he hedges his bets.[107]) For now, Syrian political support for the recognition of Palestinian rights is undefined.[108]

Damascus has been much more circumspect in concrete support for the Palestinian cause. Syrian territory has been used intermittently by the Palestinian guerrillas in operations against Israel and has been open to Palestinian military support of Syrian military operations. However, such activities have been infrequent, determined by strategic considerations of the Syrian-Israeli relationship or, occasionally, by domestic factors. Syria has not fought for the Palestinians since 1947. The pressure that exists within Syria to fight for the Palestinians can be, and has been, eased by political support and by the melange of Syrian-Palestinian justifications the government has used as a rationale for essentially national-interest actions. In 1976 Syrian armed forces were used in military operations in Lebanon that were justified as support for the Palestinian cause. In fact, the army, the PLA, and Sa'iqa all operated against a coalition of PLO and Lebanese leftist forces. Substantial Syrian opposition was encountered — predictably — but largely overcome by Assad in this instance. As is discussed below, Syrian military operations in 1976 answer the second of the four questions posed by the Palestinian issue, and in such a way as to respond as well to the other three.

Sectarianism

A central problem in Syria is sectarianism. Virtually since the inception of Ba'ath power — even under the Sunni Amin al-Hafez from 1963 to 1966 — Sunnis have been concerned over favoritism shown 'Alawis and 'Alawi-populated areas. In May 1967 serious sectarian demonstrations took place. They followed from an atheistic (but typically Ba'athist) article in an army magazine. The crisis preceding the June War overshadowed the demonstrations. Since the "setback," as Syria and other Arab regimes referred to the outcome of the 1967 conflict, Sunni rumors throughout the Middle East attribute the loss of the Golan Heights to an 'Alawi "deal" with Israel involving a large sum of money in exchange for the Heights.[109] In the aftermath of the June War disaster, there was little overt religious unrest in Syria, however. Only in the early 1970s did such troubles begin to surface — in the spring of 1972, when a radio commentator's minor error in reporting a religious celebration led to some disturbances, and throughout the early months of 1973 when substantial violence broke out in connection with a new draft of the constitution that did not identify Islam as the state religion.[110] Riots erupted in late February, when the People's Assembly ratified the constitution, and again around the Prophet's birthday in April.

Undoubtedly the major Syrian foreign-policy activity that has abetted the reawakening of religious unrest in Syria is Syrian behavior in Lebanon. The spectre of an 'Alawi-Maronite alliance in Lebanon against the Palestinian and Lebanese Sunnis was particularly grating to the Syrian Sunni majority. At the same time, it is true that the sectarian unrest that grew during the period in which Syria maintained an active military presence in Lebanon did not focus on or protest the Lebanese intervention.

One of the complicating factors of the religious schism within Syria is the involvement of other regional powers in that issue. The Muslim Brotherhood, for example, is supported by Saudi Arabia and Jordan. Iraq, too, is believed to provide financial support to Sunni dissidents in Syria. Since Syrian leaders have had to look to Jordan for military and political cooperation, and to Saudi Arabia for vital financial assistance, they have been frustrated by these connections.[111] Indeed, some of the senior Syrian leadership has consistently feared Saudi Arabia precisely because of the potential magnitude of the sectarian problem and of the Saudi ability to influence its denouement. Yet, to lead a consciously sectarian foreign policy would be to exacerbate the domestic differences and provide a rationale for dissent.

Foreign Relations

The Syrian relationship with the world outside the Middle East has been limited in recent years. After the Ba'ath, and particularly the neo-Ba'ath, came to power, Syria became increasingly isolated, with ties of growing strength and number to the Soviet Union and its East European allies. Following the June War, disagreement over the role of the Soviet Union and the degree of reliance on it continued as a major issue. Ba'ath ideologues, Communists, and some other groups favored greater alliance with Moscow and the severance of Syrian relations with regional "reactionaries." Some nationalists, however, with tacit support from conservative elements and groups within the military, argued in favor of cooperating more with all Arab countries rather than with the socialist commonwealth, and of placing more traditional limits on Syrian reliance on non-Arab supporters. Assad, for example, opposed the terms of some economic agreements with the Soviet Union, on the ground that they were overly favorable to Moscow.[112]

Prior to his final coup, Hafez Assad had sided rather consistently with the nationalists against overreliance on, and excessive concessions to, the Soviet Union. He had attacked the Jadid regime for improper contacts with the Soviet embassy, undue economic concessions to Moscow, and collusion with Syrian Communists. The army had acted openly against Syrian Communists and pro-Soviet elements throughout much of 1970. Nevertheless, the Soviets did not hesitate to support Assad once his dominance became clear.

Since his accession to power, Assad has at times been placed in the position of supporting the Soviet Union against anti-Soviet elements. Following the July 1972 expulsion of Soviet advisors and other military personnel from Egypt, a debate ensued in Syria over the future of the Soviet personnel in that country. Despite some problems that had arisen from time to time, however, Soviet-Syrian military relations never reached the level of animosity characterizing Soviet-Egyptian problems. Assad did more than strongly support the retention of Soviet personnel: he tried to serve as intermediary to bridge the Moscow-Cairo gap, and undertook new and substantially expanded military agreements with the Soviet Union, under the terms of which some important Soviet strategic needs (unrelated to the Arab-Israeli conflict) previously met by Egypt were filled by Syria.[113]

After the October War, Syrian-Soviet relations were complicated first by the entry of the United States into the Syrian political scene, then by the Lebanese civil war. Renewal of U.S.-Syrian relations was not the result of Syrian frustration with the Soviet Union. Indeed, while there had been intermittent problems of military supply, Assad believes and has consistently indicated that maintenance of strong ties between Moscow and Damascus is crucial to the realization of Syrian objectives. At the same time, neither of the Assad brothers trusts the Soviets; Syrians and Arabs in general have difficulty in understanding or identifying with the Soviets; and the Syrian leadership is typical in its belief that American technology is superior to its Soviet counterpart. Moreover, Soviet influence over Israel was known to be negligible, while that of the United States was thought to be sufficient to assist in securing a negotiated settlement that met Syrian terms.

Following the resolution of Syrian-Soviet differences over the Syrian role in Lebanon, Syria began to find itself isolated in the Middle East. An attempted rapprochement with Iraq aborted, leaving the two countries at odds once again. Jordan, Syria's closest ally from 1973 to 1979, began to look to Iraq for political and economic support, and relations between Damascus and Amman cooled substantially. Syria's active participation in the anti-Camp David alignment left relations between Egypt and Syria almost nonexistent. Finally, Saudi Arabia, Assad's principal financial backer until 1980, but ever distrustful of Syria, became impatient over the nature of Syrian behavior in Lebanon, Syrian ties with the new regime in Iran, and the suddenly passionate Soviet relationship.

Thus, notwithstanding the Assads' perceptions of Moscow, in spite of their recognition of Soviet impotence in influencing Israel, and in the face of a blatant and bloody Soviet intervention in Afghanistan that shocked the Muslim world, Syrian foreign policy in 1979 and 1980 reflected a pronounced Soviet orientation.[114] On October 8, 1980, the two countries signed a "friendship treaty." Massive military aid, including unusually advanced weapons systems such as the

T-72 and MiG-25, helped to buttress the relationship.[115] One result has been the identification of the Soviet Union as an "'Alawi" ally by Sunni opponents of the Assad government, leading to the targeting of Soviet advisors by armed dissidents.[116]

By contrast with political relations, the stagnation of Soviet-Syrian commerce and economic relations has been apparent for some time. Assad initiatives to attract Western capital investments and technology enjoyed some success — partly at the expense of Soviet-Syrian economic cooperation — in 1975. Indeed, prior to the intervention in Lebanon, Syria's economy was booming. Since 1976, however, the Syrian economic picture has been bleak, and Soviet-Syrian economic relations have remained relatively unimportant. The cost of closer relations with Moscow and increasingly hostile links with the United States has been steep, however: reduction of Saudi support, and diminution of the transfer of U.S. technology. The financially strapped Assad regime was forced into the munificent arms of the Libyan Arab Jamahariyah by 1980, though the relationship was clearly a marriage of convenience.

The thaw in relations with the United States between 1974 and 1978 was less uncontroversial than recent dealings with the Soviet Union. Despite a reservoir of good feeling toward the United States and Americans (in general, Syrians can more easily identify with Americans than with Soviets), U.S. relations with and support of Israel, suspicions about the trustworthiness of the United States and the reality of its evenhandedness, ideological preferences, and the recognition of the need for continued economic and military backing from the Soviet Union led diverse groups to oppose the warming trend between Damascus and Washington.[117]

Events in Lebanon, where there was some substantial cooperation between the two capitals, served to maintain a useful dialogue, however, because by 1978 the relationship was on a rapidly accelerating downward spiral again. Syria's opposition to the Sadat initiative and the later Camp David agreements, which seemed to leave little room for Syria's vital concerns on the Golan and to give away too much to Israel for too little, placed Damascus in the role of opposing a major U.S. foreign-policy initiative once more. As Syria's regional isolation forced Assad to turn more and more to the Soviet Union, relations with Washington worsened, although the personal good feelings of individuals involved in the diplomatic contact continued.

For centuries, historians have observed a pattern in which Egypt and Iraq compete for Syria. This pattern bears a striking resemblance to contemporary Syrian politics. (Indeed, the principal error of viewing Egypt as the conservative or moderating force, and Iraq as the revolutionary, is that these positions have been much less stable than the rivalry itself.) Even before the definitive ouster of Jadid, however, Assad was Cairo's choice.[118]

Syria's relationship with Egypt has been a major issue, the importance of which is underscored by Syria's inability to fight Israel alone — which means, in practice, Syria's need for a military alliance with Egypt at the time of full-scale hostilities or of threat of force. Egypt's relatively moderate role after Sadat came to power and the fluctuation of Egypt's relations with the Soviet Union during that same period have been troublesome for Syria, whose role as the "irreconcilable" and whose close ties to Moscow were both prejudiced, thus leading to domestic debates over the wisdom of following Egypt. At the same time, it should be pointed out that when Damascus did not follow Cairo − as in the 1972 expulsion of Soviet advisors − the debate was no less strident.[119] For approximately a year in 1972-73, Egypt and Syria were at odds; but sometime in the spring of 1973, when Assad and Sadat apparently took their decision to use war to prevent further solidification of the status quo, Syria's relations with Egypt − and others − were repaired, bringing about the familiar debate over dealing with "reactionary" Arab regimes.

Following the October War, which significantly improved Assad's domestic position, the debate was reopened. Assad was careful not to follow Sadat's virtual about-face in his relations with the superpowers; but the Syrian policy trend toward close coordination with Cairo and greatly improved relations with the United States was the subject of intense debate, mitigated only by the gradualness of the new policy toward the United States and the maintenance of close and cooperative ties to the Soviet Union. Bilateral negotiations and agreements between Egypt and Israel aroused Syrian suspicion and resentment. Generally, the same faction that favored negotiation with Israel, disengagement, and a U.S. role in the settlement favored coordination with Egypt. Some, on the other hand, felt that Syria had already gone too far in pursuing Sadat-like policies. Syrian Communists, too, were alarmed by the drift toward cooperation with countries like Saudi Arabia and Egypt, even while recognizing the key role these states play in exerting indirect or direct pressure on Israel. Most of the leftist thought in Syria accepts some cooperation as necessary, but there is substantial attention paid to the Soviet view.[120]

Cooperative relations with Egypt and the debate over Egypt's direction were mooted by the second-stage Sinai withdrawal in the fall of 1975. After "Sinai II" and on the basis of certain provisions of that accord, Assad and other Syrians concluded that Egypt was no longer an active factor in the confrontation with Israel. The implications of Sinai II for Syrian politics and policy toward the Arab-Israeli conflict, for inter-Arab cooperation generally, for the Palestinians, and for Lebanon were very far-reaching indeed. Here we shall confine ourselves to the impact on Syrian foreign policy.

Accepting the withdrawal of Egypt from the Arab frontline meant, as it has always meant, no credible strategic threat any longer confronted Israel. Given the Syrian conviction that Israel will never relinquish control of the Golan without such a threat, the defection of Egypt constituted a mortal blow to Syrian policy, which favored a settlement, but one in which the Golan was evacuated by Israel.

Later events brought about brief tactical respites in Syrian opposition to Egyptian policy and Egyptian resistance to Syrian initiatives, but Sadat's trip to

Jerusalem in 1977, the Camp David accords of 1978, and the Egyptian-Israeli peace treaty of 1979 all served to confirm Assad's 1975 view that Egypt had withdrawn from the confrontation with Israel. By no means did Syria accept the view that the Camp David accords were designed or destined to bring about a regional settlement. From Sinai II to the March 1979 treaty, Assad perceived a straight line of thinking that centered on a separate peace between Egypt and Israel.[121]

Despite certain sectoral economic cooperation, military cooperation against Israel, Iraqi economic aid to Syria, Syrian political support for Iraq in its dispute with Iran before the deposition of the Pahlavis, and some strong pro-Iraqi interest groups in Syria, relations between the two Ba'ath regimes have never been very good and often have been bitter. Each country has plotted against the other on several occasions, and each is blamed by the other for antiregime action that may or may not originate on the other side of the border. While Syria was the key country in the Middle East, and then as Iraq assumed that mantle, the antipathy of the two Ba'ath regimes has only grown.

Because Baghdad and Damascus rationalize their dispute on ideological grounds, many observers have drawn the conclusion that the problems separating the two countries are based upon a disagreement as to the real path of, or even the real identity of, Ba'athism. However, any study of Iraqi and Syrian politics, including the present one, demonstrates clearly that Ba'athism is used in both countries largely to legitimize minority or narrowly based governance, and is not the compass guiding policy or practice. Ba'athism did not hinder the impassioned romance of 1979, when the two governments spoke of uniting, or the rapid and bitter estrangement that followed.

It has been a consistent and unfortunate custom of Western analysts to assess and compare Arab regimes on the basis of their policies toward the Arab-Israeli issue, despite the fact that policies and performance with respect to that problem are notoriously poor predictors of behavior in the foreign-policy arena generally. Chapter 4 above demonstrates this fact vividly for the case of Iraq. But Iraqi-Syrian relations manifest the same phenomenon. The motive force behind much of the foreign policy of each government has been its opposition to the other, yet both defend their policies under the rubric of anti-Zionism, opposition to the Camp David accords, and support of the Palestinians.

In the immediate aftermath of Camp David, and partly in response to the accords reached there, Iraq and Syria worked together to block the implementation of the agreements. Yet, throughout this period of cooperation, neither government trusted the motives or individuals involved in the process on the other side. When Syrian leaders went to Baghdad to join those opposed to the Camp David accords they did so on their own terms — continued acceptance of U.N. Security Council Resolutions 242 and 338, and this fact was reassuring to Assad. Yet, the immediacy of the Jerusalem trip and Camp David waned, and soon the basic and essential rivalry between Iraq and Syria reemerged. Now, which is the moderate: Syria, which accepts the U.N. resolutions and the concept of peace with Israel, and has even advanced a number of concrete suggestions in that regard, or Iraq, which has turned cold toward the Soviet Union, has urged the Palestinians to participate in such Geneva negotiations as might take place, and pressed the leftist-Palestinian forces to work with rather than fight Israel's Christian allies in Lebanon? The point is, the Arab-Israeli issue is a highly inappropriate measuring stick for Iraqi-Syrian relations.

The countries most important to Syria after Egypt and Iraq are Jordan and Lebanon. Syria's ties to Lebanon are ancient, the latter having formed part of traditional Syria. Many of the customs and much of the commercial philosophy of the two countries have been similar in the past, and personal and family ties are transnational. Lebanon and Syria have, however, had very different postwar histories. Lebanon's military role in the region is minimal, although its commercial role, and in some respects its political situation, are of some importance. The transnational issue regarding Lebanon that has arisen in Syria concerns the plight of the Palestinians. The Syrian government, which generally gave verbal backing to the Palestinians in their complaints against the Lebanese government and occasionally resorted to economic measures to demonstrate support for the Palestinians,[122] conducted "peacekeeping" operations in Lebanon in 1976 that were a facade for military actions against an alliance of Palestinians and Lebanese leftists. Syria, historically the greatest supporter of the Palestinian cause, clearly had made some decisions that constituted a key turning point in Syrian-Palestinian relations.

Jordan has had a less fraternal relationship with Syria than Lebanon has. The two have a long-standing territorial conflict (although that dispute has been of little import for over two decades). The Hashemite kingdom was a consistent target of Syrian rhetoric from the advent of the Ba'ath regime until the 1970s. Long-standing tension between Palestinians, on the one hand, and the Jordanian government, on the other, resulted in a civil war in September 1970[123] ("Black September" to Palestinian guerrillas), in which Syrian armored units participated without air cover. The Syrian operations in Jordan led to the final Assad coup in November 1970. Assad later sent the regime's second most powerful leader, Mustapha Tlas, to meet with the Jordanians. Tlas is a conservative Sunni with personal ties to both Jordan and Saudi Arabia.[124] Each attempt to improve relations with Jordan was at first low-keyed; nevertheless, they encountered substantial opposition, especially among younger Ba'ath military officers. Thus, Syria did not hesitate to use economic sanctions or allow the Palestinians to "punish" Jordan, even though relations between the Hashemite monarchy and the 'Alawi regime were in fact relatively good from the outset of Assad's rule.[125]

With the development of a new Syrian foreign policy in the aftermath of the Sinai II accord, Jordanian-Syrian relations improved dramatically. Despite internal resistance to this change at first, the regime imposed its views. Considering the emerging rift with Egypt and the gulf between Iraq and Syria, and in the face of the Israeli problem, the rapprochement with Jordan declined as a rallying point of dissension. Until 1980, the Jordanian-Syrian entente held as perhaps the firmest, even if one of the quietest alliances in the region.[126] Then, however, sensing the changing political winds in the Middle East and the rise of Iraq, King Hussein began to move toward Baghdad, leaving Syria totally isolated in the Arab East.

Relations with Saudi Arabia, like those with Jordan, have fluctuated widely since Assad came to power. Both the Assad brothers have felt Saudi Arabia has the capability to cause substantial unrest in Syria through the Muslim Brotherhood and other conservative Sunni elements of society. As a result, Assad has endeavored to maintain cordial relations with the Saudis and to avoid a split with Riyadh of any magnitude. However, as Syria became increasingly isolated in 1979 and 1980 and turned more toward the Soviets for support, Saudi patience wore thin. Assad's refusal to attend the Islamic summit in 1980, for example, angered the Saudis and led to private threats and counterthreats.[127]

SYRIAN OBJECTIVES AND POLICIES

In the highly heterogeneous society that is Syria, consensus on national objectives — or even whether national Syrian (as opposed to national Arab) objectives should exist — cannot be expected. The following constitute objectives of the current Syrian regime:

- Recovery of Syrian territory presently occupied by Israel (Golan Heights);
- Maintenance of the current regime and, associated with that goal, development of popular support for the regime and government;
- Resolution of the Palestinian issue;
- Economic development of Syria and, in support of that policy, the attraction of private and foreign government investment;
- Maintenance and improvement of relations with Arab countries;
- Improvement of economic, political, and social relations with the West; and
- Acceptable termination of the conflict with Israel.

Hafez Assad's approach to governance of Syria showed positive results until about 1979-80. Clearly the most popular regime in the country for many years, his government has been characterized by a stability remarkable by Syrian standards. Many of those in key positions in 1970 remained as important advisors, formally or informally, to Assad a decade later. However, as we have pointed out, by 1979 it was clear that the Assad government was no longer accepted by the majority of Syrians. And, ironically, Syria found itself in 1980 as it had found itself in 1970 — isolated, tense, riven by conflict, and suffocated under tight security.

Although Assad continues to attempt to legitimize his government, current policies emphasize short-term control more than long-term legitimacy. Quasi-military sweeps through major cities, a proliferation of security and intelligence organizations, summary abductions and executions − these are not the foundations on which stability rests over time. Casting the blame for unrest and violence on the Muslim Brotherhood and the United States provides an excuse for Assad's supporters, but Syria's Sunni majority remains unconvinced. Recognizing the magnitude of the opposition, Assad has also resorted to government shuffles, since part of the complaint against his regime concerns corruption. (In fact, however, it is as much the Damascene Sunni society that benefits from corruption as any other single group.) Yet, since Rifaat Assad is widely believed to symbolize the corruption (as well as the oppression) of the government, and since Hafez depends upon Rifaat's security forces, middle-level shake-ups do not impress public opinion.

It is unlikely that the unpopular 'Alawi minority can continue to control Syria indefinitely. It is even more unlikely that Hafez Assad, given the level of domestic opposition that has developed over the past few years, fails to recognize this fact. He is an astute political leader who mastered the complex political machinations traditional in the country, who brought Syria an unprecedented level of progress and stability, a leader who dared to think about, talk of, and plan for a peaceful settlement of the conflict with Israel. There is substantial evidence that Assad recognizes the end of 'Alawi leadership in Syria is near, and that he is giving attention to the possibility of 'Alawi autonomy or independence in the area in which 'Alawis are the majority.[128]

Political Policies

Under the rubric of "political programs" we shall consider both domestic and foreign policies of the Assad government. Separation of domestic from foreign policies is arbitrary and misleading, in that foreign issues frequently are of domestic significance. Nevertheless, we shall first discuss questions of internal Syrian politics.

Hafez Assad's primary domestic objective has been to preserve his regime and to establish its legitimacy. To this end, the president endeavored to build a constitutional foundation in the "permanent constitution" promulgated in 1973. Moreover, added legitimacy is sought in the direct election of the president by universal suffrage.[129] At the outset of his administration, Assad introduced democratic reforms, undertook new economic policies more in line with majority Syrian wishes and values, and opened the legislative and public political arenas to parties other than the Ba'ath.[130]

Assad refers to his 1970 coup as a "corrective movement," thereby suggesting the continuity of Ba'athism. However, the president placed heavy emphasis on the relaxation of internal security measures and reduction of the government's isolation from the people. The visibility and importance of the secret police were reduced,[131] as was the stridency of public discussion and the extreme secularism of the Ba'ath party.[132] Indeed, the role of the Ba'ath itself changed, partly because of the history of the Assad-Jadid conflict[133] and partly because Assad recognized and wished to reduce the vulnerability that derived from the conservative Sunni suspicions of the "Godless Ba'ath."

The inclusion of non-Ba'ath parties in the People's Assembly and NPF was only part of Assad's attempt to broaden the base — that is, to increase the representativeness — of his regime. Equally important, anti-Ba'ath groups were not overlooked in cabinets: Assad made a real effort to secure popular unity behind his government, to make it "a government of the people."[134]

The reduction of domestic revolutionary rhetoric carried over to domestic coverage of foreign affairs. Assad curtailed much of the polemic in the public media. His effort to develop better relations with all his Arab neighbors was attended by a noticeable decline in the temperature of public political discourse on foreign affairs.

While we do not propose to discuss foreign-policy considerations in the context of domestic political programs, a significant policy change under Assad has been the approach taken to the conflict with Israel. Whereas previous governments had insisted on military confrontation and on the unacceptability of a peaceful solution, Assad softened this stand virtually from the time he assumed direction of the government. Often assailed by Jadid for his desire to concentrate on the development of the armed forces before undertaking hostilities with Israel, Assad all but formally accepted Resolution 242 of the Security Council after his coup. Following the October War, Assad accepted Resolution 338. Later, his government entered into negotiations with Israel that culminated in a disengagement agreement. This approach is a radical departure. Domestically, Assad's policy is characterized by a totally different perspective in the media. The Syrians have secured Soviet support and now accuse Israel of wanting war, suggesting that recurrent hostilities between Israel and its Arab neighbors benefit Israel through Zionist expansion. Thus, "we Arabs must put an end to the chain of wars."[135]

Syria's primary concern in its confrontation with Israel is the recovery of the Golan Heights, occupied by Israel in 1967. There are major differences of opinion among the Syrian population on various issues between the two countries. With respect to Golan, however, there is no difference. All Syrians want, demand, and expect return of the Golan to Syrian control. Cession of any part of it, even on the basis of a long-term lease, is unacceptable to virtually any Syrian. Syrian sovereignty and the termination of Israeli control over the Heights are a sine qua non of any settlement. The incessant public insistence by Syrian leaders on return of the Golan is sincere; no agreement is possible for less.[136]

The straightforward Golan issue explains much of Syrian policy. It explains Syria's rejection of the negotiation concept after 1967, for Syrians were convinced that Israel would never agree to return the Golan. Thus, negotiation was refused because it would reduce Arab support for Syria (as others' needs were met). This also explains Syria's insistence on rejection of the concept of "minor adjustments" to the pre-June 5 borders, since Golan (it was felt) would be one such sacrifice.[137]

Given the determination to reacquire the Golan, one can understand the importance the Syrians have placed on blocking any solidification of the status quo. Syrian spokesmen have attacked Israel's demand for secure borders, probably not so much from lack of understanding as from thorough understanding of the logical conclusion — that much of the Israeli-occupied Golan would be claimed by Israel as necessary to security.[138] This, too, is the basis for Syria's demand that disengagement be explicitly tied to a peace settlement requiring withdrawal to pre-June 5 boundaries.[139] Although the disengagement accord was so linked, to the satisfaction of the Syrians,[140] later problems in negotiations have reinforced Syrian doubts concerning the likelihood of a peaceful settlement including restoration of the Golan. Thus, Syrian Golan refugees have not resettled to any extent in that portion of the Golan returned through the 1974 disengagement accord. There are several reasons for their retaining refugee status,[141] but the continued depopulation of the Golan effectively underscores the proximity of war and the readiness of the Syrian government[142] to accept it as a means of regaining control — or ending Israeli occupation — of Syrian territory.

Recognizing the balance of forces, Syria has from the outset insisted upon an Israeli guarantee of total withdrawal before entering "negotiations." Since such a guarantee is unlikely, Syria will continue to demand it.[143]

We have already described the fundamental change in Syrian policy toward Israel. Before the Assad regime, Syria led the opposition to peaceful settlement, rejecting Security Council Resolution 242.[144] From its inception, the Assad regime has looked upon peaceful settlement as the preferable approach,[145] if Israel would relinquish territory occupied in 1967 and recognize the rights of the Palestinians.[146] Moderation was no more successful than the extremist policy Syria had followed, however; and when Egypt's initial attempts in 1971 and 1972 to secure American backing for progress failed, Assad was prepared to consider war. Indeed, the new Syrian position facilitated war planning, for agreement on objectives was easy — war aims were limited, and the destruction of Israel was not even considered.[147] Nor has Syrian policy reverted to its pre-Assad "irreconcilable" image. Since the October War, the Syrians have consistently and publicly favored peace talks. (This implicitly means the acceptance of Israel's existence.)[148] As we have seen, today Syria suggests it is Israel that favors war, while "we are above all for a political solution."[149] It is Israel's unwillingness to return the occupied territories and recognize Palestinian rights, the Assad regime maintains, that makes the use of force inevitable.

That Assad's change in Syrian policy on a peaceful settlement rests on values fundamentally different from Jadid's must be clear. Jadid's Syria was isolated in the Arab world (except for the Palestinians). The Syrian leadership feared Egypt or Jordan might reach a separate accord with Israel. Since Israel was less concerned about Sinai and the West Bank than about the Golan, either Egypt or Jordan or both might settle; but nothing short of war could bring back the Heights. No one even seriously tried to persuade Syria to accept a peaceful solution.[150] The new leadership placed a high priority on Arab cooperation. Recognizing strategic threat (potentially effective use of force) as the key factor likely to persuade Israel to negotiate withdrawal from the occupied territories, Syria initially depended upon cooperation with Egypt to compose that threat. Thus, as it became clear that Egypt would remove itself from the combined strategic threat to Israel, the Syrian leadership seized upon the remaining alternative — an eastern front.[151] The Egyptian agreement — Sinai II — has been opposed and condemned in order to increase the costs of such an option. (Indeed, although preferring a peaceful resolution, Assad has never hesitated to disrupt Egyptian attempts at single-front settlements.[152])

Syrian foreign-policy decision makers — and this clearly means Assad — have been unable to deal with the situation resulting from Sinai II and the Camp David agreements, including the Egyptian-Israeli peace treaty of March 26, 1979. They are convinced that an acceptance of this approach guarantees permanent Israeli occupation of the Golan. Yet, as Jordan gravitated toward Iraq in 1979 and 1980, any semblance of the chimera of an eastern front dissolved. From the Syrian perspective, step-by-step and single-front approaches have created a political situation far less conducive to a settlement acceptable to Syria than even the circumstances antecedent to the October War.

Another major element in Syrian policy toward Israel is Soviet support. Such backing is necessary not only because Syria's military forces depend upon Soviet materiel, training, and support, but also because of the exigencies of domestic Syrian politics.[153] Thus, while Syria does not subordinate its own policies toward Israel to those of its superpower provider, Damascus' position certainly is strongly influenced by Moscow's. In the past, Syria has not been able to mount either war or peace policies seriously or effectively without Soviet support.

Soviet policy has viewed the Geneva conference, under the joint chairmanship of the United States and the Soviet Union, as the best vehicle for a settlement in accordance with Moscow's interests. Soviet superpower status would thereby be underscored, and the Soviet Union might be able to exert considerable influence on the outcome. This policy is very much in line with Syrian interests as well, for a multilateral framework would bring the Arab alliance (and solidarity) into Syria's bargaining hand, ensure that Egypt is not proceeding too far toward a separate accord, and — if Palestinian presence were effected — reduce Assad's vulnerability to the Palestinians and to his countrymen.

Whatever the forum of settlement, Syrian policy stresses the importance of the threat or use of force as the talks proceed. The clearest example of this policy was in the extended hostilities around Mt. Hermon preceding the conclusion of the disengagement agreement in the spring of 1974. "Fighting while talking" confers several benefits: it reduces the strength of domestic groups opposing settlement and favoring resumption of hostilities; it adds to the pressure on Israel; it maintains readiness; it forces Israel to absorb higher costs in continued occupation; and it demonstrates the unacceptability of the status quo.[154]

To what could the status quo give way? Syria's views of the shape of an acceptable settlement are ambiguous. Given the bitterness of the policy debate, it is unlikely that Syria will take the initiative. Rather, Syrian leaders will respond to Israeli initiatives, trying to refine proposals that hold out the possibility of success. Generally, Assad will accept a demilitarized Golan or even one occupied by international forces. He is prepared to end the state of belligerency with Israel, to recognize that nation, and perhaps even to establish diplomatic and commercial relations, although he would prefer to broach these separately. Israeli forces must withdraw totally from occupied Golan, possibly in stages but not over an unduly extended period. Although Syrians have pointed out that neither demilitarization nor continued occupation is of avail in preventing violence in an age of missiles, Assad has already given indications of his willingness to accept demilitarization of the Golan.[155] Syria will not take a firm position on Jerusalem. With respect to the Palestinian question, it defers to the PLO and other Palestinian sentiment. It is likely that Assad will continue to search for means to disarm his perceived potential opponents. Certainly he can be expected to require Soviet approval at each step, as well as some sort of Palestinian "blessing." Moreover, he will give substantial weight to the opinions of his brother, Rifaat, minister of defense Mustapha Tlas, and Foreign Minister Abdel Halim Khaddam.[156]

Rather than reject the concept of peaceful settlement on the one hand, or take the lead among the moderates on the Arab-Israeli (and occupied territories) issue, on the other, Assad probably will continue to attack those who move far ahead of him in coming to terms with Israel; deny any credit to Israel for the outcome of agreements Syria may reach; claim a Syrian victory (a victorious zero-sum game) for any such agreements; confront Israel militarily, politically, and economically in every possible way during the negotiations; and take few initiatives and make very few initial compromises, opting instead to deal on others' terms and his own often-stated basic objectives. This approach facilitates defense of ongoing bargaining, and has been used to defend past negotiations. In view of its relatively weak bargaining position vis-a-vis Israel, Syria would much prefer to deal from the strength of a united Arab front that includes: Egypt and Jordan, the two other Arab belligerents bordering on Israel; Saudi Arabia, as the financial backbone and the country with leverage on Israel's primary external supporter; and the Palestinians. Such a strategy has encountered important obstacles:

- Egypt, traditionally the most powerful Arab country but also the confrontation state most insulated from Levantine currents, could — and did —

reach separate agreements largely detracting from Syria's bargaining power;
- Saudi Arabia could not be counted on to deliver an embargo against the United States in many circumstances;
- The PLO would — and did — react like Syria to any negotiations to which it was not a party and that might remove an Arab belligerent; also, with substantial independence of action in Lebanon and as a transnational force throughout the Middle East it could obstruct settlement initiatives Syria considered viable — thus threatening Syrian independence of action; and
- The Syrians too have noted that the USSR becomes less interested in a settlement directly as the possibilities for one increase.

Assad's attempt at a solution to these problems was a united eastern front with elements weaker than (and therefore dependent on) Syria.[157] Such a front necessarily consisted of Jordan, the PLO, and Lebanon.

Jordan's troubled relations with the Palestinian movement[158] complicated the Syrian-Jordanian relationship. The Palestinian cause is important in Syria, where support for it is a matter of faith; and the bitter Palestinian feelings resulting from the September 1970 Jordanian civil war placed a strain on Syrian policies toward Jordan. In 1970, Syrian armor intervened in Jordan;[159] but the ambivalent and ill-coordinated (or uncoordinated) thrust was aborted largely because of the opposition of Assad, who within three months took over the leadership of Syria. Assad's orientation and policies regarding Jordan were almost diametrically opposed to Jadid's.

Ever conscious of the power of the Syrian Palestinian constituency, and therefore offering nominal support to the Palestinians, Assad sought to improve relations with Jordan immediately after he came to power. Although Syria closed its borders with Jordan during the July 1971 Jordanian mop-up of the civil war, and left them closed for about a year and a half, this action should not be allowed to overshadow the fact that the Syrian government made considerable efforts to improve both its own relations and those of the resistance with Jordan.[160] All evidence suggests that Assad was enormously relieved to be able to reopen the borders on December 1, 1972, with widespread Arab support for the action. The justification employed by Damascus for reopening the borders — even though Palestinian guerrillas at that time continued to view Hussein's government with almost more bitterness and fury than was directed at Israel — was unity against Israel.[161] After the lifting of the border measures, relations between these Arab neighbors were good. Although Jordan was a reluctant and minor participant in the October War, Jordanian soldiers saw action on the Golan front.

Jordan and Syria began to interact openly on a major scale in early 1975, as it became apparent that the Syrian-Palestinian unified command was inadequate to the task of creating a credible strategic threat to Israel. In mid-1975, Assad visited Jordan, and the Arab world soon heard rumors about agreements on Syrian-Jordanian military coordination. These plans, as well as rapid political and economic cooperation, matured over the next few months. As the Sinai II accord was signed, the Syrian-Jordanian alliance was sealed. Jordan's redeployments also reflected the new policy. Although the program of coordination presented a concrete approach to specific areas and types of political, economic, and military cooperation, the broad strategic meaning was clear — Syria and Jordan were thenceforth to constitute a single front. The new eastern front would stretch from Ras an-Naqoura on the Lebanese coast to the Gulf of Aqaba.[162]

Extension of a united front into Lebanon, however, would create a new peril: Israel might hold Syria responsible for Palestinian attacks launched from southern Lebanon. Indeed, from almost any perspective, the Palestinians and Lebanon constituted two major complexes of problems.

We have already reviewed the importance of the Palestinian issue in Syrian politics. Before 1967 the Syrian Ba'ath had established the (Ba'athist) Vanguards of the Popular War of Liberation Organization. The military element of the Vanguards was known as Sa'iqa. Originally formed from Palestinian elements in, and linked to, the Syrian army, Sa'iqa was later joined to the Ba'ath Party apparatus. From 1967 to 1970 Sa'iqa was perhaps the most active of the guerrilla organizations, and therefore rapidly attracted a large number of adherents. It played a major role in Syrian politics, but it also attracted support from other Palestinian organizations as an alternative to Fatah. Sa'iqa even attempted a coup in Jordan and was a major irritant in Lebanon, where it enjoyed a large following and played a key role in bringing about the Lebanese-Palestinian clashes in April and October 1969.[163]

Assad's coup led to a change in Syrian policy toward the resistance. Over a period of six months, Sa'iqa was purged of Jadid elements. Assad was attempting to repair relations with regimes alienated from his predecessor, and a major concern was Jordan. Soon after July 1971, Syria began to restrict the Palestinians. The number and severity of the restrictions varied, but generally the guerrillas' political activities in Syria were proscribed and operations against Israel had to be approved by the army command. Syria exercises strict supervision over the PLA.

In late 1972 and early 1973, Syria had begun to exert even greater control over the Palestinians in the country. Almost unprecedented restrictions came into play.[164] In this perspective, Assad needed a stage on which to dramatize his continued support for the Palestinian cause. Also, he was determined "to convince the peace-makers in Cairo that any agreement with Israel which does not take the Golan into account will be bound to fail."[165]

As the planning for the October War reached its final state, Syrian relations with the Palestinian movement neared a nadir. The Assad government seemed to take issue with the quasigovernmental status of the PLO and objected to the PLO claim to be the only legitimate representative of the Palestinian people. New restrictions were placed on the commandos, and Syria refused to allow the transfer of some PLA units to Iraq.[166] Clearly, these initiatives were part of the war preparations. Some were related to political ends and were designed to help shore up the eastern front against Israel. Others were related to Syrian military preparedness.

Since the October War, Syria has tried to reinforce Syrian in the Palestinian leadership. Although Sa'iqa has waged a long struggle to wrest the leadership of the Palestinian movement from Fatah, in recent years Sa'iqa's main role has been to represent Syrian views.

In July 1972 Syria first agreed to allow Yassir Arafat to control all of the guerrilla groups in southern Lebanon.[167] From then until 1976, Sa'iqa usually supported Fatah. (We shall consider the later Syrian-Palestinian problems after reviewing Syrian-Lebanese relations.) Syria's current foreign policy on the Palestinian issue must be understood: Syria will accept what "the Palestinians" agree to. Likewise, Damascus will oppose what the Palestinians oppose. (This policy masks substantial Syrian influence over — sometimes control of — the PLO.) A Syrian foreign ministry official said:

> Syria . . . cannot sign any agreement unless the Palestinians agree to it. If they do not agree . . . Syria could not acknowledge any "organization" or "group" . . . called "Israel." Syria . . . was a third party and could no more legitimize Israel than could a third party legitimize one individual's usurpation of another's house. Without Palestinian acquiescence the recognition of Israel by Syria or any other Arab state would be legally invalid and politically without value.[168]

Lebanese-Syrian relations are something of an anomaly. Although there is a strong kindred feeling between the peoples of the two countries, and traditions and customs carry over from one people to the other without any clear distinction based upon arbitrary political demarcations, the recent histories of Syria and Lebanon have been so divergent that a number of disputes have arisen. The relatively open political forum in Lebanon has been a particular source of problems at times, as have the vagaries of Palestinian-Lebanese relations. Syrian political refugees have joined the numerous middle-class emigres in Lebanon, and their feelings about the Damascus regimes often have not been muffled. Despite some isolated individual problems of this sort, Assad generally followed a policy of improving relations with Lebanon. The principal difficulty, as with his Jordanian rapprochement, was the Palestinians. In cases of Palestinian-Lebanese conflict, Assad — at least publicly — supported the Palestinians.

Lebanon has long been viewed as the most Western-oriented country in the Middle East, and therefore has perhaps been given disproportionate attention outside the region. Syrians have perceived their role as growing in importance and that of Lebanon as declining. Indeed, there was a widespread feeling in Syria after the October War that Lebanon might disintegrate over the succeeding years while Syria consolidated.[169] It is in the context of this perception that Syrian policy toward the Lebanon conflict must be considered.

After the June War, and particularly after "Black September," the Palestinian leadership increasingly concentrated its political and military activities in Lebanon. Commando operations brought Israeli shelling to southern Lebanon; the influx of mostly Muslim Palestinians threatened the Lebanese religious political system; internal and international migrations, some caused by the shellings in the south, altered the social structure of the country; Palestinians and private militias imported large quantities of firearms. By 1975 the authority of the central government was minimal, and that of traditional leaders of society was threatened. Lebanon remained at the edge of anarchy, and only a small incident was needed to push it over the brink. That incident was a protest by fishermen in Sidon in February 1975. From March to September 1975, an intermittent civil war fought between a complex coalition of forces arrayed along religious, political, socioeconomic, and other dimensions raged through Lebanon. Although the various participants received some outside support, the conflict was primarily internal, concerning domestic issues and problems.[170]

The renewal of fighting in Lebanon in September 1975 ushered in a new, international stage of the civil war. Syria had participated in helping to settle the initial phase, and Syrian good offices led to a compromise resolution, under the terms of which greater representation was to be accorded certain Muslim elements of the population, while overall leadership was returned to the hands of the traditional Lebanese leaders. Syrian support for traditional Lebanese leaders – the Christian and Sunni "establishment" – was designed to safeguard stability in the country while rearranging the political system to allow for the rise of a few younger leaders. Yet, Assad could not totally withdraw Syrian forces from Lebanon for two reasons. First, and officially, Syria was concerned about Israel's use of Lebanese territory to launch an attack upon Syria that would circumvent the stiff defenses of the Golan. Second, and privately, in the event the many 'Alawis who had moved from Latakia-Tartus to Damascus were forced to retreat to their own area as a result of developments within Syria, they would require a secure access. The best escape route is certainly through Lebanon's Bekaa Valley, and that is where Syria deployed its units, most of them commanded, and many of them largely staffed, by 'Alawis.

The 1975-76 Syrian political strategy to establish an eastern front combining Syria, Jordan, Lebanon (under Syrian influence), and the Palestinians ran aground. The Palestinian leadership was to be restructured to accommodate Syrian policy, and Syria was to emerge as a dominant factor in a Middle East settlement, able to deliver Syrian, Jordanian, Lebanese, and Palestinian blessing to a settlement that, presumably, would see Israeli withdrawal from, and the establishment of international forces and early-warning devices in, the Golan; the creation of a Palestinian entity in the West Bank and Gaza acceptable to the PLO and Jordan (and probably linked in some way to the latter); and recognition of and the signing of treaties with Israel. Instead, Syria was never able to completely dominate the Palestinian leadership; Israel intervened in Lebanon and created its own "new facts" in the south of that country; and Jordan left its alignment with Syria to establish better relations with Iraq. The only positive achievement of the Syrian policy constellation of 1975-76 was the rapprochement between Jordan and the PLO, which did open some new settlement possibilities, although those possibilities could be pursued outside Syria influence.[171]

Syria's own "eastern front" has also been troubled. Rather than being the object of Syrian intervention, Iraq has had substantial influence on, and attraction for, a large constituency within Syria. Northeastern Syria and northwestern Iraq are really a single area, and numerous Syrian exiles remain in Baghdad today. Despite some cooperation over the years, Iraqi economic assistance to Syria, and the pragmatism of Assad and Saddam Hussein, the two Ba'athist governments have been primary antagonists. A brief rapprochement in 1978-79 featured calls and announced "plans" for union, but analysts who understand Arab political dynamics recognized the reservoir of suspicion and distrust that still separated the two regimes.

The renewed conflict in September 1975 seriously threatened the territorial integrity of Lebanon. Syria was concerned for three reasons. First, the mountains in southern Lebanon form a natural defensive frontier. Properly armed, they could tie down substantial numbers of Israeli troops. If Israel were to annex southern Lebanon, however, the defense of Syria would be jeopardized, the defenses of Golan outflanked. A second and related concern was that Palestinian freedom of action in southern Lebanon might ignite another Arab-Israeli war, a war Syria did not want and was not prepared to fight, a war that would undoubtedly destroy whatever bargaining power Syria had left. Third, Damascus feared that Lebanese sectarianism might prove contagious, spreading to Syria where 'Alawi-Sunni relations were then relatively pacific and constructive. Thus, after several unsuccessful attempts at mediating the conflict, Assad resorted to the dispatch of Sa'iqa, PLA, and finally Syrian army units into Lebanon. Although these troops were purported to be "keeping the peace," in fact, they began almost immediately to coordinate with the Phalangists in offensive operations against Palestinians and Lebanese leftists.

Analysts of the Syrian involvement since 1975 and 1976 at times voiced perplexity over the vacillation of Syrian policy. However, Syrian policy was quite consistent from the outset of the Lebanon venture, and only tactics changed in accordance with circumstances. Initially, the Syrians believed they could restore the traditional Lebanese leadership to power, but weakened sufficiently to still depend upon Syrian support. When the Palestinians and leftists opposed the negotiated settlement arranged by Syria, Assad used his army to try to bring them to accept his terms. Later, Syrian armed forces attempted to bring the Christian rightists under control, but Syria's political strategy had centered on an agreement with the Phalange to enable the latter to dominate the Christian areas, while another force (early, Damascus pinned its hopes on the SSNP and Palestinians; later, on the Shi'a militia, 'Amal) dominated the Muslim areas of Lebanon. Both would be weak, both would need Syrian support or could be used by Syria to prevent anti-Syrian activities.

The Syrian policy lines we have described became a necessity as the domestic situation within Syria deteriorated. Withdrawal of Syrian forces was required both to reduce Syrian vulnerability in Lebanon and to allow the flexibility of armed forces employment inside Syria. After al-Bakr "retired" (see Chapter 4), relations quickly worsened again. Iraq was concerned about the relationship of the Syrian 'Alawi leadership to the Shi'a Iranian leaders.[172] (And with some reason.)

Relations between the two Ba'ath regimes had always been touchy, but had first reached their nadir in 1975 when a dispute erupted over the waters of the Euphrates River. The erection of a dam at Tabqa has been the principal economic development project in Syria, yet the dam's effect on the flow of Euphrates water has adversely affected Iraq. The merits of this and other disputes between Baghdad and Damascus are in fact of much less importance than the central element in Iraqi-Syrian relations, which is the competition for leadership in the Fertile Crescent. While Syria was the dominant party from 1973 until the end of the decade, the mantle of leadership has now passed to Iraq.

The last regional object of Syrian attention is the Arabian Peninsula. Assad sought to improve Syria's relationship with peninsular regimes for four reasons. First, a principal objective of his government was the reversal of the isolation in which Syria found itself at the time of his accession to power. Second, given the inability of their economies to productively absorb the vast funds accruing to them as a result of the petroleum trade, these countries represented important potential (and now actual) contributors to the Syrian economy, which has badly needed capital investment and hard currencies, and to the Syrian military.[173] Third, after the war, Assad recognized that King Faisal was not only a Syrian financial benefactor but was also in a unique position to help bring American pressure to bear on Israel, and thus to assist Syria in the realization of its political goals. Finally, both the Assad brothers were concerned about the potential role Saudi Arabia could take in assisting Sunni opposition to the 'Alawis.

Syria's most important nonregional ties are with the Soviet Union. Beginning in the late 1940s, Syrian governments moved increasingly toward the Soviet Union. The Jadid government pursued a policy of particularly close cooperation with Moscow; indeed, Assad criticized his predecessor for some of his regime's actions in this connection. However, once in power, Assad abandoned his role as critic and generally continued Syria's good relations with the Soviets. When the Soviets were forced to leave Egypt, they increased their presence in Syria.

The Syrian rejection of Security Council Resolution 242 was a major point of disagreement between Moscow and Damascus; but eventually, Assad indicated more flexibility on the question of a peaceful settlement, eliminating the most serious point of contention between the two countries.[174] The rift between Egypt and the Soviet Union in the summer of 1972 (including Egypt's expulsion of its Soviet military advisors) discomfitted Syria. Faced with the prospect of his two most important allies (in the effort to recover the Golan) taking separate routes, Assad played an active role in trying to reconcile them.[175] At the same time, Syria was endeavoring to get additional military assistance from the Soviet Union and yet to maintain a safe distance from Iraq, toward which it was being pushed by Moscow. Syria's loyalty was rewarded: the Soviet Union and Syria reached an agreement under the terms of which Syria would receive an advanced, integrated air defense system similar to Egypt's; the Soviet Union would have the right to use several airfields for strategic purposes related to the U.S. Sixth Fleet, and would also receive extensive privileges in Latakia and Tartus.[176]

From late 1972 until 1976, President Assad maintained his cooperation with the Soviet Union rather easily.[177] The post-October War environment brought a new policy toward the United States; but unlike his counterpart in Egypt, Assad took care to maintain close Syrian-Soviet cooperation. Indeed, in his own interest, Assad has seen fit to give Moscow as high a profile as possible in disengagement and peace talks. Although Syrians have occasionally objected to what they have seen as undue Soviet restraint in providing arms and applying pressure on the Middle East issue,[178] Assad recognizes that Syrian military forces depend on Soviet materiel and training, and that there is no near-term prospect of replacing that Soviet function. Moreover, Soviet support can provide the greater bargaining latitude vis-a-vis domestic critics (as well as Israel) that is essential to a settlement. Thus, however Assad may try to improve Syria's relations with the West, he will not replace Soviet ties — at least not until the Israel problem is resolved.

Syria, needing Soviet support, will likely continue to press for the preferred Soviet approach to a Middle East peace: the Geneva Conference. Besides the advantages already identified, Syria can thus be assured of Soviet support. In return, Syria will continue to be a Soviet mouthpiece, insisting on the importance of Soviet participation, and will provide Moscow high visibility at the conference and in any separate agreements.[179] Similarly, it can be anticipated that when the Soviets take a more cautious policy toward peace — by opposing the personal diplomacy of U.S. leaders, by rejecting the Camp David approach, by demanding an overall approach to settlement, or because they fear American inroads — Syria will not publicly go beyond the most conservative Soviet position. (Indeed, sometimes Assad will intentionally remain far to the rear of Soviet policy on settlement — at least publicly — in order to secure political, economic, or military concessions.)

Circumstances — namely, the failure of Syrian forces in Lebanon to achieve a clear-cut victory over either the Palestinians or the Christians; the Sadat initiative and Camp David accords; the emergence of Iraq as a regional heavyweight and the shift of Jordanian alignment; the even greater military superiority of Israel and the deterioration of conditions within Syria — have pushed Assad toward Moscow as the only available and useful Syrian ally. More than ever before, the core of the Soviet-Syrian relationship remains military. Even the Soviet-Syrian friendship treaty is based on Syrian perceptions of military requirements and its residual belief that the IDF (possibly in conjunction with Egypt or Egyptian political initiatives[180]) may attack Syria. Assad seeks some sort of Soviet guarantee, but Moscow is unwilling to proceed that far out on the Syrian limb, especially when its own internal weakness is ever more in evidence.

As we have indicated elsewhere,[181] close Syrian-Soviet relations have not been without controversy in Syria. For example, the 1976 conflict between Damascus and Moscow exacerbated existing disenchantment with Soviet weapons systems and resentment against the Lebanese Communist Party for its criticism of the Assad regime.[182] More recently, Sunni opposition to 'Alawi governance has manifested itself in violence against (indeed, assassinations of) Soviet military advisors. A dilemma for Soviet leaders is that the closer relations between the minority government and the USSR become, the more unpopular the Soviets become. The Syrian government must, however, preserve good relations with the Soviet Union for some time in the future, especially in a period of regional isolation.

Syrian policies toward the United States are more ambiguous. While President Assad is known to have sought better relations with the West than Syria has had in recent years — or in 20 to 25 years — he also recognized the costs. (In this context, the cost of a clear-cut and ambitious all-out rapprochement with the United States before a Middle East settlement is reached would have been severe: loss of Soviet backing at a crucial time in Arab-Israeli relations, a time when Syrian leaders believed Syria must, and could, deal from a position of strength. Recognizing that they could not have expected untrammeled support from Washington in return, there was no persuasive reason to go too far toward rapprochement. No one could have filled the Soviet role in military supply; and Washington would not have, even if its production capacity allowed of such an option.) In the absence of an acceptable settlement, these costs were too high. Although Assad definitively concluded in late 1975 that the American approach would abort rather than support the chances for settlement, he remained aware of the criticality of the U.S. role. Yet, Sinai II, the "Sadat initiative," the Camp David accords, and the Egyptian-Israeli peace treaty appear to him and other Syrians a systematic and integrated U.S. policy direction designed to guarantee Israeli security, thwart any meaningful resolution to the Palestinian issue, and consolidate and legitimize Israeli control of the Golan Heights.[183] In other words, Assad and many other Syrians perceive American policy to be the construction of a viable *non*resolution to the problems of the Palestinians and of the occupied territories, a nonresolution to be paid for by the Syrians (and Palestinians). Most of the trust Secretary of State Kissinger labored long and hard to win has now been dissipated by Kissinger (Sinai II) and his successors. Consequently, Syrian behavior toward the United States has been correct and cold, even when (as during the Lebanese intervention) it was cooperative.

Military Policies

Until Assad took over, the objective of Ba'ath policy in the military was the creation of an "indoctrinated army." That goal was never achieved, except at the higher ranks, which were subject to political purges and control.[184] Assad has been less concerned with party loyalty than with regime loyalty. With fewer and less consequential challenges than Jadid had to meet until recently, and with much greater popular support, he also worked toward the improvement of the army's military capabilities.

The foregoing notwithstanding, the Syrian army remains the guarantor of the Assad regime. We have indicated the pervasive presence of 'Alawis throughout the armed forces. They occupy key positions in every major element of the army, and constitute the true command and control network, bypassing (when necessary) the official unit commanders. Although the army has been infrequently used for domestic purposes, it retains a primary capability for regime security.[185]

From June 1967 until October 1973, Syria placed primary emphasis on upgrading its defense, particularly its air defense. The extent to which this stress devolved from Soviet doctrine or to which it grew from Syrian military calculus is not clear. The results of the Syrian development of defensive capability were evident in October 1973, when the Syrian army held the Israeli ground forces in a stubborn defensive battle less than 20 miles from Damascus, and Syrian surface-to-air missles (SAMs) exacted a high toll of Israeli aircraft.

Since the October War, highest priority has been placed upon increasing the mobility of the ground forces — mechanization of infantry (large numbers of armored personnel carriers), and upgrading and modernizing existing equipment. Other areas of concentration have dealt more with manpower.

Like all of the combatants in the Middle East, Syria has suffered from the dearth of trained manpower.[186] The impact of this shortage has been particularly acute in the air force, where modern aircraft and air combat demand increasing sophistication on the part of command, combat, and maintenance personnel. Indeed, although Arab air forces possess a combined numerical superiority over Israel, the IAF has consistently dominated the skies in air-to-air combat. The manpower problem — a "qualitative" problem at base — has also been keen in the other services. In the army, armor and artillery have consistently suffered from the educational level of officers and enlisted personnel, and support (both combat support and combat service support) branches suffer the same problem. The extent to which the Soviet Union in its large training effort in Syria has been able to overcome these hurdles to military effectiveness is unknown, but performance of Syrian forces in Lebanon has been less than exemplary.

Soviet policy before the October War was to provide equipment that was, at best, one generation behind Israel's. Since 1973, however, Syria has received MiG-23s, MiG-27s, T-72s, SA-8s and SA-9s (SAMs), and other advanced weapons.

These systems may not be the equal of Israel's most sophisticated materiel, but they are among the best the Soviet Union has developed even for its own forces.[187] There are approximately 2,500 Soviet advisors in Syria attached at all levels of the military.[188] In addition, North Korean and Cuban advisors have actively assisted the Syrian armed forces.[189]

The most important military decision Syria has taken in many years was the determination to go to war in October 1973. Although the reason for this decision was political — the apparent impossibility of securing any movement toward the return of the Golan Heights — it is unclear precisely how much Assad really believed Syrian forces could accomplish. Syrian forces carried out an aggressive attack on the Golan at the outset of the war, but command, control, and other aspects of coordination (except withdrawal) seem not to have improved sufficiently. The SAM air defense system, and the Syrian defense line east of Sassa, consisting of concrete emplacements linked by trenches (and mine- and wire-screened), held relatively well, although Israeli aircraft had control of the skies in several sectors by the war's end.[190]

Notwithstanding increases in size and improvement in capabilities of the Syrian armed forces since October 1973, they probably have at best a marginal offensive capability against Israel.[191] Certainly, they cannot undertake a sustained offensive role. Because of the effectiveness of their defenses, however, and the consequent toll they could exact on limited Israeli resources, Syrian forces are a crucial component of the Arab military threat. To what extent will Syria be willing to resort to force again for the return of the Golan? Without question, if Egypt decided to return to the Arab alliance and turn to the ultimate recourse — war — Syria would join in the effort. It is unlikely that Syria would take on Israel alone or, in effect, without Egypt, although it is perhaps conceivable that hostilities may be used to cover an 'Alawi secession from the rest of Syria. Assad will not go to war with Israel over the Palestinian issue; recovery of the Golan is a higher priority. However, in the event no further movement is made on the Golan and Egypt is open to further military cooperation, war with Israel certainly cannot be excluded.

A substantial military deployment to the east (against Iraq) and in Lebanon has also weakened the Syrian capabilities significantly. There is little chance Syria will initiate active hostilities against Iraq, since too many of Assad's forces are and must remain tied down in the west (Israel and Lebanon), Jordan's role could prove an important imponderable, and, principally, Iraq's military strength may be more than a match for Syria. It is our view that neither of these countries has the military power at this time to effectively project itself far into the other's territory. Both have a two-front problem; both are more capable in static defense than on the offense.

In Lebanon, Syrian policy has been to draw back from urban areas and, indeed, from the bulk of Lebanese territory in favor of controlling the Bekaa Valley. Control of the Bekaa is a means to secure access to 'Alawi areas of Syria on the part of those 'Alawis who may flee Damascus in the event of a Sunni takeover. Syrian armed forces policymakers remain concerned about Israel's capacity to outflank Golan defenses by a move through Lebanon, but the deployment of tens of thousands of Syrian troops to Lebanon significantly weakens the Golan defenses anyway.

NOTES

1. As one book puts it:

> The consciousness of a Syrian nationality is not well developed. Both among Arabs and minority groups, the primary loyalty of the individual is to the local ethnic or religious community. In effect, cooperation tends to be restricted to traditional family, ethnic, and religious groups. . . . Those not belonging to [one's] family or religious or ethnic community (depending on the context) are outsiders, not to be trusted and, therefore, not to be cooperated with.

Richard F. Nyrop, ed., *Syria: A Country Study* (Washington, D.C.: Foreign Area Studies Division, American University, 1979), p. 54.

2. For instance, Michael H. Van Dusen, "Political Integration and Regionalism in Syria," *Middle East Journal*, 26, no. 2 (Spring 1972), pp. 123-36.

3. One of the concrete results of this policy was the overrepresentation of minorities in the Syrian military. This development is discussed later in the text.

4. Moshe Ma'oz, "Attempts at Creating a Political Community in Modern Syria," *Middle East Journal*, 26, no. 4 (Autumn 1972), p. 398.

5. We do not mean to suggest that sectarianism is a new phenomenon. Rather, the renascent salience of sectarianism has detracted from earlier progress toward a national consciousness. Nikolaos Van Dam's excellent monograph, *The Struggle for Power in Syria: Sectarianism, Regionalism and Tribalism in Politics, 1961-1978* (New York: St. Martin's Press, 1979), provides many insights into the problem. However, it can be argued that sectarianism helps to identify and define a nation, too, and in fact it is conceivable (though unlikely) that sectarian dissent and unrest will unify Syria around the dominant symbols of Syrian nationality — Arabism and Sunni Islam. (Cf. Nyrop, ed., *Syria*, pp. 54-55.)

6. Van Dusen, "Political Integration," pp. 123-28; Richard F. Nyrop et al., *Area Handbook for Syria* (Washington, D.C.: Foreign Area Studies Division, American University, 1971), p. 163.

7. See especially Van Dusen, "Political Integration," pp. 126-27.

8. Gordon H. Torrey, *Syrian Politics and the Military 1945-1958* (Columbus: Ohio State University Press, 1964); Patrick Seale, *The Struggle for Syria* (New York: Oxford University Press, 1965); Itamar Rabinovich, *Syria Under the Ba'th 1963-1966: The Army-Party Symbiosis* (Jerusalem: Israel Universities Press; New York: Halsted Press, 1972).

9. Nyrop et al., *Area Handbook*, p. 163.

10. P. J. Vatikiotis, "The Politics of the Fertile Crescent," in Paul Y. Hammond and Sidney S. Alexander, eds., *Political Dynamics in the Middle East* (New York: American Elsevier, 1971), p. 237.

11. Ma'oz, "Attempts," pp. 399-402; Van Dusen, "Political Integration," pp. 132-33.

12. It should not, however, be inferred that the Qutriyin were alike. They represented a heterogeneous group of Ba'athists united mainly by opposition to the established Ba'athists.

13. Nikolaos Van Dam, "The Struggle for Power in Syria and the Ba'th Party (1958-1966)," *Orient*, XIV, no. 1 (March 1972), pp. 10-11; Rabinovich, *Syria*, pp. 24-39.

14. These are described in detail in Van Dam, "The Struggle for Power," passim.

15. However, only 75 to 80 percent of these could be viewed as supporters of Jadid; the remainder followed Mohammed Umran.

16. See Van Dam, "The Struggle," pp. 16-17; Van Dusen, "Political Integration," p. 145; Rabinovich, *Syria*; Eliezer Beeri, *Army Officers in Arab Politics and Society* (New York: Praeger, 1969), pp. 336-38; William Hazen and Peter Gubser, *Selected Minority Groups of the Middle East: The Alawis, Berbers, Druze and Kurds* (Kensington, Md.: American Institutes for Research, 1973), pp. 81-82, 97-98; Martin Seymour, "The Dynamics of Power in Syria Since the Break with Egypt," *Middle Eastern Studies*, VI, no. 1 (January 1970), p. 40; George Haddad, *Revolutions and Military Rule in the Middle East: The Arab States*, vol. 2 (New York: Robert Speller, 1971), p. 45; Gad Soffer, "The Role of the Officer Class in Syrian Politics and Society" (Ph.D. diss., American University, 1968), p. 26; and the excellent article by Hanna Batatu, "Some Observations on the Social Roots of Syria's Ruling Military Group and the Causes for Its Dominance," *Middle East Journal*, XXXV, 3 (Summer 1981), pp. 340-43.

17. The Syrian experience proved the validity of what Ba'athists should have learned from the Aref coup of November 1963 in Iraq — the impossibility of maintaining civilian party control over the military. As Michel Aflaq said, "We wish to alter the army's role by precluding the formation of a bloc of military officers within the party's leadership. When the party chooses as a leader someone from the military, he should not retain his military position. Rather, he should devote himself to civilian leadership." *Al-Hayat*, February 25, 1966, pp. 7-8. Also see A. I. Dawisha, "The Transnational Party in Regional Politics: The Arab Ba'th Party," *Asian Affairs*, LXI, no. 1 (February 1974), pp. 23-31.

18. Michael H. Van Dusen, "Syria: Downfall of a Traditional Elite," in Frank Tachau, ed., *Political Elites and Political Development in the Middle East* (Cambridge, Mass.: Schenkman, 1975), pp. 115-55; Gordon H. Torrey, "Aspects of the Political Elite in Syria," in George Lenczowski, ed., *Political Elites in the Middle East* (Washington, D.C.: American Enterprise Institute, 1975), pp. 151-61.

19. Although the change in Ba'ath outlook began to be confirmed as early as 1963, old line Ba'athists attacked it most vehemently immediately after the neo-Ba'ath coup of 1966, when Aflaq, for example, accused the new Syrian Ba'ath of deviationism, of subverting true Ba'athism. He accused the Syrian leadership of slavishness, comparing them to Arab Communists. *Al Hayat*, February 25, 1966, pp. 7-8.

20. See Van Dam, *The Struggle*, for a detailed discussion of the sectarian aspects of the attempted coup.

21. We shall not chronicle the progressive stages of Assad's control. It should only be noted here that his move in November 1970 was the last step of a multiple-stage change of power.

22. Rabinovich, *Syria*, pp. 215-17; Tabitha Petran, *Syria* (New York: Praeger, 1972), p. 240; Avigdor Levy, "The Syrian Communists and the Ba'th Power Struggle, 1966-1970," in Michael Confino and Shimon Shamir, eds., *The U.S.S.R. and the Middle East* (Jerusalem: Israel Universities Press, 1973), pp. 407-8; Aryeh Yodfat, "The End of Syria's Isolation?" *World Today*, XXVII, no. 8 (August 1971), pp. 332-34.

23. See *Al-Nahar, As-Sayyad, Al-Anwar* from March 1969 through November 30, 1970. Also see "The Civilians Win," *An Nahar Arab Report*, I, no. 37 (November 16, 1970), pp. 1-2; "The Loser Wins," ibid., no. 38 (November 23, 1970), pp. 1-2; Yodfat, "The End," p. 335.

24. Syrian constitution, Art. III.

25. Ibid., Art. 112.

26. Ibid., Art. 8.

27. Ibid., Arts. 71, 84.

28. See Raymond A. Hinnebusch, "Local Politics in Syria: Organization and Mobilization in Four Village Cases," *Middle East Journal*, XXX, no. 1 (Winter 1976), pp. 1-24.

29. Ibid., p. 6. *Al Hayat*, December 7, 1971, p. 10.

30. Van Dam, *The Struggle*. Also, see below.

31. "It is true that 99 percent may draw snickers in certain circles, but it must be remembered that the Syrians were very enthusiastic in their support of the new regime" ("Assad Opens New Paths"). "The masses said yes . . . to Hafez Assad because he disagreed with the Ba'ath. . . . He also said that 'the party will no longer be that of a special group because the cornerstone is individual freedom' " (*Al-Hayat* [Beirut], March 15, 1971, p. 3).

32. See Paul Balta's articles in *Le Monde*, March 23-26, 1971 ("La Syrie baasiste, An VIII": I. "Détente, ouverture, réalisme," March 23, pp. 1, 15; II: "L'armée, source du pouvoir," March 24, p. 5; III: "Un vast chantier," March 25, p. 6; IV: "L'épine dorsale," March 26, p. 5).

33. See Art. 8 of the Syrian constitution; David Holmstrom, "Syria — Unity, Liberty, and Socialism," *Middle East International*, no. 22 (April 1973), p. 11; Balta, "La Syrie baasiste," *Le Monde*, March 23, 1971, pp. 1, 15; Petran, *Syria*, p. 251; Mahmoud al-Ayyubi, "Syrian Government Policy Statement," *Foreign Broadcast Information Service* (*FBIS*), February 28, 1973, Supp. 6, pp. 1-2; Dawisha, "The Transnational Party," p. 27; Malcolm H. Kerr, "Hafiz Asad and the Changing Patterns of Syrian Politics," *International Journal*, XXVIII, no. 4 (Autumn 1973), pp. 702-3.

34. "The New Cabinet," *An Nahar Arab Report*; Rabinovich, *Syria*, p. 217. In Homs and Hama, traditional Ba'ath opposition and the Muslim Brotherhood attempted to persuade the Syrians to boycott the spring 1973 legislative elections.

35. Alain Cass, "Cool Head in Damascus," *Middle East International*, no. 60 (June 1976), p. 7.

36. Only Ba'ath recruitment may take place in the army or among students, however.

37. The Ba'ath Party exerts itself to ensure that information flows "down" to the people and up to the hierarchy. Such a communications system is subject to the problems in human behavior, however. Thus, assistance from the other parties and "popular organizations" is very useful.

38. See R. D. McLaurin, ed., *The Political Role of Minority Groups in the Middle East* (New York: Praeger, 1979).

39. Cf. Lewis W. Snider, "Minorities and Political Power in the Middle East," in ibid., Chap. 10.

40. Marvine Howe, "Assad's Star Fades in City Where He Was a Hero," *New York Times*, April 3, 1980, p. 3; Ihsan A. Hijazi, "For Syria, Religious Killings Mean Political Trouble," ibid., July 10, 1977, Section 4, p. 3; Bruce Van Voorst, "Syria Strife Grows from Sects Rivalry," *Washington Star*, September 10, 1979, p. 9.

41. See Martin Kramer, *Political Islam* (Washington, D.C.: Georgetown University Center for Strategic and International Studies, 1980); R. Hrair Dekmejian, "The Anatomy of Islamic Revival: Legitimacy Crisis, Ethnic Conflict and the Search for Islamic Alternatives," *Middle East Journal*, XXXIV, no. 1 (Winter 1980), pp. 1-12; and Daniel Pipes, "This World is Political!! The Islamic Revival of the Seventies," *Orbis*, XXIV, no. 1 (Spring 1980), pp. 9-41. In relation to Syria, see Itamar Rabinovich, "Damascus: The Islamic Wave," *Washington Quarterly: A Review of Strategic and International Studies*, II, no. 4 (Autumn 1979), pp. 139-43.

42. "Syria's Tough Decisions," *Middle East*, no. 60 (October 1979), p. 20; Van Voorst, "Moslem"; Edward Cody, "Terrorists Pursue Campaign Against Syrian Leadership," *Washington Post*, October 26, 1979, p. 23; Helena Cobban, "Sectarian Strife Faces Syria's Assad at Home," *Christian Science Monitor*, July 6, 1979, p. 6; James M. Markham, "Economic Woes and Assassinations Buffet Assad Leadership in Syria," *New York Times*, August 31, 1977, p. 1. Among the prominent victims have been Sheikh Youssef Sarem and Nader Hosri, leading 'Alawi clerics; Sheikh Mohammed Chami, one of Syria's most prominent Sunni clergymen; Mohammed al-Fadhel, former president of Damascus University and an advisor to Assad; Brigadier Abdel Hamid Razzuk, chief of Syria's missile forces; and Mohammed Naama, head of the dentistry syndicate and a cousin of Assad. In addition, numerous middle-level bureaucrats and military personnel have been killed. See, e.g., John Kifner, "Syrian Clinic Is Killed, Apparently by Foes of Regime," ibid., February 4, 1980, p. A3; John Kifner, "Strains in Damascus Weaken Assad Rule," ibid., October 14, 1979, p. 17; Markham, "Economic"; Hijazi, "For Syria"; Van Voorst, "Moslem"; Helena Cobban, "More Sectarian Killings Threaten Stability Assad Has Brought Syria," *Christian Science Monitor*, September 7, 1979, p. 7; Thomas W. Lippman, "Slayings in Minority Sect Shake Syria," *Washington Post*, April 7, 1978, p. 20. Also, *FBIS* reports of Iraqi, Egyptian, and Lebanese broadcasts disclose many of the assassinations.

43. For a report of the Aleppo artillery school attack, see the statement of the Syrian minister of the interior, 'Adnan Dabbagh, broadcast on June 22,

1979 (*FBIS*, June 25, 1979, pp. H3-H5). Events in Hama, Aleppo, Latakia, Homs, Tartus, and even Damascus are discussed in William Branigin, "Aleppo: Old Stronghold, New Resistance," *Washington Post*, February 19, 1980, p. A13; Marvine Howe, "Moslem Extremists in Syria Trying to Destabilize Government with Terrorist Attacks," *New York Times*, August 20, 1979, p. 12; Marvine Howe, "Syria Concedes Wide Unrest over Policies," ibid., March 28, 1980, p. 1; "Blasts Mark Start of a General Strike in Syrian City," ibid., April 1, 1980, p. 6, and "Syrian Leader Eases Unrest and Strikes," ibid., April 13, 1980, p. 8; Helena Cobban, "Syria Debates Strength, Impact of Its Muslim Fanatics," *Christian Science Monitor*, September 10, 1979, p. 8; "Syria Seethes with Unrest, Discontent," ibid., December 10, 1979, p. 4; and "Syrian Unrest Highlighted by Aleppo Strife," ibid., February 1, 1980, p. 3; William Stewart, "Assad Seeks to Rally Syrians in Face of Religious Challenge," *Washington Star*, March 14, 1980, p. 9; and "Wave of Unrest Presents Serious Threat to Syria's Assad," ibid., April 9, 1980, p. A-6; Howe, "Assad's Star"; Kifner, "Strains"; *FBIS*, July 16, 1979, p. H1, September 4 (pp. H1-H2), 7 (p. H1), 9 (p. H1), 10 (p. H3), 11 (pp. H4-H5), and 15 (p. H1), 1979, December 14 (p. H2), 18 (p. H1), 21 (p. H1), 1979, and January 15, 1980, p. H4; *An Nahar Arab Report and Memo*, III, no. 27 (July 2, 1979), pp. 2-3; ibid., 38 (September 17, 1979), pp. 6-7; ibid., 41 (October 8, 1979), pp. 4-5; and "Syria's Tough Decisions." After this chapter was written, a major outbreak of civil resistance occurred in Hama. In some respects, the Hama uprising can be considered the definitive "beginning of the end."

44. See Stanley Reed III, "Dateline Syria: Fin de Regime?" *Foreign Policy*, no. 39 (Summer 1980), p. 176 and sources in note 43 above.

45. Nyrop et al., *Area Handbook*, p. 140. Cf. Petran, *Syria*, p. 236. (Quotation is from Nyrop et al.)

46. "Waiting for War," *An Nahar Arab Report*, V, no. 41 (October 14, 1974), pp. 2-3.

47. See Graham Allison, *Essence of Decision: Explaining the Cuban Missile Crisis* (Boston: Little, Brown, 1971), passim.

48. Joseph Dunner, ed., *Dictionary of Political Science* (New York: Philosophical Library, 1964), p. 261.

49. It is incorrect to assume that the Arab-Israeli conflict is an exception. If this were the case, the Syrian government, the position of which has been relatively consistent on this subject, would have enjoyed much greater stability.

50. Riad N. el-Rayyes and Dunia Nahas, eds., *The October War: Documents, Personalities, Analyses and Maps* (Beirut: An-Nahar Press Services S.A.R.L., 1974), pp. 178-80; "Waiting for War"; "Syria: Two Years Under President Assad (1)," *An Nahar Arab Report*, III, no. 39 (September 25, 1972): "Backgrounder"; "Jordan: Unwelcome Hand," ibid., no. 26 (June 26, 1972), p. 3; "Syrian Front: Tense but Calm," ibid., no. 51 (December 18, 1972), pp. 2-3.

51. See Raymond A. Hinnebusch, "Local Politics in Syria: Organization and Mobilization in Four Village Cases," *Middle East Journal*, XXX, no. 1 (Winter 1976), pp. 1-24. Ba'ath effectiveness at the local level has substantially deteriorated since this article was written, however.

52. Until recently at least, lower and middle-level Ba'ath members were motivated by ideological zeal. The senior party members, however, are "subsidized" by Rifaat or others close to Hafez Assad.

53. "Rifaat Ali Suleiman Assad," *An Nahar Arab Report*, VI, no. 32 (August 11, 1975); "Profile."

54. In his unofficial but real position as Syria's second-in-command, Rifaat has not hesitated to confront leftists, rightists, Palestinians, Sunnis, or other 'Alawis — in Syria and Lebanon — to retain the Assads' grip on power. His lifestyle of ostentatious wealth is widely seen in Syria as the epitome of corruption. (However, much of Rifaat's "income" is in fact diverted to regime-support purposes. See note 52 above.)

55. Paul A. Jureidini and R. D. McLaurin, *Beyond Camp David: Emerging Alignments and Leaders in the Middle East* (Syracuse: Syracuse University Press, 1981), p.

56. "Syria: The Ball Starts Rolling," *An Nahar Arab Report*, V, no. 9 (March 4, 1974), p. 1.

57. Michael H. Van Dusen, "Syria: Downfall of a Traditional Elite," in Frank Tachau, ed., *Political Elites and Political Development in the Middle East* (Cambridge, Mass.: Schenkman, 1975), Chap. 3, is the best portrait of the social revolution that has taken place in Syria over the last decade so far as it affects elite values.

58. E.g., *FBIS*, July 2, 1979, p. H1; ibid., September 6, 1979, p. H1; Helena Cobban, "Assad Tries to Placate Syria's Hard-Hitting Dissidents," *Christian Science Monitor*, March 26, 1980, p. 10. Cf. Van Dam, *The Struggle*, for earlier accusations along similar lines. The regime names Egypt, Israel, and the United States, particularly the latter two, as the fomenters of the sectarian strife. Although our information confirms the internal sources of the unrest, there is no question Israel, for one, has at times sought to exacerbate intercommunal tensions. See Nikolaos Van Dam, "Israeli Sectarian Propaganda Against Syria During the October 1973 War," in R. D. McLaurin ed., *Military Propaganda* (New York: Praeger, 1982).

59. Balta, "La Syrie baasiste," *Le Monde*, March 23, 1971, pp. 1, 15.

60. Ibid., "Potential Trouble"; "The National Front," *An Nahar Arab Report*, III, no. 18 (May 1, 1972), pp. 2-3; "Military Moves," ibid., IV, no. 20 (May 14, 1973), p. 1; "Syria-U.S.S.R.: Crisis is Brewing," ibid., no. 30 (July 23, 1973), p. 2; "Domestic Fears," ibid., no. 39 (September 24, 1973), p. 2.

61. See Petran, *Syria*, p. 151; Rabi' Matar, "Socialist Union of Ba'ath and Nasserites under the Leadership of Assad," *Al-Hawadith*, March 19, 1971, pp. 16-18.

62. Balta, "La Syrie baasiste," *Le Monde*, March 23, 1971, pp. 1, 15; R. D. McLaurin and Mohammed Mughisuddin, *The Soviet Union and the Middle East* (Washington, D.C.: American Institute for Research, 1974), pp. 248-49; Aryeh Yodfat, "The U.S.S.R., Jordan and Syria," *Mizan*, XI, no. 2 (April 1969), p. 87; "The Ba'th: Allergic to Advice," *An Nahar Arab Report*, I, no. 27 (September 7, 1970), p. 4, "The National Front," ibid., III, no. 18 (May 1, 1972), pp. 2-3; "Cautious Approach," ibid., no. 32 (August 7, 1972), p. 2; "Domestic Fears," "SCP: Titoist Trends," ibid., V, no. 5 (February 4, 1974), pp. 3-4;

Levy, "The Syrian Communists," pp. 404-6; *FBIS*, December 15, 1974, p. 143; Joe Alex Morris, Jr., "Syria's Ties with Russ Show Signs of Cooling Off," *Los Angeles Times*, March 16, 1976, pt. I, pp. 1, 10.

63. Petran, *Syria*, pp. 150, 155, 203, 230, 243, 250.

64. Syrian Interior Minister Ali Zaza responded to a question on whether antiregime groups were still active in Syria as follows: "Which groups? Do you mean groups such as the Muslim Brotherhood or others? None of them has any grassroots now, for the [Assad] regime reached the popularity spirit." Interview, *Al-Bayraq*, March 30, 1974, p. 7. This vision is far removed from Syrian political realities, however, and was even in 1974.

65. See sources in notes 42 and 43 above.

66. An unusual feature of these transnational pressures is their visibility. The Beirut press provides a guide to the current views and inclinations of each major Arab state with a political following inside Syria.

67. Vatikiotis, "The Politics of the Fertile Crescent," pp. 227-37.

68. Petran, *Syria*, p. 234.

69. Amnon Sella, "Soviet Military Doctrine in the October War," unpublished ms., 1974; Sella, "Soviet Training and Arab Performance," *Jerusalem Post Magazine*, February 8, 1974, pp. 6-7.

70. R. D. McLaurin and Mohammed Mughisuddin, *Cooperation and Conflict: Egyptian, Iraqi, and Syrian Objectives and U.S. Policy* (Washington, D.C.: Americn Institutes for Research, 1975), pp. 195-96; Roger F. Pajak, "Soviet Military Aid to Iraq and Syria," *Strategic Review*, IV, no. 1 (1976), p. 57; D. K. Palit, *Return to Sinai: The Arab Offensive, October 1973* (New Delhi: Palit and Palit, 1974), passim; Charles Wakebridge, "The Syrian Side of the Hill," *Military Review*, LVI, no. 2 (February 1976), p. 27; *U.S. News and World Report*, March 17, 1975, p. 14.

71. Moshe Ma'oz, "Syria Under Hafiz al-Asad: New Domestic and Foreign Policies," *Jerusalem Papers on Peace Problems*, no. 15 (1975), p. 7.

72. Riad N. el-Rayyes and Dunia Nahas, eds., *Guerrillas for Palestine: A Study of the Palestinian Commando Organizations* (Beirut: An Nahar Press Services S.A.R.L., 1974), p. 143; *Arab World*, XXI, no. 5166 (March 28, 1974), pp. 11-12; "Syria: Ball Starts Rolling."

73. There are so many intelligence and special purpose army units that translation and nomenclature are problematical. Commander of the Special Forces is 'Ali Haydar, but the "defense units" are Assad's praetorian guard. Another unit of these forces is commanded by Jam'l Assad; also Hafez' brother. The "Struggle Companies" appear to have regime protection functions as well, but are less prominent than Rifaat's troops. They are commended by Adnan Assad, a cousin of the president. See Batatu, "Some Observations," pp. 331-32.

74. McLaurin, ed., *The Political Role*, p. 282.

75. For a more detailed description of 'Alawi beliefs and societal role, see Peter A. Gubser, "Minorities in Power: The Alawites of Syria," in McLaurin, ed., *The Political Role*, Chap. 2.

76. See Eric Pace, "Northern Syria Finds New Prosperity, Thanks to Help from Its Neighbors," *New York Times*, November 17, 1975, p. 10; Howe, "Assad's Star."

77. Ma'oz, "Syria Under Hafiz al-Asad," pp. 6-7; Ma'oz, "Alawi Military Officers in Syrian Politics," in H. Z. Schiffrin, *The Military and State in Modern Asia* (Jerusalem: Academic Press, 1976), pp. 285-86.

78. Abbas Kelidar, "Religion and State in Syria," *Asian Affairs*, LXI, no. 1 (February 1974), p. 19.

79. Hijazi, "For Syria"; Ma'oz, "Syria Under Hafiz al-Asad," pp. 10-11.

80. The Assad regime allowed the *Ikhwan* to operate rather openly as a political safety valve in its strongholds for several years. Thus, the Brotherhood was represented by candidates in the People's Assembly elections of 1973. By the late 1970s, however, the government decided, perhaps correctly, that the *Ikhwan* constituted a threat too significant to be tolerated.

81. Among other fundamentalist Islamic opposition groups are the Islamic Liberation Movement, the Islamic Liberation Party, the Salah ad-Din Commando, the Youth of Muhammad, Islamic Youth, and Denouncers of the Infidels. (The Youth of Muhammed in particular is suspected of many assassinations.) Some of these and other groups may be related to, sponsored by, or even organic elements of, the Brotherhood. "Islamic Extremist Leader Admits Plans to Precipitate Civil War," *An Nahar Arab Report & Memo*, III, no. 38 (September 17, 1979), pp. 6-7; Cobban, "More Sectarian Killings"; Cody, "Terrorists Pursue Campaign"; Cobban, "Syria Seethes."

82. "Islamic Extremist Leader," cited note 81 above.

83. E.g., see Howe, "Assàd's Star Fades" and Cobban, "Syria Seethes." Our own interviews have disclosed the same phenomenon.

84. See Van Dam, *The Struggle*, passim.

85. See Paul A. Jureidini and R. D. McLaurin, "Political Disintegration and Conflict Reduction in the Eastern Mediterranean Area," Abbott Associates SR51 (October 1979), pp. 2-3.

86. Andrew Bordwiec, "Syria Opening Doors Despite War Threat," *Washington Star-News*, November 17, 1974, p. A6.

87. Nyrop et al., *Area Handbook*, pp. 66-67.

88. See Nyrop et al., *Area Handbook*; Petran, *Syria*; "Syrian Front: Tense But Calm"; "The Military in the Arab World: Syria," *An Nahar Arab Report*, II, nos. 28 and 29 (July 12 and 19, 1971): "Backgrounder"; Vatikiotis, "The Politics of the Fertile Crescent," pp. 226-27.

89. Petran, *Syria*, pp. 228-30; Hinnebusch, "Local Politics," passim.

90. Petran, *Syria*, pp. 230-32.

91. Nadav Safran, "Arab Politics, Peace and War," *Orbis*, XVIII, no. 2 (Summer 1974), p. 394.

92. Indeed, the role of the PFLP-GC and DPFLP (like that of Sa'iqa and the PLA) in Lebanon in 1976 is enlightening, as these organizations were placed in a difficult position by the Syrian military offensive against the PLO.

93. Safran, "Arab Politics," p. 399; el-Rayyes and Nahas, eds., *Guerrillas for Palestine*, p. 143; "Disengagement Accord: Syrian Precautions," *An Nahar Arab Report*, V, no. 22 (June 3, 1974), p. 1; "Syrian Front: Tense but Calm," pp. 2-3; "Taking Sides," *An Nahar Arab Report*, I, no. 25 (August 24, 1974), pp. 3-4; "Syria and the Palestinians," ibid., IV, no. 23 (June 4, 1973): "Backgrounder"; "Jordan: Hussein's Peace Efforts," ibid., V, no. 6 (February 5, 1974),

p. 3; "The Commandos: Plan for Action," ibid., IV, no. 7 (February 12, 1973), p. 4; Petran, *Syria*, pp. 253-54.

94. At the same time, it must be recalled that Syrian policies in this instance were justified on the basis of their contribution to the Palestinian cause. (See Hafez Addad's major speech on the issue, reprinted in full in *FBIS*, July 21, 1976, pp. H-1 to H-23.) The Assad position is most likely not incredible to Syrians, for it is true that the Palestinians could achieve major benefits from a consolidated eastern front that led to a negotiated settlement, including some form of Palestinian entity.

95. There are approximately 250,000 Palestinian refugees in Syria.

96. Syria has over 100,000 Syrian refugees from the conflicts of 1967 and 1973, as well as 250,000 Palestinian refugees.

97. Additional territory occupied by Israel in October 1973 and some of the Golan land taken in 1967 have been relinquished to Syria.

98. John Cooley, "Syria Opens Windows to the Outside World," *Christian Science Monitor*, December 27, 1971, p. 5.

99. See R. D. McLaurin, Mohammed Mughisuddin, and Abraham R. Wagner, *Foreign Policy Making in the Middle East: Domestic Influences on Policy in Egypt, Iraq, Israel, and Syria* (New York: Praeger, 1977), p. 243.

100. John Cooley, "Syria-Israel Disengagement: Soviets Take Part This Time," *Christian Science Monitor*, February 1, 1974, p. 1; *FBIS*, January 31, 1974, p. F-1. Also see "Syrian Ba'ath Party Congress Begins Today: Internal Troubles Reported," *Arab World*, XXI, no. 5215 (June 7, 1974), p. 5.

101. Safran, "Arab Politics," pp. 396-98.

102. "Is it a War of Attrition on the Golan?" *Arab World*, XXI, no. 5166 (March 28, 1974), pp. 11-12.

103. See Joseph Kraft, "The Divided Arab World," *Washington Post*, April 16, 1974, p. A-17.

104. Ironically, Syria and the PFLP have had a very tumultuous relationship.

105. See "Syria: A Waiting Game," *An Nahar Arab Report*, V, no. 13 (April 1, 1974), pp. 1-2.

106. The dissent was centered in the armed forces and some factions of the Ba'ath. Both the negotiation of an agreement per se and the terms were debated before and after the fact. Marilyn Berger, "Mideast Signing Today," *Washington Post*, May 31, 1974, p. A-1; Berger, "Syria Seems Ready to Free POWs," ibid., May 2, 1974, p. A-1; Bernard Gwertzman, "Kissinger is Given Syrian Proposals on Opening Talks," *New York Times*, January 21, 1974, pp. 1, 6; "Syrian Ba'th Congress: Assad Criticized," *An Nahar Arab Report*, V, no. 24 (June 17, 1974); "Disengagement Accord: Syrian Precautions," p. 1; "Syria: The Ball Starts Rolling"; *Arab World*, XXI, no. 5123 (January 28, 1974), p. 7. In order to still the dissension caused by the disengagement accord and the newly exhibited moderate tendencies, Assad's regime insisted that the initial agreement and talks leading to and following from it be predicated on the direct and close link between these steps and both total Israeli withdrawal from occupied Arab territory and reestablishment of the rights of the Palestinian people. This conceptual connection was particularly important to Syria for another reason: Israel's greater reluctance to relinquish the Golan Heights than to leave the Sinai or West Bank. The link between initial steps and ultimate goals was supported as well by

the United States, in order to provide the firm ground deemed necessary to Assad's continued ability to negotiate. The Assad government, in control of all Syrian media, spared no effort to communicate to the population the importance of disengagement as a step toward a Syrian victory. Indeed, the agreement was portrayed as a Syrian victory, in that the costs were depicted as few and the benefits — especially Israeli evacuation of some of the territory occupied in 1967, including Kuneitra — great. In addition, Soviet support and Palestinian acquiescence were sought to legitimize the agreement (and to shield it from radical and Palestinian-based criticism). "Disengagement Accord: Syrian Precautions"; "Syrian Ba'ath Congress: Assad Criticized"; "Syria's Crucial Position in Mideast Situation," *Arab World*, XXI, no. 5129 (February 5, 1974), pp. 11-12; "Syria-Israel: Where They Disagree," *An Nahar Arab Report*, V, no. 21 (May 27, 1974), p. 1; Jim Hoagland, "Kissinger Plan Key to Syrian Shift on Talks," *Washington Post*, March 3, 1974, p. A-25; Jason Morris, "Kissinger Breaks Syria Stalemate," *Christian Science Monitor*, February 28, 1974, p. 1. Iraq and Libya led opposition to the disengagement agreement.

107. See the "Objectives and Policies" section below.

108. Safran, "Arab Politics," pp. 394-96; Levy, "The Syrian Communists," p. 399; "Syria-Jordan: A Much Needed Detente," *An Nahar Arab Report*, III, no. 50 (December 11, 1972), pp. 2-3.

109. The Egyptian fundamentalist leader, Abdul Hamid Kishk, repeated this common allegation in his sermon no. 326. See Paul A. Jureidini, *The Themes and Appeals of Sheikh Abdul Hamid Kishk* (Alexandria, Va.: Abbott Associates, 1980), p. 22.

110. Past constitutions had not done so either.

111. At the same time cooperation with Sunni regimes has been at least partially an attempt to legitimize 'Alawi rule.

112. Levy, "The Syrian Communists," pp. 401-6; 408-9; McLaurin and Mughisuddin, *The Soviet Union*, pp. 248-49; Yodfat, "The U.S.S.R., Jordan and Syria," pp. 83-89.

113. Specifically, basing for Soviet aircraft engaged in surveillance of the U.S. Sixth Fleet and Soviet naval use of Syrian ports for a variety of needs.

114. See William Branigin, "Isolated Syrians Tighten Soviet Ties," *Washington Post*, February 22, 1980, p. A17; Doyle McManus, "Syrians Not Entirely Comfortable in Their Marriage of Convenience with Russia," *Los Angeles Times*, March 2, 1980, I, p. 18.

115. Branigin, "Isolated Syrians"; McManus, "Syrians"; Roger F. Pajak, "Soviet Arms Aid in the Middle East Since the October War," in *The Political Economy of the Middle East: 1973-78* (Washington, D.C.: U.S. Congress, Joint Economic Committee, 1980), pp. 476-85.

116. Helena Cobban, "Opposition to Russian Advisors Mounts in Syria," *Christian Science Monitor*, January 31, 1980, p. 1; McManus, "Syrians."

117. U.S. Congress, "The Middle East Between War and Peace," staff report for subcommittee on Near Eastern Affairs, 93d Cong., 2d Sess. (March 5, 1974), p. 6.

118. "Egypt's New Ally," *An Nahar Arab Report*, I, no. 39 (November 30, 1970), pp. 2-3.

119. In that case, the sides were also chosen on the basis of consequent benefits and costs to Syria: agreements reached soon after the Soviet departure provided more and better Soviet military materiel, especially in return for Soviet use of Syrian airfields for strategic purposes, special naval facilities at Latakia and Tartus (replacing Mersa Matruh in Egypt), and an increased presence and freedom of action in coordinating Syrian air defense. "Syrian-Libyan Relations," pp. 2-3; "Syria: Two Years Under President Assad (1)"; "Syria: New Policy Lines," *An Nahar Arab Report*, III, no. 35 (August 28, 1972), p. 1.

120. "Assad Meets with Party Leaders," *Arab World*, XXI, no. 5122 (January 25, 1974), p. 3; Safran, "Arab Politics," pp. 398-99; el-Rayyes and Nahas, eds., *Guerrillas for Palestine*, p. 296; Salim al-Lawzi, "The Disengagement as Understood by Kissinger Means Bargaining on Damascus," *Al-Hawadith*, February 22, 1974, pp. 20-22; "Syria: A Waiting Game"; "Disengagement Accord: Syrian Precautions," *An Nahar Arab Report*, V, no. 22 (June 3, 1974), p. 1; "Syrian Ba'ath Congress: Assad Criticized"; *Svenska Dagbladet*, August 9, 1974, p. 3.

121. Marvine Howe, "Assad Rejects Sadat Effort, Saying It Delays Peace," *New York Times*, November 29, 1977, p. 2; John K. Cooley, "Why Syria Stays Firmly Opposed to Sadat Talks," *Christian Science Monitor*, December 14, 1977, p. 6; Jonathan C. Randal, "Syrian Suspicion of Sadat and U.S. Is Deep Seated," *Washington Post*, December 14, 1977, p. A20; James Reston, "Assad, in Interview, Voices Doubt of Gain in Any Carter-Begin Talk," *New York Times*, March 14, 1978, p. 16; Anthony Lewis, "The View from Damascus," ibid., May 8, 1978, p. 19; Ziad Shawky, "Staying Afloat in Troubled Waters," *Middle East*, 53 (March 1979), pp. 45-48; Helena Cobban, "Assad Steers Syria Toward Harder Line," *Christian Science Monitor*, January 15, 1980, p. 7.

122. Kerr, "Hafiz Asad," p. 705; *An Nahar* issues of Spring 1973; "Lebanon-Commandos: New Formula Sought," *An Nahar Arab Report*, III, no. 27 (July 3, 1972), pp. 3-4.

123. See Paul A. Jureidini and William E. Hazen, *The Palestinian Movement in Politics* (Lexington, Mass.: D. C. Heath, 1976); Paul A. Jureidini and William E. Hazen, *Six Clashes: An Analysis of the Relationship Between the Palestinian Guerrilla Movement and the Governments of Jordan and Lebanon* (Kensington, Md.: American Institutes for Research, 1971); John K. Cooley, *Green March, Black September* (London: Frank Cass, 1973); William B. Quandt, Fuad Jabber, and Ann Mosely Lesch, *The Politics of Palestinian Nationalism* (Berkeley: University of California Press, 1973).

124. Anti-Soviet activities and Jordanian and Saudi intelligence collaborators have been linked to Tlas. "Syria: Two Years Under President Assad (1)."

125. El-Rayyes and Nahas, eds., *The October War*, pp. 178-80; "Soviet Experts: Another Eviction?"; "Syria: Domestic Fears"; "Syria: Two Years Under President Assad (1)"; "Potential Trouble"; "Syria-Jordan: A Much Needed Detente," *An Nahar Arab Report*, III, no. 50 (December 11, 1972), pp. 2-3; Kerr, "Hafiz Asad," pp. 702, 705; John K. Cooley, "Syrian Move Brings Praise – and Apprehension," *Christian Science Monitor*, December 4, 1972, p. 4; Jim Hoagland, "Syrian Leaders Call on Hussein to Join Battle Against Israel," *Washington Post*, December 6, 1972, p. A-19.

126. Paul A. Jureidini and R. D. McLaurin, "The Hashemite Kingdom of Jordan," in Haley and Snider, eds., *Lebanon in Crisis*, p. 153.

127. The Saudis reportedly threatened to cut off budgetary aid to Syria. It is in this context that the Syrians' threat to pull "peacekeeping" troops out of Beirut in early 1980 must be understood. See John Kifner, "High Stakes, High Risks in Syria's Threat to Beirut," *New York Times*, February 10, 1980, pp. E-1, E-5.

128. See Jureidini and McLaurin, "Political Disintegration," passim.

129. A Syrian political "first." Balta, "La Syrie baasiste," passim.

130. Ba'ath Party Provisional Regional Command Statement, *FBIS*, November 17, 1970, pp. F-1 to F-4. Jebran Chamieh, ed., *Record of the Arab World (Documents, Events, Political Opinions)* (Beirut, March 1971), pp. 1584-85.

131. Jesse W. Lewis, Jr., "Syria Makes Cautious Overture to West," *Washington Post*, August 26, 1971, pp. H-1, H-7. Reduction of the police role should not be taken to mean that Assad has reduced the level of security forces protecting the regime. On the contrary, he has added Struggle Companies (of about 30,000 men) led by his nephew, Adnan Assad, to the Defense Units led by his brother Rifaat Assad. Both clearly are regime security forces. "Syrian Front: Tense but Calm."

132. Nyrop et al., *Area Handbook*, p. 165; Ma'oz, "Attempts at Creating," p. 404. Ba'ath secularism has returned to the emphasis on the importance of Islam in Arab culture.

133. Thus, the Ba'ath is scarcely a coherent and effective political organization any longer. See Lewis, "Syria Makes Cautious Overture."

134. Balta, "La Syria baasiste"; "Syria: The New Cabinet"; Cooley, "Syria Opens Windows."

135. *Jaish al-Shaab*, October 1974, p. 3. Similarly, the disengagement agreement was defended as an Israeli retreat, an Arab victory. *Al-Ba'ath*, June 3, 1974, p. 1.

136. See, for instance, Assad's interview by Milhelm Karam, *Al-Bayraq*, February 21, 1974, p. 1; his earlier interview in *An Nahar*, March 17, 1971, p. 1; "Is it a War of Attrition?"; Petran, *Syria*, p. 201; "Syria's Crucial Position in Mideast Situation," *Arab World*, XXI, no. 5129 (February 5, 1974), pp. 11-12; Seymour Topping, "Egypt and Syria Divided on U.S. Peace Proposals," *New York Times*, December 18, 1974, pp. 1, 17.

137. "Syria's Ayoubi Demands Israel Get Off Arab Land," *Christian Science Monitor*, March 12, 1973, p. 2.

138. For example, see the interview with Syrian Information Minister George Saddiqni, *Svenska Dagbladet*, August 9, 1974, p. 3.

139. See Foreign Minister Khaddam's statement in "Saudi Arabia and Kuwait Give Syria Pledge on Oil Embargo," *New York Times*, February 5, 1974, p. 3.

140. The disengagement agreement meets this criterion by being tied to Resolution 242, which Syrians view as requiring withdrawal from all occupied territories. In other words, the ambiguity of the resolution has been employed to bring about a disengagement agreement acceptable to both Israel and Syria.

141. Israel destroyed Kuneitra before withdrawing in 1974. To rebuild it would be expensive, especially with Israeli guns on surrounding hills threatening

the new city. Topping, "Egypt and Syria Divided," p. 17; *FBIS*, June 26, 1974, p. H-9; *Al Ba'ath*, September 17, 1974, p. 1. Second, it should be recalled that Kuneitra's population increased to some extent because the area was militarized. Many inhabitants were armed forces personnel and dependents. With the present order of battle, it is unlikely that many military dependents will move to Kuneitra, in effect beyond the front lines. Many other inhabitants were farmers, tending land still occupied by Israeli troops. The proximity of the front is a disincentive to resettlement in Kuneitra for all former inhabitants, particularly since Israeli military forces are ensconced on the surrounding hills. *Al-Ba'ath*, September 17, 1974, p. 1.

142. As both sides recognize, the pressure of a sizable Syrian population in the Golan would add to the costs Syria would have to bear if hostilities broke out again.

143. John K. Cooley, "Syria Hopes Kissinger Brings Pullout Solution," *Christian Science Monitor*, February 26, 1974, p. 2. The fact that Israel has set up 30 new settlements in the Golan, several of them built on the remains of Syrian towns, is well known in Syria and does not facilitate negotiation. See John K. Cooley, "Syria-Israel Disengagement: Soviets Take Part This Time," ibid., February 1, 1974, p. 1.

144. It should be pointed out that Assad, even before his coup, was in favor of reducing the level of confrontation. "Syria could no longer afford the luxury of threatening Israel and playing at extremism; 'it would be better,' [Assad] said, 'to refrain . . . from . . . gratuitous acts of provocation which the enemy could use as a pretext to challenge the Syrian Army and force upon it a battle which it is in no position to undertake.' " Kerr, "Hafiz Asad," p. 699.

145. See Khaddam's press conference, March 13, 1971, in Chamieh, ed., *Record of the Arab World*, pp. 1586-87, in which the foreign minister avers that war will be necessary because Israel is not amenable to peaceful settlement: "The Arabs have tried to pursue a course leading to a peaceful settlement." Assad had just previously suggested that Syria was ready for negotiations. "The Soviet Union and the Arab World (3)," *An Nahar Arab Report*, III, no. 23 (June 5, 1972): "Backgrounder."

146. John K. Cooley, "Syria Joins Arab 'Peace Policy,' " *Christian Science Monitor*, March 10, 1972, p. 3.

147. Walter Laqueur, *Confrontation: The Middle East War and World Politics* (London: Wildwood House and Abacus, 1974), p. 54. Also see "Hussein's Peace Efforts," *An Nahar Arab Report*, IV, no. 6 (February 5, 1973), p. 3. Virtually all sources on October War planning indicate the limited objectives intended by the Arab combatants.

148. U.S. Congress, "The Middle East Between War and Peace," p. 28; Raymond H. Anderson, "Syrians Cautious on Hopes for Talks," *New York Times*, March 1, 1974, p. 7. Assad has, however, stressed that Syria is engaged in peace talks, not negotiations. *FBIS*, October 30, 1973, pp. F-1 to F-6, *Al-Ba'ath*, September 17, 1974, pp. 1, 7.

149. Minister of Information Ahmad Iskander Ahmad, October 11, 1974. See also Henry Tanner, "Syrians Gloomy on Mideast Outlook but They Pledge to Continue Trying," *New York Times*, December 7, 1977, p. 10; Ray Vicker,

"Proud Syria Sees No Hope in Israel-Egypt Talks but Still Believes Peace in Mideast is Possible," *Wall Street Journal*, March 2, 1978, p. 36.

150. "Growing Isolation," *An Nahar Arab Report*, I, no. 14 (June 8, 1970), p. 1.

151. See Fehmi Saddy, *The Eastern Front: Implications of the Syrian/ Palestinian/Jordanian Entente and the Lebanese Civil War* (Alexandria, Va.: Abbott Associates, 1976), pp. 4-6.

152. Marvine Howe, "Assad Rejects Sadat Effort, Saying It Delays Peace," *New York Times*, November 29, 1977, p. 2; Lewis, "The View from Damascus," p. 19; Marvin Kalb, "The Syrian Connection," ibid., July 17, 1979, p. 17.

153. "Disengagement Accord: Syrian Precautions"; "Syria: Moscow Helps Out," *An Nahar Arab Report*, III, no. 29 (July 17, 1972), pp. 3-4.

154. "Syria's Crucial Position," p. 11; *Svenska Dagbladet*, August 9, 1974, p. 3; Henry Kamm, "Syrian Guns Seen in Political Role," *New York Times*, March 21, 1974, p. 11. Also see Assad's speech to the Ba'ath, April 17, 1974; *FBIS*, no. 68, April 18, 1974, pp. H2-H4.

155. Cooley, "Why Syria"; Kalb, "The Syrian Connection"; Henry Tanner, "Syria Has Not Lost Its Pivotal Role in the Mideast," *New York Times*, April 24, 1977; Shuart Averback, "Assad Underlines Offer to Accept Demilitarized Zone," *Washington Post*, May 6, 1977, p. A12. In general, see R. D. McLaurin, "Golan Security in a Middle East Settlement," Abbott Associates SR47 (July 1979).

156. As we have indicated, the most important individual in the regime after the president is his brother. It must be assumed that Rifaat's views are weighed on a variety of important issues. However, the reservations of Tlas and Khaddam are important to the extent that they reflect the feelings of significant publics.

157. However, it has been suggested that Egypt was weaker after Nasser's death and that Syria joined the Federation of Arab Republics to strengthen Egypt. Leonard Binder, "Transformation in the Middle Eastern Subordinate System After 1967," in Michael Confino and Shimon Shamir, eds., *The U.S.S.R. and the Middle East*, p. 259.

158. The best analysis of these relations is Jureidini and Hazen, *Six Clashes*.

159. The intervention followed from Syrian determination not to be the new home of the guerrilla forces (not to turn a Jordanian-guerrilla conflict into a Syrian-guerrilla conflict), the urge of the 'Alawis to demonstrate their "revolutionary virtue," and a direct concern about the Palestine movement. See Jureidini and Hazen, *Six Clashes*, p. 157; Stephen Oren, "Syria's Options," *World Today*, XXX, no. 11 (November 1974), p. 474.

160. Binder, "Transformation," pp. 256-67; Kerr, "Hafiz Asad," p. 705; Petran, *Syria*, pp. 253-54; Cooley, "Syria Opens Windows," p. 5; John K. Cooley, "Syria Chides U.S. Leadership," *Christian Science Monitor*, November 19, 1971, p. 10. Those who seek perfect consistency as the key to explanation of government motives will be frustrated in this case. The Syrian blockage (closure of borders) had deleterious effects on several economies. Maintaining the blockade at some cost to Syria must appear a matter of principle. Yet, immediately before the July 1971 clashes, Syria seized and confiscated a large shipment of arms destined for the Palestinian guerrillas, apparently at least partially

because allowing completion of the transaction through Syria would have imperiled relations with the Amman regime. Moreover, Syrian efforts to improve these relations were not interrupted by the border closure. "Arab Borders: Brotherly Blockades," *An Nahar Arab Report*, III, no. 36 (September 4, 1972): "Economic Brief"; "Syria-Jordan: A Much Needed Detente," ibid., no. 50 (December 11, 1972), pp. 2-3; Kerr, "Hafiz Asad," p. 705; Petran, *Syria*, pp. 253-54. See also Geoffrey Godsell, "Behind Hussein-Arafat Handshake," *Christian Science Monitor*, March 10, 1977, p. 3 for a typical discussion of Syrian efforts to effect a Jordanian-Palestinian rapprochement. By 1979 these efforts succeeded, but limited Palestinian-Jordanian cooperation might outlast Syrian-Jordanian cooperation.

161. John K. Cooley, "Syrian Move Brings Praise — and Apprehension," *Christian Science Monitor*, December 4, 1972, p. 4; Jim Hoagland, "Syrian Leaders Call on Hussein to Join Battle Against Israel," *Washington Post*, December 6, 1972, p. A19; "Syrian-Jordanian Border Reopened to Facilitate Battle," *FBIS*, December 1, 1972, p. F-1; 'Amid Khuli, "Why Were Our Borders with Jordan Opened?" *Al-Ba'ath*, December 3, 1972, p. 3. However transparent this rationale with regard to the (un)likelihood of Jordan's actively joining any near-term military effort against Israel, it is certainly true that the economic consequences of the closed borders were undermining the Arab anti-Israeli boycott and were forcing the Jordanian government to deal increasingly (and more publicly) with Israel. "Arab Borders: Brotherly Blockades."

162. "Consolidating Trend," *An Nahar Arab Report*, VI, no. 24 (June 16, 1975), pp. 1-2; "Closing the Ranks," ibid., no. 25 (June 23, 1975), pp. 2-3; "Prospects for Disengagement," ibid., no. 34 (August 25, 1975), pp. 1-2; "Facing the Future Together," ibid., pp. 2-3; "Serious Determined Effort," ibid., no. 35 (September 1, 1975): "Chronology: Syria-Jordan Supreme Commission, Joint Statement, July 30, 1975"; Elizabeth Picard, "La Syrie du 'redressement' et les chances de paix au Proche-Orient," *Politique etrangere*, LXI, no. 2 (1976), pp. 174-75; Saddy, *The Eastern Front*, pp. 9-16.

163. El-Rayyes and Nahas, eds., *Guerrillas for Palestine*, pp. 49-52.

164. Ibid., pp. 144-45. The restrictions became even tighter in mid-1973 ("Syria and the Palestinians," *An Nahar Arab Report*, IV, no. 23 [June 4, 1973]: "Backgrounder"); but these later restrictions probably were directly related to the October War, which by then was already in the planning stage. In January and February, stories concerning alleged Syrian "incitement" of villagers against the commandos circulated. These rumors probably grew out of the increased restrictions, but one cannot discard the idea of a government-inspired or -spread canard. See "Hussein's Peace Efforts," ibid., IV, no. 6 (February 5, 1973), p. 3; "The Commandos: Plan for Action," ibid., no. 7 (February 12, 1973), p. 4.

165. "A Front Reopened," ibid., no. 38 (September 18, 1972), p. 1.

166. "Syria and the Palestinians"; "Cairo Summit: Splits and Alignments," ibid., IV, no. 38 (September 17, 1973), pp. 1-2.

167. "Lebanon-Commandos: New Formula Sought," ibid., III, no. 27 (July 3, 1972), pp. 3-4.

168. U.S. Congress, in "The Middle East Between War and Peace," p. 29. See the interview of Assad by Arnaud de Borchgrave, *An Nahar Arab Report*, June 3, 1974, p. 1.

169. McLaurin and Mughisuddin, *Cooperation and Conflict*, p. 235. These views are based on discussions with a variety of individuals in the Middle East.

170. Marius Deeb, *The Lebanese Civil War* (New York: Praeger, 1980); Haley and Snider, eds., *Lebanon in Crisis*; Youssef al-Hashem, *Sawt Lubnan fi Harb al-Sanatayn* (Beirut: Manshurat Idha'at Sawt Lubnan, 1977); Leile Badi' 'Itani et al., *Harb Lubnan* (Beirut: Dar al-Masira, 1977); Paul A. Jureidini and William E. Hazen, *The Dissolution of Lebanon* (Alexandria, Va.: Abbott Associates, 1976); Hasan Khalid, *al-Muslimum fi Lubnan wa al-Harb al-Ahliya* (Beirut: Dar al-Kindi, 1978); Walid Khalidi, *Conflict and Violence in Lebanon: Confrontation in the Middle East* (Cambridge, Mass.: Center for International Affairs, Harvard University, 1979); Antoine Khuwairi, *al-Harb fi Lubnan 1976*, 3 vols. (Junee: al-Berlusinger, 1977); Markaz at-Takhtit Munazzamat at-Tahrir al-Filastiniya, *Yawmiyat al-Harb al-Lubnaniyya*, 2 vols. (Beirut, 1977).

171. One of the remarkable attributes of Syrian leadership has been its paranoia. Assad has sought out situations in which Syria could mediate between two parties in conflict or, at least, not in communication. Yet, typically, the Syrian role has been seen in Damascus as the sine qua non of the dialogue. Thus, Assad exerted great efforts to engineer a rapprochement between Jordan (then aligned with Syria) and the PLO, but objected to separate Jordanian-PLO contacts.

172. The Jordanian role in the dissolution of the Iraqi-Syrian "union" project should not be overlooked. See Joseph Chaim, "La Jordanie et l'Irak font tandem contre la Syrie," *Journal de Genève*, October 15, 1979.

173. R. D. McLaurin and James M. Price, "OPEC Current Account Surpluses and Assistance to the Arab Front Line States," *Oriente Moderno*, LVIII, no. 11 (November 1978), pp. 533-46, discusses the level of aid.

174. "The Soviet Union and the Arab World (3)"; Lenczowski, *Soviet Advances in the Middle East* (Washington, D.C.: American Enterprise Institution, 1972), p. 117.

175. John K. Cooley, "Russian Test in Syria," *Christian Science Monitor*, September 13, 1973, p. 4.

176. "Syria: New Policy Lines," *An Nahar Arab Report*, III, no. 35 (August 28, 1972), p. 6; "Syrian-Libyan Relations."

177. Soviet Jewish emigration has become a problem because a substantial proportion of Soviet Jews who emigrated to Israel settled in the occupied Golan Heights. "Syria: Military Moves," *An Nahar Arab Report*, IV, no. 20 (May 14, 1973), p. 1.

178. Pressure frequently has been used to moderate Syrian demands or policies, but recently the Soviet Union has been more concerned to protect distinctly Soviet interests.

179. "Joint Syrian-Soviet Communique Backs Syrian Right to Liberate Occupied Land as U.S.S.R. Aid is Promised in Military and Economic Fields," *Arab World*, XXI, no. 5779 (April 17, 1974), pp. 2-3; "Is it a War of Attrition on the Golan?"; "Disengagement Accord: Syrian Precautions"; "Syria: A Waiting Game."

180. Joe Alex Morris, Jr., "Israeli-Egyptian Attack on Syria Possible: Assad," *Los Angeles Times*, September 21, 1978, pp. 1, 7.

181. McLaurin and Price, *Soviet Middle East Policy*.

182. Drew Middleton, "Syria, with Forces Built up Since '73, Maintains Alert Stance in Golan Area," *New York Times*, July 21, 1975, p. 4; "Healing the Rift," *An Nahar Arab Report*, VII, no. 23 (June 7, 1976), pp. 2-3; "The Issue of Soviet Arms Supplies," ibid., "Backgrounder."

183. Jonathan C. Randal, "Syrian Suspicion of Sadat and U.S. is Deep Rooted," *Washington Post*, December 14, 1977, p. A20.

184. Petran, *Syria*, p. 234.

185. See Joseph Chaim, "Syria: le regime sur la corde raide," *Journal de Genève*, October 7, 1979, p. 1; Stanley F. Reed, "Dateline Syria: Fin de Régime?" *Foreign Policy*, 39 (Summer 1980), pp. 176-90, passim.

186. Anthony Pascal et al., *Men and Arms in the Middle East: The Human Factor in Military Modernization* (Santa Monica: Rand, 1979).

187. Pajak, "Soviet Arms Aid"; Branigin, "Isolated Syrians."

188. In fact, over 3,000 Soviet advisors are in Syria, counting civilian and military personnel. U.S. Central Intelligence Agency (CIA), *Communist Aid Activities in Non-Communist Less Developed Countries 1978* (Washington, D.C., 1979), p. 4.

189. However, they have never been central to the defense effort, performing peripheral tasks only.

190. See Trevor N. Dupuy, *Elusive Victory: The Arab-Israeli Wars 1947-1974* (New York: Harper & Row, 1978), Book 5.

191. Cf. Steven J. Rosen, "What the Next Arab-Israeli War Might Look Like," *International Security*, II, no. 4 (Spring 1978), pp. 149-74; Geoffrey Kemp and Micheal Vlahos, "The Military Balance in the Middle East in 1978," in *The Political Economy of the Middle East*, p. 425-37.

PRESSURES, PROCESSES, AND POLICY

The foreign policies of any state tend to be viewed quite differently by its nationals (and indeed differently by different groups of nationals), foreign nationals, military observers, political scientists, religious leaders, and so forth. It is not the purpose of this chapter to summarize the foreign policies of Egypt, Iraq, Israel, Saudi Arabia, and Syria. Instead, we seek here to briefly compare the diverse ways in which external and especially the internal environments we have examined help forge foreign policy.

The "unitary rational actor" model[1] assumes for analytical purposes that there is an objectively ascertainable optimum policy that a unitary government, acting rationally, would choose and pursue. The shortcomings of such assumptions are well known and need not be overdrawn here, for we do not deny the utility of the model as a parsimonious analytical tool in many circumstances, one we have used frequently in the course of this book. In comparing foreign-policy processes and their outputs, however, it is important to remember that they are also unique expressions of political culture.

In this chapter we shall compare the nature of pressures influencing the policy process and the processes themselves.

PRESSURES

Of the five countries we have studied, Egypt enjoys greater psychological independence from external pressures than the other four states, even more than Israel, which is not part of the Arab world surrounding it. Although Egypt cannot remain isolated from the remainder of the Arab world indefinitely without direct implications for its internal political order, the country's leadership can act independently from the Arab world for some years at a time. Whether Egypt will lead the Arab world is Cairo's decision — not that of the Arab world (though whether and to what extent this leadership must be shared cannot be decided in Egypt, but depends on other factors).

The potential danger under which all Egyptian governments must operate is that foreign-policy issues may adversely impinge on or exacerbate the overwhelming domestic problems endemic to Egyptian society. Indeed, the linkage between domestic political constraints and foreign affairs is the common denominator of all five countries — the principal concern of each is to insulate foreign policy from internal problems. However, the parochial nature of Egyptian mass consciousness has precluded the realization of this potential problem. The tangible objectives of current policy, nevertheless, aim concretely at securing economic advantages from its relationship with the United States that will at least cushion the devastating economic conditions in which the mass of Egyptians find themselves.

What is unusual about the relationship of external policies and internal pressures in Egypt is the great policy latitude in time and content allowed the national government. A policy that cut off substantial existing Arab aid with the objective of greater long-term benefits would be inconceivable in most other Arab countries. Here again we see the importance of political culture to the making of foreign policy and to our understanding of it.

Iraqi policy is somewhat independent of domestic institutional pressures, but the narrow base of the government and the size of sectarian and ethnic groups that do not identify with the government renders policymakers sensitive to issues that could mobilize opposition. Internationally, Iraq is situated along the historically troubled border between the Arab world and the Persians. Moreover, since the establishment of the republic, Iraq has suffered hostile relations with many of its Arab neighbors as well as the Western powers.

Iraq's leaders today confidently looked beyond the borders of their country before the Gulf war. Their national objectives are no longer purely defensive, though certainly they continue to work to prevent foreign exploitation of their domestic ethnic and sectarian schisms. But the principal pressures Saddam Hussein experiences today are international constraints on national ambitions to establish Iraq as the primary Arab leader and the dominant country of the Gulf. These constraints are the resistance to Iraqi ambitions not so much because of Iraq, as because of the implications for Iran, the United States, Saudi Arabia, Syria, and the Soviet Union. None of these powers, each for its own reasons, sees its interests best served by permitting itself to be cowed, or extruded from power, by Iraq.

Unlike any of the other countries studied in this volume, Israel must formulate policy for a highly aware, well-informed, articulate, and politically active public. Undoubtedly, even in the fact of constant Arab-Israeli tension, the greatest pressures operating on Israeli policy are domestic. Moreover, the magnitude of Israel's economic problems may dictate foreign policy by determining the government.

A principal pressure on foreign policy has been the inability of the public or the government to deal meaningfully with the territory-versus-security issue. Are the two values in conflict? If so, how can the conflict be resolved? Because these questions go to the heart of Zionism and Israeli security they are widely debated; they are not widely agreed upon. Ultimately, the territorial issue means the West Bank (and, to a lesser extent, Gaza), but the question also necessarily brings in the Palestinians and therefore Israel's role in the Middle East as well as the country's security.

In the fact of the Sadat initiative, Israeli leaders recognize a need to evolve a policy that provides incentives to Arab cooperation but retains the elements necessary to Israeli security and safeguards the Zionist raison d'être. While conceptually easy to define, such policies are practically difficult to implement since incentives to cooperation are also concessions to potential enemies.

Finally, Israeli security has for many years leaned heavily upon the United States. During those years, American economic interests in the Middle East were of a commercial nature, and other interests often took precedence. Since the early 1970s, however, the Gulf has occupied an increasingly prominent place in Washington's Middle East strategic thinking, and U.S. dependence on Arab oil exports for Western economic, political, military, and even social security has brought forth a new and different viewpoint to the Arab-Israeli conflict. Evidence both suggests that the United States will continue to focus more and more heavily on the Gulf in the years ahead, and proves conclusively that Israel no longer enjoys the only American "special relationship" in the region. The equally important result: many Israelis distrust U.S. goals and policies in the region, significantly complicating the negotiations toward Arab-Israeli settlement.

Saudi policy problems derive from the country's wealth, which Saudi leaders fear makes the country an attractive target, and its very small population, which places severe limits on those available to defend and develop the kingdom. But pressures at least as great come from Saudi Islamic missionary zeal and social conservatism. In both these respects the royal family accurately represents the majority of the populace; but the growing educated sector has somewhat divergent social views and the process of modernization has often shown little respect for traditionalism, whether adhered to by the populace or royalty alone.

The divided body politic inside Syria remains the primary pressure on the leadership. Foreign policy must above all ensure that external forces and problems do not further exacerbate the already volatile domestic Syrian problems. All other limits on Syrian policy freedom are secondary by contrast.

PROCESSES

Among the five countries treated here, policy processes vary between the formal and the informal, the democratic and the autocratic, the reality and the facade. Interestingly, these dimensions operate independently, so that the democratic-autocratic continuum, for example, does not parallel the formal-informal or the real-false. Once again, the location of each country along each dimension is, to a surprising extent, a function of political traditions and culture.

As we have indicated, the Egyptian president is granted a virtual carte blanche by the public in his conduct of foreign policy. Strong leadership, such as that of the late Anwar Sadat, can address and overcome the hurdles of public attitudes much more easily in Egypt than in a country where active public participation in foreign policy is the norm. The institutions of Egyptian foreign policy permit executive initiative and action. Public support is expected and, with strong leadership, the legislative forums reflect this public acquiescence. (Implementation of policy initiatives when this involves bureaucratic action is a wholly different story, for the Egyptian bureaucracy has gained international notoriety for its unresponsiveness.)

By contrast, Iraqi and Syrian institutions relating to foreign-policy formulation and administration are chimeric — they have little to do with the real processes involved which are, as in Egypt, highly centralized in the presidency. Neither country lacks formal procedures for public input, but the procedures are largely without substance. In Iraq, public attention to foreign-policy issues is less active and participation historically more restricted. In Syria, the greater number of ethnic, sectarian, ideological, and regional identity groups and historically more active public participation in these issues constitute real problems for management and policy articulation. Moreover, individual contentious postures and policies undoubtedly lead to greater political problems for the Assad regime.

In both Iraq and Syria, foreign-policy decision-making processes have been revised in recent years to account for interest groups purporting to represent the "opposition." In reality, however, there are no formalized procedures through which the key interest groups, especially those unrepresented in these narrowly based regimes, can articulate their policy views for consideration or dissent. Indeed, the political existence of most interest groups apart from their government-sanctioned role, if any, is ignored.

In Israel, where many foreign-policy issues are seen to go to the heart of the state's meaning and certainly to the heart of its existence, public participation is active and vocal. The Israeli executive has less policy independence from the public than other regional governments on foreign-policy matters, particularly when the government is a weak coalition. Indeed, the diversity and number of Israeli views as expressed in the Knesset show clear-cut paralyzing characteristics as regards political domains. On military aspects of foreign policy, the executive is granted much greater freedom of action.

Israeli policy processes are complicated by the necessity for honest legislative review, but are not more (or in some cases, as) formal than (as) Arab states in which public approval is not sought. Yet, the foreign-policy processes of Israel are real — they involve submission of executive action to legislative approval.

Even if this approach is not technically democratic in nature, it does provide for the lively operation — and hindrance — of public interest groups.

Saudi Arabia's policy processes are unique and no less "real" than Israel's. They involve no pretense of public participation. Their uniqueness lies in the fact that the kingdom intends that its approach to policy formulation should remain hidden from public view. While Iraq and Syria often make decisions secretly, Saudi Arabia has institutionalized secrecy as a political process. It is, after all, *Saudi* Arabia, and key policy decisions are therefore viewed as appropriate to internal royal family consideration.

Iraq's, Saudi Arabia's, and Syria's arbitrary processes do not disregard domestic interest groups. Indeed, it is the very privacy of the process that *allows* full and balanced consideration of the perceived attitudes of all groups and expected policy impact on them, consideration that could not be permitted if the processes were public. We are not suggesting such factors are always or even usually decisive; but they are considered.

We have seen that the universe of political systems establishes means, formal or informal, secret or public, real or apparent, of accounting for the diversity of interest and identity groups and other key publics critical to the maintenance of public support. Processes may vary by issue and generally do vary over time. Yet, the widespread notion that undemocratic systems "disregard" public attitudes appears to have little empirical support and certainly makes little political sense. Even in countries like Egypt where the executive branch is given substantial latitude for action by both the masses and public institutions, the attitudes and interests of key constituencies are considered.

It is not clear that any single approach to the formulation, administration, and execution of foreign policy commends itself as superior to others. Each of the systems we have studied in this book grows out of a unique history and political tradition. It is only clear that an understanding of the political cultures that give rise to foreign policies and of the systems through which they are shaped may help us to interact and deal more effectively with other governments.

NOTE

1. Graham T. Allison, *Essence of Decision: Explaining the Cuban Missile Crisis* (Boston: Little, Brown, 1971), Chap. 1, discusses the rational actor model and its widespread application in international political analysis.

SELECTED BIBLIOGRAPHY

Ajami, Fouad. *The Arab Predicament: Arab Political Thought and Practice Since 1967*. London: Cambridge University Press, 1980.

Akhavi, Shahrough. "Egypt: Diffused Elite in a Bureaucratic Society." In I. William Zartman, Mark A. Tessler, John P. Entelis, Russell A. Stone, Raymond A. Hinnebusch, and Shahrough Akhavi, *Political Elites in Arab North Africa*. (New York: Longman, 1982).

Amos, John W., II. *Arab-Israeli Military/Political Relations: Arab Perceptions and the Politics of Escalation*. New York: Pergamon, 1979.

_____ . *Palestinian Resistance: Organization of a Nationalist Movement*. New York: Pergamon, 1980.

Aronson, Shlomo. *Conflict and Bargaining in the Middle East: An Israeli Perspective*. Baltimore: Johns Hopkins University Press, 1976.

Azar, Edward E. and Stephen P. Cohen. "Peace as Crisis and War as Status-Quo: The Arab-Israeli Conflict Environment." *International Interactions*, VI, 2 (1979), pp. 159-84.

Azar, Edward E., Paul A. Jureidini, and Ronald D. McLaurin. "Protracted Social Conflict: Theory and Practice in the Middle East." *Journal of Palestine Studies*, VIII, 1 (Autumn 1978), pp. 41-60.

Baker, Raymond William. *Egypt's Uncertain Revolution under Nasser and Sadat*. Cambridge: Harvard University Press, 1978.

Batatu, Hanna. "Iraq's Underground Shi'a Movements: Characteristics, Causes and Prospects." *Middle East Journal*, XXXV, 4 (Autumn 1981), pp. 578-94.

_____ . *The Old Social Classes and the Revolutionary Movements of Iraq*. Princeton: Princeton University Press, 1978.

309

_____ . "Some Observations on the Social Roots of Syria's Ruling, Military Group and the Causes for Its Dominance." *Middle East Journal*, XXXV, 3 (Summer 1981), pp. 331-44.

Boutros-Ghali, Boutros. "The Foreign Policy of Egypt in the Post-Sadat Era." *Foreign Affairs*, 60, no. 4 (Spring 1982), pp. 769-88.

Brecher, Michael. *Decisions in Crisis: Israel, 1967 and 1973*. Berkeley: University of California Press, 1980.

_____ . *Decisions in Israel's Foreign Policy*. New Haven: Yale University Press, 1975.

_____ . *The Foreign Policy System of Israel: Setting, Images, Process*. New Haven: Yale University Press, 1972.

Cohen, Stephen P. and Edward E. Azar. "From War to Peace: The Transition Between Egypt and Israel." *Journal of Conflict Resolution*, XXV, 1 (March 1981), pp. 87-114.

Dann, Uriel. *Iraq Under Qassem: A Political History 1958-63*. New York: Praeger, 1967.

Dawisha, Adeed I. *Egypt in the Arab World: The Elements of Foreign Policy*. New York: Wiley, 1976.

_____ . "Saudi Arabia's Search for Security." *Adelphi Papers*, no. 158 (1979).

Dekmejian, R. Hrair. *Egypt Under Nasser: A Study in Political Dynamics*. Albany: State University of New York Press, 1977.

Devlin, John. *The Ba'th Party*. Stanford: Hoover Institution Press, 1976.

Dupuy, Trevor N. *Elusive Victory: The Arab-Israeli Wars 1947-1974*. New York: Harper and Row, 1978.

El-Sadat, Anwar. *In Search of Identity*. New York: Harper and Row, 1978.

Ghareeb, Edmund. *The Kurdish Question in Iraq*. Syracuse: Syracuse University Press, 1981.

Golan, Galia. *Yom Kippur and After*. London: Cambridge University Press, 1977.

Haddad, Yvonne. "The Arab-Israeli Wars, Nasserism, and the Affirmation of Islamic Identity." In John L. Esposito, ed., *Islam and Development: Religion and Sociopolitical Change*. Syracuse: Syracuse University Press, 1980.

Haley, P. Edward and Lewis W. Snider, ed. *Lebanon in Crisis: Participants and Issues*. Syracuse: Syracuse University Press, 1979.

Hameed, Mazher, R. D. McLaurin, and Lewis W. Snider. *An American Imperative: The Defense of Saudi Arabia*. Washington, D.C.: n.p., 1981.

Handel, Michael I. *Israel's Political-Military Doctrine*. Cambridge: Harvard University, Center for International Affairs, 1973.

Harris, William Wilson. *Taking Root: Israeli Settlement in the West Bank, the Golan, and Gaza-Sinai, 1967-1980*. New York: Wiley, 1980.

Heikal, Mohammed Hassenein. "Egypt Foreign Policy." *Foreign Affairs*, 56, no. 4 (July 1978), pp. 714-27.

_____ . *The Road to Ramadan*. New York: Quadrangle, 1975.

_____ . *The Sphinx and the Commissar*. New York: Harper and Row, 1978.

Holden, David and Richard Johns. *The House of Saud: The Rise and Rule of the Most Powerful Dynasty in the Arab World*. New York: Holt, Rinehart and Winston, 1981.

Horowitz, Dan and Moshe Lissak. *Origins of the Israeli Polity*. Chicago: University of Chicago Press, 1978.

Hudson, Michael C. *Arab Politics: The Search for Legitimacy*. New Haven: Yale University Press, 1977.

Ibrahim, Saad Eddin. "Anatomy of Egypt's Militant Islamic Groups: Methodological Note and Preliminary Findings." *International Journal of Middle East Studies*, 12, no. 4 (December 1980), pp. 423-53.

Isaac, Rael Jean. *Israel Divided: Ideological Politics in the Jewish State*. Baltimore: Johns Hopkins University Press, 1976.

_____ . *Party and Politics in Israel: Three Visions of a Jewish State*. London: Longmans, 1981.

Jureidini, Paul A. and R. D. McLaurin. *Beyond Camp David: Emerging Alignments and Leaders in the Middle East*. Syracuse: Syracuse University Press, 1981.

Kerr, Malcolm. *The Arab Cold War*. New York: Oxford University Press, 1972.

McLaurin, R. D., ed. *The Political Role of Minority Groups in the Middle East*. New York: Praeger, 1979.

Mansur, Abdul Kasim (pseud.). "The American Threat to Saudi Arabia." *Armed Forces Journal International*, CXVIII, 1 (September 1980), pp. 47-60.

_____ . "The Military Balance in the Persian Gulf: Who Will Guard the Gulf States from their Guardians?" *Armed Forces Journal International*, CXVIII, 3 (November 1980), pp. 44-86.

Ma'oz, Moshe. "Alawi Military Officers in Syrian Politics." In *The Military and State in Modern Asia*, ed. H. Z. Schiffrin. Jerusalem: Academic Press, 1976, pp. 277-97.

_____ . "Attempts at Creating a Political Community in Modern Syria." *Middle East Journal*, XXVI, 4 (Autumn 1972), pp. 389-404.

Nyrop, Richard F., ed. *Iraq: A Country Study*. Washington, D.C.: Foreign Area Studies Division, American University, 1979.

_____ , ed. *Israel: A Country Study*. Washington, D.C.: Foreign Area Studies Division, American University, 1979.

_____ , ed. *Syria: A Country Study*. Washington, D.C.: Foreign Area Studies Division, American University, 1979.

_____ et al. *Area Handbook for Saudi Arabia*. Washington, D.C.: Foreign Area Studies Division, American University, 1977.

Peretz, Don. *The Government and Politics of Israel*. Boulder: Westview, 1979.

Perlmutter, Amos. *Military and Politics in Israel: Nation-Building and Role Expansion*. London: Cass, 1969.

Quandt, William B. *Decade of Decisions: American Policy toward the Arab-Israeli Conflict, 1967-1976*. Berkeley and Los Angeles: University of California Press, 1977.

_____ . *Saudi Arabia in the 1980s: Foreign Policy, Security, and Oil*. Washington, D.C.: Brookings, 1981.

_____ , Fuad Jabber, and Ann Mosely Lesch. *The Politics of Palestinian Nationalism*. Berkeley and Los Angeles: The University of California Press, 1973.

Rabinovich, Itamar. *Syria Under the Ba'th 1963-66: The Army-Party Symbiosis*. Jerusalem: Israel Universities Press, 1972.

Rubin, Barry. *The Arab States and the Palestine Conflict*. Syracuse: Syracuse University Press, 1981.

_____ . *Paved with Good Intentions: The American Experience and Iran*. New York: Oxford University Press, 1980.

Sachar, Howard M. *A History of Israel from the Rise of Zionism to Our Time*. New York: Knopf, 1976.

Safran, Nadav. *Israel: Embattled Ally*. Cambridge: Harvard University Press, 1978.

Sheehan, Edward R. F. *The Arabs, Israelis, and Kissinger*. New York: Reader's Digest Press, 1976.

Van Dam, Nikolaos. *The Struggle for Power in Syria*. 2d ed., London: Croom Helm, 1981.

Waterbury, John. *Egypt: Burdens of the Past, Options for the Future*. Bloomington and London: Indiana University Press, 1978.

PERIODICALS

News

an-Nahar. Beirut daily (Arabic).

ash-Sharq al-Awsat. London daily (Arabic).

Christian Science Monitor. Boston weekdays (English).

Foreign Broadcast Information Service. *Daily Report*, vol. V, Middle East and Africa. Washington, D.C., weekdays (English).

Jerusalem Post. Jerusalem daily (English).

Los Angeles Times. Los Angeles daily (English).

Le Monde. Paris daily (French).

New York Times. New York daily (English).

Wall Street Journal. New York weekdays (English).

Washington Post. Washington, D.C., daily (English).

Analysis

an-Nahar Arab Report & Memo (formely *an-Nahar Arab Report*). Beirut/Paris, weekly (English).

Armed Forces Journal International. Washington, D.C., monthly.

Foreign Affairs. New York quarterly.

Foreign Policy. Boston quarterly.

International Security. Cambridge, Mass. quarterly.

Middle East. Beirut quarterly.

Middle East Journal. London monthly.

Orbis. Philadelphia quarterly.

Orient. Opladen (W. Germany) bimonthly.

Oriente Moderno. Rome monthly.

Politique étrangère. Paris quarterly.

Revue de Défense nationale. Paris monthly.

Washington Quarterly. Washington, D.C., quarterly.

INDEX

Abd al-Aziz ('Abd al-Aziz ibn Fabd ar-Ruhman as-Sa'ud), 197-99, 201, 213-14, 215, 221

Abd al-Hatif, Abdal Suttar, 90

Abd-Allah ibn Abd al-Aziz, 203

Abd al-Majid, Hamdi, 90

Abd al-Sharif, Tahir, 103

Abdullah, Amir, 106

Abu Musa, 18, 20, 101, 111, 211

Abu al-Wafiya, Mahmoud, 42

Afghanistan, 62, 107, 117, 121

Aflaq, Michel, 81, 90, 242, 243

Agranat, Shimon, 181

Ahmad, Ahmad Iskander, 250

Ahmad, Ibrahim, 101

Algeria, 15, 21, 22, 23, 59, 60, 104

Ali, (Sheikh) Baba, 97

Ali, Kamal Hassan, 44

Ali ibn abi Talib, 75

Ali ibn Hussein, 197

Allon, Yigal, 148

"Allon Plan", 163

Amer, Abdel Hakim, 45

American-Israel Public Affairs Committee (AIPAC), 161

Amin, Idi, 62

Ammash, Salih Mehdi, 91

Aqrawi, Aziz, 103

Aqrawi, Hashem, 103

Arab-Israeli conflict, 3-5, 7-8, 15-16, 18-19, 33-36, 40, 45, 48, 49-50, 51, 55-56, 58-59, 64-65, 115-16, 119-20, 122, 131-34, 136, 138, 139, 149, 161-62, 164-65, 166-69, 170, 172, 177, 178-82, 195, 205, 208-11, 214-16, 217-18, 219-20, 222, 227, 243-44, 255, 257, 259-65, 266-69, 275-78, 282, 283-85, 304-5

Arab-Israeli Wars: First (1948-49), 3-4, 133, 161-62, 164-65, 166-67, 172, 179; Second (1956), 3, 34, 133, 168-69 (*see also* Egypt-Suez Crisis); Third (1967), 4, 5, 13, 37, 45, 48, 49-50, 133, 180, 138, 149, 162, 166-67, 169, 170, 177, 178, 180, 208, 211, 216, 243, 255, 261, 263-64, 279, 284; Fourth (1973), 4-6, 13, 35, 36, 49-50, 51, 55-56, 65, 116, 133, 136, 170, 180-81, 195, 220, 227, 244, 255, 257, 260-61, 265, 267, 272-74, 276, 277-79, 284-85; Military balance, 3-4, 18-19, 219, 247; Peace Initiatives, 4, 13-14, 33, 35-37, 43-44, 49, 51, 52, 56, 58, 62, 66, 117-18, 133, 139, 161, 182, 210, 214, 220, 261, 266-68, 271, 273-74

Arab League, 119, 120, 169

Arab Liberation Front (ALF), 115

Arab Military Industries Organization (AMIO or AOI), 60-61, 220

Arafat, Yasser, 159, 278

Aref (Arif), Abdel Rahman, 106

Aref (Arif), Abdel Salam, 89, 91, 100, 105-6

Assad, Adnan, 256

Assad, Hafez, 4, 19, 33, 55-56, 120, 242-44, 246-48, 249-52, 253-54, 256-58, 259-62, 264-66, 266-67, 269-70, 270-71, 273-74, 275-78,

ABOUT THE AUTHORS

R. D. McLaurin, Senior Associate at Abbott Associates, Inc., is the author of *The Middle East in Soviet Policy*; coauthor of *Foreign Policy Making in the Middle East* and *Beyond Camp David: Emerging Alignments and Leaders in the Middle East*; and editor of *The Political Role of Minority Groups in the Middle East*, *The Art and Science of Psychological Operations*, and *Military Propaganda*. Formerly, Dr. McLaurin was on the staff of the Assistant Secretary of Defense (International Security Affairs). He continues to consult with a wide variety of clients in the public and private sectors.

Don Peretz, Professor of Political Science at SUNY-Binghamton, is a member of the board of advisory editors of the *Middle East Journal* and a frequent contributor of articles to a wide range of professional publications. He is author or coauthor of *Israel and the Palestine Arabs*, *The Middle East*, *A Palestine Entity?*, *The Palestine State: A Rational Approach*, *The Middle East Today*, and *Government and Politics of Israel*.

Lewis W. Snider is Associate Professor and Chairman, Department of International Relations, Claremont Graduate School. He is also a research associate at Abbott Associates, Inc., and a consultant to several corporations. The author of *Arabesque*, he coedited *Lebanon in Crisis: Participants and Issues*, and has contributed to a variety of journals, newspapers, research reports, and other books on a number of political and military issues.